Where the Past meets the Future
The Politics of Heritage in Xi'an

Since the incidental discovery of the head of a terracotta warrior, Xi'an's archaeological and historical importance has been spotlighted in the national, provincial and municipal political discourse. The city is glorified as 'the cradle of civilization', 'the ancient capital', and 'the start of the Silk Road'. At the same time, Xi'an is undergoing intensive urban development as it strives to be a modern cosmopolitan city. The city is expanding at breakneck speed, constructing 'new heritage', creating 'Central Business Cultural Districts' and building new metro lines. In today's Xi'an, both history and modernization affect the urban development process, and neither component can be separated from the other.

Based on a year of ethnographic fieldwork in the city, this book investigates how tradition, history, and modernization interact in the heritage projects and the changing cityscape. By analysing the heritage policies and projects taking place in this ancient capital and conveying the voices of different social actors, from city officials to ordinary residents, this book demonstrates the meaning of history and heritage in both the official representation and the everyday life of a contemporary Chinese city.

Halle Studies in the Anthropology of Eurasia

General Editors:

Christoph Brumann, Kirsten Endres, Chris Hann, Burkhard Schnepel,
Lale Yalçın-Heckmann

Volume 37

LIT

Leah Cheung Ah Li

Where the Past meets the Future

The Politics of Heritage in Xi'an

LIT

Cover Photo: Terracotta warrior on the Christmas Market in Xi'an (Photo: Leah Cheung Ah Li, December 2013).

This book is a revised version of a dissertation manuscript, submitted to the Faculty of Philosophy I at Martin Luther University Halle-Wittenberg in 2016.

This book is printed on acid-free paper.

Bibliographic information published by the Deutsche Nationalbibliothek
The Deutsche Nationalbibliothek lists this publication in the Deutsche Nationalbibliografie; detailed bibliographic data are available in the Internet at http://dnb.dnb.de.

ISBN 978-3-643-90887-2 (pb)
ISBN 978-3-643-95887-7 (PDF)

©LIT VERLAG Dr. W. Hopf
Berlin 2019
Fresnostr. 2
D-48159 Münster
Tel. +49 (0) 2 51-62 03 20
Fax +49 (0) 2 51-23 19 72
E-Mail: lit@lit-verlag.de
http://www.lit-verlag.de

LIT VERLAG GmbH & Co. KG Wien,
Zweigniederlassung Zürich 2019
Flössergasse 10
CH-8001 Zürich
Tel. +41 (0) 76-632 84 35
Fax
E-Mail: zuerich@lit-verlag.ch
http://www.lit-verlag.ch

Distribution:
In the UK: Global Book Marketing, e-mail: mo@centralbooks.com
In North America: Independent Publishers Group, e-mail: orders@ipgbook.com
In Germany: LIT Verlag Fresnostr. 2, D-48159 Münster
Tel. +49 (0) 2 51-620 32 22, Fax +49 (0) 2 51-922 60 99, e-mail: vertrieb@lit-verlag.de

e-books are available at www.litwebshop.de

Contents

List of Illustrations ix

Acknowledgements xi

Note on Transliteration xiii

1 **Introduction** **1**

Field Situation: A City of the Past 4
Contributions 7
Methodology 18
Chapter Structure 22

2 **From Chang'an to Xi'an – Urban Transformation
and Heritage Preservation** **27**

Tracing the Roots of the City 28
From *Gucheng* to Da Xi'an: Urban Transformation
in Xi'an 32
From Cultural Relics to Cultural Heritage – The History
of Heritage Management in China 37
Heritage Management in Xi'an 40

3 **The City of Civilization – Archaeological Heritage** **45**

Doubting Archaeology 48
Archaeology and Everyday Life 52
The Boom of Archaeological Parks 56
The Segregation of the Professional Community 61
The Ambivalence between Archaeology and History 67
The Uses of Archaeology in China 72

4 **The City of 'China' – Imperial Heritage** **75**

History and Everyday Life 77
Revitalizing an Imperial China 82
The Dilemma of 'Authenti(c)-city' 91
'His'-story? 'Her'-it-age? 96
'Re-membering' the Past 100

5   **The City of Connectivity – Silk Road Heritage**   **103**

         The Silk Roads as World Heritage   106
         The Politics of the Silk Roads Nomination   109
         The Myths of the Chinese Silk Road   122
         Silk Road on the Ground   126
         From the Ancient Silk Road to the Modern Silk Road
         Economic Belt   131

6   **The City of Copies – Modelized Heritage**   **137**

         The Rise of Qujiang   139
         'Xi'an City, Qujiang Province'   144
         Anti-Qujiang Sites   153
         2014: The Fall of Qujiang   155
         Local Views of Qujiang   158
         Branding the City   162

7   **The City of Communities – Urban Heritage**   **165**

         The Calligraphy Quarter   168
         The Muslim Quarter   170
         Comparison between the Two Quarters   173
         Historic Quarters in Change   179
         Social Strategies against Change   183
         Social Resilience with Chinese Characteristics   186

8   **The City of Construction – New Heritage**   **191**

         A New Old Xi'an   193
         China or Chai-na?   200
         Remaking the Urban Landscape   210
         The Dilemma between Pride and Shame   215

9   **Conclusion: The City of Cosmopolitanism**   **219**

         A Chinese View of Cosmopolitanism   220
         Connecting World Cities   224
         'Once a Cosmopolitan City, Forever a Cosmopolitan City'   225
         The Making of Cosmopolitanism   229

National Rejuvenation: Fulfilling the 'China Dream'
in Xi'an   231
Xi'an as the China Dream   233

Appendices   237

Bibliography   239

Index   275

List of Illustrations

Maps

1 Xi'an City in Shaanxi Province   5
2 Tang Chang'an   30
3 Four master plans for Xi'an   34
4 Greater Xi'an under Strategic Development   36
5 The sphere of influence of the Qujiang Model   145
6 Three historic conservation areas in Xi'an   167

Plates

1   Iconic view of Pit One   50
2   Floor Plan, Shaanxi History Museum   84
3   Timeline of Chinese history and mental timelines   85
4   Pre-tentative lists for the Silk Roads nomination   112
5   Salespersons in front of a reconstructed building in Silk Road Street 128
6   Reconstructed building in Silk Road Street   129
7   Model in the Silk Road Museum   134
8   Structure of Qujiang Corporation   142
9   Bird's-eye view over Qujiang District   144
10 High rises with neo-Tang rooftops   197
11 Signboard in Daming Palace Heritage Park   208
12 Reconstruction of a house from the Daming Palace area   210
13 'China Dream' slogans in Xi'an   232

(all photographs were taken by author [2013-2014])

Acknowledgements

Conducting my fieldwork in Xi'an and finishing this manuscript has not been easy, but fortunately, I was never alone through all the ups and downs. Without the invaluable support of the following people, this book would not have been possible. I would like to thank all of those whom I came across during my research from the bottom of my heart.

First and foremost, I am indebted to my supervisor, Prof. Christoph Brumann, head of our research group, 'The Global Political Economy of Cultural Heritage', in the Department 'Resilience and Transformation in Eurasia' of the Max Planck Institute for Social Anthropology, Halle (Saale), Germany. He inspired my work and showed remarkable faith in me from the beginning to the very end. He has been a truly supportive, inspiring and thoughtful teacher, who guided me patiently and encouraged me to overcome all challenges. Furthermore, I would like to express my thankfulness to my thesis committee members, Prof. David Berliner, Prof. Francois Bertemes, Prof. Sidney C. H. Cheung, and Prof. Chris Hann, for the insightful suggestions and comments. I am also grateful to the Max Planck Institute for Social Anthropology for providing me with an institutional home and to the research cluster and graduate school 'Society and Culture in Motion' of Martin Luther University of Halle-Wittenberg for giving me academic and financial support that enabled me to continue my exploration of anthropology.

I would like to express my sincere thanks to Prof. Erwin Emmerling and Dr. Catharina Blänsdorf for their great help in introducing me to the Terracotta Army Museum, which paved the way for the success of my fieldwork. A special thank you goes to Dr. Jennifer Cash, for her diligent editing and constructive criticism for this manuscript. Without her help, the publication of this book would not have been possible. My debt is equally great to the many people in Xi'an who welcomed me like a family member and shared their knowledge and social networks with me. I am also thankful to local scholars from different research institutions and museums who provided me with support in getting established in the field and carrying out my research. Without the support of my informants, my fieldwork would not have been possible.

I am similarly indebted to other members of my research group: Dr. Vivienne Marquart for her tireless support helping me especially in the last phase of my work; Dr. Pierpaolo de Giosa for his encouragement; Dr. Elisa Kohl-Garrity for being the sweetest and most caring office mate; and many other members – Dr. Mustafa Coskun, Dr. Lucia Facchini, Dr. Miriam Franchina, Dr. Hami Gümüs, Nadine Holesch, Dr. Daniel Pateisky, Dr. Sascha Roth, Dr. Daria Sambuk, Dr. Simon Schlegel, Dr. Jakub Stofanik,

Dr. Hendrik Tieke, Dr. Özgür Ucar, Dr. Ruijing Wang, and Dr. Fan Zhang –
for much guidance and assistance. It would be amiss if I did not
acknowledge the support of Jutta Turner for the wonderful maps and
German lessons. Anett Kirchhof, Ronald Kirchhof, Armin Pippel, Oliver-
Pierre Rudolph, Oliver Weihmann, and the student assistants of Department
II, including Ronny Klawunn, are due thanks for their inputs, technical
support and understandings. All my friends and colleagues in Halle made
memorable contributions to my stay in Germany being enjoyable and
rewarding.

Finally, I have to express my deepest gratefulness to my family
members. In particular, I have to thank my father and mother for providing
me with years of encouragement to pursue my passion. I am thankful that
they have continued to respect my decision to study anthropology – a very
unfamiliar field to them – for so many years. Lastly, my gratitude goes to
Konstantin Kinast who has always been there giving me support and
comfort. His kindness, care, patience, and intellect are imprinted on this
manuscript and myself.

Note on Transliteration

The main language spoken during my field research in the city of Xi'an was Mandarin. However, as older Xi'anese and people from the suburban areas speak a strong local Shaanxi dialect, this dialect is sometimes recorded here instead of Mandarin. I Romanize Chinese terms according to the pinyin system for both Mandarin Chinese and the Shaanxi dialect.

Personal names follow the Chinese order where the family name precedes the given name. Mostly, I refer to my informants as Mr. or Ms. with a fictive surname. I use real names only for famous politicians, government officials, academics, or artists.

This book is dedicated to my parents
Lok Sang Cheung and Ho Yi Cheung, with love.

Chapter 1
Introduction

In December 2013, Xi'an organized a German Christmas market in the city centre for the first time. Beneath the Bell Tower, locals experienced an 'authentic' German Christmas, taking glühwein, beer, and sausages from stands decorated with fake snow. Sponsored by Zwilling, a German kitchen utensils company, the central stand sold pots and cooking utensils, while the other stands sold other German-branded products. Yet, the most eye-catching element of the market was neither the cute huts with foreign products, nor the exotic food. It was a terracotta warrior dressed up with seasonal adornments. Every time I passed by the market, I saw many people queued to take photos with it.

A week after my first visit to the Christmas market, I met the woman who had supplied the statue of the warrior. The meeting was incidental. I had an internship at the world-famous Emperor Qin Shihuang Mausoleum Site Museum. The mausoleum is also sometimes referred to as the Mausoleum of the First Qin Emperor, and the museum on its site is more simply referred to as the Terracotta Army Museum. It was one of the museum guards who had supplied the market's statue. The woman also owned a warrior replica factory. After work, the same day I met her, she drove me to her factory. There, warrior replicas of different colours, materials, and sizes were produced. She told me that she was very proud of her job as a guard at the World Heritage site, but when I asked about her own business, she expressed even more excitement, particularly about this warrior she had provided for the Christmas market. She said with a big grin on her face: 'I have not been to the market myself yet, but I heard that the organizer dressed him up as Santa Claus!' She was amazed that her warrior's historical image had been so easily cast off.

Indeed, the set-up of the Christmas market with its German huts contrasted against the Ming Dynasty Bell Tower[1] and the warrior's trans-

---

[1] For the Bell Tower, as with many of the sites that appear in this book, it is sometimes important to call attention to their form or appearance in a particular era. Normally, I have

formation into Santa Claus demonstrates how tradition, history, and modernity harmonize with each other in Xi'an. It shows too how historical images are given modern meanings to align with the changing society. As Xi'an, the ancient capital, has become more globalized and modernized, its citizens have witnessed a vivid moment of social transformation.

Xi'an, like many other Chinese cities, has undergone intensive and rapid modern development under the state's modernization discourse and programs. In particular, Xi'an has been transformed under the Four Modernization Plan, which aims at strengthening industrial, agricultural, military, scientific and technological development (Rofel 1999). Schemes under this and other plans have altered the cityscape in many places throughout China. However, Xi'an differs from other cities because it is home to many important heritage sites and archaeological remains which the state uses to enhance nationalism and economic development. Consequently, Xi'an has to balance between the demands of heritage preservation and urban development. Its historical sites are confronted with endless construction works, while the population's traditional practices are challenged by elements of modernity on a daily basis.

The relation between heritage and development is not always one of contrast or opposition. As Lisa Rofel (1997) pointed out, 'history has not been erased by the search of modern' (173). And, the presence of 'history' is even one of the most important signs of modernity (Dirks 1990). In Xi'an, one can observe how history and modernity coexist and are strongly inter-linked. Accordingly, this book analyses the dynamic interaction between heritage preservation and modern development and investigates how various social actors perceive the 'dilemma' between history and modernity.

Since the 1990s, China has experienced a heritage boom. In addition to promoting its own national heritage projects, China has also participated actively in the international heritage arena. China ratified UNESCO's Convention Concerning the Protection of the World Cultural and Natural Heritage in 1985 (World Heritage Convention), much later than many Western countries. Yet it quickly caught up with the nomination of World Heritage sites. As of 2015, China boasted the second highest number of sites on the UNESCO World Heritage List with 48 items listed (Italy had 51 sites listed) (UNESCO 2015). At the time of this book's publication, Italy had only one more site listed than China (54/ 53) and it is foreseeable that China

---

done this by preceding the site's name with the relevant dynasty (e.g. Qin, Han, Tang, Ming, Qing) but without stressing 'dynasty'. Appendix 1 provides a chronology of China's imperial dynasties; Plate 3 provides a visualization of the more local reckonings of the dynastic past. Sometimes, too, I refer to a historical period or dynasty only by its name (e.g. 'in the Tang' or 'after the downfall of the Tang'); this follows Chinese usage.

will soon lead the UNESCO list. There are at least two motivations for the rise of heritage in China. First, China's participation can be seen as a bid to participate in a global phenomenon. Gaining the title of 'World Heritage' does represent an 'expert' valuation, but more importantly, it boosts the international recognition of a country's past. Such recognition helps establish a good reputation for China and helps strengthen nationalism. Second, World Heritage functions as a brand and can attract financially lucrative tourism. For these political, diplomatic, social, and economic advantages, many sites in China have been nominated and inscribed on the World Heritage List since the 1990s.

However, the term 'heritage' evokes various images in different sectors of society. Heritage projects are executed according to different interests and understanding of the concept. International organizations assess heritage sites by their aesthetic, historical, ethnological, and scientific value (what is called by UNESCO, 'Outstanding Universal Value'). The state looks for potential to boost its international reputation, pursue nation-building, or both. The provincial government wants to increase its national competitiveness. The city aims to construct a common local identity among its residents. Developers uses heritage to increase the price of real estate. Local citizens have personal attachments to sites, associated with memories. Even in a country like China, where the state plays a dominant role in heritage projects, decisions are not solely made by one party. There is limited space for other heritage actors to use social media, specific professional knowledge, and other strategies to negotiate with the government. The rich resources of cultural heritage, the increasing development of historical attractions, the diversity of heritage sites, and the freshly listed World Heritage sites in Xi'an create a dynamic interface of heritage development between local, national, and transnational levels.

My research was conducted within the framework of the research group 'The Global Political Economy of Cultural Heritage' at the Max Planck Institute for Social Anthropology in Halle, Germany. This group centred its attention on contestations around cityscapes and heritage sites. My research in Xi'an complements two other studies – on Istanbul and Melaka – undertaken within the group (Marquart 2015; De Giosa 2016). Our group leader was Christoph Brumann, who observed that the scope of World Heritage has been significantly broadened in the first decade of the twenty-first century. Emphasis has shifted from elite and monumental sites – palaces and cathedrals – to other forms of heritage, including vernacular architecture, cultural routes, and intangible cultural heritage (Brumann 2012b, 2015). Like my colleagues, I explored not only the elite heritage sites of the Terracotta Army Museum and other ancient palaces, but also shop houses, urban neighbourhoods, and public traditions. With the shared interest in uncovering the instrumental purposes of heritage, the present-day uses of the past, and the contested socio-politics, our group explored the dynamic inter-play between transnational, national, and local agencies. As a result, all our studies challenge the official understanding of heritage provided by UNESCO. Heritage is not just 'remains from the past'; nor is World Heritage just that which presents outstanding universal value. 'Heritage' is made, and recognized, and it bears important political, social, and economic dimensions.

During my research, I was also a member of the International Max Planck Research School for the Anthropology, Archaeology, and History of Eurasia. Accordingly, this research was developed under an inter-disciplinary framework, and I discuss the roles and use of archaeology and history in heritage making, alongside my anthropological insights. Taken together, this book, based on one year of ethnographic fieldwork from August 2013 to September 2014, aims to explore how experts and ordinary residents of Xi'an envision the city's past and respond to its transformation under the twin-projects of urbanization and heritagization.

Field Situation: A City of the Past

When introducing my field site to non-Chinese friends, many said that they had never heard of the city. However, once I told them that 'it is the place where the terracotta army was buried', then they suddenly knew it. One of them even tried to correct me: 'Oh! You mean Chang'an!' The city's past fame seems to have exceeded its present status. Xi'an was formerly called Chang'an. In the present, Xi'an is the capital city of Shaanxi Province, located geographically at the heart of China (see Map 1).

According to a census conducted in 2010, the population of Xi'an consists of 8,467,837 people (Xi'an City People's Government 2011). The great majority (99.1 per cent) are ethnic Han Chinese, and the remaining 81,500 ethnic minorities are mostly Hui (50,000).[2] In the late 1990s, the state emphasized Xi'an's economic development as it carried out the Open Up the West Program (Xibu dakaifa). This program, which aimed to strengthen the economy of western China, allowed Xi'an to re-emerge as an important cultural, industrial, and educational centre. The population soared and high residential buildings mushroomed. Echoing the state's Four Modernization Plan, industrial factories, scientific research centres and national security

---

[2] The Hui are one of China's 56 officially recognized ethnic groups. They are also known as 'Chinese Muslims' because they practise Islam but (unlike other Muslim groups in China) speak Chinese. In Xi'an, most Hui reside in the city's Muslim Quarter.

facilities were relocated to Xi'an. Since then, Xi'an has relied on the production of heavy machinery, a light secondary manufacturing industry for electronic products, and a tertiary tourism industry. The total GDP of the city was 628.3 billion CNY in 2016, which has increased steadily at the rate of 8.6 per cent per year.[3] The tertiary industry developed constantly and accounted for 61.3 per cent of the whole GDP composition.

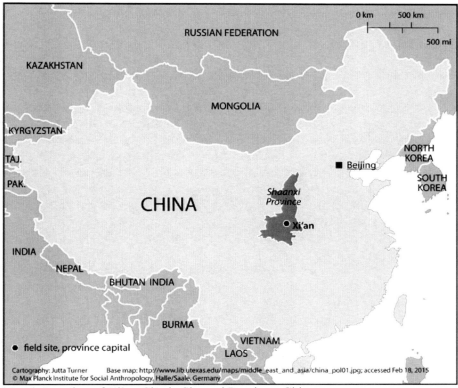

Map 1. Location of Xi'an City in Shaanxi Province, China.

The tourism industry developed so quickly and became so important to the economy by capitalizing on the city's historical and cultural resources. Xi'an is one of the oldest cities in China. Its history has been documented for more than 3,100 years, and it is regarded as 'the cradle of Chinese civilization' (Feighery 2011). It was the seat of power for thirteen dynasties, including

---

[3] Based on statistics through 2018. http://china-trade-research.hktdc.com/business-news/article/Facts-and-Figures/Xi-an-Shaanxi-City-Information/ff/en/1/1X000000/ 1X0A14EA. htm. Last accessed 28 February 2019. See also HKTDC (2011).

the Western Zhou (eleventh century BCE to 771 BCE), Qin (211 BCE to 207 BCE), Han (206 BCE to 24 CE), Sui (581 CE to 618 CE), and Tang (618 CE to 907 CE) (see Appendix 1). During the Han Dynasty, Xi'an was known as Chang'an, meaning 'Eternal Peace'. It served as the eastern end of the Silk Road, and it was one of the biggest cities in the world during its peak era under the Tang Dynasty (around 690 CE) when it reached an estimated population of one million inhabitants (Beckwith 2009). Chang'an's layout also served as a blueprint for other ancient cities, like Kyoto and Nara, which were built in Japan around 794 CE. Today's Xi'an abounds in places of archaeological and historic interest, including the Mausoleum of the Yellow Emperor, the Mausoleum of the First Qin Emperor, Xi'an City Wall, the Forest of Steles, the Big and Small Wild Goose pagodas, the Banpo Museum, Han Chang'an city remains, and numerous temples and palaces.

The Chinese state has long been aware of Xi'an's historical significance. In 1982, the government designated it a 'national historic city' (*lishi wenhua mingcheng*) and acknowledged the city's efforts to preserve its rich collection of cultural relics and architectural structures (Wang 2000). On the World Heritage stage, Xi'an experienced its first fame in 1987. Just two years after China ratified the World Heritage Convention, the Mausoleum of the First Qin Emperor was inscribed in the UNESCO list. This made it one of the first World Heritage sites to represent China, along with the Great Wall and the Forbidden City. However, Xi'an had no new inscriptions until 2014. For years, a few items from the city lingered on China's Tentative List: such as some Silk Road-related historical sites dated back to the Chang'an era, the Mingqing City Wall, the Forest of Steles, and Mount Hua.[4] In June 2014, as parts of the trans-boundary Silk Roads World Heritage nomination, Xi'an contributed five sites for the heritage route: Big Wild Goose Pagoda, Small Wild Goose Pagoda, Xingjiao Temple, Daming Palace, and Weiyang Palace.

The city's heritage has been recognized on other terms as well. The national government classified three-quarters of the city as 'historic conservation areas' in order to preserve the traditional townscape, and has designated shop houses as 'living heritage' (see chapter 7). Moreover, Xi'an has preserved a number of intangible cultural heritage forms, including the

---

[4] The Tentative Lists drafted by states include sites which the state considers suitable for inscription on the World Heritage List. The Tentative List must be submitted to the World Heritage Centre at least one year before the submission of any nomination to be considered for World Heritage status. In World Heritage discussions, Xi'an's City Wall is often referred to as the Mingqing City Wall, referring to its structure with reference to both the Ming and Qing dynasties. In other contexts, as reflected by terminology in this book, only the Ming structure is emphasized. However, the building and architectural style across the two dynasties is considered distinct, as Mingqing.

Xi'an wind and percussion ensemble which was inscribed on the Representation List of Intangible Cultural Heritage of Humanity in 2009.[5]

Geographically speaking, Xi'an and its surroundings are dotted by heritage sites, not only in the densely populated urban setting, but also in the rural perimeters. For example, the terracotta army lays 37.5 kilometres away from Xi'an's centre and the Han Chang'an city remains located in the north-western corner of Xi'an were designated as rural and restricted zones for construction work (to protect the archaeological treasures). The zoning shows that the city government values certain archaeological remains and prioritizes the preservation of historical sites. Similarly, the city government decided to construct the Xi'an airport almost 40 kilometres away from the city centre in a different direction for the same reason: to avoid disturbing archaeological remains. However, at the same time, the city has intensified urbanization in the past decade and the urban area has expanded rapidly. The urban development projects have a huge impact on the cityscape, the historical and archaeological sites nearby, and the local inhabitants. In Xi'an, many of these projects took place in the late 1990s, putting many heritage sites at risk (see chapter 2).

Contributions

Previous regional research projects on Xi'an have mainly focused on archaeology and history, studying very specific topics of a site or a limited time frame (Song 1990; Fong 1991; Shatzman Steinhardt 1991, 2004; Chung 1996, 1998; Guo and Guo 2001; Louis 2005; Han 2006; Chen, Wang and Chen 2009). These works examine archaeological finds from excavations and historical archival documents in order to develop a better understanding of the culture, society, political system, and mode of production in the prehistoric and imperial periods. Yet, only limited research has been conducted on the role of archaeology and history in contemporary Xi'an. Hence, this thesis focuses on the modern use of history and archaeology, and on how the two disciplines construct the past. It questions the production of historical knowledge and archaeological 'facts' and critically analyses the information and layout of the displays at the heritage sites. In fact, in present-day Xi'an, both history and archaeology play an important role in the construction of the city's identity and of urban social life.

---

[5] The Xi'an wind and percussion ensemble denotes a type of religious music that integrates drums, wind instruments, and male chorus. It has been played for more than a millennium in Xi'an. The music is played usually on religious occasions, such as temple fairs or funerals, and its texts describe local life or religious belief.

Contemporary social scientific studies on Xi'an tend to investigate industrialization and its impact on the city (Ge and Zhang 1998; Wan, Wang and Zhu 2001; Zhang H. N. 2001), conflict between Han and other ethnic groups (Gillette 2008; Dorsten and Li 2011), private and public housing (Wang 1992, 1995), and the increasing environmental problems (Han et al. 2006; Li and Feng 2010). These academic works identify various changes caused by modernization and urbanization. However, very little attention has been paid to the dilemmas of conjoining urban planning with historical preservation. In the 2000s, there have been a number of publications on the individual themes of urban planning (Yin and Liu 2002), tourism development (Wang and Liu 2011; Xu and Chu 2012), and heritage conservation in specific urban districts (Gillette 2000, 2008; Wang 2000; Feighery 2008, 2011). Only one, so far as I can tell, puts urbanization and heritagization into a common critical framework. Wang (2000) used Xi'an to illustrate how the conservation of historic cities in China brings together the apparatus of the state, socialist ideology, and market reform to effect policies on heritage protection.

My research thus sheds light on the general understanding of heritage development in Xi'an as a reflection of overall heritage development in China. Instead of just focusing on a specific site, it applies a holistic approach to uncover the politics of heritagization in the whole city. Moreover, this work contributes to the regional studies of Xi'an and Shaanxi Province by providing an in-depth ethnographic account of negotiation and decision making in processes related to social change. It aims to contribute to four broad fields: the anthropology of China, heritage studies, urban anthropology, and multi-disciplinary studies.

The Anthropology of China

As China continues with its economic development, the authorities have increasingly used the terms 'modern' (*xiandai*) and 'modernization' (*xiandaihua*) in political slogans and propaganda since the late 1990s. In an ancient city like Xi'an, where history plays an important socio-political role, how do the city government and the inhabitants react to the state's modernization discourse? What is the relationship between modernity and history? Does modernity erase history? So far, not many studies in China have addressed social change and the interplay between history, tradition, and modernity. This research, hence, aims to contribute a case study demonstrating a possible interrelationship between modernity and history in heritage development.

Modernity normally appears in an oppositional relation to what is of the past and 'traditional', but its relation with history is never straightforward. Many scholars have insisted that traditions are invented, formally instituted, and used to serve present-day agendas (e.g. Hobsbawm 1983; Salvatore 2009: 6). History too is highly fluid, constructed to fit national discourse, and closely related to modernity. From the other side of the relation, Robert Schreiter understood modernity as a 'selective use of traditions' (2000: 302), and Nicholas Dirks (1990) asserted that history is one of the most important components of modernity. Thus, history, tradition, and modernity do not oppose but rather sustain each other. Even Clement Greenberg pointed out the interrelationship between modernity and the past: 'I cannot insist enough that modernism has never meant, and does not mean now, anything like a break with the past' (1993: 92). I have observed exactly that connection in Xi'an. Although the Chinese regime and its people consider tradition as something backwards[6], history and modernity are interlinked in today's Xi'an.

The majority of literature from the West regards 'modernity' as comprised of specific modes of social life and organization, liberalism, and progress, which emerged in Europe from about the seventeenth century onwards (Giddens 1990: 1). The idea of modernity has been criticized by many anthropologists because of its Euro-centric connotations and its implied unilineal and uniform formation (Therborn 2003; Thomassen 2012). Shmuel Eisenstadt (2000) has proposed the concept of 'multiple modernities' to argue against the longstanding associations of modernization with Westernization and of Western patterns of modernity as its 'authentic' form. In this research, I follow the understanding of modernity proposed by Lisa Rofel: 'modernity is a struggle that takes place in specific locations and a process that knits together local/ global configurations' (1999: 18).

Historians and social scientists have debated vehemently about China's modernity. Numerous studies argue that China entered modernity in the late Qing period around the early 1900s, when it encountered globalization and was strongly influenced by colonialism (Cochrane 2000; Yeh 2000; Fong, Qian and Zurndorfer 2004; Qian 2004). Others argue that China only experienced modernity in the postsocialist era, namely after Deng Xiaoping advocated the Open Door Policy in 1978 (Rofel 1999; Kam 2008). Stephan Feuchtwang (2004) distinguished three modernizations in China: first, a late dynastic native modernization in the mid-nineteenth century; second, a planned and anti-capitalist modernization from 1953 to 1978; and third, since the 1980s, the fastest modernization 'with private Chinese and transitional corporations supplementing state-backed corporations' (p. 16). The last phase of modernization continues to change

---

[6] Tradition is associated with the Four Olds (old customs, old habits, old culture, and old thinking) that were to be abolished during the Cultural Revolution (1966–76).

urban planning, style of architecture, and consumer behaviour. In general, most scholars consider that China is still seeking its own way to understand modernity. Some assert that China's way of pursuing material and moral parity looks towards the West and is highly linked to the Western understanding of production, technology, and rationality (Rofel 1999: 9–10; Feuchtwang 2004: 15). Others highlight the Chinese characteristics of modern culture, including elements from the historical imperial era (Kam 2008: 6). In fact, both 'Western' and 'native' approaches to modernity exist in China, as will be demonstrated in this study.

Certainly since the 2000s, an increasing number of studies have asserted China's modernity from specific angles. For example, there has been attention to the changing gender relationship (Rofel 1999; Duara 2000), family and kinship structure (Yang 1996; Greenhalgh 2003), industrial development (Kirby 2000), and consumption patterns (Yan 1997; Lee 2000; Yeh 2000; Sabbon 2014). Whereas the coastal cities in China used consumption habits to demonstrate modernity and cosmopolitanism to 'keep pace with other urban cities around the world' (Yeh 2000: 8), provincial cities located inland achieve modernity through projects of municipal bureaucracy and planners (Kirby 2000; Strand 2000; Yeh 2000). As David Strand (2000) observed, the urban status of cities like Lanzhou was eroded when compared to the coastal ports.

As we will see in this study, Xi'an, despite its inland location, manifests 'modernity' at both levels of local consumer behaviours and through municipal and provincial government-led projects. Moreover, modernity is under discussion across all social segments. During my fieldwork in Xi'an, the term 'modern' was used often in daily conversation. Terms such as *xiandai*, and the obviously borrowed *modeng*, are invoked often to describe various aspects of architectural style or lifestyle. Hence, this study investigates modernity in the emic way, as it is used by government and local inhabitants to refer to urbanization and development, as well as to a new 'style', that dates not much further back than the 1990s.

The core topic of this thesis – the politics of heritage in Xi'an – relates to the concept of modernity in two ways. First, 'heritage' itself is a concept that adheres to the 'modern' period of Xi'an. That is to say, the heritage boom in China took place only in the late 1990s. Before that, the state did not see much value in historical or archaeological sites. Second, a shift from 'heritage conservation' to 'heritage development' shows another aspect of modernity. Conceptually, heritage and development are opposed to each other: heritage refers to old sites and things that need to be preserved, but development implies change and advancement. Although the government emphasizes the conservation of cultural relics in official documents, it regards heritage projects as development-oriented in its slogans and propaganda. This use and perception of heritage is an expression of modernity in China.

The politics of heritage in Xi'an show a clear connection between modernity and nationalism. In many countries, not least China, the state becomes interested in preserving (or developing) sites that promise to enhance nationalism and patriotism (Abu el Haj 1998; Henderson 2002; Flath 2004). The narration and display of heritage sites are highly controlled by the state and linked strongly to national education and nationalism (Therborn 2003: 301). Just like heritage development, nationalism, too, is a product of modernity (Ong 2005). And, nationalism ties the past together with modernity: 'Nationalism, is a modern phenomenon, although there is some controversy about its roots and precedents. However, there is no nationalism without some resurrection of a past, however imagined' (Therborn 2003: 296).

Certainly nationalism has been one of the most common themes addressed within Chinese studies. It has been treated through the diverse lenses of 'bio-politics' (Greenhalgh 2009; Salter and Waldby 2011) and policies concerning ethnic minorities (Harrell 1995; Gladney 1998, 2004; Oakes 1998). Nationalism in China is always linked to the power of the state: it can be understood as a form of governance to regulate the population and as a part of the state-building project (Duara 1995, 2009; Anagnost 1997; Ong 2005). Again, in the state-building project, we find a strong link to heritage making and historical narration. As Stevan Harrell observed, 'Chinese nationalism, ever since its inception in the late nineteenth century, has combined an odd mix of pride in its ancient and marvellous civilization, its moral, social, and culinary superiority to the rest of the world, with self-loathing for not being able to keep up with the West, or even more shamefully, with Japan' (Harrell 2013: 289). Xi'an's politics of heritage exemplifies the state's attempt to constitute nationalism and a common historical narration through the glorification of certain historical periods or sites. By placing stress on the long and splendid civilization of China, Chinese people develop a strong feeling for the nation and Xi'an locals become proud.

Heritage Studies

The Convention Concerning the Protection of the World Cultural and Natural Heritage defines cultural heritage as 'monuments, groups of buildings or sites, which are of Outstanding Universal Value' (UNESCO 1972). The definition is widely used by heritage conservationists, architects, restorers, and government officials. However, the definition only refers to the physical manifestation and so-called value of heritage. It would be hard enough to create a more precise definition of the 'things' that constitute heritage, as 'heritage today all but defies definition' (Lowental 1998: 94). But, a definition like UNESCO's ignores the social continuity of a heritage 'site', its relation to nearby communities, and the political implications of recognizing its value. Therefore, as an anthropologist, I follow a broader understanding of heritage as a 'fluid matter', the invocation of which contributes to social, political, and economic needs (Ashworth 2011: 3). Moreover, when heritage is 'practised' on the ground, it is defined and conceived differently due to multiple interests, and the criteria for recognizing heritage differ. Laurajane Smith opined that 'there is no such thing as heritage' (2006: 13, my emphasis). Rather, heritage is 'a cultural practice involved in constructing and regulating a wide range of values and understandings' (ibid. 11). The 'authorized heritage discourse' that emerges from this practice, continued Smith, is inherently political and discordant; it performs the legitimation and de-legitimation of cultures. Others who have insisted that heritage is both more and less than a 'valuable site' have called it –a social phenomenon (Breglia 2006: 16), a label (Fyall, Garrod and Leask 2003: 207; Ryan and Silvanto 2009: 290; Yaniv, Arie and Raviv 2010: 483), a political tool (Silberman 1989: 8; Trigger 1989: 13; Flath 2002: 57; Henderson 2002: 337; Denton 2005: 581), an economic means (Ashworth and Larkham 1994: 22), [a set of] discourses (Clifford 2004: 5; Smith 2006: 14), and a 'use of the past' (Silverman 2010: 203). As we shall see in Xi'an, it is not only heritage, but also other related concepts – such as 'authenticity', 'identity', 'history', and 'archaeology' – that are bound up with power relations and used as tools to serve political discourses.

As Christoph Brumann (2009) pointed out, the recognition of 'heritage' has social consequences involving four typical phenomena: falsification, petrification, desubstantiation, and enclosure. Turning a place into a heritage site involves the beautification of the past, suppression of cultural change, the branding of the heritage label and self-aggrandizement of the proclaimed 'owner' of the heritage. That is to say, as Lisa Breglia did, that 'heritage' is not a singular practice, but involves several practices (2006: 11). I follow this lead to underline the social relationships and contingent practices in the heritage city.

Taken together, these practices constitute a process of heritagization. This process entails dynamic interactions between different social actors who interpret the meaning and uses of the sites differently. Heritage is created to fit the needs of many: people, communities, and government authorities (Harvey 2001; Ashworth and Graham 2005; Smith 2006). My research avoids showing a one-sided-story of the heritage issues in Xi'an and demonstrates the embedded social background and meanings of heritage.

For the moment, let us follow Brumann's (2014) classification of actors in the heritagization process according to their 'belief'. There are three types of person, he wrote: the believer, the atheist, and the agnostic. Heritage believers are those 'who are tacitly or explicitly committed to cultural heritage in general or to specific heritage items of whose intrinsic value they are convinced and whose conservation they endorse' (ibid.: 173). They firmly believe that heritage does good to society in economic and educational terms. A number of my informants, including government officials, experts, and architects, were 'heritage believers' – at least in their professional capacity. By contrast, heritage atheists are sceptical and have a 'fundamental doubt about the value of specific heritage items or heritage as such' (ibid.: 174). I met few such individuals. Most of the local residents in Xi'an are better described as 'agnostic'; they were not critical about heritage. They agreed with the values of heritage, but were not committed to their realization.

Helaine Silverman (2010) concluded that heritage is highly contested. Indeed, many ethnographies highlight the 'dark side' of heritage, full of tension and conflicts between the empowered and the powerless (Herzfeld 1991; Bartu 2001; Joy 2012; Probst 2011; Franquesa 2013). To take just two examples: Lisa Breglia (2006) presented how private and public actors in Chichén Itzá compete for the right to benefit economically and to gain control of heritage, while Charlotte Joy (2007) examined the struggles faced by a majority of local residents as Djenné, Mali gained in historical renown. Disharmony and ambivalence dominate contemporary ethnographic accounts to an extent that heritage would seem only to be a field of disputes and conflicts. I too found it easier to spot disputes than to identify (sometimes secret) alliances between groups. Heritage is contested and ambivalent, but it is at the same time formed due to the support, collaboration, and networks between different actors. James Clifford (2004) highlighted this possibility for teamwork, but few studies have looked for cooperation (Herzfeld 1991; Grimwade and Carter 2000; Cheung 2003). This book therefore attempts to display not only the conflicts but also the collaborations and compromises. These are made between and within actors at local, national, and global levels. This book shows too how networks for such collaboration are made, and how tactics are applied in order to maintain heritage sites.

Concerning heritage studies in China, there are few that go beyond asserting the value and history of the sites. The investigation of cultural heritage policies, debates, and practices – antagonistic or cooperative – is rare. There are studies of touristic development. Most such studies explore the phenomenon of globalization and tourism development in rural China (Siu 1989, 1990; Park 2014). There has been concern for the impact of tourism on the local traditions and lifestyles of ethnic minorities (Oakes 1998, 2006, 2013; Notar 2006). These studies show the increasing influence of Han institutions and government organizations and a tendency towards the Sinicization of minorities (Mackerras 2003; Nyiri 2006; Li and Wall 2008; Su and Teo 2008, 2009; Li 2011). They also demonstrate how local communities frequently welcome tourism and exoticize themselves to cater to it (Oakes 1997, 2006; Dombroski 2008). Such studies offer, unfortunately, little direct ground for comparison with the overall politics of heritage in an urban setting like Xi'an, where tourism has become one of the major industries and has been used to boost the real estate market.

Furthermore, just as this book aims at breaking through the conflictual approach of most critical heritage studies, it aims to break through the top-down approach applied by most of the studies concerning heritage in China. This approach has been assumed valid because of the government-led nature of the existing management model for heritage development in China (Lu 2008). These studies examine the role of government departments and institutions and demonstrate the national interests of heritage projects (Goodman 2002; Du Cros and Lee 2007; Gruber 2007; Wang and Zan 2011; Tang 2013). The top-down approach eschews the involvement of and consultation with other social actors affected by developmental projects (Lu 2006, 2008). Only a few anthropologists have investigated heritage projects from local perspectives (Svensson 2006; Blumenfield and Silverman 2013; Nitzky 2013). Therefore, this work puts emphasis on the ground and attempts to cover the opinions from as many social actors as possible, not overlooking the negotiation with and even resistance to the government-dominated heritage management model. It adapts a holistic, both top-down and bottom-up, approach in demonstrating the dynamic interaction between international, national, provincial, municipal agents, the market, pro-fessionals, as well as ordinary residents and community members. It fills the gap of missing local voices and points to the interrelations between the different levels of society.

Urban Anthropology

Due to increasing urbanization everywhere, anthropological research has shifted gradually from studying 'tribes' in remote areas to studying cities (Southall 1973; Antweiler 2004). Theoretically and methodologically, the study of cities can be challenging. Rather than only focusing on segments, particular sites, communities, or neighbourhoods within a city, I attempted an 'anthropology of the city' (Hannerz 1980: 248), following a holistic approach to the study of urban space and social life. In viewing the city as a whole, I apprehend its residents as the social actors who effect change, and are affected by change, in the planning and transformation of urban spaces and life-ways. I look at how Xi'an's residents use the city's past, brand it, and construct a local and urban identity for it.

In this endeavour, I have drawn from many of the dominant strands in urban anthropology. These include poststructural studies of race, class, and gender; political economic studies of transnational culture; and studies of the symbolic and social production of urban space and planning (Low 1999). The concept of space has been particularly important. Spatial relations can be understood as cultural, political, and economic practices (Harvey 1989; Holston 1989; Rabinow 1989; Davis 1990). Like heritage, space is also 'not a thing but rather a set of relations between things [objects and products]' (Lefebvre 1991: 83). This definition highlights the interactions that take place in and around urban heritage sites.

Take the ancient city wall in Xi'an as an example. If the city wall were to be analysed as 'a thing in space', it would be studied as a historical feature. Applying Henri Lefebvre's approach of the 'production of space', the ancient city wall participates in a number of spatial relations along the vectors of human action, history, and political economy. As heritage sites become developed and commercialized as 'things', their socio-spatial relations change. To trace such relations and changes, I adopted Setha Low's (1996a) four foci for the analysis of spatial relations: historical emergence, socio-political and economic structuring, patterns of social use, and experiential meanings. This study concentrates most on the social uses, drawing further inspiration from other anthropological approaches to the social production and construction of space (Liggett 1995; Low 1996b) and the use of urban space (Whyte 1980).

China is devoted to an intensive phase of urbanization as the state promotes urban renewal and regeneration projects as part of its modernization agenda. Demolition, urbanization, and reconstruction serve as a tactic that the government uses to achieve modernization (see chapter 8). Hence, urban designs are perceived as an epitome of modernity (Rabinow 1988: 361) and are an important component of China's contemporary political economy. Consequently, there has been an upsurge of studies on Chinese cities over the past two decades. These cover issues ranging from rural-urban migration (Yang 1994; Zhang Li 2001, 2012; Guang 2003; Xiang 2005), urban consumer culture (Yan 1997; Davis 2000; Latham, Klein and Thompson 2006), ethnic identities (Honig 1992; Schein 2000b; Gladney 2004), family composition and kinship matters (Ikels 2004; Whyte 2004), spatial reconstruction (Zhang Li 2006; Li 2010), urban hierarchy (Guldin and Southall 1993; Jankowiak 1993), and political economy (Auty 1992; Johnson 1993; Gustafsson and Li 2000). However, these studies focus only on a specific group, district, or community within Chinese cities and, moreover, only cover a narrow topic. They do not portray the social life and characteristics of the studied city as a whole. Only two ethnographies in China, Charlotte Ikels' (1996) research project in Guangzhou and Björn Kjellgren's (2002) work in Shenzhen, manage to conduct an 'anthropology of the city' which, in refraining from singling out one specific issue, contribute towards a broader understanding of contemporary Chinese culture and society on multiple points.

Most research projects on urban heritage in China choose cities with a colonial background as the field of study. These include Shanghai (Zhang 2000; Pan 2005; Shen 2009; Farrer 2010; Lagerkvist 2010), Tianjin (Marinelli 2010), Harbin (Clausen and Thogersen 1995), Qingdao (Hiery 1999; Huang 1999; Biener 2001; Demgenski 2018), and Hong Kong (Cheung 1999, 2003; Henderson 2002; Lu 2003, 2009). These studies analyse the social changes in cities, and address the problems of Westernization and modernization. However, their time depth is relatively shallow. For instance, Tracey Lie Dan Lu's (2003) work on the changing heritage discourse in Hong Kong considers only the period after 1997, when Hong Kong was returned to China; in this context, society began to treasure the colonial heritage and to stress their colonial identity. Similarly, Tianshu Pan's (2005) study of Shanghai shows how local inhabitants developed a nostalgic feeling towards 'colonial heritage' as a counterpoint to 'Mao nostalgia'.

The interaction between history and urban spaces has only been addressed for a handful of ancient Chinese cities without foregrounding a colonial experience. Beijing has been the best studied (Sit 1996; Abramson 2001; Winston Yan 2006; Currier 2008; Zhang 2008; Li 2010), but Nanjing (Li 2010), Kashgar (Li 2010), and Kunming (Zhang 2006) have been studied too. Hence, in-depth studies on urban heritage and social life and their complex interplay in Chinese cities remain limited. As a second-tier city geographically removed from central power, Xi'an enjoys more freedom in the making of urban planning and heritage preservation policies than cities such as Beijing and Shanghai. While the glorification of the city's imperial past is imposed from a top-down level by the provincial authorities, the locals are also genuinely proud of their own past and regard themselves as descendants from the dynasties. By examining the implication of modern heritage development in an ancient capital, my research project will add to the literature on contemporary urban China.

Multi-Disciplinary Studies

A further goal of this study was to achieve cross-fertilization between the three disciplines of anthropology, archaeology, and history. The three disciplines are natural partners for any interrogation of the relationships between the past and society. After all, archaeologists use excavated findings and material culture to imagine the societies of a distant past, historians traditionally analyse textual materials to imagine and interpret past society, and anthropologists – though they mostly work on contemporary societies – consult historical materials to understand present behaviour and values. My anthropological study of Xi'an's cultural heritage development, however, requires a more direct engagement with history and archaeology. This is because both archaeological and historical sites play a dominant role in heritage politics and everyday life.[7] The presence of these sites deeply impacts the government's vision and the locals' worldview about the past, present, and future. Thus, studying the perception of heritage and the accompanying negotiation with modernization in the present cannot ignore the shape and role of archaeology and history.

Indeed, most scholarly articles and books about Xi'an have been published by archaeologists and historians. Such studies typically provide in-depth knowledge of a specific time or site (Song 1990; Fong 1991; Shatzman Steinhardt 1991, 2004; Chung 1996; Guo and Guo 2001; Louis 2005; Han 2006; Chen, Wang and Chen 2009). However, they do not highlight the social aspects of their research objects. In contrast, my research turned to examine how modern society views, remembers, narrates, and uses the past as it has been recorded by historians and archaeologists. By undertaking a qualitative study of a community's symbolic aspects of culture from a historical point of view, I used the concept and methods of 'historical anthropology' (Burke 1987). I drew on oral history and secondary sources on policies, laws, and regulations on urban planning and heritage preservation. I also collected old photographs from the archives to study the changing townscape. The social history narrated to me by locals challenges the national official historical narrative. Yet I also document how the past is being constructed by certain government agencies, through the narration of history at heritage sites and in other elements of the cityscape.

Although the scientific literature on Xi'an has been conducted to-date within tight disciplinary boundaries, I had many streams on which to draw

---

[7] Though excavations may be undertaken at all sites, I distinguish 'archaeological' sites as those pre-dating the existence of written records. 'Historical' sites, to the contrary, are likely to be mentioned, described, and documented in detail by official and unofficial Chinese records.

for inspiration in crossing these. Archaeology itself presents many models as the discipline has, like history, long intended to study 'society' in addition to artefacts. Early in the 1930s, for example, a group of European archaeologists established the field of social archaeology with the intention to explore the intersection of temporality, spatiality, and materiality in past societies (Meskell 1998, 2005). One of the earliest social archaeologists, Gordon Childe (1946) stressed that the study of 'past societies' should be the goal of archaeology and insisted that human consciousness could not be separated from social organization. Since the 1990s, there have also been attempts to develop 'archaeological ethnography' which consists of putting together 'a mosaic of traditional forms, including archaeological practice and museum or representational analysis, as well as long-term involvement, participant observation, interviews, and archival work' (Shankland 2012: 135) to understand the past. A large number of such archaeological ethnographies have been put towards studying the role of archaeology in modern societies and to examining the relationships between local communities and decision-makers. Specifically, they have investigated how archaeology empowers local communities and leads to changes at higher levels of power structures, which in turn leads to new forms of collaborative archaeology (Stoffle, Zedeno and Halmo 2001; Lilley and Williams 2005; Colwell and Ferguson 2007; Lilley 2009). Moreover, archaeology and anthropology have already crossed in the production of ethnographies devoted to the consideration of how transnational issues and priorities related to heritage and the protection of archaeological sites are decided in local terms (Herzfeld 1991, 2009; Abu el Haj 2001; Benavides 2005; Breglia 2006; Wynn 2007). And, in the reverse on how transnational organizations, such as UNESCO, are brought into play in local arenas and how locals and national policies are made and unmade through international regulations (Arantes 2007; Lafrenz Samuels 2009). However, very few studies that critically combine archaeology with ethnography have been conducted in China. There is Erika Evasdottir's (2004) work about the practice of *guanxi* (social network) among Chinese archaeologists, but that still tells us little about society's reception of the past.

Methodology

In summer 2007, I visited Xi'an for the first time. It was during a fieldtrip to assess the impact of tourism development in Chinese cities along the Silk Road. I travelled from Kashgar, through Xinjiang and Gansu Province, and finally arrived in Xi'an. Although Xi'an is known as one of the most ancient Chinese cities, it was the most visibly 'modern' of all the cities I visited. The contrast stimulated me to think about the role of historical sites and the negotiation between history and modernity in this ancient city. In August 2013, I embarked on a 13-month-fieldwork trip to Xi'an for my Ph.D. project. As I re-entered the city, it was even more advanced and developed than I remembered. On the way from the airport to the city centre, I saw endless blocks of high rises and construction sites. Revisiting the heritage sites, I was struck again by the degree to which their presentation had become standardized and commercialized. My personal encounter with the city's urban changes reinforced my commitment.

It was daunting to be a stranger entering a city with a population of over eight million people and hundreds of heritage sites. I spent the first three months exploring the city to 'map' the general development of these sites. I visited World Heritage sites, nationally and provincially ranked historical sites, traditional urban districts, heritage-parks-to-be under construction, quarters at risk of gentrification, and other places that locals told me were 'historical' and meaningful. On these visits, I tried to talk to as many people as I could and traded contact details for future conversations.

In a second phase, I narrowed my focus to a handful of specific sites. Here, I eschewed the 'official' value-based categorization of the sites and made my own list distinguishing religious heritage, political heritage, archaeological heritage, Silk Road-related heritage and so on. I picked some sites from each category for further study, but most had a clearly historical-dimension: the terracotta army, Big Wild Goose Pagoda, the Han Chang'an city remains, Daming Palace, Small Wild Goose Pagoda, Xingjiao Temple, and Xi'an City Wall. I also picked some urban districts to continue studying, specifically Qujiang District, the Muslim Quarter, and the Calligraphy Quarter. I visited the selected sites regularly a few times a month for the rest of my stay (or in some cases, more intensively for just a few months), but I also tried to visit other unselected sites once every few months to observe changes.

After narrowing down the sites I wanted to study, I also began to approach government departments and institutions for interviews. I found myself being turned down all the time, and realized the need to strengthen my own *guanxi*. With the help of François Bertemes, Professor of Archaeology at Martin Luther University of Halle-Wittenberg, I was introduced to some German restorers involved in conservation collaboration in Xi'an. I then had the chance to participate in the Symposium of Qin Terracotta Warriors and Polychrome Cultural Relics Conservation and Research in September 2013, and it was here that I made my first personal contacts in Xi'an with archaeologists, restorers, and government officials. Afterwards, I joined five other conferences to expand my social network across various professional communities: the International Euro-Asia

Economic Forum in September 2013; the International Conference for Modern Architectural Heritage Conservation in October 2013; the International Conference on Archaeology and Conservation along the Silk Road in May 2014; the UNESCO World Heritage Forum on Tourism Development and Rural Social Economic Prosperity at World Heritage Sites in Kunming in June 2014; and lastly, a summer workshop on Socio-Cultural Geography in China in July 2014. All these conferences provided me with connections to staff at international organizations, national, provincial and municipal government officials, and experts from various fields related to urban development and heritage preservation. In the end, I managed to broaden my network to include government officials from different departments, academics, urban planners, architects, heritage site developers, site administrators, activists, archaeologists, conservationists, museum curators, tour guides, project managers, journalists, religious leaders, farmers, local residents, tourists and other users and keepers of heritage sites.

Based on the network I had established through conferences and on-going everyday exploration in Xi'an, two local institutions agreed to host me as their guest researcher, the Shaanxi History Museum starting from November 2013 and the Terracotta Army Museum in January 2014. With the affiliation of these two museums, I gained access to various archives, libraries, institutions, organizations, and other opportunities in Xi'an. I joined and helped to organize heritage-related activities including archaeological excavations, heritage assessment excursions, and press conferences on archaeological findings. I also forged close relationships with the history, archaeology, restoration, and architecture departments of North West University and Xi'an University of Science and Technology.

Once I could boast of affiliations with the two museums and universities, locals became more willing to talk to me and to introduce me to further useful contacts. With the snowball effect, my social network expanded quickly and I could reach out to yet more important contacts. Moreover, I had the opportunity to give two talks to introduce the contro-versial topics of my research and stimulate discussions with the audience. For example, I made one presentation on heritage projects and urban transformation, 'Xi'an – *wenhua yichan haishi wenhua yihan*?' (Xi'an – Cultural Heritage or Cultural Shame?), in a language centre. In August 2014, I gave another presentation about the insights of my fieldwork called 'The Past of the Future; The Future of the Past' in the Terracotta Army Museum. After these talks, more people became interested in my topic, gave me related information, and volunteered to be my interviewees.

The main methodology I employed during my fieldwork was par-ticipant observation. I took part in as many social activities in the city as possible. I rented an apartment in the centre of the city so that I could access a variety of sites easily. I utilized a number of tactics to join local communities and conducted participant observation in various forms. I joined gatherings, socialized with shopkeepers, participated in archaeological work, and attended events and festivals. Because very personal information is often disclosed to an ethnographer, ethics is one of the most important issues to address while conducting anthropological fieldwork. My informants came from different backgrounds and had different views of state and market policies. Some of them were organizers of resistance; some had been involved in corrupt practices. I made sure to state my purpose at the beginning of our encounters.

I also employed several fieldwork techniques, including conducting structured and semi-structured interviews and asking my informants to draw mental maps and timelines (see chapter 4).[8] I also showed my informants photographs of various sites and asked to be told about them. Surprisingly, even some of the most famous heritage sites were sometimes not identifiable. Some informants had only heard of the names, but had never visited or otherwise seen the sites. In some cases, they did know that the site actually existed. This experiment shows that heritage development in Xi'an has been conducted so rapidly that the public is not even up-to-date with their city's 'heritage'.

For my part, I did my best to keep up-to-date with the latest developments in heritage. I checked the media landscape every day, not only television news and newspapers, but also social media including online blogs. I read the three main newspapers, namely *Huashang Daily Huashang bao* (Huashang Daily), *Shaanxi ribao* (Shaanxi Daily), and *Xi'an ribao* (Xi'an Daily). All of these newspapers reported only pro-government news, but they informed me about the most recent and trendy issues concerning archaeological excavations, heritage celebrations, and urban development. Moreover, I consulted secondary sources including history textbooks and statistical reports on selected topics.

My position as a Hong Kong researcher from a German institute had both advantages and drawbacks. I easily entered the mainland and did not need any permits to conduct research. In addition, I did not have to report my activities to the local government authorities and I could conduct my research freely. Moreover, my identity raised many locals' curiosity. To them, Hong Kong, although politically belonging to China, remains very

---

[8] Voice recording during interviews was only used if permission was obtained from the informants. I also asked for consent for all interviews and photos. With the exception of well-known professionals or public figures who would be difficult to anonymize, all informants have been given pseudonyms in order to protect their identities.

Westernized and metropolitan. They were impressed and could not believe that I would leave such a city, nor that I would choose to stay in Xi'an. However, since Hong Kong is a special administrative region of China with its own government and currency, I was regarded as a foreigner in most aspects of everyday life. For example, without a Chinese residence card the government authorities could not issue me a city bike rental card nor the permission to use internet at home. When accessing archival materials, I had to pay 20 CNY per document while locals could do so for free. My Hong Kong identity presented the greatest difficulty in relations with government departments and institutes. For instance, I could not work for the Terracotta Army Museum at the beginning because I was considered a foreigner, and the state does not allow foreigners to handle national relics. It took almost half a year of getting recommendation letters from professors and different departments and building up my network with government officials in order to get the needed permission. Towards the end of my stay in Xi'an, my background as a Hong Kong person worsened the relationship between me and some of my informants as the so-called Umbrella Revolution for greater democratic reforms broke out in Hong Kong in September 2014.

Chapter Structure

The present book is divided into nine chapters. After this introduction, the second chapter presents a historical background of my field site. It briefly illustrates the history of the city from the prehistoric period to the modern era and gives an in-depth account of the city's management and regulations of heritage preservation and urban planning – the two core topics of research. Chapters 3 through 8 display the main content with in-depth ethnographic material, discussing the political economy of heritage making in Xi'an. These six chapters classify the heritage sites into six different types, according to their uses and functions. Heritage sites in Xi'an are not only used as a goldmine to boost economic development, but are also celebrated to acknowledge the national historical narration and to glorify China's greatness. Hence, the classification of heritage sites displays the trends of heritage development in Xi'an. The typology of heritage provides a guide to the diverse ideas, concepts, and frameworks that I use to analyse and write about Xi'an and becomes the lens to display the contested relationship between heritage development and historical preservation in an urban landscape.

Chapter 3 focuses on archaeological remains and explores the interplay between the discipline of archaeology, archaeological sites, and society in Xi'an. By using the Terracotta Army Museum and some other archaeological sites as examples, the chapter dissects the role of archaeological heritage and how it is used to reinforce national and local identity. It also demonstrates the dominant role of the state in choosing which archaeological projects to finance and which historical periods to highlight. By displaying the locals' perception of archaeological heritage and powerful social actors' influence on heritage projects, this chapter aims to portray how the state narrates and shapes Xi'an as 'the city of Chinese civilization' to build up nationalism.

Chapter 4 moves the emphasis from archaeological remains to historical sites. The provincial and city governments not only promote imperial palaces and royal tombs to represent China. They have also replaced many original Ming-style vernacular houses in the city centre with neo-Tang buildings of standardized colours, patterns, and rooftops. In this chapter, I describe how locals have developed an infatuation for particular historical periods and identify themselves as descendants of an imperial past. This chapter explores the symbolic meanings and political implications of three celebrated eras: the Qin, Han, and Tang, in transmitting the greatness of the nation's glorious past. By narrating a selective history, the Chinese state reinforces its political discourse of China as a civilized and strong nation. Imperial history and heritage, hence, play a significant role in boosting nationalism and building a common identity in Xi'an.

Chapter 5 draws attention to the historical sites related to the Silk Road, especially sites which were included in the Silk Roads World Heritage candidacy. It uncovers the politics of heritage nomination at the local, national, and global levels. The notion of the Silk Road in China means more than just a historical route and the long-term cultural exchange within Eurasia. It serves as a tool to lionize China in world history. My ethnographic materials show how the Silk Road is romanticized and Sinicized. The Silk Roads World Heritage nomination is no longer about promoting intercultural understanding, but a way for China to revitalize its leading role economically and politically.

Chapter 6 shifts the focus from the political uses of heritage development to its economic potential. It investigates the unique heritage phenomenon in Xi'an known as the 'Qujiang Model', which commercializes historical sites into large-scale heritage parks to enhance future real-estate development in the surrounding area. This model influenced many historical sites, changed the cityscape, and strengthened the touristic economic development of Xi'an. Locals started to perceive historical remains as cultural resources instead of 'useless garbage'. This locally-developed model also brought national attention to Xi'an and many cities wanted to copy the concept. Based on the rise and fall of the Qujiang Model, this chapter discusses the political-economy of heritagization.

Chapter 7 is concerned with living urban heritage forms preserved and maintained by communities. The chapter compares the social life and the inhabitants' relationship with the historical sites within two urban quarters: the Calligraphy Quarter and the Muslim Quarter. Both quarters located at the heart of Xi'an share similar architectural styles, economic patterns, and a lively social life. However, the community members of the quarters understand 'heritage' very differently. Facing internal and external threats to the harmony and continuity of their communities, local residents adopted completely opposite attitudes and strategies. Whereas the Calligraphy Quarter remained silent, the Muslim Quarter employed various tactics to resolve the problems and improve the situation. By focusing on two micro-units of the city, this chapter reveals the diversity of the heritage-scape and the interaction and negotiation between different levels of heritage management and ownership in Xi'an.

Chapter 8 tackles the problems involved with the 'new heritage' in Xi'an. I divide this new heritage into three types: new heritage with old meanings; original heritage with new meanings; and brand-new construc-tions. From the view of the city government and certain officials in power, all three categories will become 'cultural heritage'. To produce this new heritage, the city engages in intensive urban transformation, including large-scale demolition (to build heritage parks) and the construction of a metro. The second part of the chapter dissects the social consequences brought about by urbanization, heritagization, and gentrification, specifically the creation of ghost towns, slums, and invisible boundaries within the city. This chapter introduces the complexity of the developmental discourse in Xi'an and unfolds how the city uses its past to build its future.

Lastly, chapter 9 draws attention to China's overall political economy through Xi'an's heritage politics. It argues that the national, provincial and city governments' ultimate goal is the pursuit of cosmopolitanism. Through the revitalization of the cityscape, a variety of heritage projects, and participation in the Silk Roads World Heritage nomination, Xi'an aims at recuperating its historical cosmopolitan status. This quest is complemented by other forms of modernization and economic development to achieve cos-mopolitanism for today's Xi'an.

In Xi'an, economic development does not dominate the process of heritagization. Here the socio-political uses of heritage are of paramount importance. Despite conflicts, nearly all social actors are invested in the construction of a cosmopolitan identity for Xi'an. As the city's inhabitants actively repossess 'their' glorious past from the Tang Dynasty, they are aligned with the goals and aims of the national government. Together, with local heritage projects, China builds its reputation on the international stage and Xi'an resurrects a strong local identity. The combination of archae-ological, imperial, and Silk Road heritage with intensive commercialization and modernization all add to the reinforcement of an image of a great and open China.

Chapter 2
From Chang'an to Xi'an – Urban Transformation and Heritage Preservation

During my fieldwork, many people were fascinated by my research. I was told repeatedly that I had chosen the right city for my topic; people in Xi'an firmly believed that their city would be the best place for me to learn about Chinese history and culture. Mr. Cao, a retired man in his seventies, told me: 'if you want to know about how China grew in the past 50 years, you should go to Shanghai. If you want to study the past 500 years of history, then visit Beijing. And if you are interested in learning about the over 5,000 years of ancient Chinese civilization, come to Xi'an'. Indeed, most people, including scholars, drew attention only to the ancient and imperial history of Xi'an before the Chinese capital city moved eastwards in 904 CE. They shifted their interest to other cities as Chinese history evolved. Of course, Xi'an also has a history of the last 500 years. Here too there were changes and development with rises and falls in prosperity, expansion and reduction in size, and other socio-political changes. Nowadays, as the largest city in north-west China, Xi'an is undergoing massive urban transformation.

How has the city transformed over these years? How does it identify as both a '5,000-year-old civilization' and a modern technological centre in Western China and balance between historical preservation and modernization development? What are the roles of the national, provincial, and municipal governments regarding city planning and heritage management?

In order to answer these questions, this chapter presents the essential background information through the following four sections. The first section provides the historical framework and briefly traces the formation of the city and the changing townscape from prehistory to the modern era. The second section focuses on the urban transformation of Xi'an from the early 1950s till the present. It introduces the city's ongoing and upcoming urban projects, which will turn Xi'an into an international metropolis. The third section turns to the topic of cultural heritage and explores the development of cultural heritage preservation and management in China on a macro and national level. Finally, the last section zooms in on Shaanxi Province to discuss the situation of heritage preservation regionally. By displaying the policies concerning heritage preservation and the history of city development, this chapter unfolds how Xi'an has tackled the dilemma between urban transformation and heritage preservation.

Tracing the Roots of the City

Without some appreciation of the historical background of Xi'an, it is very difficult to make sense of what is happening in the city today. The historical legacy and remains continue to influence the government's development and locals' everyday life. Archaeological evidence of the Banpo Neolithic settlement suggests that the history of Xi'an can be traced back 3,100 years (Chang 1986). Even though we can hardly regard the Banpo settlement as a city setting, archaeologists argue that the settlers established an organized society with land use planning and social hierarchy (Allan 2005). Hence, it is typically depicted as a precursor to Xi'an in the city's historiography. After the Neolithic period, during the Bronze Age, the Western Zhou Dynasty (1046–771 BCE) and Qin Dynasty (221–206 BCE) situated their capitals in the surrounding area. These two capitals, not exactly congruent with Xi'an, similarly are drawn into historiographical narratives about the city's growing political status. Xi'an today continues the presentation of its history with reference to city settings in four subsequent historical periods: the early imperial, imperial, late imperial, and modern periods.

The Early Imperial Period: From 221 BCE to 220 CE

After the first emperor of the Qin Dynasty, Qin Shihuang, unified China (221 BCE), he consolidated the language, political system, military administration, transportation network, and defence system (Lewis 2007). During his reign, China constructed a national highway, the Grand Canal, and the first part of the Great Wall. As the capital of the Qin Dynasty, the area surrounding Xi'an contains the archaeological remains of Epang Palace, some city remains, and numerous imperial mausoleums of Qin emperors including the famous terracotta army.

In 206 BCE, Han troops overthrew the Qin Dynasty, and established one of the strongest dynasties in Chinese history. They founded the city of Chang'an in what is today the north-western part of Xi'an. Based on remains and archival material, archaeologists and historians have been able to reconstruct the whole of Chang'an. Approximately 70 per cent of the city was occupied by the palace-complex (including the Weiyang and Changle palaces) and 30 per cent was occupied by commoners (Zhu 2010). There was a strong division between commoners' and royal areas. For instance, commoners could only enter the city through the East or West gates while the noble families could only use the South Gate (Zhu 2010). Due to wars and uprisings, the Han Dynasty was overthrown. Chang'an deteriorated and was eventually abandoned.

The Imperial Period: From 500 to 1400

The rulers of the Sui and Tang dynasties (581–618 CE, 618–907 CE) placed their capitals at the centre of today's Xi'an. Historians speculate that the population of Chang'an reached one million at its peak during the Tang Dynasty, making it the biggest city in the world (Beckwith 2009). A Tang poet, Bai Juyi, described the layout of Chang'an as a chess board with its twelve main streets as orderly as broad ploughed fields (Harris 2009).[9] The whole city was divided into 134 grids as shown in Map 2. Each grid had its own characteristics and function, reflecting social variation and hierarchy. The palace areas were bigger than normal grids to show the imperial power of the emperor and the royal family who lived there. Government officials lived in the central area of the city along Vermilion Bird Road. Foreigners resided in a district close to the West Market, where international trading activities were conducted.

Abundant Tang historical sites remained in Xi'an until today. These include various imperial mausoleums, the Big and Small Wild Goose pagodas, Daming Palace, Xingqing Palace, Qujiang Lake, remains of the city wall and gates, and countless ritual and religious venues. The underlying grid also still influences city planning and urban development (see chapters 4 and 8).

---

[9] The description comes from the poem, 'Viewing the City from Guanyin Tower' (登观音台望城). The original formulation for the metaphors of chessboard and broad plowed fields is 百千家似围棋局，十二街如种菜畦。

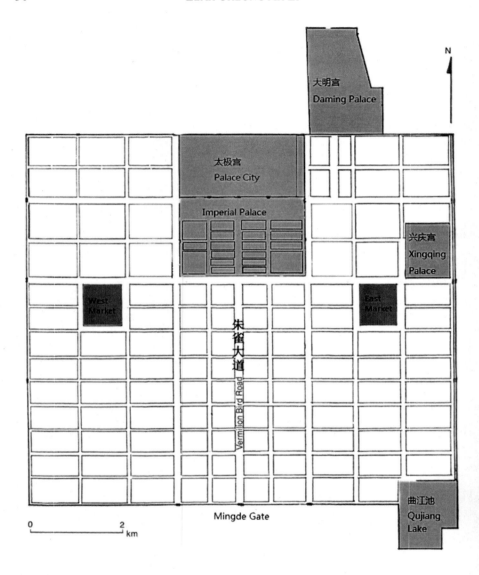

Map 2. Map of Chang'an City during the Tang Dynasty (Source: Jing Xie. 2016. Figure 1 in Disembodied Historicity: Southern Song Imperial Street in Hangzhou. *The Journal of the Society of Architectural Historians* 75 (2): 182–200 [June 2016]; https://www.researchgate.net/figure/Schematic-plan-of-Tang-Changan-Imperial-Street-Zhuque-Street-is-gray-authors_fig1_304031037).

In 904 Emperor Zhao decided to move the capital from Chang'an to Luoyang. Houses in Chang'an were destroyed and people were forced to move to the new capital. Since Tang Chang'an was mainly composed of government officials and foreigners, including students, monks, ambassadors, and diplomats, they too moved out of the city as Xi'an lost its political status. After the Tang Dynasty came to an end, Xi'an's role in Chinese history declined. Subsequent capitals were established eastwards – at Luoyang, Nanjing, Beijing. In 989, merely 86,900 people lived in Chang'an (Jing 2014). The Tang layout of Xi'an and many of its structures remained almost untouched but were buried underneath new construction as time went by. The population of Xi'an only grew slowly during the Song Dynasty (960–1176) as it could not attract any new migrants (Jing 2014).

The Late Imperial Period: From 1400 to 1949

By the Ming Dynasty (1368–1644), the size of the city shrank by at least 80 per cent. At this time, the city covered barely the area of the former central palace (the middle light grey box in Map 2). Xi'an rebuilt the Ming city wall based on the remains and foundation of the Tang Chang'an city wall. Furthermore, the Bell Tower was relocated to its current location, becoming a vital landmark of the city (Zhu 2010). In 1932, Xi'an faced a tremendous loss of population because of plague. In the mid-1930s, Xi'an regained its political significance as it served as a political area for both the Guomindang Party and the Communist Party to collaborate. Shaanxi Province and the area of Xi'an later evolved as the base for the Communist Party's military retreats (i.e. the Long March).[10] In the 1940s, due to the Henan flooding hazard and the Japanese invasion during the Second World War, flocks of refugees rushed to Xi'an because of its relatively safe location (Jing 2014).

The Modern Period: From 1949 to Present

After the establishment of the People's Republic of China, Xi'an entered the era of modernization. The state started to advocate industrialization in the western part of the country and to carry out large-scale construction of infrastructure, such as building road systems (Li 2010). According to the first five-year plan (1953–57), the central government promoted light and precision machinery as well as textile industries in Xi'an (Yin, Shen and Zhao 2005). The Third Front Construction (1958–65) encouraged coastal industries to move their factories from cities such as Guangzhou and

---

[10] The Red Army of the Communist Party of China undertook the Long March in order to evade the Chinese Nationalist Party (Guomindang). The march lasted for a year from October 1934 to October 1935. It started in Jiangxi and ended in Shaanxi Province.

Shanghai to Xi'an (Chen 2003). As a result, Xi'an became a base for heavy industry, aerospace, and military facilities. This series of reforms transformed Xi'an from a western, geographically remote town to one of China's most technologically advanced cities.

Urban planning accompanied nationally-led development. In 1954, Xi'an City Urban Planning Bureau (hereafter Xi'an City Planning Bureau) divided Xi'an into six sectors: the central old city area, an industrial area in the west, an industrial area in the east, a residential area between the old city and industrial areas, a cultural area in the south, and a yet-to-be-developed area in the north (Zhu 2010). Xi'an City Planning Bureau intended to preserve the historical layout of the old city. Therefore, industrialization took place mostly at the outskirts of the city. Ming streets and architecture remained in place until the early 1990s.

Until the early 1990s, Xi'an would seem to have merited being known, as it is across China, as *gucheng* (ancient city). The naming refers to the city's long tenure as a site for imperial capitals, but well into the modern period, the city also looked 'ancient' with its preponderance of two-storey Ming buildings (and no high rises) in the city centre. However, from 1998, new state policies for developing the western part of China began to change the city's look. Xi'an played a central role in the new economic program, attracting hundreds of thousands of migrant workers and investors.

Many of my informants were prepared to offer their own versions of a chronology of national policies that had led to their city's transformation. For example, Mr. Guo, a tour guide in his mid-twenties, explained to me that there had been three stages to the development of contemporary China. In the first stage, he said, Deng's Open Door Policy introduced a series of economic developments in eastern coastal cities such as Shanghai and Guangzhou during the 1980s. The second stage took place in the late 1990s with the national program Open Up the West that encouraged companies from the east to invest in the western part of China. Then in the mid-2010s, he explained, China had entered a third stage, as it aimed to develop the central part of the country and foster economic links between the east and the west. Both the second and third stages, he said, were responsible for the intensification of industrialization, urbanization, and economic development in Xi'an.

Through chronologies and attributions of causation will surely differ, what is sure is that within 50 years, Xi'an had expanded significantly. Its population increased eight times from less than 400,000 inhabitants in 1949 to more than 3 million in the late 1990s (Sanjuan 2000). Also compared to the 1950s, the size of Xi'an expanded 140 times.[11]

From *Gucheng* to Da Xi'an: Urban Transformation in Xi'an

Xi'an now advertises itself as Da Xi'an (Greater Xi'an). The new name invokes both the enlargement of the city and its rising status as a modernized international metropolis. Xi'an's urban expansion, caused mainly by the central government's development policies, has been met by four stages of city planning: 1953–1972, 1980–2000, 1995–2010, and 2008–2020.[12] Urbanization worked almost hand-in-hand with cultural heritage preservation in the early 1950s because the city government could not ignore the presence of the large number of archaeological sites – stone foundations and relics populated the soil. In 1954, Xi'an City Planning Bureau launched the first master plan for Xi'an from 1953 to 1972 under the guidance of Soviet experts (Zhu 2010). The plan was proposed to build Xi'an as a socialist city of inland industrial production with physical expansion to the east and west (Fayolle Lussac, Høyem and Clément 2007). In 1980, under Deng's influence, the city government implemented the second master plan, which continued to put economic development in the foreground. It intended to expand the city based on a concentric system with three rings.[13] In 1995, the city introduced the third master plan, which increased the urban area significantly to accommodate the influx of migrants. In the latest plan drafted in 2008, the city further enlarged the urban area in order to make room for the constantly growing population. Map 3 shows the drastic growth of the city throughout the four stages of city planning. Nowadays, the city of Xi'an covers a total area of 9,983 square kilometres, with 1,964 square kilometres zoned as an 'urban area'. It is now 22 times larger than Chang'an at its peak during the Tang Dynasty.[14]

---

[11] Xi'an city government's website: http://www.114huoche.com/zhengfu_XiAn. Last accessed 1 May 2016.

[12] I was unable to obtain a clear explanation as to the missing years between the first and second stages and the overlaps of the subsequent years. Probably the missing years reflect the relative unimportance of urban planning in the 1970s, while the later phases reflect a continual process of 'updating' as planning became more urgent.

[13] Xi'an was built in a ring system. The first ring is the Ming city wall surrounding the old city area (4.5 kilometres by 2.8 kilometres). The second ring circulates the outer area of approximately 84.39 square kilometres. The third ring encompasses the new districts that the city developed including Qujiang District, with a total area of 385,95 square kilometres.

[14] Xi'an city government's website: http://www.114huoche.com/zhengfu_XiAn. Last accessed 1 May 2016.

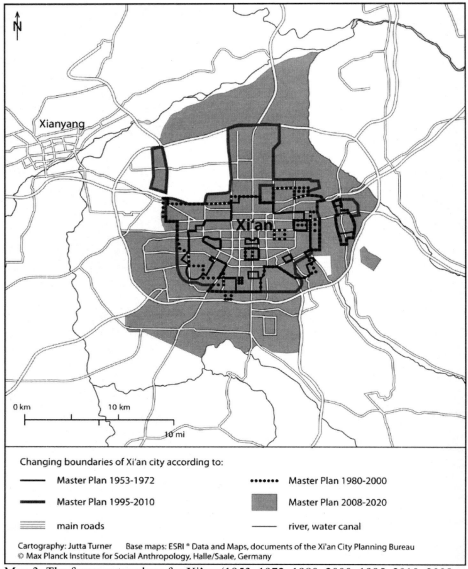

Map 3. The four master plans for Xi'an (1953–1972, 1980–2000, 1995–2010, 2008–2020).

Following the four master plans, the city has executed extensive construction and urban renewal projects. The majority of Ming-style buildings in the old city were demolished in the 1990s and replaced by modern ones (Fayolle Lussac, Høyem and Clément 2007). In 2009, Xi'an took a further step to transform the 'ancient city' to Da Xi'an, when the state approved the Greater Xi'an Strategic Development Plan proposed by Shaanxi Provincial Bureau of Housing and Urban-Rural Construction (Xi'an City Planning Bureau 2014a). The objectives of the plan include increasing the economic productivity of the area and expanding the urban area of Xi'an, so as to transform the city into an international metropolis. The plan suggests the merging of Xi'an with the city of Xianyang across the Wei River. Map 4 shows the sphere of influence of the Da Xi'an project, which stretches northward to and southward to the Qin mountain area. The dark line on Map 4 encloses the core urban area of development, three times as big as the one suggested in the fourth master plan (2008–20) (area filled in gray in Map 3). According to the Da Xi'an proposal, Xi'an will be established as a leading city in different fields including: inland economic development, techno-logical research management, heavy industry, modern agricultural develop-ment, and historical and cultural tourism (Shaanxi Provincial Bureau of Housing and Urban-Rural Construction 2010).

According to the National Land Ownership Law of the People's Republic of China enacted in 2004, all urban areas are owned by the state. Therefore, the state and the provincial government can exercise their power over urban transformation projects (Legislative Affairs Office of the State Council 2004). If the state decides to conduct a construction project and remove a neighbourhood, the people living there have no right to resist. They do, however, have the right to negotiate a better compensation from the city government departments (Xi'an Municipal Government 2014). The government uses this power over land to carry out urbanization projects, though it contracts private companies to develop real estate projects. Many districts were re-planned, new districts were created, and old districts were gentrified. Although urbanization signifies modernization and the improve-ment of the city to many local residents, the rapid urban transformation has also resulted in numerous problems, including rising land prices, the widening of the gap between rich and poor, the creation of ghost towns, and the presence of *chengzhongcun* (slums). Xi'an is no exception to the emergence of these urban problems (see chapter 8).

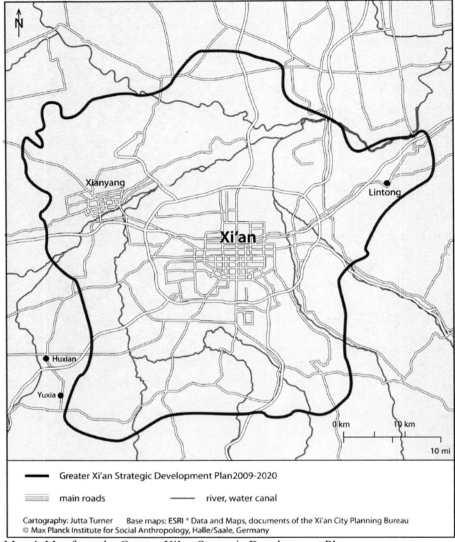

Map 4. Map from the Greater Xi'an Strategic Development Plan.

In general, the Da Xi'an plan maximizes urbanization, however, it left a few specific areas in the city aside due to heritage preservation. Since the first master plan introduced in 1954, the city has restricted any sort of development in northern and western Xi'an, where Zhou, Qin, Han, and Tang city and palace remains are located. The second master plan proposed the protection of a few historical monuments in the city centre and attempted to create three 'visual corridors' (*shijue zoulang*) between the Bell Tower, Big Wild Goose Pagoda, and Small Wild Goose Pagoda. These corridors would enable people to see another historical site clearly from the top of any one monument. No high rises or other obscuring construction is allowed between the historical features along the visual corridor. For instance, the government restricted developers from building any high rises between Big Wild Goose Pagoda and the Bell Tower, so that the pagoda can be seen from the tower on a clear day. The master plans also effectively banned some urban development projects that might have harmed heritage sites and the historical townscape of Xi'an (see chapter 3). The next sections will describe the heritage management system in China, Shaanxi Province, and Xi'an City.

From Cultural Relics to Cultural Heritage – The History of Heritage Management in China

The history of heritage management and the relevant legal background in China serve as the grounds for understanding urban heritage politics in contemporary Xi'an. Due to the strong and state-oriented nature of governance in China, regional authorities' decisions and plans are often dependent on the state's policies, laws, and systems. In 1930, the Republic of China passed the Law on the Preservation of Ancient Objects, which was the first law on archaeological preservation in China (Murphy 1995). According to the law, ancient objects are regarded as 'cultural relics' (*wenwu*). This term is used explicitly to describe tangible objects, but was extended by the 1982 Cultural Relics Protection Law of the People's Republic of China to include all historic landmarks as cultural relics and assets from the past (National People's Congress of People's Republic of China 1982). As stated in the first guideline of the law, its goal is to 'strengthen the protection of historical relics, sustain the distinct cultural heritage of China, promote scientific research, enhance nationalism and communist education, and build up a socialist spiritual and material civiliza- tion' (National People's Congress of People's Republic of China 1982). The law, which is still active, illuminates the state's ambition to use heritage as a way to boost nationalism. The concern for 'relics' remained dominant in the field of heritage preservation until the late 1980s, even as other acts and regulations were made, including Protection of Historic Interests Act of the People's Republic of China (1982), Regulation on Building Heights (1985), and Height Controls for Ancient Cities (1987).

In 1985, China ratified UNESCO's Convention Concerning the Protection of the World Cultural and Natural Heritage, which enables China to nominate World Heritage sites. When the country began to participate actively in the nomination of World Heritage sites in 1987, the notion of 'cultural heritage' (*wenhua yichan*) began to enter national discussions. Since then, it has become increasingly popular and is widely used in official documents. However, *wenhua yichan* becomes problematic on the ground, as it highlights the relationship between 'ancestors' and 'descendants'. 'Intangible cultural heritage' is yet more problematic, as people may refuse to recognize their customs as 'heritage' because they still practise them (cf. Overmyer 2003). They would choose to use terms such as *chuantong* (tradition), *yishu* (art), or even more generally *wenhua* (culture) (Cheung 2019). In Xi'an, people also did not accept the term *wenhua yichan* until the late 2000s and rather used more specific terms, such as *wenwu* or *yizhi* (remains) to refer to heritage sites. Since 2009, people in Xi'an have become more familiar with the term 'cultural heritage' in tandem with the city's engagement with the Silk Roads World Heritage nomination.

In the 2000s, China has also reacted to international laws and conventions. In response to UNESCO's Convention for the Safeguarding of the Intangible Cultural Heritage adopted in 2003, China set up the National Intangible Cultural Heritage Law in 2011 (State Council of the People's Republic of China 2011).

Heritage governance permits the state to pursue its goals of national integration and political stability by promoting cultural autonomy and preservation at the national level (Svensson 2006). The responsible authorities are several, all linked to the Central Committee of the Party or the State Council. The key government department for cultural heritage affairs is the State Administration of Cultural Heritage. It is in charge of regulating the preservation of historical sites, managing all archaeological projects, administering the museums, and nominating World Heritage sites for China (State Administration of Cultural Heritage 2014a). State Administration of Cultural Heritage divides heritage management into six levels: national, provincial, city, county, district, and site. The system indicates a site's importance and the government or administrative level that is responsible for its management.

As of 2014, 233 sites in Shaanxi Province, including 51 sites in Xi'an, were sites of 'national' importance (State Administration of Cultural Heritage 2014b). The Terracotta Army Museum, Daming Palace, and Big Wild Goose Pagoda are among these. These nationally ranked heritage sites have to follow strictly the Cultural Relics Protection Law, and they cannot be demolished or altered without permission from the national government. As for provincially ranked heritage sites, Xi'an harbours 115 (e.g. Xingqing

Palace and Dapiyuan Mosque).[15] At the city level, Xi'an has 176 sites (Xi'an Municipal Government 2005), including Lama Guangren Temple and the Tang Hongqing Tomb. The county government, the district committee, and the site administration manage the remaining sites.

In reality, two or more administrative levels often co-manage the sites. For instance, the Terracotta Army Museum is officially a nationally ranked heritage site, but Shaanxi Provincial Bureau of Cultural Heritage, the Lintong district government, and the site's own administrative committee all have power over its management. Another example is the Qian Imperial Mausoleum from the Tang Dynasty. It is also a nationally ranked heritage site, but when the museum's administration (at the site level) decided to withdraw from the Silk Roads World Heritage nomination, neither the national nor provincial government could change its decision (see chapter 5). Although the national title is the highest, when it comes to the administrative process, the national governmental departments are only the symbolic heads. The regional government levels or even the administrative units have more executive power. In addition to governmental units specifically responsible for cultural heritage, other government departments including the Ministry of Culture, National Tourism Administration, and the Ministry of Land and Resources, are all responsible for some aspects of the administration of heritage sites. Each of these departments can draft laws or set restrictions that influence heritage management. For example, Tang (2013) pointed out the role of the Ministry of Land and Resources in controlling land use and property rights, which includes the management of land related to heritage projects.

While State Administration of Cultural Heritage ranks all heritage sites for a systematic administration, other government departments also grant different rankings to outstanding heritage sites to glorify their various accomplishments. For example, the entrance hall of the Terracotta Army Museum welcomes its visitors with one wall displaying the UNESCO logo and another wall with other rankings: National Patriotic Site (Quanguo aiguo zhuyi jidi), First-Class National Museum (Guojia yiji bowuguan), National Civilization Unit (Quanguo wenming dawei), and National AAAAA Tourist Attraction (Guojia AAAAA lvyou jingqu). All these rankings were granted by national government departments which hold the shared goal of promoting cultural heritage in China. The title of National Patriotic Site, for instance, was given by the Publicity Department of the Communist Party of

---

[15] 'Shaanxisheng renmin zhengfu guanyu gongbu di liu pi sheng wenwu baohu danwei de Tongzhi' ([2014] Notice from the Shaanxi People's Government about heritage protection departments). Available online, http://www.shaanxi.gov.cn/0/103/10464.htm. Last accessed 1 May 2016.

China, which announced its first list of 100 national patriotic sites for patriotic education in June 1997 and its second list of 258 sites in 2010 (Matten 2012). (Xi'an hosts six national patriotic sites.) The A-rating system for tourist attractions in China comes from the National Tourism Administration. Tourist attractions are classified into five categories (A, AA, AAA, AAAA, or AAAAA sites) based on quality. According to the Code of Categories and Rating Standard of Tourist Attractions (Chris, Gu and Fang 2009), AAAAA attractions fulfil all twelve criteria of touristic development on which the system is based (e.g. transportation accessibility, hygiene, marketing strategies). (In Shaanxi Province there are 6 AAAAA tourist attractions, but 22 AAAA attractions.) The following section and beyond considers the intertwinements and collisions between these various government departments and agencies.

Heritage Management in Xi'an

The location of government buildings in Xi'an reflects how the regional government values its heritage development. As Ms. Yuan, an architect in her early thirties, explained: 'the more important cultural heritage is to a city, the closer its office of cultural heritage is located to the central city government'. Unlike many Chinese cities where the cultural heritage bureaus are located far away from the central authorities (and neglected), in Xi'an, both the City Office of Cultural Heritage and Shaanxi Provincial Bureau of Cultural Heritage are located directly in the city centre next to the central government buildings. This reflects that Xi'an's city development is highly linked to its cultural heritage. Due to the large number of archaeological finds in the city, Shaanxi Province has considered cultural heritage preservation a main concern of policy making since the 1950s. At that time, most Chinese cities prioritized industrial and economic development above all, but Xi'an was especially alarmed by the high risk of damaging important hidden archaeological sites when carrying out construction works. Hence, Shaanxi Province considers itself to have long been ahead of other regions in cultural heritage preservation. Certainly, the province holds a privileged position and plays a leading role in the field of heritage preservation in today's China.

Even before the national survey of historical architecture conducted in 1961, the Shaanxi Provincial Committee had identified its own list of important heritage sites within the province in 1956. The Shaanxi Provincial Archaeological Institute was established in September 1958 to monitor and conduct all archaeological excavations.[16] Also, the Xi'an City Planning Bureau integrated urban heritage sites into the first master plan from 1953 to 1972 (Fayolle Lussac et al. 2007). In the 1980s, the city government decided that the borders of major archaeological sites had to be framed by strips of green (i.e. undeveloped) land for protection (Fresnais 2001), and it instituted further regulations on the environment and building height around the historical sites to ensure a harmonious townscape (Ren 1998). In 1988, Shaanxi Provincial Bureau of Cultural Heritage enacted the Regulations of Shaanxi Province on the Protection of Cultural Relics. This was the first legal document concerning heritage protection made at the provincial level in China. It forbids the demolition of old architecture from urbanization and modernization. In 2002, the Xi'an city government introduced the Regulations on Protection and Management of the Xi'an Historic City. The successful World Heritage inscription of five heritage properties in Xi'an further drove the city government to set up new regulations to monitor the management of heritage sites and the development around the properties. For example, Xi'an City Planning Bureau and the City Office of Cultural Heritage introduced new regulations on height control around the five nominated sites in October 2013.

Within Shaanxi, the most powerful government department regarding cultural heritage development is Shaanxi Provincial Bureau of Cultural Heritage. It exercises the direct management over nine institutions in the province including four museums and heritage sites, including the Shaanxi History Museum and the Terracotta Army Museum. Since the distribution of resources within the province is hierarchical, these nine institutions directly under the control of Shaanxi Provincial Bureau of Cultural Heritage receive privileged benefits and financial support. During my fieldwork, I was fully affiliated with the Terracotta Army Museum and Shaanxi History Museum, and partly affiliated with Shaanxi Provincial Research Institute for Cultural Heritage Conservation. As all three institutions are managed under the provincial bureau of cultural heritage, I was allowed to access many governmental documents and non-public information.

Other provincial bureaus also affect the management of cultural heritage sites. Shaanxi Bureau of Price Control coordinates the entrance ticket fees and other prices at all the heritage sites within the province to prevent commercialization.[17] Shaanxi Provincial Bureau of Religious Affairs

---

[16] Historical details are taken from the institute's website, http://www.shxkgy.cn/contents/3/1.html. Last accessed 1 May 2016.

[17] For example, when Big Wild Goose Pagoda intended to raise its entrance ticket by 10 CNY, the Bureau of Price Control intervened, arguing that any fee increase had to take into consideration the living costs of the general public.

regulates all the religious sites and their activities. Shaanxi Provincial Bureau of Cultural Heritage is in charge of the management and promotion of the intangible cultural heritage of the province. Shaanxi Provincial Tourism Administration promotes touristic development.

Mr. Tao, an urban planner, told me about the difficulties he faced as a planner for heritage projects. He had to work with all the implicated government bureaus, and he was cynical about the situation. 'There is a lack of communication between all these authorities even though they are all responsible to a certain extent for the heritage sites. So, we have to approach different departments to get permissions to make certain changes. Yet when we face some serious problems, all departments deny their responsibilities'. Mr. Tao gave me examples of how these authorities make contradictory decisions. For example, Shaanxi Provincial Bureau of Housing and Urban-Rural Construction approved a construction project around a heritage site in Lintong District, but Shaanxi Provincial Bureau of Cultural Heritage objected, claiming that the constructions would violate the heritage protection law. In another instance, Shaanxi Provincial Tourism Administration approved the development plan of the God of Fortune Temple, but Shaanxi Provincial Bureau of Religious Affairs found the plan unacceptable because it would lead to the commercialization of a religious site. In such instances of conflict, negotiation and compromise take place between the various government departments. Governmental levels, real estate developers, various professionals, and sometimes even the local community are all involved.

Similar to the national and provincial levels, the City Office of Cultural Heritage also collaborates with other government departments. In fact, in Xi'an, the city government assigns heritage projects to departments other than the Xi'an City Office of Cultural Heritage, since the duty of the latter is limited to the maintenance and restoration of historical buildings and artefacts (Xi'an City Office of Cultural Heritage 2009). Consequently, the City Office of Cultural Heritage has to cooperate with other government departments to manage the heritage sites. For example, the Municipal Bureau of Culture and Broadcasting declares the intangible cultural heritage forms of Xi'an, and is responsible for constructing cultural venues, such as theatres or theme parks. Xi'an City Planning Bureau is in charge of all city planning projects, including urban renewal projects, heritage projects, and the planning of resettlements due to urban renewal projects. The Municipal Urban Landscape Office takes over the gardening work of all heritage parks and also the construction of some archaeological heritage parks.

Besides all of these offices concerned with heritage, Xi'an hosts the International Conservation Center (IICC-X) of the International Council on

Monuments of Sites (ICOMOS).[18] This gives the city an advantage over others in China concerning various matters of heritage management and preservation. IICC-X was established in 2006, following the Fifteenth General Assembly of ICOMOS held in Xi'an in October 2005, during which the Xi'an Declaration on Conservation of the Settings of Heritage Structures, Sites, and Areas was adopted.[19] The offices of IICC-X are located at Small Wild Goose Pagoda; its activities are overseen by ICOMOS (it has to submit regular progress reports on its major development and projects to the Executive Committee of ICOMOS), but its operations are funded by the Xi'an city government. It aims to support international and regional cooperation for research, training, and education concerning the conservation of monuments and sites in Asia and the Pacific. Within this aim, IICC-X also gives advice on heritage projects in Xi'an. The leadership of the office is divided into three organizational levels: the highest level is a steering committee composed of representatives from ICOMOS, ICOMOS China and Xi'an City People's Government; the second level is a management committee including representatives of partner organizations such as ICOMOS, ICOMOS China, State Administration of Cultural Heritage of the People's Republic of China, and the Xi'an City People's Government; and the final level is an international scientific advisory board composed of experts. Operationally, IICC-X is divided into six departments: secretariat, information centre, project department, exchanging and training department, secretariat for the Silk Road information centre, and a coordination committee.

The activities of IICC-X are certainly diverse. I was able to secure an interview with the Silk Road secretariat, and was told about IICC-X's engagement in the Silk Roads World Heritage nomination. It coordinated the provision of advice for the nomination from experts, created an online platform to enhance the collaboration between the involved countries, and organized regular events to educate the public about World Heritage, including exhibitions, conferences, and workshops. IICC-X is also interesting because it brokers local, regional, national, and international relations without being in a direct line of subordination to China's national government. It is part of an international organization, but most of its employees are Chinese who – in fact – originated in Xi'an. I look a bit more at its role and activities in chapter 5.

To sum up, China integrates a state-oriented mechanism to govern, regulate, make decisions, and implement policies and projects concerned

---

[18] The main office of the National Committee of ICOMOS is located in Beijing.

[19] A historical overview appeared on the website of the ICOMOS International Conservation Center. http://www.iicc.org.cn/Column.aspx?ColId=30. Last accessed 1 May 2016.

with heritage preservation. Because all land and heritage sites are owned by the state, it would appear inevitable that the government would take the lead in urban transformation and heritage preservation projects. However, decisions concerning heritage involve unpredictable dynamics because of the many heritage-related actors across government departments which, moreover, work with development agencies and other experts in unclear chains of institutional command as they draft, implement, and evaluate each and every project. The following six chapters will illustrate the pragmatic interplay between government levels, international organizations, developers, local communities, experts, and different kinds of individuals, thereby exploring the socio-politics of urban heritage in Xi'an.

Chapter 3
The City of Civilization – Archaeological Heritage

Due to the vast and significant archaeological findings unearthed in Xi'an, such as Lantian Man[20] and the 3,000-year-old Banpo Neolithic settlement, Xi'an is known as the 'cradle of Chinese civilization' (Feighery 2011). As mentioned in chapter 2, many Xi'an residents insist that Xi'an represents 5,000 years of civilization – the whole history of the Chinese nation. As archaeological evidence thus far only proves the city's existence for 3,100 years, the city and provincial governments devotes itself (and significant funding) to conducting further prehistoric archaeological excavations to extend the timeline backwards. Their hope is even to show that China was the oldest civilization in the world.[21] At the time of my research, there was new hope.

Mr. Zhang, a local archaeologist in his mid-forties in charge of an archaeological excavation in Lintong District shared excitedly with me about his team's newest archaeological discovery. In spring 2014, they had unearthed a complete Neolithic settlement with an area that measured more than twenty square kilometres; it had been identified as Yangguanzhai. Mr. Zhang and many other archaeologists in Xi'an found the excavation highly significant because it could potentially push Xi'an's history 2,000 year earlier and support the '5,000 years' claim.

---

[20] Lantian Man (*Homo erectus lantianensis*) was discovered in 1963 in Lantian County. Lantian Man is dated back to the Palaeolithic, approximately 1.15 million years ago (Woo 1964). It is the second oldest *Homo erectus* site found in China.

[21] There is no clear date for the beginning of Chinese 'civilization'. According to museum descriptions (of the Shaanxi History Museum, Xi'an City Museum, and Banpo Museum), Xi'an's civilization (which also represents China's) started in the Neolithic with the evidence of cultivation and agriculture. Evidence of a more complex social structure with cosmologic beliefs was found for this period as well. Evidence of the production of pottery as well as other ornaments (instead of only stone tools to survive living) is taken as another sign of 'civilization'. Therefore, Lantian Man, who used only simple stone tools, was not included in the civilization discourse.

The city's desperate wish to fulfil 5,000 years of history mirrors the importance of a long civilization in the national discourse. Moreover, it reflects the political use of archaeology in Xi'an. Why does China, specifically Xi'an, aim to become the longest civilization? Why is the claim of 5,000 years of civilization so important to the nation and to the city? What is the role of 'civilization' in the socio-political life in China?

Since the 1980s, the term 'civilization' has dominated political discourse in China. Civilization (*wenming*) has a range of meanings in its wide use from government slogans to daily conversations (Shen 2015). Politically, the term relates to modernity and advancement (Harrell 1995). Many social scientists have studied the meaning of civilization in the Chinese context and have distinguished two layers of understanding: material civilization (*wuzhi wenming*) and spiritual civilization (*jingshen wenming*) (Lynch 2006). According to Børge Bakken (2000), 'material civilization' represents the growth and development of the nation in relation to modernity, while 'spiritual civilization' refers to social control and individual commitment to the values of civility, order, and stability. For example, the 'civilizing project' undertaken by the state with respect to ethnic minorities has treated non-Han ethnic groups as in need of civilization, education, and advancement (Harrell 1995). In its social use, *wenming* conveys two meanings when ordinary Chinese people use it. The first one refers to the quality of the population (Tomba 2014), which mainly points at social behaviours such as politeness and at the cleanliness of cities. For instance, Paul Festa's (2006) ethnography reports that the local neighbourhoods regarded the poor sanitation of streets where loud mahjong games were played in southern China as something 'uncivilized' (*bu wenming*). The second meaning of 'civilization' used by ordinary people, especially in Xi'an, is related to archaeology, the origin of Chinese culture, and historical continuity from the ancient past till present. Martin Jacques (2009) pointed to this use of 'civilization' in ordinary parlance. He claimed that contrary to Western understandings in which ancient 'civilization' is felt only as a distant and indirect influence on the present, in China, 'it is not only history that lives but civilization itself: the notion of a living civilization provides the primary identity and context by which the Chinese think of their country and define themselves' (ibid.: 201). I too observed a similar self-identification with 'living' civilization and sense of historical continuity in Xi'an. Finally, the term is connected to cities in scientific literature and the popular imagination: Zhu (2010) emphasized that civilization is a process through which human beings transformed from barbarians, specifically through the formation of cities.

Since archaeology serves as the only way to prove the long presence of civilization (Chinese Civilization Center 2007), archaeological excavation and its resulting sites are under the spotlight of heritage development in Xi'an. Archaeological remains account for more than 80 per cent of all the heritage sites in and around the city. The ancient archaeological sites are showcased as early settlements and forms of the city, and with increasing funding from the central government, local authorities conduct further archaeological research and develop sites into tourist attractions.

Chapter 2 introduced the most common terms used for cultural heritage sites in China: *wenwu* and *yizhi*. Ordinary people assigned distinct meanings to these two terms when they use them. They regard *wenwu* as grand and complete sites with high historical values, such as Forbidden City, the Great Wall, and the terracotta army. They think that *wenwu* are rare and have the potential to represent the nation as World Heritage sites. However, *yizhi* implies archaeological and historical remains from the past that are 'useless' and not as significant to the country. Due to Xi'an's long historical background, to the locals, the city is full of *yizhi,* as many historical sites were destroyed in the long run of history by natural hazards, erosion, or during wars. Yet, from my observation in Xi'an, I found out that *yizhi* were not totally 'useless' to locals, but were socially important. What does archaeology actually mean to the people and how do they relate to the archaeological sites? This chapter explores the interpretation of archaeology by different social actors, ranging from outsiders like tourists to insiders who work closely with the archaeological objects every day.

This chapter aims to enrich the field of archaeological ethnographies in China by examining the socio-political implications of archaeological heritage sites in Xi'an. My fieldwork entailed museum cooperation, site visits, interviews, as well as continuous interaction with numerous social actors related to the development of archaeological sites. Through a hybrid set of practices, drawing on archaeology and ethnography, I attempt to present the interface between archaeology and society in China. This chapter demonstrates the construction of archaeological data, the politics of archaeological heritage sites, and the view of archaeology by different social actors. It focuses on the archaeological sites in Xi'an, and looks into how the state constitutes the idea of 'civilization' through the discipline and in ordinary social comprehension and use. The first part of the chapter in-vestigates the perceptions of ordinary people, including Chinese tourists and locals, about archaeology and the archaeological sites in Xi'an. The second part discusses the trends of archaeology in the city and how the state and other social actors influence the uses of the discipline.

Doubting Archaeology

Xi'an's most well-known heritage site is undoubtedly the Terracotta Army Museum. Since the site hosts more than ten million visitors per year, the scale of the site has expanded massively in the past twenty years. Nowadays, visitors have to walk for over 15 minutes from the parking lot or bus stop to reach the first entrance gate of the museum. There is an eight-metre tall statue of Emperor Qin statue in the parking lot. Many souvenir shops, restaurants, and photo booths (all built to a standardized look in red brick) use replicas of terracotta warriors to attract customers, while souvenir shops sell warriors of different sizes and colours. At the photo booths, tourists can dress as warriors themselves or take photos with employees dressed like warriors. None of this is incidental: the grounds outside the site have been planned by a developer hired by the museum administration. In the near future, the developer plans to provide more entertainment activities for the tourists in the outlying areas with the construction of a Qin music and dance theatre and an 'intangible cultural heritage' garden.

Despite the fame of the site, the feedback from visitors is surprisingly negative. A number of tourists used the same phrase to describe their ex-perience: 'If you missed visiting the army, you might regret [it] for your whole life, but after you visit the army, you would definitely regret more! (*Buqu yihan cisheng, qule yihan zhongsheng*!)'. They lamented the commer-cialization of the site and its surroundings with the hundreds of shops and restaurants. Although they had to pay an entrance fee of 150 CNY[22], they could not take a close view of the army because of the massive number of visitors. Mr. Feng from Guangdong Province moaned to me, 'it is impossible to take a photo without other tourists in it'. Ms. Shi, who visited the site during the national day holiday period[23], said that she could barely see any warriors in the pit because there were seven rows of people in front of her and she could hardly squeeze to the front row. Even those who managed to see the whole pit told me that since they had too high expectations before the visit, they found the army not as impressive as they had imagined. Many others grumbled about the small number of warriors displayed in the pit. Visitors found the view of the terracotta army not as impressive as in the booklets or in the documentaries, thus they regretted paying the visit to the site.

---

[22] The entrance fee was equivalent to about 22 euros or US dollars. During my fieldwork, the Chinese yuan (CNY) or renminbi averaged about 0.14 euros or 0.16 US dollars.

[23] The national day holiday period is also known as the gold week. People enjoy one week free from work starting 1 October.

In the past, the first pit – with its more than 700 life-size terracotta warriors in tidy lines – used to impress visitors (Plate 1). They were astounded by the number of warriors and by the display of detailed ancient craftsmanship. I remember how the hall was filled with 'aahs', 'oohs', 'wows', and 'wahs' when I entered the pit during my first visit in summer 2007. However, in summer 2014, when I revisited the museum during my fieldwork, the site had shifted from an impressive iconic site to a 'doubt site'. Tourists were still amazed by the scene at the beginning, but very soon, they started to question, 'is it real?' and 'is it authentic?' Some foreigners doubted the authenticity of the display because they remembered when reporters had revealed in 2007 that the Museum für Völkerkunde in Hamburg was exhibiting numerous terracotta warrior replicas as if they were real. The museum had to terminate the exhibition and refund the entrance tickets to 10,000 visitors, who had intended to see the original terracotta warriors (Fiskesjö 2015). But most of the doubts were raised by Chinese tourists. Many visitors from outside Shaanxi Province told me that they believed the displayed warriors were replicas. Mr. Hong from Shandong exclaimed that these warriors 'must be fake' because 'the warriors are supposed to be more than 2,000 years old and it is simply impossible to keep them in such a good shape!' Mr. Li from Henan said: 'these warriors cannot be real because they are national cultural relics. The state would not exhibit original objects just like that'. He thought only the warriors displayed in the museum area protected by glass screens were real, but those in the pit were copies.

To-date, merely half of Pit One has been excavated and the excavation of the second half is still on-going. Therefore, the museum uses Pit One to showcase the different stages of archaeological and restoration work involved. The very front rows exhibit the completely well-preserved warriors to create the iconic view. From the twentieth row on, visitors can find some slightly tilted, headless, and incomplete figures. From around the fortieth row, visitors can only see partly excavated warriors lying in pieces in situ. In the second half of the pit, visitors can observe how archaeologists and restorers conduct excavation work.

Plate 1. The iconic view of the terracotta army at Pit One.

Visitors view the pit first from above, and then have the chance to walk from the front of Pit One back towards the unexcavated Pit Two. Overseas visitors generally appreciated this presentation, and after traversing the site no longer questioned the originality of the warriors. However, many Chinese tourists did not feel the same way. They believed that even the pit was a recon-struction that served as a 'show' for the tourists. They thought that the real and original warriors were either still buried beneath the earth or kept in the storage of the museum under tight security.

In my observations, an obsession with 'authenticity' and the con-sumption of 'real' products goes far beyond the touristic moment and dominates everyday life for people in China. During my fieldwork, every time I commuted between Hong Kong and Xi'an, my informants asked me to buy 'real' (branded) products for them, including I-pads, cosmetics, instant noodles, and even soya sauce. They had lost trust that 'authenticity' could be found within China after the numerous and widely-publicized scandals involving the adulteration of food, including that of industrial cooking oil and baby formula.[24] Questioning the authenticity of the

---

[24] See Li. L. 'In the Tank, Not on the Table'. *The Beijing Review*, 17 November 2011. http://www.bjreview.com.cn/nation/txt/2011-11/14/content_405509.htm. Last accessed 1 May 2016. And, Cao Y. and W. Luo. 'Rotting Meat Used to Make Illegal Oil'. *China Daily*, 4

terracotta warriors, and other heritage sites, is thus part of a broader relation between political economy and heritage development. At one level, it mirrors the people's lack of trust in the Chinese market. But there are at least three other components of a 'political economy' of heritage development that are discernible in the question of authenticity.

First, and simply, the massive scale of tourism development in China has made it hard for tourists to distinguish 'real' attractions. They are confronted by the self-exoticisation of many attractions (Nyiri 2006; Dombroski 2008; Mclaren 2010; Li 2013), as well as intentional copies. Perhaps the most widely known of these copies is a town in southern China that reconstructed the Austrian UNESCO town of Hallstatt – and even built a snow mountain for its background.[25] In Xi'an, there are also plenty of examples of reconstructed palaces and heritage sites, such as Ziyun Palace in Tang Paradise, and the entrance gate of Daming Palace. Historical sites are turned into tourist attractions with authentic and inauthentic elements mixed in such a way that visitors can no longer tell what is real and what is not. The general tendency to reconstruct and commercialize tourist attractions creates the illusion that all sites must have been beautified and are no longer displaying original artefacts.

Secondly, even within Lintong District, where the Terracotta Army Museum is situated, there are two similar attractions which have been reconstructed. These are the Eight Wonders Museum and the Underground Palace of the Qin Shihuang Emperor. Both sites invoke the Emperor Qin Shihuang Mausoleum as a selling point to attract visitors. The Underground Palace is a clear reconstruction. The original palace has not yet been excavated, so this one was constructed on the imaginative interpretation of historical records. For its part, the Eight Wonders Museum showcases reconstructions of famous historical icons from all over the world, such as the Great Pyramid in Egypt, alongside replicas of the terracotta army. Surprisingly, Chinese tourists preferred these two 'theme-park-like' sites over the official museum. Mr. Fei, a local taxi driver in his late forties, told me that he always recommended his passengers to visit the two recon-structed sites; he claimed that people enjoyed them much more because the experience was more exciting; it was as if they explored the past during their visit to the site. Other tourists found the replicas they encountered on the

---

April 2012. http://www.chinadaily.com.cn/china/2012-04/04/content_14975475.htm. Last accessed 1 May 2016. The problems with baby formula even caught the attention of Western social science (Gong and Jackson 2012; Sabbon 2014).

[25] 'Xeroxed Village: Chinese Secretly Copy Austrian UNESCO Town'. *Spiegel Online*, 16 June 2011. http://www.spiegel.de/international/europe/xeroxed-village-chinese-secretly-copy-austrian-unesco-town-a-768754.html. Last accessed 1 May 2016.

way from the bus stop to the main entrance of the Terracotta Army Museum much better than viewing those in the pit. Ms. Luo said, after seeing the replicas in different sizes and colours in the commercial street before entering the museum, the pit was no longer impressive. The warrior replicas found everywhere in the district and the two clearly 'fake' sites further mislead and confuse tourists' judgment of 'authenticity', to the point that the museum with the real warriors and the various reconstructed sites and their replicas do not differ much – except that the imaginative and fanciful dimensions of the 'fakes' present an unexpected appeal.

Lastly, the limited understanding of archaeology and World Heritage among the general public resulted in the questioning of authenticity. As Magnus Fiskesjö wrote, 'going to museums to see exhibitions is an acquired taste, originally cultivated and intimately embedded in modernity, in the European configuration of our era' (2015: 162). Most of the visitors from China have not yet acquired this 'modern taste' and approach World Heritage sites as a must-try form of entertainment. They visit the site because of its fame and the UNESCO brand, but they do not know much about the history of the site, nor how the site fulfilled the criteria of UNESCO. They view the archaeologists and restorers working in situ as staged for tourists. Ms. Ouyang pointed out: 'the tools that the restorers used to measure the warriors seem so simple and look like what I used for my office work!' Those who doubted the site believed that archaeologists should be working in the wild without cover; Pit One does not fit their imagination.

Interestingly, although Chinese tourists wondered if the displayed warriors were real, they had no question about the historical value of the site. They opined unconditionally that the site represents China as it symbolizes the first imperial dynasty and civilization. The pursuit of historical and archaeological traces they took as sincere, even as they doubted and critiqued its display. Thus, regardless of its perceived 'authenticity', the site still succeeds as a political instrument for boosting the understanding of Chinese civilization.

Archaeology and Everyday Life

In contrast to the visitors' doubt about archaeological artefacts, local Xi'an people were convinced that all heritage sites in Shaanxi are real. When I first arrived in Xi'an, I asked locals to recommend the most worth-seeing sites. The top three suggestions were all related to archaeology: the terracotta army, Emperor Huang's Mausoleum (also known as the Mausoleum of the Yellow Emperor), and Qian Imperial Mausoleum. The recommendation of the terracotta army and Qian Mausoleum did not surprise me, as both serve as the resting place of significant historical figures: the first emperor in the former one and the first empress in the latter one.

However, I did not expect locals to recommend Emperor Huang's tomb so strongly. In contrast to the 'real' first emperor and empress, Emperor Huang is a legendary figure. Glorified as a hero of Chinese culture, it is said that he reigned for one hundred years (2698–2598 BCE) after defeating a foreign barbarian monster and saving China (Veith 2002). Back in the 1920s, Chinese historians stated that Emperor Huang was a mythological figure, originally worshiped as a god and only later depicted as a human (Chang 1983). The People's Republic of China narrates the legend of Emperor Huang as part of its national history, and uses it to reinforce a unified Chinese identity (Leibold 2006). According to Wang (1999), because *huang* (yellow) is the skin colour of the majority, he was narrated as the common ancestor of Han Chinese. Later, in order to integrate the ethnic minorities, the character of Emperor Yan (the Red Emperor) was created as the brother of Emperor Huang. In any case, the Mausoleum of Emperor Huang was built before the Han Dynasty as a temple for the emperor's worship. Later, a Han emperor changed the temple to a mausoleum by putting some garments into the 'tomb' as a symbolic gesture to commemorate the ancient ancestor.

Xi'an locals perceived Emperor Huang as a real historical figure. Very few people questioned whether he actually existed, and no one ever doubted that the mausoleum was real. When I challenged Mr. Shi, a worker in his late sixties, he responded: 'That is our national story. Sometimes, it is better when you do not question if things are real. We are told so and we just believe so!' Another restorer in his early thirties also stated: 'it is wrong and disrespectful to question the site's origin! He is the greatest ancestor of China!' My informants, including those who were highly educated, saw me as wrong for posing such questions. When I asked why there were no remains in the tomb, they told me that Emperor Huang had ascended to heaven.

A strong affinity for archaeology was nurtured by the environment in which locals grew up. In Xi'an, many people grew up as amateur 'archaeologists'. Mr. Han, a businessman in his early twenties, who lived in the eastern part of the city, recalled playing around the fields close to the Banpo Neolithic site and discovering ancient pottery pieces all the time. He said that the government did not bother to control these fields because there were so many artefacts and because they were in such poor condition. Ms. Lin, a student who resided in the northern part of the city around the remains of Daming Palace remembered that as a kid, she liked to climb up and down the palace remains. On a lucky day, she could unearth a tile or a brick from the former palace. Mr. Gong, a tour guide in his mid-thirties who grew up in the Han Chang'an city remains area, recalled how he and his friends found Han dynasty coins, and tied them up to make Chinese hacky-sacks (*jianzi*). These childhood stories exemplify the close relationship between locals' everyday life and archaeology. In fact, informants did not only grow up with archaeology, but when they approached the end of their life, they also preferred to be buried with the archaeological remains. Mr. Lei, a hotel manager in his late thirties, told me that his grandfather wished to be buried inside the city wall of Han Chang'an. Mr. Lei said:

> My grandfather was not alone, many people chose to be buried that way. [Others] simply dug [out] holes from the wall to put the bodies inside.[26] The city wall has hence become a mass cemetery. He made that decision because nothing could be more honourable than being buried in an ancient city like Han Chang'an and resting together with the thousand-year-old heritage and the historical emperors.

Besides, the linkage between archaeology and everyday life is also demonstrated by the rich local knowledge of heritage sites and ancient history. When I visited some museums with locals, my correspondents told me extensively about the background of each item we viewed. Ms. Tang, an English teacher in her late twenties, had developed a strong interest for Tang architecture. When we visited the Daming Palace Museum together, she could identify every architectural part of the palace structure. Mr. Sun, a student majoring in finance, told me that he enjoyed hanging out at antiquity markets in Xi'an in his free time because he could appreciate ancient art and learn a lot about antiquities. Mr. Wang, who grew up in the Han Chang'an city remains area, said that it was not difficult to find real archaeological relics in the antiquity market in Xi'an, and that not all of the real artefacts were rare or expansive. He claimed that Xi'an people tended to have a feeling for what was real or valuable. He gave an example from the Shaanxi History Museum, 'the stone lying in the pond at the main entrance of the museum is an original piece from Weiyang Palace in the Han Dynasty. Yet, the museum kept it there in the public space because it knows no one would steal it, as it is common sense in Xi'an which cultural relics are worth more and which ones are worthless'. These strong interests and deep knowledge, which locals regard as 'common sense', reflect how archaeology and archaeological knowledge have merged in Xi'an people's everyday life.

During social interactions, people often commented on recent archaeological excavations. Never have I been to a place where archaeological sites and excavations would be discussed so much in an everyday

---

[26] The city wall of Han Chang'an was estimated to be more than two metres thick.

context. Local newspapers reported about excavations taking place in the province on average every three days. Locals discussed these reports and their implications in daily conversation. Furthermore, the public participated keenly in archaeological events, such as press conferences on the most recent excavations and talks given by archaeologists. Ms. Mei, an entrepreneur in her early thirties, whom I met during my internship at the Shaanxi History Museum, volunteered every week at the museum because she wanted to learn more about Xi'an's history. She admired the hard work of the archaeologists and restorers and decided to devote her free time to heritage preservation. Two years previously, she had even put her business aside and enrolled in a Masters program in antiquities studies at Tsinghua University in Beijing. She said: 'I realized that I did not have "culture" when I was purely a businesswoman, and that is a shame as a Xi'an person!' Mr. Zhao, a primary school teacher who had joined the volunteering program at the museum in 2008, told me that he chose to study history in university because he had always dreamed of becoming an archaeologist, like many other Xi'an people. He said that he would never forget his first summer volunteering (in 2008) which he had spent excavating with archaeologists at nearby Shigu Mountain. Such respect for archaeologists and archaeology as a discipline is common in Xi'an.

Apart from those who volunteered, many local Xi'an people choose to become a professional in the field of heritage preservation. Mr. Cha, an antique collector who grew up in the Han Chang'an city remains area, told me that his birth place gave him the inspiration to engage in the preservation of cultural relics. The moment when his father, a farmer in the region, handed in thirteen Iranian coins, which he found while farming, to the Xi'an City Archaeological Institute, was unforgettable to Mr. Cha. After that, he wanted to devote his lifetime to heritage preservation. He also remembered the moment when he collected his first piece of antiquity – a brick from the roof of a Han palace, which nurtured his passion for archaeology and antiquity. Mr. Zhang, a restorer at the Terracotta Army Museum, told me that he had wanted to work for the museum since he was a child because he lived next to the mausoleum. Every time locals learned of my affiliations with the Terracotta Army Museum and Shaanxi History Museum, they expressed admiration and recognition of my work. They believed that these institutes are prestigious places to work because there one can contribute to society, even if one cannot earn a lot of money.

The high degree of engagement with archaeology and respect for it among the general population in Xi'an is unusual. In other parts of China, people prefer work in the sectors of finance and industry because of the money such work brings. That many Xi'an natives dream of working in the fields of archaeology and restoration, perceiving these as stable and respectable jobs regardless of their salary, confirms that the state's idea of civilization has been taken up here. The locals recognize Xi'an as representative of China's ancient civilization and accept a personal and social responsibility to protect the heritage sites, in order to prove the nation's glorious past. The next section discusses the role of the government and the uses of archaeology at higher levels.

The Boom of Archaeological Parks

Embarking on my fieldwork, I aimed to explore every corner of the city and to discover as many historical sites as possible – not only the famous touristic ones but also the unknown places. When I studied the map and city development plan of Xi'an, I realized that there was a vast and undeveloped piece of land located less than 10 kilometres north-west from the city wall. Few local residents could tell me anything about the area. After extensive research, I found out that the provincial and city governments had disapproved a plan to build an automobile factory there in the 1970s, and in the 1990s, they had again banned construction there of a highway.[27] The government's repeated hesitation over potential development aroused my interest. I wondered: were there archaeological sites out there?

On a hot summer day in September 2013, I decided to explore the area. I took a bus to its terminal station, and arrived in a semi-urban district. I asked local residents about the archaeological sites around. They told me that I had to walk for half an hour and cross through the woods to see some remains. One man warned me not to go alone because drug addicts and robbers were active in the woods. I went anyway.

When I reached what I understood to be the remains, I found a group of local women harvesting wild cabbages. They told me that the area had been occupied by a few villages until a year previously, but the government had removed them all for some development projects. I decided then to visit the area every two weeks to observe the progress of the 'project'. Indeed, there was one. Gradually, the city government allocated guards to the

---

[27] Later in my fieldwork, I met some urban planners who had dealt with the area. They confirmed that the area has been a taboo area for urban development because of the Han and Qin palace remains beneath. Developing the area, they said, would have meant not only a huge destruction of the city's history but also a high cost for any archaeological excavations that were conducted. Articles containing information on this history appeared in local newspapers during the time of my fieldwork. One published in 2015 that is still accessible is 'Han Changan de zhengti baohu tiqu zhilu' (The general restoration portfolio of Han Chang'an city). http://www.xiancn.com/zt/content/2015-01/19/content_2912021.htm. Last accessed 28 February 2019.

archaeological sites, beautified the sites, built roads and sightseeing platforms, planted trees, put up signs, and arranged food and drink booths. By June 2014, the site had its own entrance gate with the UNESCO logo on it. In barely nine months, the place had been transformed from an unknown shanty slum to a 36-square-kilometre national archaeological park, and then even to a World Heritage site. This case study demonstrates the speed of heritage park construction in Xi'an and shows the increasing role that archaeological sites play. Since 2010, Shaanxi and Xi'an governments have carried out an increasing number of heritage projects with the support of the national government, which resulted in the boom of archaeological parks.

In fact, the legal grounds for the development had been some years in the making. In 2009, State Administration of Cultural Heritage announced the National Archaeological Parks Law (State Administration of Cultural Heritage 2009) and officially categorized some heritage sites as 'national archaeological parks' (*kaogu yizhi gongyuan*). These were to be organized around large-scale archaeological remains considered valuable and important for scientific research and national history education (State Administration of Cultural Heritage 2009). Provincial bureaus of cultural heritage could nominate sites that fit these criteria for assessment by State Administration of Cultural Heritage. After obtaining the title of national archaeological park, the site must follow the rules outlined in the Act. Among these, all national archaeological park candidates have to be listed as nationally-ranked heritage sites (see chapter 2), they must have an on-going archaeological excavation project and valid heritage preservation plans for the site, and they must adopt all the advice given by experts from the national level.

In October 2010, after a year of preparation and evaluation, State Administration of Cultural Heritage announced the first list of 35 national archaeological parks. Three of these are located in Shaanxi Province – Qin Shihuang Mausoleum National Archaeological Park (together with the Terracotta Army Museum), Yang Mausoleum of the Han Dynasty National Archaeological Park, and Daming Palace National Archaeological Park (State Administration of Cultural Heritage 2010). In December 2013, State Administration of Cultural Heritage published the second list of national archaeological parks; this time the Han Chang'an city remains (by that time already enclosed within a cultural scenic area) also appeared among forty sites (State Administration of Cultural Heritage 2013). As a consequent, Xi'an City Tourism Board highlighted in its tourism plan for the period between 2013 and 2020 that it will develop Xi'an as a 'world-class archaeological park city' (Xi'an City Tourism Board 2013a).

The central government grants the management right to the provincial governments to monitor the national archaeological parks and to reduce the possibility of destructions (State Administration of Cultural Heritage 2009). For example, the sites are advised to be equipped with only the most basic facilities. The Han Chang'an City National Archaeological Park, for instance, did not construct any permanent buildings within the area of the archaeological remains; even the washrooms and restaurants were movable. The movable toilet cabins and snack vans do not require water or electricity supply, which would potentially disturb the underground archaeological remains. Moreover, the design and planning of national archaeological parks are usually joint projects between the provincial government and the archaeological, restoration, or heritage studies departments of universities to ensure the holistic planning and preservation of the parks.

The rise of national archaeological parks has created a wave of other 'archaeological parks'. Since 2010, private developers in Xi'an have started to extend at least seven heritage sites as 'archaeological parks' (*yizhi gongyuan*). These include Tang City Wall Archaeological Park, Qujiang Lake Archaeological Park, Love Cave Archaeological Park, Du Mausoleum Archaeological Park, Mausoleum of the Second Qin Emperor Archaeological Park, Da Ci'en Temple Archaeological Park, and Han Chenghu Archaeological Park. These parks are more commercialized and focus much less on archaeology and heritage preservation than the 'national archaeological parks'. Mr. You, an urban planner involved in the design of national archaeological parks, criticized the unofficial parks for using the name 'archaeological park'. Not only is the term too similar, but it is against national law. 'National archaeological park', he said 'represents the national standard with set criteria and a complicated process'.

There are six unofficial archaeological parks in Qujiang District alone (see chapter 6). Among them, Mr. You regarded Love Cave Archaeological Park, built by Qujiang Corporation, as the most ridiculous one. Organized on principles similar to those of Juliet's House in Verona, the Love Cave presents a classic love story from the Tang Dynasty. The story is about a rich girl who falls in love with a poor but brave young man against the will of her family. The young couple elopes to Love Cave because the groom cannot afford a house, and shortly after their betrothal, the young man must join the army to invade foreign lands. The girl waits for him eight harsh and cold years in the cave, but not in vain. The young man returns to become the emperor of the Tang Dynasty, and his bride joins him as empress in the palace. The story is set in Chang'an, but as Mr. You said, 'the story is purely a legend and it never happened in history. The characters in the story also never existed. How can you name this totally artificial site without any historical basis an archaeological park? The term "archaeological park" does not fit at all!' He proposed that the six 'archaeological parks' without national standing would be better called 'cultural theme parks' as they have nothing to do with archaeology, nor do they have any preservation plans. As with the other reproductions in the area, Mr. You was concerned that the wide application of the term 'archaeological' misleads visitors into thinking that these sites are real.

But, how do visitors and locals perceive the two types of archaeological parks? Do they know the differences between them? According to my observation, the domestic visitors and locals actually preferred the unofficial archaeological parks. Domestic tourists found unofficial archaeological parks more entertaining and exciting. Statistics from the one-week national day holiday in 2013 shows that Qin Shihuang Mausoleum National Archaeological Park received 364,500 visitors, while Qujiang Lake Archaeological Park hosted 1,897,000 tourists (Xi'an City Tourism Board 2013b). I use the golden week statistics because mainly Chinese domestic tourists travel during this period. The unofficial archaeological parks (or cultural theme parks) are free to enter, which may explain some of their greater attraction over the official ones. But they offer many other advantages too. One visitor, Mr. Chen, said: 'Qujiang Lake is well-equipped with many restaurants and shops, and we even took a ride in the Qujiang air balloon to have an overview of Xi'an. It was spectacular. The lake has a beautiful night view and the water fountain show at Big Wild Goose Pagoda was not far. I highly recommend this place'. He compared Qujiang District and the Terracotta Army Museum and found the latter one not as attractive in terms of their facilities and entertainment.

Indeed, some of the local farmers from the Han Chang'an city remains area expressed disappointment over the development of the new national archaeological park. Mr. Chang, for example, was initially very happy when he heard about the government's plan to develop the area as a national archaeological park in 2010. However, the finished park let him down. He grumbled that the park was too simple and that the government had not even tried to turn it into a popular touristic site. Following the regulations set in the national act, urban planners and heritage experts had decided to refill the excavated areas. They used stones of different colours to indicate the layout of the underlying city; the roads were marked with light brown sandstone and the walls of the palace buildings were marked by grey rock. Experts had advised refilling the site would protect the original content while the stone markings would suffice to help visitors reconstruct the past palace. However, locals complained that the site had been turned from Han cheng (City of Han) to Hai cheng (City of disaster). They expected that the development of the archaeological heritage site would transform the site to a famous attraction, and that it would bring in visitors on a par with the Terracotta Army Museum or Qujiang District.

Dissatisfaction among locals correlates with a low educational background. Presumably, one must know about archaeology to value its rigours. But, dissatisfaction also points to other things that locals hope to gain from heritage-related development. Mr. Wei, a former farmer from the area, also felt dissatisfied about the development of the new national park. It had failed to boost tourism, he said, and not raised the price of land as had happened in Qujiang District (see chapter 6). He had counted the price of land rising, so that he could rent his apartments and gain a higher income. To him, the national archaeological park was not worth visiting. Indeed, during my visits to the archaeological park, I rarely found tourists. Although the site is inscribed on the World Heritage List, it mainly served as an area for evening and weekend walks by the local residents.

Moreover, because they perceived the development of national archaeological parks in the area as a 'failure', Xi'an farmers were no longer enthusiastic about other national or provincial heritage projects. I was invited to join a provincial heritage-site-evaluating team on a visit to Ping Mausoleum of the Han Dynasty in June 2014. The site is only an hour away from Xi'an by car, but the local farmers did not show any eagerness to protect or develop the area into a heritage site. They even shouted at our team and tried to drive us away! The local officials who accompanied us found the farmers' attitude embarrassing. Another day, I went to the site again and a farmer told me: 'everywhere underneath the ground here lie cultural relics. When we farm in the field, we always find artefacts, but we do not tell the government departments about them, because otherwise, we cannot farm anymore'. The farmer argued that the development of the site into an archaeological park would disturb their everyday life. Xi'an, he said, has too many mausoleums already and this one would not matter to Xi'an's tourism economy.

In fact, the locals' opposition could not stop the construction of archaeological parks. Shaanxi Provincial Bureau of Cultural Heritage makes all the decisions regarding if and how to develop the archaeological sites. Han Chang'an City National Archaeological Park, for example, was executed by the Heritage Site Protection and Planning Centre, which was established by Shaanxi Provincial Bureau of Cultural Heritage and North West University. The centre consulted restorers, archaeologists, and planners at different stages of the park's construction, but most importantly, the centre had to take advice from the national administration and follow the instructions given by national experts. In the end, the central government evaluates and decides if the site can be classified as a national archaeological park.

Nevertheless, the boom of archaeological parks, whether the official or unofficial ones, reflects the growing importance of archaeology and archaeological sites to the national, provincial, and city governments, as well as to the developers and part of the local population. It also displays the role of archaeology in Xi'an's urban and touristic development.[28]

The Segregation of the Professional Community

Just like the unearthed terracotta warriors – broken into pieces – the professional community related to heritage management and preservation is fragmented. As described in the previous sections, the making of archaeological parks and site conservation involves consultation between experts from various fields, including archaeologists, historians, restorers, urban planners, architects, and even engineers. However, the diverse educational backgrounds and professional training result in different interests, focuses, as well as misunderstandings and even conflicts. For instance, restorers pay attention to the practical techniques of restoring broken parts; archaeologists concentrate on the findings and their implications; engineers focus on the technical components of the archaeological parks; some architects and urban planners follow international standards and conventions, but others do not. Professional, educational, social, and even family background determines how one perceives heritage preservation. During my fieldwork, I observed that the segregation between certain types of specialists was particularly strong. The next subsections will disclose the tension between Chinese and foreign restorers, as well as those between archaeologists and restorers.

Restoration: West versus China

In Xi'an, even when original heritage sites are given new outlooks and new decorations, they are still accepted and seen as 'real' and 'authentic' by locals. Most of my correspondents, no matter at the public or professional levels, did not distinguish between the concepts of 'restoration', 'preservation', and 'reconstruction'. Only a very few experts in heritage studies, restoration, architecture, or urban planning define these concepts clearly and apply them in practice. Mr. Xu, an architect in his late thirties, is one who does. He found it dreadful that many urban planners, architects, and even restorers mixed different concepts when designing plans, implementing heritage projects, and even conducting restoration work. In his free time, he

---

[28] Information about the Bureau's structure, organization, and some changes is provided on its website. http://www.wenwu.gov.cn/. Last accessed 1 May 2016.

lectured at universities in Xi'an to teach young professionals his concepts of restoration.

Here are his definitions and implications of the terms. The act of preservation, (*baohu*), has to follow national guidelines strictly. No original parts or colours can be removed or changed. Similarly, in the process of renovation (*chongxiu*), only original materials and techniques can be used. In his view, restoration (*xiufu*), rebuilding (*chongjian*), and reconstruction (*gaijian*) provide the room for new technology and creativity. Restoration implies the repairing of old and broken parts, where new material and scientific methods are often applied. Rebuilding refers to the building of a new structure in a historical architectural style according to historical sources and records. Lastly, reconstruction is a way to renew old buildings for modern use.

The national government and State Administration for Cultural Heritage laid emphasis on the heritage restoration principle of *xiujiurujiu* (lit. restore historical objects to old original look). This principle was coined by the famous Chinese architect Mr. Liang Sicheng (1901–72), who studied architecture at Harvard University, and is regarded as the saviour of Chinese cultural heritage. In the 1950s, he persuaded the PRC to make laws to protect a list of endangered sites, resulting in the survival of many that were damaged from wars and instabilities. In Xi'an, I had the chance to meet his niece. She too is an architect and devoted to heritage preservation. She teaches at a university in Xi'an. But she criticized Liang's concept of *xiujiurujiu* as too vague and the government of over-using it without fully understanding the four component words. In her view, the definitions of 'old' (*jiu*) and 'restoration' (*xiu*) should be clarified before applying the concept to every heritage issue. In her opinion, 'restoration' should be conducted only when it is urgent and absolutely needed to save a site. In contrast, she said, many 'restoration projects' carried out in Xi'an are unnecessary and even harmful to the historical sites. On the other hand, she was not wedded to the belief that restoration is always best achieved with the use of old materials: in the West, she pointed out, restorers may replace broken parts with new ones of a different material; but, they use another colour to indicate the difference between the original and new parts.

In practice, the technique and guidelines of restoration in China are still seeking their path. Xi'an organized numerous international cooperation projects on heritage restoration to facilitate the exchange of technology, skills, and ideas of restoration. One example is the Sino-German cooperation project between Germany's Federal Ministry of Education and Research and China's State Scientific and Technological Commission, carried out from 1990 to 2014. The project aimed to preserve and restore various historical sites in Shaanxi Province, including the terracotta army. According to the German restorers who participated in the program, a lot of friction was caused by differences in the perception, interpretation, and execution of heritage restoration. Whereas the Germans tried to minimize restoration, their Chinese counterparts were much less concerned about repairing broken parts, and they even filled in new parts based entirely on speculation. A clear example of their different approaches can be seen in the restoration of the walls of Bewusheng Study Hall, which dates back to the mid-eighteenth century.[29] The Chinese team restored the right wall by applying bright colours and repainting the details of the characters which had eroded over time. The German restorers conserved the left wall with light colouring and left the weathered and distorted parts empty. They explained that the condition of the wall was so bad that the faded faces and hand gestures could not be repainted without resulting in a potential misrepresentation of the past. Another team of German restorers working in Shuilu Nunnery located in Lantian District also found it difficult to work with their Chinese partners. In this case, they tried (unsuccessfully) to convince the Chinese not to use new material to replace the broken arm of a wooden sculpture.

The German team was not always very diplomatic in expressing their frustration. 'This is a very backward way of restoration', said Ms. Maier, one of the German restorers. In contrast to the Chinese government's use of *xiujiurujiu*, the German restorers claimed to follow the prescriptions of the Venice Charter adopted in 1965 by ICMOS. This document states that conservation and restoration must consider the harmony with the original composition and its relation with its surrounding. No demolition, construction, modification, or additions are allowed (ICOMOS 1965). However, without actualizing distinctions between 'restoration', 'repair', and 'reconstruction', the creative approach taken by the Chinese team to restoration can be said to be much closer to the nineteenth-century style of Eugène Viollet-le-Duc, who combined historical accuracy with romanticized modification.

There are many reasons for the more creative and seemingly 'random' approach to restoration pursued by Chinese specialists. One cause is the lack of standardization; unlike restorers in the West, they do not follow international charters. Education in restoration is also not standardized. The courses of study that are offered are, moreover, highly scientific. They focus on the operation of certain machines and chemicals, and not on the principles

---

[29] Differences in restoration were discussed in a Chinese article featured on the webpage of the Chair in Conservation-Restoration of the Technical University of Munich in 2015. 'Ziyang Beiwusheng huiguan' (Beiwusheng Hall in Ziyang village). Available online, https://www.rkk.ar.tum.de/index.php?id=250. Last accessed 1 May 2016.

or theory of restoration and conservation. Hence, the way to restore remains unstructured, and depends on other circumstances, such as the general political discourse, the background of the restorers, and even traditional beliefs. This last point is important: in China, people renovate temples and ancestral halls regularly by repainting the buildings with bright colours. An 'old-looking' building with pale colours signals that a village is not prosperous or that the villagers disrespect their gods and ancestors.

Archaeology versus Restoration

Like their Western counterparts, Chinese restorers feel tension with archaeologists. An Austrian archaeologist, Ms. Rosenberg, noted that the relationship between archaeologists and restorers is like an arranged marriage. The two professions work very closely with each other, but they are not drawn together by true love. Each has a prejudice against the other. To archaeologists, restorers are not professional; they think restoration requires only handiwork and that restorers lack knowledge about the past and the objects they treat. To restorers, archaeologists do not handle artefacts correctly and are always too rough with the historical relics. Restorers regard every archaeological excavation as destruction and think archaeologists exploit sites and relics to enrich their discipline. When I asked restorers for their own views about their work and role (especially during a restoration conference in which I participated), they described themselves as 'doctors'. They diagnose the disease of a site or a relic, they said, and find the right solution to preserve it.

Even though this tension between archaeologists and restorers is universal, my observation indicates that it is stronger in Xi'an than elsewhere. During my internship at the Terracotta Army Museum, I worked with the department that researches ways to preserve the colours on the excavated warriors. The longer I worked at the museum, the more I realized that the duties and tasks of the restorers and archaeologists overlapped. Restorers might excavate and archaeologists also performed restoration on unearthed objects. But the relationship was not one of cooperation. With the slow progress of excavation and limited amount of unearthed material, restorers and archaeologists were constrained to use the same objects and data in their work. Furthermore, the museum administration assessed the quality and productivity of both based on their research and publication. Hence, at a very important level, the archaeology and restoring teams were in competition. One archaeologist told me, 'even though we work in the same museum, we are not supposed to work together. We work in one team and restorers work in another. However, we share the same findings from the excavations, so it all depends on who can publish faster'. A restorer told me that because of this same rivalry, they rarely had contact with each other. Another restorer who had worked for two years in the museum had never talked to any archaeologists: 'they work in the pit and their office is not in our building. During lunchtime, I sit together with the other restorers'. Mr. Lu, a senior restorer, blamed the museum system for the hostile relationship: 'it is a pity that we cannot share our research data with each other, which might actually be more beneficial to the preservation of the objects. However, we have to keep our findings confidential'. Indeed, when I asked the senior restorers if they could introduce any archaeologists to me, they hesitated. What were the other reasons for this tension?

In Xi'an, the tension between archaeologists and restorers is highly institutionalized, and at the end, even the state is involved. The tension is linked to a strong hierarchy between archaeologists and restorers, which is in turn formed by the educational and administrative systems. That is to say, archaeology has a much longer academic tradition than does restoration in Xi'an. The archaeology department at North West University is among the best in China and was established in 1956. The restoration department was founded only in 1989.[30] As a result, archaeologists received high-level education and training much earlier than did restorers. They are regarded as academics while restorers have not yet shaken their image of being skilled workers. Moreover, the state has delayed in expanding its institutional support to professional restoration. State Administration of Cultural Heritage and the central government upgraded Shaanxi Provincial Archaeological Centre (Shaanxi sheng kaogu yanjiushuo) to Shaanxi Provincial Archaeological Institute (Shaanxi sheng kaogu yanjiuyuan) in 2006 and promoted Xi'an City Archaeological Centre to an institute in 2011. However, the central government did not grant the Provincial Restoration Research Centre the institute title until 2012 and has not yet granted it to the City Restoration Centre. Although the change of title from 'research centre' to 'research institute' does not result in any practical changes, it signifies the state's recognition of a centre's contribution and importance. The researchers considered it as an honour if their centres get upgraded. Both the education and administration systems reflect that archaeology has gained more attention from the state, is perceived as a proper profession, and enjoys more privileges than restoration.

Besides, the ranking and assessment systems of the two professions also vary, which impact the individual archaeologists and restorers. Mr. Yao, a chief restorer at the Terracotta Army Museum, shared his bitterness with me:

---

[30] A brief history is provided on the website of the Cultural Heritage Preservation Faculty. http://mainpage.nwu.edu.cn/unit/uwbxy. Last accessed 1 May 2016.

I feel like no matter how hard I work, I do not get recognized. It is different for the archaeologists. They have very clear ranking systems and examinations to climb up the ladder. Restorers, on the contrary, do not. We remain restorers without any rankings no matter how long we have worked or how much we have achieved.

Indeed, archaeologists are classified with a rank of one (highest) to five (lowest). They are assessed and promoted based on examinations, experiences, and the number of published articles. Such a grading system does not exist for restorers. Though restoration also requires a lot of knowledge, experience, and research skills, without a ranking system restorers do not feel acknowledged. If restorers want to be known, they have to work on different projects, teach at the universities, and publish as much as they can to gain the recognition from the museum administration. Ms. Guo, a senior restorer who worked in the Terracotta Army Museum for eight years, explained that the restoration work in the museum was initially conducted by workers without any education. Therefore, the payment is lower compared to similar professions, and especially to the archaeologists who are regarded as experts. However, as heritage preservation becomes more important due to the changing heritage policies, restorers also have to attend university and conduct research. Their work is no longer a mere handicraft, but they are still anonymous.

This hierarchy influences the view of undergraduate students of the two disciplines as well. Mr. Bao, a restoration undergraduate, said: 'my uncle is an archaeologist, and he told me that it is much better to become an archaeologist. So, I applied for archaeology as my first choice, but I did not manage to get into the program and now I study restoration instead'. He insisted that he would keep trying to transfer to archaeology for a more promising future. Ms. Han, who also majored in restoration, told me: 'I will not become a restorer after my graduation. Even if I find a job as a restorer, it is impossible to become famous or to get promoted!' Due to this fact, China has lost many gifted and capable restorers. Mr. Bi, a young restorer at Shaanxi History Museum, secretly looked for better and more challenging job options because he felt he was 'wasting time' as a restorer. These young restorers actually still have passion for conducting restoration work, but at the same time, they seek chances of promotion and further development opportunities. Hence, some of my informants chose to leave the field.

Thus it can be concluded that the tension between archaeologists and restorers in Xi'an is caused by a state-imposed system. While the state confirms archaeology as a professional discipline, acknowledges the value of archaeological research, and rewards archaeologists with a universally-recognizable system of titles and rankings, it continues to treat restoration as a helper-discipline. Restoration should assist archaeological work, but has little independent status. If the tension between archaeologists and restorers in Europe can be best understood as arising from misunderstandings of, or prejudice against, each others' work, the hostility in China has clear institutional roots in national, provincial, and regional administrative levels, as well as within museum administration. At the individual level, it has even passed from one generation to the next. To a certain extent, the state and government authorities prefer archaeology because 'it has an obvious political dimension and nationalism that manifests the character of archaeology as social, historical, and political enterprise' (Silberman 1995: 249). As a consequence, the state attaches importance to archaeology as a discipline, as its findings and research results can prove and support the national discourse. The next part discusses why the state underlines archaeology and history in its civilization discourse and explores the relationship between the state and the disciplines.

The Ambivalence between Archaeology and History

Previous studies have shown the wide political uses and implications of archaeology. Michael Shanks and Chris Tilley (1987a, b) have gone so far as to argue that only political goals are viable in archaeological research. In part, the political nature of archaeology can be ascribed to its research methods and way of interpretation (Trigger 1995), which is to say that archaeologists interpret their findings based on their own knowledge and imagination of the past, which is already highly subjective. The most prominent political aspects of archaeology are national – so much that Nadia Abu el Haj (1998) described archaeology as a 'national project'. Perhaps archaeology is so often paired with nationalism because the discipline creates social solidarity as it highlights tradition (Clark 1957). At any rate, the topic of nationalism and archaeology has been intensively discussed since the 1990s (e.g. Shennan 1994; Diaz-Andreu and Champion 1996).

Others use more concrete examples to demonstrate the importance of archaeology to political leaders. For instance, despite Israel's weak economy and constant danger of war, the early Israeli government still poured efforts into archaeological works and spent lavishly on publications and exhibitions (Mandelbaum, Lasker and Albert 1963). Nazi Germany also used archaeology to shape the ideology of the society (Härke 2000). For all the attention to various aspects of the interrelation between archaeology and nationalism, very few studies have shown the methods applied by government agencies to construct nationalism through archaeology in China. This section attempts to display how the Chinese state and institutions use archaeology and history to accomplish nationalism education.

In Xi'an, archaeology is portrayed as an 'objective' science. When I first visited Shaanxi Provincial Archaeological Institute, its head, Mr. Wang, showed me the facilities and emphasized the technologies utilized in archaeological analysis. He guided me through one laboratory after another and showed off their latest equipment for dating artefacts and carrying out long-distance monitoring. Knowing that I was pursuing my doctoral degree in Germany, he asked: 'how would you rate our technological level of archaeology when compared with Germany?' The state underlines archaeology as scientific through museums, education, and the media. In North West University, whose archaeological department is considered to be the best in China, the discipline is classified among the sciences. The portrayal of the discipline as science, as opposed to arts, reflects how the state values the findings of archaeology and its potential use as evidence for national discourse. By emphasizing the scientific aspect of archaeology and underlining the scientific methods adopted by archaeologists, it hides the interpretative and imaginative nature of how the discipline draws conclusions. The displays at two national archaeological parks in Xi'an, the Terracotta Army Museum and Daming Palace Heritage Park, however, can be investigated to demonstrate how archaeological data and historical material are interpreted to support the national narrative.

The Terracotta Army Museum attracts millions of tourists every year and up to 100,000 visitors per day during the peak seasons. Images of the warriors feature as a national icon on travel brochures. Yet many questions about their presence and significance could be asked. One is about their relative importance to the overall site: the impressive Pit One, together with the excavations conducted in six other pits open to the public, account for barely 3 per cent of the whole mausoleum complex. But, there is also a problem of historical corroboration of their placement (Davis 2012). The written history in China started more than two thousand years ago, and it could be expected that such a major feat as creating and burying an army would have been recorded. The historical classic *Shiji* (*The Records of the Grand Historian*) compiled by Sima Qian in 109 BCE, records a detailed history of China during the Zhou, Qin and early Han periods (Watson 1993). However, there is no mention of the terracotta army. Sima Qian did mention the construction of the mausoleum for the emperor in *Shiji*, yet nothing about the grave army. Mr. Zhang, a restorer, insisted that a section of the *Shiji* does describe the terracotta army in the context of an account of the overthrow of the Qin Dynasty by the Han. He even quoted to me a sentence of six characters in classical Chinese, and interpreted the meaning as 'at the beginning, the Han soldiers were frightened because they thought the warriors were real'. Mr. Zhang told me that this sentence described a moment when the Han army attempted to destroy the mausoleum and discovered the underground army. However, the historians among my informants disagreed with Mr. Zhang. They said that the sentence was too short and unclear. They stressed that there are many different interpretations and Zhang's might not be true. Thus far, historians still have not discovered a single historical source that directly documents the terracotta army. Without such corroboration, it remains just possible that the First Qin Emperor and the terracotta warriors are not related – some historians have asserted as much, even in special television programs.[31]

Why does the state use the warriors as a national icon despite the site's lack of historical support? What strategies did the museum apply to cover this historical defect? Do the visitors realize this when they visit the museum? Visitors generally do not realize the archaeological uncertainties concerning the warriors because the museum displays insist that the function of the terracotta army was to serve the emperor, while other elements distract a visitor from raising particular kinds of questions. The museum combines archaeology with a discourse on the 'splendid ancient culture' (*gudai de canlan wenhua*) of China to impress the visitors (see also Davis 2012). It tries to overwhelm them with the impressive visual experience of seeing hundreds of the warriors lined up in the trenches in battle formation. It invokes an emotional feeling for a splendid past by having visitors face the warriors and horses directly from the top, as if participating in a military review with the emperor. Statues of the Qin emperor are everywhere in the museum and its perimeters. With such a display, the visitor can hardly think to ask: if not by and for the emperor, then why? At the same time, visitors are presented with a large amount of detailed archaeological information, in display captions and other texts, describing the locations, measurements, and structure of the pits as well as of their excavated content. For example, the introductory panel at the entrance of Pit Three reads,

> Pit 3 was discovered in June 1976, located north of Pit 1 at the western end. It is 25 metres to the south of Pit 1 and 120 metres to the east of Pit 2. It is of U-shape about 520 square metres, measuring 28.8 metres long from east to west, 24.57 metres wide from north to south and 5.2-5.4 metres deep. Investigation shows that Pit 3 was seriously damaged at some point in history. Only 68 pottery figures, one chariot and 34 bronze weapons were unearthed from this pit. Pit 3 is now known as the command centre of Pit 1 and Pit 2.

---

[31] In 2009, China Central Television (CCTV) produced a special, *Who Did the Terracotta Warriors Really Belong To?* http://english.cntv.cn/program/newfrontiers/03/03/index.shtml. Last accessed 1 May 2016.

In contrast to this level of technical detail, the information boards provide very limited historical background of the site. The museum only displays historical facts of the site after 1974, when the first warrior was discovered by a farmer. This story is told over and over again. However, little information is given about the Qin Dynasty. The visitor learns little about how the army was related to the Qin emperor, what roles the soldiers played in the society, or who designed and produced the pottery figures. What the texts do stress is the support received for the site's preservation after 1974 from the national government and the involvement of the provincial government. Furthermore, the museum stages the archaeologists as stars and highlights their hard work with detailed technological descriptions of the many processes from excavation to restoration.

Both the presence and absence of archaeological evidence, like that of historical documentation, can be used to support national narratives. Heritage sites in Xi'an tend to use what is most available. The terracotta warriors are displayed with an emphasis on archaeological findings, interpreted and presented to emphasize a splendid Chinese past, in disregard for the dubious historical evidence. Daming Palace Heritage Park emphasizes historical records without recourse to much archaeology.

Daming Palace served as an imperial palace in the Tang Dynasty (634 CE–896 CE). Here, important decisions were made and ambassadors from other countries were greeted. In operation at the peak of the Tang and the political domination of China along the Silk Road, abundant historical records have been found. Archaeological findings are limited. Moreover, the possibility for archaeological recovery was comprised deeply by the site's development.

In 2008, the provincial government invited a developer called Qujiang Corporation to conduct the Daming Palace project.[32] The developer aimed to make use of heritage sites in Xi'an for surrounding real estate development (see chapter 6). As it treated heritage sites as nothing more than tools for economic development, it built the heritage park in a rush without careful consideration of the archaeological material lying underneath. It made no long-term plans for excavation or preservation. Mr. Wang, an archaeologist and the curator of the Daming Palace Museum located in the heritage park, witnessed the making of the park from the removal of local communities to

---

[32] Daming Palace refers most specifically to the remains of the Tang Palace. However, it is also used to refer to the general area of the contemporary city. The remains were also granted the official status of 'national archaeological park', but the project under discussion here refers to the construction of a heritage park. Here, then, is just one of many examples of the overlapping designations with various degrees of official oversight and regulation that characterize Xi'an's heritage landscape.

the large-scale construction: 'it resulted in huge destruction of the archaeological remains. The workers dug every day in the park area, not for archaeological excavation, but for the sewage system or electricity supply for the
future park!' At the time, he had expressed his resentment and reported the
harm to the archaeological content to the provincial government and the
developer, but he received no responses and the construction continued. He
said, 'I felt so desperate and helpless that I went to the construction sites to
scold and condemn the workers for destroying the archaeological findings
every day. They stopped working when I was yelling at them, but afterwards, their boss ordered them to work again'. After a while, he realized that
he could not change the decision makers' minds and could only remain silent
and observe how the valuable archaeological remains and original palace
foundation were destroyed to make the park.

In 2010, Daming Palace Heritage Park was finished and opened to the
public. The 56-square-kilometre park consists of two museums (the main
museum and the gate museum), an archaeology experience centre, an
information centre, and a cinema. The rest of the park is very spacious,
occasionally showcasing rebuilt models of palace buildings, modern
sculptures, and artworks. When I visited the park for the first time, I could
hardly find any archaeological traces of the palace. The only preserved
remain is the Danfeng Gate, which serves as the main entrance and a
museum.

As at the Terracotta Army Museum, Daming Palace Heritage Park
distracts visitors from looking for evidence that does not exist. There are
fewer than ten signs with information concerning the archaeological
excavations of the whole park area. In contrast, there are hundreds of
signboards and illustrated pictures to provide historical details, giving a
comprehensive view of the role of the palace in the Tang Dynasty. Signs are
placed on average every ten metres and include information about the
military, architecture, everyday life in the royal palace, events that took
place in the area, and stories from the Tang period. The following is
illustrative; it appears on a tablet next to Taiye Pool:

> Located in the north of Daming Palace, Taiye Pool, also named
> Penglai Pool, was the most significant royal pool during the Tang
> Dynasty. One year on Mid-Autumn Day, Emperor Xuanzong and his
> favourite concubine, Yang Guifei, came to Taiye Pool to enjoy the
> romantic moonlight. However, the platform was not high enough to
> delight Xuanzong and his concubine, so the emperor issued an order
> to the servants, 'another platform hundreds of feet in height shall be
> constructed to entertain me and my concubine next year'. However,
> the Anshi Rebellion happening afterwards intruded on the estab-

lishment of the high platform, leaving only a stylobate. In another autumn, one day when Emperor Xuanzong was treating his honourable relatives by Taiye Pool, white lotuses were in their prime, winning extensive compliments among the crowd; while Emperor Xuanzong pointed to Concubine Yang and said to the people, 'is the white lotus better compared to my flower of ex-planation?' Concubine Yang proudly carried the title of 'Flower of Explanations'.

Taking two national archaeological parks as examples, we can see how archaeology and history are each used to fill the narrative gaps of the other. Importantly, both historical and archaeological data are 'edited' in the parks to support national discourse. Through site organization, text illustrations, the photographing and filming of objects, and the creation of exhibitions, park staff 'interven[e] on images, objects, and texts in order to make them appropriate for public display' (Manoukian 2012: 64). This editing produces one narrative, where there could be many (or none). Because archaeology is widely considered 'objective', and all the more so in Xi'an where the general population values archaeology, the invocation of even a small amount of technical data from excavations renders a narrative authoritative.

The Uses of Archaeology in China

So far, this chapter has demonstrated different social actors' perceptions of archaeological heritage in Xi'an: from short-term tourists' doubts to the local residents' social attachment to the sites, from restorers' anxieties to archae-ologists' concerns, and from the state's boosting of national archaeological parks to the museums' selective way of displaying information. As an archaeological ethnography, this chapter has revealed the role of archae-ology in modern Xi'an.

Along with the rise of heritage in China, archaeological sites have come under the spotlight of the national, provincial, and city governments. The boom in archaeological parks is just the first sign. Xi'an, home of hundreds of unearthed archaeological sites, will conduct many more excava-tions in the future. From the view of the state and the city, the development of archaeological heritage is favoured for political discourse and for economic growth. Economically, the city government and developers see the potential of the remains for the tourism market. The making of Xi'an as a 'museum city' and 'national archaeological park city' (Xi'an City Tourism Board 2013a) will attract more tourists, for longer stays, spending more, and raising the city's GDP.

Politically, by increasing the budget of and efforts on archaeological excavations, developing more archaeological sites and designating new national archaeological parks, the state establishes the image of China as the home to the most ancient civilization in the world. In some parts of China, the historical narratives and interpretations highlighted by museums have shifted from displaying a macro-national history to focusing on local living stories and regional memories (Pan 2016). However, that is not true for Xi'an. Here, museums and archaeological parks have expanded on the portrayal of national history. They have been constructed around symbols of Chinese civilization and culture, following political discourse.

Although the use of archaeology to constitute nationalism has been observed in many countries, the emphasis on civilization is quite unique to China. It is partly because Chinese civilization is long, continuous, and relatively unified and uncontested, making it easier for the Han regime to impose an imperial and civilizational discourse. From the mythological character of Emperor Huang, to Qin, to Tang, China was ruled by the same 'Han Chinese'. Moreover, the idea of civilization is 'expressed in history, ways of thinking, customs and etiquettes, traditional medicine and food, the role of the government and family' (Jacques 2009: 249). Hence, the state finds the concept of historical civilization useful for its political agenda to represent the greater Chinese identity.

Yet, the making of parks and other heritage sites cannot just be made in the state's image. It faces a number of locally-based constraints. Some are pragmatic, such as the need to relocate residents when a site is to be created, formalized, or expanded. Also, there are the divergent expectations of various stakeholders to be addressed (or not) during the process of site development and management. These have been addressed above.

But there are also local conceptions of civilization, self, and heritage that complicate the state's claim to Xi'an's past. One conception is perhaps only a nuance: for people in Xi'an, archaeological sites show China's greatness, but evidence of cultural exchange between China and the outside world. 'Their' ancestors are 'Chinese' – but with this additional history of contact. When I visited the terracotta army with locals, they were eager to tell me the story of the Qin emperor unifying China, emphasizing how Qin conquered the neighbouring kingdoms. They paid close attention to the facial features of each warrior and tried to spot the 'foreign' ones. Mr. Su, an engineer in his early thirties, explained his questing: 'the Qin Empire's power reached to the West. I am sure the army recruited some foreigners'. Another conception may be more limiting. Alongside the general veneration of archaeology and Chinese civilization, and the desire for economic growth, there is also a concern for the sacrality of the past and the dead. A heritage management student, Ms. Jing, who considered the development of archaeological sites into tourist attractions as immoral, quoted to me a local saying:

'the earth in Shaanxi Province is not for farming, but for burying emperors!' Every Xi'an person knows this idiom and normally uses it to reference the 72 imperial mausoleums in the province as a point of pride and superiority to other provinces. In this case, Ms. Jing invoked the saying to preserve the land's consecration to mausoleums against the development of heritage parks. 'After [tourists'] visit, they might not even know who was buried in the site! From the point of view as a [future] site manager, I am not sure if it is right to make money out of the dead'.

Nevertheless, this chapter shows the ways in which the state controls the discipline of archaeology and ensures its prestige. The education and training of archaeologists is highly institutionalized and monitored. The provincial government monitors and standardizes the curriculum for both archaeology and restoration. Archaeologists have to take standardized examinations and publish articles to get recognized. During my stay, I found out that every archaeologist and restorer who worked in the provincial museums or institutes had to submit an annual report of up to 50 pages in length, not only on personal achievements and scientific findings, but more importantly, on their contribution to the party and the state. For this exercise, my informants studied the current doctrines of the Communist Party and applied them to their work.

As Randall McGuire has written, 'Archaeology is a weak weapon for political action, because it cannot be wielded directly in the struggles over land, life, liberty, and wealth that drive the political process'. Equally, it is 'a powerful weapon in ideological struggles that have real consequences' (McGuire 2008: 21). In China, archaeology is a powerful weapon to reinforce the ideology that China is among the most ancient and 'advanced' civilizations in the world. To the extent that archaeology can be made to 'prove' China's civilization extends back 5,000 years in Xi'an, the consequences are very real. Institutes of archaeology and archaeologists receive significant benefit and attention from the government as well as from the public. The national, provincial, and local governments see value in archaeological heritage as it can generate income and bolster the political claim. For people in Xi'an, archaeology merges into social life, instilling self-esteem in an identity as the descendants of a long civilization. The next chapter will discuss the uses of history and imperial heritage in Xi'an.

Chapter 4
The City of 'China' – Imperial Heritage

Xi'an, with its 3,100 years of history, plays an important role in the making of 'Chineseness'. Many terms that describe 'Chinese people' are directly or indirectly related to Xi'an. For instance, in almost every big city in the world, overseas Chinese form an enclave known as Chinatown. In Chinese, this place is called Tangren jie, literally 'the street of Tang people'. Thus overseas Chinese have used the Tang Dynasty (618–907 CE), which was regarded as the most open and flourishing era of Chinese history, to represent their identity. There is a massive list of vocabulary in the Chinese language to express the meaning of 'Chinese people' including *Zhongguoren* (people from the People's Republic of China), *huaren* (civilized people)[33], *zhonghua ernv* (the sons and daughters of the civilized), *Hanren* (people of Han), *Tangren* (people of Tang), *long de chuanren* (descendants of the dragon), and *yanhuangzisun* (descendants of the Red and Yellow emperors). These notions highlight the long civilization of China as most of these terms are deeply rooted in history or ancient myths dated back thousands of years.

Xi'an is considered a second-tier city in China because of its comparably slow development after the establishment of the People's Republic of China.[34] Nevertheless, when foreign presidents or political leaders visit China, Xi'an is among one of the must-visit places. When India's prime minister visited China in 2015, his first stop was Xi'an, before Beijing and Shanghai. The second stop of then-US First Lady Michelle Obama's tour in China in 2014 was Xi'an. The local government officials showed her the Terracotta Army and Xi'an City Wall, which impressed

---

[33] The term *hua* is understood by many scholars in China as an antonym of 'barbarian', thus meaning 'civilized' or 'cultured' (Qian 1988; Ge 2011).

[34] Zhongguo kexin erxian chengshi PK paixing bang (The ranking of second tier cities in China). *Tencent Finance*, 20 November 2015. Available online, http://finance.qq.com/cross/20151120/V0p8RQ62.html. Last accessed 1 May 2016.

her.[35] The heritage sites and imperial background of Xi'an serves the state to illustrate the national historical discourse and shape the imagination of China by foreign visitors.

Xi'an was the seat of power throughout Chinese history for 13 dynasties, and perhaps for as many as 16 (Zhu 1996), 17 (Zhang 2010) or even 19 (Shi 1990). Though it has not been the capital since the Tang Dynasty, local residents continue to regard Xi'an as the country's western capital (*xijing*), distinguishing Beijing as the northern capital; Nanjing as the southern one; and Tokyo as the eastern one. The sense of continued importance pervades the city. Restaurants, hotels, and theatres bear the name 'Western Capital'. The Xi'an City Theatre performs a play entitled *Xijing Story* all year long. Nor is this identity even slightly inferior to that of China's other 'capitals'. People in Xi'an believe the city to be the 'real' Chinese capital because it was the seat of 'real' and 'pure' Han emperors (such as the Qin, Han, and Tang dynasties). In contrast, Beijing was the capital of the Manchu-ruled Qing Dynasty (Elliot 2001), and – for my informants – considered less able to represent *Chinese* history.

In some places, the past is a foreign country (Lowenthal 1985). However, in Xi'an the past has blended in with the present. In fact, some Chinese historians have pointed out that Chinese history is unique because it is alive and expressed through everyday life. Jin Guangtao (Zhang Y. N. 2004: 81) argued that 'China's only mode of existence is to relive its past. There is no accepted mechanism within the culture for the Chinese to confront the present without falling back on the inspiration and strength of tradition'. Wang Gungwu (1968) also indicated that no matter how distant history is, Chinese live in and through their history to a degree which is different from other societies. Another Chinese scholar, Huang Ping (2005), suggested 'Chinese (…) is a living history. Here almost every event and process happening today is closely related to history, and cannot be explained without taking history into consideration' (cited in Jacques 2009: 6). Similar to these observations by historians, Xi'an's past in all dimensions is expressed through everyday social life, urban development, heritage projects, and the mind-set of its residents.

This chapter displays how the past is being remembered and romanticized in the setting of Xi'an. The Xi'an city government features imperial heritage in order to narrate a selective national historical discourse and to construct the city image as a representation of China. While the previous

---

[35] The visit was also covered by the international press. Finley, J. C., 'Michelle Obama and Daughters Tour Xi'an, China'. *United Press International*, 24 March 2014. Available online, http://www.upi.com/Top_News/World-News/2014/03/24/Michelle-Obama-and-daughters-tour-Xian-China/9441395681335/. Last accessed 1 May 2016.

chapter elucidated the role of the state and provincial government in using archaeological heritage to shape national and local identity, this chapter places stress on the city government's effort to create Xi'an as the 'city of China' and shows the meanings of history to Xi'an people. During my fieldwork, I observed the high degree of historical consciousness among locals. Their rich knowledge about and intensive references back to history is both a top-down implementation and bottom-up anticipation. Xi'an highlights its historical background not only for the historical discourse but also for commercial activities. What strategy does the government use to underline the specific historical aspects? How does it select and showcase the past? Which elements of the past should be recuperated? How do locals perceive Xi'an's history? How do they connect and interact with history? Is their version of history the same as the national narrative and in what ways is history alive in Xi'an? By examining the role of history and imperial heritage, this chapter demonstrates the process of history making and remembrance by the state, the city, and other heritage actors.

History and Everyday Life

The city of Xi'an constantly reminds people of history, not only through the historical sites everywhere, but also through the names of modern constructions. Restaurants and hotels are named Chang'an, Daqin (Great Qin), Datang (Great Tang), and Gucheng (Ancient Capital). Just like archaeology, history is omnipresent in Xi'an. More importantly, history is alive. Locals referred to and quoted historical figures in daily conversations as if they talked about friends. History is discussed or mentioned in many kinds of social situation, from high-level governmental official meetings, to everyday family dinners. Even in taxi rides, the drivers often started to introduce the background of the city and showed off their historical knowledge, perhaps even with classical literature references or a thrown-in Tang poem. Why do local residents know so much about history, and why are they so eager to talk about it?

Xi'an people learn about history through the standardized national education system, but also from everyday life experiences. Stafford's (2000) study in Shandong Province on how rural children develop historical consciousness shows the critical role of home environment (and language use). In Xi'an too, I found evidence that historical knowledge was accumulated through family education and also shaped by the townscape. Mr. Cai, a businessman in his late twenties, told me that he developed an early and strong interest in history because of his father. They enjoyed reading historical classics like *Shiji* together. Even now, *Shiji* was like a bible to Mr.

Cai that he put next to his bed and read before going to sleep. Ms. Qian, a marketing professional in her early twenties, said:

> I find history really interesting and it was the favourite subject for me and my classmates in school because we could see and almost experience everything that we learnt. History is just around the corner and not distant at all! For example, if we learnt about a historical figure from the Qin Dynasty, we could visit his mausoleum easily, or we just live around the sites where historical events took place.

She thought that history would have been much more boring if people could not relate to it. The city itself with the heritage sites became a lively history book. My informants shared eagerly with me what the city taught them, such as the origin of various idioms. For example, *mai dongxi* means 'to buy things'. *Mai* is the verb, but they told me that *dongxi* (lit. east west) referred to the Tang layout of Chang'an. In the city at that time, people could go shopping only in the East or West markets (see Map 2). Therefore, 'to buy east west' was a general term for going to market that has now been spread to the whole of China. This story is considered 'common sense' (*changshi*) in Xi'an.

At the beginning of my fieldwork, Xi'an people recommended me to look into the names of places and streets in the city to understand its 'soul'. I found that many street names originated in the Tang Dynasty. Old Xi'anese (*lao Xi'an ren*) who had grown up in the city treasured these names because they conveyed the original function of the places. They told me many stories when we walked around the city centre. For example, Mr. Chang, who grew up in the Calligraphy Quarter, said that Xiamaling Street was where government officials had dismounted their horses to march the remaining distance to the palace on foot to show their respect to the emperors. Mr. Cai, who grew up around the Bell Tower, showed me the inner city enthusiastically, and when we arrived at Fen Street he asked me if I knew what the street was famous for. I answered, 'it is a street full of cafés and bars with live music'. No. *Fen*, I was reminded, means powder and the name refers to the street's function in the Tang as an area selling cosmetics. It was the street of fashion. After the downfall of the Tang, people respected the street's name and sold flour (*mianfen,* lit. noodle powder) there. But as the city evolved, the land price in the inner quarter became too high for such simple shops, and that is how it came to be filled with bars and nightclubs. My trips around town, spliced with historical references and etymologies, were nothing unusual. Older generations continually tell the younger ones the original meanings of the named places around them. Such oral history shortens the distance between the past and present as it enriches local understanding and imagination of history.

Locals' historical 'common sense' is not limited to the stories of places in Xi'an, but extends to a general knowledge of early imperial China. Xi'an people enjoyed watching soap operas based on history. My informants suggested me titles of soap operas and of drama and comedy series so that I could gain historical background knowledge about different dynasties in a quick way. One television series focused on the Qin was particularly loved because of its detailed production and closeness to real history. My informants were particularly sensitive to historical mistakes. Mr. Mai, an engineering student, told me that he could not stop laughing at the blunders in historically themed movies produced in Hong Kong. He told me about the mistakes in a war scene from one drama: soldiers threw their enemies into the river, but this could not have happened because there was no river around the place where the war took place. He wondered why the producers or production assistants did not notice such obvious mistakes and considered it shameful to produce such movies. Mr. Lang, a language teacher in his mid-twenties, made a similar criticism of a Taiwanese produced movie about Empress Wu; it showed her reading a bound book from paper, but she should have been reading one made from bamboo. While the rest of China commented on the beauty of the actress portraying Empress Wu, in Xi'an, audiences made fun of the careless anachronisms and other inaccuracies.

The city's strong identity is also reflected in the local dialect. Locals speak a strong Shaanxi dialect known as *Shaanxi hua* or *Chang'an hua*. It sounds very different from standard Mandarin, *putonghua* (commoners' language), and elsewhere in China it is considered a rude language because of it is 'hard and dominated by falling tones' (Jia 2011: 38). But in Xi'an, the dialect with its distinct vocabulary and expressions is another point of pride. 'Our dialect was the language spoken in the Qin Dynasty, when the first Qin emperor united China. His prime minister Li Si had to unify the language, they spoke the Xi'an dialect. So, it has existed for more than 2,000 years', exclaimed Mr. Cao, a book writer in his seventies. Mr. Wang, a shop owner in his mid-fifties, asserted: 'in order to learn about Chinese culture, you need to master the Shaanxi dialect!' Many of my informants proudly recited Tang poems in Shaanxi dialect and claimed that the poems rhymed much better and sounded smoother in Shaanxi than in Mandarin. This was because, they said, the people in the Tang Dynasty spoke a language much closer to Shaanxi dialect. Indeed, even though the state promotes Mandarin as the standard language to unify China, locals remain reluctant to speak it in daily life. Even a government official, Mr. Hao, argued '*Putonghua* is only for commoners! Yet, here in Xi'an, we speak the royal and classical language of the Tang Dynasty: the official language of the past'. He maintained that the local dialect kept the use of many ancient words with historical connotations from previous sources or stories that have faded out in Mandarin. Hence, the city and its residents had turned also to language preservation in order to preserve their historical connections, even risking overt opposition to state policies.

Xi'an people claimed the city's distinctiveness on many fronts. They boasted, for example, of being 'open-minded' (*kaifang*). They emphasized how they welcomed and accepted outsiders and migrant workers. Indeed, in contrast to the extensive documentation of hardships faced by migrant workers in other Chinese provinces (Wang and Zuo 1999; Knight and Yueh 2006; Wong, Li and Song 2007; Halegua 2008; Chan and Ngai 2010), migrant workers and students in Xi'an told me that they felt at ease in the city and that they could integrate very well. Once again, Xi'an locals claimed their openness as a legacy of their imperial background. They had, they said, tolerated outsiders since the Tang Dynasty when Chang'an hosted many resident foreigners as well as Silk Road travellers.

More recent history was marshalled to explain intense dislike for two kinds of outsiders. The first category of outsider, abhorred by a large number of Xi'an people, is the Japanese. This dislike was manifest during the Senkaku Islands incident of 2012 which – admittedly – stimulated anti-Japanese feelings across China with anti-Japanese protests in more than 50 cities.[36] The protest in Xi'an was among the largest, causing the most damages. The demonstrators blocked a main road of more than five kilometres from Big Wild Goose Pagoda to the Bell Tower. They destroyed shops and products related to Japan, including attacking Japanese hotels, burning Japanese cars, and even beating up owners of Japanese cars.[37] When

---

[36] Located in the East China Sea between Japan, the People's Republic of China, and the Republic of China (Taiwan), the Senkaku Islands are a group of uninhabited islands. Both China and Japan mark the islands as part of their maps. In 2012, the Japanese government purchased three of the disputed islands from their private owner, prompting large-scale protests in China. These protests were covered by the international press; 'More than Fifty Chinese Cities Organize Anti-Japanese Protests'. http://www3.nhk.or.jp/nhkworld/chinese/top/news01.html. Last accessed 12 April 2015.

[37] Coverage of the protests in Xi'an was also wide. See 'Muji zhe: Xi'an fangri youxing dakeng zhe duowei wensheng nanzi' (Witness: The Anti-Japanese protesters mostly had tattoos). http://news.163.com/12/0919/05/8BO7QQ7L0001124J.html. Last accessed 12 April 2015. 'Fangri youxing Xi'an Shicheng Jiudian beikang' (Anti-Japanese demonstration resulted in the burning down of the Lion City Hotel in Xi'an). Trip-J Online, 18 September 2012. http://www.trip-j.net/html/Hot-News/Hotel-industry/2012918/20129181217547055.html. Last accessed 1 May 2016. 'Yangshi ping Xi'an dakang rixiche: fanzui yu aiguo wu renhe guanxi' (Xi'an demonstration critiques: Committing crime and patriotism should not be

I asked why he had taken part in the demonstration, one informant exclaimed: 'the adverse relationship with Japan did not result from the Senkaku Islands incident, but it is a historical problem. The Japanese have never felt sorry for what they did during the Second World War and remain hostile!' Another informant said: 'there were big demonstrations in Xi'an because we cared about our country and history!' Several informants even asked me to spread the message that 'Japan should respect history' when I returned to Germany.

The second category of unpopular outsiders is people from Henan Province, which borders Shaanxi Province on the east. Here, the proximate cause of the dislike was even more recent, but explained with reference to a more distant past. Xi'an locals complained that people from Henan had caused a huge problem in Xi'an because they occupied some urban quarters and formed slums in the late 1980s (see chapter 8). Ms. Dan, who was a third generation Henanese in Xi'an, told me that she intentionally hid her linkage to Henan in school. Disdain towards Henanese can be observed throughout China in stereotypes: the Henanese are said to be 'cheaters' and 'cunning'. But in Xi'an, the disdain has a historical layer of rivalry. Like Shaanxi Province, Henan Province is also rich in heritage. Henan has eight cities listed as 'national historic cities' (*lishi wenhua mingcheng*), whereas Shaanxi has only six (see chapter 7).[38] My informants told me, 'do not go to Henan Province, the cities there all look very ugly!' And they told me of how Henan had 'stolen' Xi'an's prestige. During the Tang, Empress Wu Zetian set two capitals: the western capital of Chang'an and the eastern capital of Luoyang. Today's Henanese city of Luoyang attracts particular hatred.

As these examples have demonstrated, history and historical knowledge are not limited to elites. In Xi'an, they form part of common sense and everyday life. Locals insist on speaking their 'imperial' dialect. They keep telling the next generations the stories and the historical correlations of the cityscape. The high consciousness of history is said to determine worldview and behaviour, responsible for the city's 'open-minded' and cosmopolitan features, and justifying certain intolerances towards, for example, the Japanese and Henanese. The next section will illustrate the remembering of history at a higher level and investigate the relationship

---

not related). Xinhua Net, 27 September 2012. http://news.xinhuanet.com/local/2012-09/27/ c_123767331.htm. Last accessed 28 March 2015.
[38] 'Guojia lishi wenhua mingcheng' (National historical and cultural cities). Xinhua Net, http://news.xinhuanet.com/ziliao/2003-08/12/content_1022232.htm. Last accessed 1 May 2016.

between the identity-building processes pushed forward by the city government and the state's selective historical narrative.

Revitalizing an Imperial China

The evidence that Xi'an utilizes elements from the imperial dynasties to
represent itself is undeniable. I have already given several examples. Here is
another one: in 2006, Xi'an City organized an international sporting event
and invited several Olympic athletes. As a welcome present, the organizer
gave to each sportsman a life-size terracotta warrior figure with his face
carved onto it and to each sportswoman a personalized Tang princess
ceramic figure.

This approach to representation began in the early 1980s, a decade
after the discovery of the terracotta army. At this point, the Xi'an city
government started to glorify the imperial dynasties and spotlight the
'splendid history' of China. Later planning has been explicit. For example,
the tourism development plans, proposed by Xi'an City Tourism Board, state
clearly that the main aim of the city is to promote Qin and Tang imperial
culture (Xi'an Municipal Tourism Board 2007). This aim is supported by
Xi'an City Planning Bureau's Tang Imperial City Renaissance Plan (Datang
fuxing jihua) to revitalize the city in neo-Tang style (Xi'an City Planning
Bureau 2008). The website of Shaanxi Provincial Bureau of Cultural
Heritage was also renamed as 'Han Tang Net' to underscore the city's
imperial background. Xi'an's image became inseparable from the imperial
past.

To understand the process through which the imperial past has
become inseparable from Xi'an's present, I have found it useful to consider
Setrag Manoukian's (2012) research in Shiraz in Iraq. Manoukian examined
the process of knowledge production and the reformulation of history in
order to create 'a city of knowledge'. He also looked into ways in which the
locals have integrated their historical memories into urban spaces. He
proposed the concept of 'reversal', a political and a mental process that puts
new meaning and significance to old cultural symbols so as to secure the
ideological position of the new order. In Xi'an, symbols of imperial China
are used to reinforce the present political discourse. Similar to Shiraz, Xi'an
underwent a process of history production as the government attempted to
create a common understanding of Chinese history. While the city government transmits the national discourse through the cityscape and its heritage
projects, Xi'an people actively inscribed the city's historical memories onto
urban spaces. Parts of the history are highlighted but other parts are
completely neglected. Why does the Chinese state choose to elevate certain
periods of time? How does the city government use heritage to glorify and

narrate a selective history? What do the selected dynasties symbolize to the city and the nation?

National history museums act as places of historical knowledge production. A large amount of literature deals with the role of museums in narrating an official version of history with the goal of strengthening nationalism (Kaplan 1994; Errington 1998; Broun 2004; Coombes 2004; Kaufman 2004; Kennedy 2004). Kirk Denton (2005) suggested that Chinese museums are mainly for political legitimation. Tracey L-D. Lu's (2014) book explored the role of museums in the formation of the modern Chinese state and nationalism. The Shaanxi History Museum, as one of the most celebrated museums in China, illustrates the state's 'splendid ancient civilization' discourse in every way. Built as an evocation of neo-Tang architecture, the museum 'is located in the heart of classic Han Chinese civilization' and – strikingly – 'evinces no ideological conflict or political pressure in its exhibit scripts' (Blumenfield and Silverman 2013: 12). The permanent exhibition of the museum is divided into five parts, namely prehistory, Qin, Han, Sui, Tang, and Ming dynasties. The floor plan (Plate 2) shows that the museum spares the most space to present the Zhou, Qin, Han, and Tang dynasties. The museum glorifies these dynasties by displaying the best artefacts of those times and gigantic reconstructions of the relics as eye-catchers. However, the museum then skips more than 460 years and exhibits only a few artefacts of the Ming Dynasty. The modern and contemporary history of the city is not shown at all. The whole exhibition is highly selective and aimed at impressing national and international visitors with Xi'an's long civilization and influential dynasties.

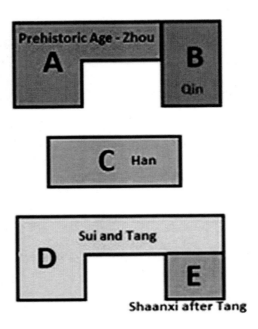

Plate 2. Floor plan of Shaanxi History Museum.

Like the Shaanxi History Museum, the Xi'an City History Museum introduces Xi'an as the capital city of thirteen dynasties, including Zhou, Qin, Western Han, Xin, Eastern Han, Western Jin, Early Zhao, Early Qin, Late Qin, Western Wei, Northern Zhou, Sui, and Tang dynasties. The claim in both museums, made with such apparent transparency is not quite accurate. Xi'an was not continuously a capital city across the thirteen-named dynasties. The Zhou Dynasty positioned its capital in Haojing (Shaughnessy 1999) and the Qin Dynasty in Xianyang (Bodde 1986). These are neighbouring cities, but neither Xi'an's authorities nor its inhabitants admit this detail. Almost everyone firmly believed in the claim to Xi'an's 13-dynasty-long role as capital. I found too that when I asked informants to name all the dynasties, not a single person could do so. I was curious. What did people really know about Xi'an and its 13 dynasties?

I turned to eliciting 'mental timelines'. I drew on the idea of 'mental maps' which allow researchers to explore local perceptions of space by having interviewees draw maps from memory (Nas and Sluis 2002; Low and Lawrence-Zúñiga 2003; Damir-Geilsdorf 2005). I requested interviewees to draw a historical timeline of the city and indicate the duration and name of the dynasties when Xi'an was the capital.

Plate 3 shows the accurate proportional historical timeline of China, alongside three examples of the mental timelines drawn by my informants. The filled areas indicate the time when Xi'an was the capital city. Informants aged twenty to thirty were willing to undertake this task, but older informants preferred to narrate the history orally because they were afraid to make mistakes. Their hesitation reflects an inclined historical knowledge focused on stories from selected glorified dynasties. Older people admitted that they knew few substantial historical facts, such as the length and ordering of the dynasties. The timelines drawn by younger informants turned out to be vague too, briefly mentioning the Qin, Han, and Tang dynasties. Moreover, despite the short duration of the Qin Dynasty (merely 15 years), many informants tended to believe that it was much longer because of its historical significance. These mental timelines mirrored influence of the state's master narrative on locals' perception of history. The next subsections examine the three glorified dynasties: Qin, Han, and Tang, separately and look into their meanings in the historical narrative and to the locals.

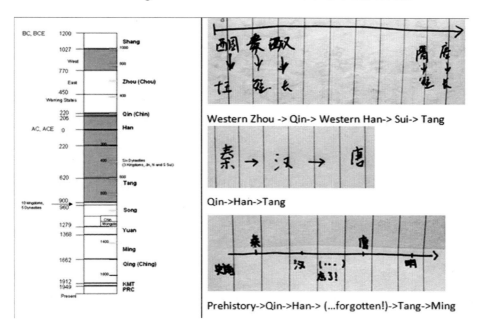

Western Zhou -> Qin-> Western Han-> Sui-> Tang

Qin->Han->Tang

Prehistory->Qin->Han-> (...forgotten!)->Tang->Ming

Plate 3. Timeline of Chinese history (marked periods indicate when Xi'an was the capital city, juxtaposed with three mental timelines drawn by informants).

The People of Qin

In China, every province has an official abbreviation which stands for its characteristics. Shaanxi Province chose the character *qin* (秦) to depict the historical significance of the province as the origin of the powerful Qin Empire. This choice is well supported by the fame of the Mausoleum of the First Qin Emperor and its terracotta army. Along with the terracotta army's inscription on the World Heritage List in 1987, the state glorified the Qin Dynasty and promoted the site as 'splendid ancient culture' of China (Davis 2012).

In China's national discourse, the Qin Dynasty is important because the first Qin emperor unified China's separate kingdoms. Under the government's increased boosting of the Qin Dynasty's importance, Chinese people have developed a feeling of 'self-respect and ethnic pride' linked to the figures of the emblematic terracotta warriors (Davis 2012: 38). Mr. Sun, a tour guide in his early twenties, told me that he felt emotional every time when he saw the terracotta warriors because he realized the greatness of his country. He said: 'now, the majority Chinese ethnicity is called Han. However, if we could go back in history and prolonged the Qin Dynasty, maybe just one hundred years more, our ethnicity might have been called Qin instead!' Some other informants simply identified themselves as 'people of Qin' (*Qinren*) *after* visiting the museum.

Chinese visitors do not merely treat the warriors as archaeological artefacts, but as their ancestors. They described the visit of the pit as a 'journey through civilization'. As mentioned before, they scrutinized the faces of the warriors. If Xi'an people looked for the 'foreigners' among them, non-Xi'an tourists looked for (and found) similarities to the features of today's Xi'an people – proof of the continuity of Chinese civilization. By celebrating the Qin Dynasty and using the image of the terracotta warriors, the state immerses history into people's minds and reinforces national identity.

Furthermore, museums in Xi'an narrate only the strengths of the empire and the unification story. The exhibitions provide details of how the first emperor succeeded and employed intelligent officers to assist him, as well as how he standardized the transportation network, political system, and writing system, which still influences present China. However, the Qin dynasty was one of the most brutal eras in Chinese history. The first emperor is known to have burnt all the books of which he disapproved, buried scholars and opponents alive, and forced the population into slave labour, such as building the Great Wall, the palace, and his mausoleum (Chan 1972; Goldin 2005). These brutalities led to the downfall of the dynasty. However, mention of these incidents is rare, and I noted it in only one privately curated exhibit in Xi'an. The selective narrative magnified the unification aspect of the Qin Dynasty but omitted the darker side of history.

The Dream of Tang

While the Qin Dynasty is mainly represented by the terracotta army, heritage sites of the Tang Dynasty are scattered around the whole city of Xi'an. Therefore, the Tang Dynasty plays a key role in shaping the cityscape and local identity. The Tang heritage sites located in the city area include Big Wild Goose Pagoda, Small Wild Goose Pagoda, Daming Palace, and various mosques and temples. Peter Hopkirk regarded the Tang Dynasty as 'China's golden age' because it maintained a long period of peace and stability with neighbouring countries (2006: 28). The state too deems the era as a time of prosperity, and it is this association which leads the city to foster not only the promotion of Tang heritage sites, but also the revitalization of the city with neo-Tang styles in urban planning projects.

On the artistic side, the city romanticizes the Tang Dynasty through Tang-theme music and dance performances. Every evening, different dance troupes perform in at least seven theatres and venues in Xi'an. Among the works performed during my fieldwork were 'Great Chang'an' in Xi'an City Theatre, 'Dream Back to Tang' in Tang Paradise Theme Park, and 'The Song of the Everlasting Sorrow' in Huaqing Palace. These performances featured imperial royal life during the Tang Dynasty with grand stage settings and glittering costumes, outlining the famous stories of that time. They were tailored as tourism packages, but locals told me that they enjoyed these shows too because they felt like they were living in the Tang Dynasty. Some elements of the costumes, music, sets and dance moves were based on historical documentation (including images from artefacts and mural paintings), but they were also highly imagined, beautified, and romanticized. As with the elaboration of the Qin for its resonance with narratives of the legacy of unification, the Tang arts are elaborated because this period is often considered to mark a peak in China's literary, musical, and artistic traditions. Mr. Fan, a professor from Shaanxi Academy of Art (and expert on the cultural continuity from the Tang Dynasty) concluded: 'Chang'an style is Chinese style!'

Just as they were attached to Qin heritage, my informants also expressed personal attachment to the Tang Dynasty. Ms. Fu, a housewife in her mid-thirties, even told me that sometimes she felt bad for her ancestors because Xi'an has lost its status as the centre of the world. She said that the Tang Empire was so strong that it had a cultural, economic and political influence all the way to the West, but today's Xi'an is not even remotely important to Chinese politics. Younger informants in their twenties, too, expressed nostalgic feelings towards 'their' imagined Tang society.

I recorded many instances of my informants engaging directly with the Tang past, inhabiting elements of it in their very modern present lives. For example, when Ms. Yin, a restoration student, graduated from North West University in March 2014, she wore an ordinary graduation gown, but after the ceremony, she and her classmates chose to take graduation photos in Tang costumes. She said they found this style representative of their identity as Xi'an students. Another informant, Ms. Pang also decided to hold a Tang-style wedding in Tang Le Gong (Tang Happiness Palace), a high-class event venue built on a Tang theme, in August 2014. The event organizer coordinated her wedding entirely in Tang style with a Tang wedding dress, Tang dance and music performance, and Tang royal food. As another example, Mr. Cai and his family invited me to celebrate Chinese New Year's Eve together in the Tang Paradise garden and restaurant. The evening was a package-dinner with Tang music and dance shows, Tang tea appreciation ceremony, and a Tang banquet. As our dining room was located in a glass house on the palace garden lake, looking at the garden and recon-structed palaces in Tang Paradise, I indeed felt like a member of Tang royalty that night. This commercial trend of revitalizing the Tang culture and traditions is seen as a form of high-class consumption in Xi'an. Even though local residents know that they cannot go back to the past, they try to recreate it, at a high cost. Examples like these (and from tourism), show that the past has a high commercial value, even beyond its political implications.

The Rise of Han

Since 2008, the Xi'an city government started to promote the heritage sites of the Han Dynasty in addition to those of the Qin and Tang. Although being the longest and most influential dynasty in Chinese history, after which the ethnicity of the majority of Chinese people is named, the city took up its Han heritage belatedly. Why did Xi'an only start to boast of the Han Dynasty and heritage in 2008? What does Han culture symbolize in Xi'an?

I was told that the national and city government had prioritized the preservation of Qin and Tang heritage due to limited financial resources. It chose to develop the terracotta army as it was listed as a 'patriotic site' by the state and had the potential to become a worldwide tourist magnet. As for Tang heritage sites, located right in the city centre, they faced an urgent need for preservation and development to facilitate the city's urbanization plan. Since Han heritage sites were located at the outskirt of the city, the govern-ment simply adopted a 'frozen policy'. It inhibited development projects in the Han heritage area until 2008.

However, the rise of archaeological parks as discussed in chapter 3 contributed to the boosting of Han heritage. The National Archaeological Parks Law enacted in 2009 gave the provincial government the opportunity to develop Han archaeological remains. In addition, the highlighting of Silk Road heritage (since 2008) brought further government interest to Han heritage sites as part of the cultural route (see chapter 5).

Since 2008, the city gradually inserted Han elements and opened Han heritage sites. These include the archaeological remains of Han Chang'an and various mausoleums of Han emperors. In 2010, Xi'an City Water Resources Bureau built a Han theme park called Han Chenghu Cultural Scenic Area. It contains a Han history museum and a gigantic statue of Emperor Wu, the most influential emperor of the Han Dynasty who proposed an expansion to the west and, according to Chinese narratives, established the Silk Road. In addition to these sites, the provincial government supported the development of other ones, sending assessment teams composed of officials and archaeological experts to evaluate various mausoleums. Xi'an City advertised especially Yang Mausoleum, as 'the second Terracotta Army Museum'.

During my fieldwork, I encountered at least four scholars from the disciplines of archaeology, restoration, and history who conducted comparative studies between the Han Yang Mausoleum and the Qin Shihuang Mausoleum because of their striking similarities. When I visited Yang Mausoleum Museum, my tour guide kept emphasizing the resemblances between the two mausoleums. She told me that archaeologists also excavated thousands of pottery figures that depict the emperor's afterlife. Although the human figures are only around 50 centimetres tall, they wore silk garments as decoration when they were buried. The Han emperor intentionally built the mausoleum in a smaller scale, it is said, because he learnt from the mistakes of the Qin emperor, who – in spending all the money and resources on building the mausoleum – led to the end of the Qin Dynasty. Thus Yang Mausoleum is considered to serve as an important site to portray the social and political situation in the Han Dynasty. However, since it, like the other Han sites, is located far away from urban Xi'an, it has been a challenge for museum administrations and city government to promote them.

Consequently, Xi'an City added new transportation links to connect those sites and the city centre. Xi'an attempted to headline and popularize the idea of Han through infrastructure. On top of Qin-Tang Avenue built in 2008, which connects the Terracotta Army Museum and Tang Huaqing Palace, the city government built a new east-west road called Qin-Han Avenue linking the Terracotta Army Museum and the Han Chang'an city remains in 2014. Furthermore, the city government also planned to build more Han-related parks and infrastructure. During a private advisory session for the construction of West Gate Silk Road Cultural Park, the project manager and the senior planner from Xi'an City Urban Landscape Office showed a historian and me their plan and asked for feedback. The planner told us that the project aimed at underlining the Silk Road culture and his team planned to characterize Han culture through the park. The historian criticized the plan vehemently because the focus on Han for the West Gate was historically wrong. The West Gate and the selected location of the park both belong to Tang Chang'an and had nothing to do with the Han era. However, the planner insisted that it was necessary to highlight Han culture because his supervisor and the members from the higher level of the urban landscape office ordered him to design the park to portray the Silk Road and the Han Dynasty. Indeed the widespread insistence on promoting Han culture came from (city) government.

Moreover, the city organized regular Han-themed events, including ceremonies and festival celebrations. For example, Han Chenghu Cultural Scenic Area organizes a Han-style coming-of-age ceremony for teenagers turning 18 years old every month; Small Wild Goose Pagoda hosts the Dragon Boat Festival celebration annually, during which participants revitalize the traditions practised in the Han Dynasty, including dance performances and a series of rituals to worship the heavens. Most of the participants belong to the Han Costume Association (Hanfu hui). Ms. Yuan, the 24-year-old chairwoman, stated:

> There are 56 ethnicities in China in total, and each ethnic minority group has its own unique costumes, but it is not fair that we, Han people, the strongest ethnic group of China, have no national costumes. Therefore, we aim to revitalize the oldest and most traditional costumes that belong to the Han people dating back to the Han Dynasty.

Her statement focused on Han as an ethnicity and ignored the aspect of Han as a dynasty, but it reflected the nationalist aspect of the revitalization movement.

In spite of the city's attempts, the Han Dynasty is still far less influential than the Qin or Tang in present-day Xi'an. The Han heritage sites that the city promoted are much less popular than the Qin and Tang sites, failing to attract either domestic or foreign tourists. At most of the Han sites, I only found locals going there for a walk. The Han mausoleum museums were not well-visited and usually empty. Xi'an people on the whole did mention that the Han Dynasty was a strong era, but they thought that the Han Dynasty could not represent the city of Xi'an because it signifies the whole

China and the Han ethnicity. Most locals could not even name a single Han heritage site. For example, Mr. Yang, a businessman in his thirties, was surprised when I told him that Yang Mausoleum was a Han heritage site. He said: 'I have heard of Yang Mausoleum, but I always thought it was a Tang mausoleum!' Another example is the Han-style pagoda called Danfeng Ge, which belongs to Han Chenghu Cultural Scenic Area. Mr. He, a lecturer from Shanghai who used to study in Xi'an and revisited the city as a presenter at the International Euro-Asia Economic Forum, commented: 'I have never seen this pagoda. Xi'an is building so many historical sites and it is hard for me to keep up with it!' He anticipated that the pagoda might be related to the Qin Epang Palace, but when I told him the full plan, he was surprised: 'Han Chang'an City? Weiyang Palace? I have been there a few years ago and I saw nothing but a vast empty area! I cannot imagine that they have built that pagoda there now!' Visitors were puzzled to hear that the pagoda is a neo-Han building because they initially linked the site to Qin or Tang heritage. However, little by little, the national, provincial, and municipal governments started to introduce Xi'an as a Han-heritage city too.

The cases of the glorification of the Qin, Tang, and Han heritage in Xi'an demonstrate that the popularity of the three dynasties are shaped by both top-down imposition and bottom-up anticipation. While the rise of Han is mostly implemented by the national, provincial, and city governments for political discourse, the popularity of Qin and Tang are generated with a bottom-up force from the locals. They have internalized and endorsed the Qin and Tang discourse promoted by the government, and willingly spread the message and consume Tang culture as a way to express their identity. Since the imperial heritage and history of Xi'an do not contradict the central state's historical narrative, all levels of government from the municipal up to the central government are involved in bolstering the three dynasties. After exploring the different driving forces that result in the selective historical narration, we will now move to discuss the execution of the state's historical discourse at the city level and look into the ways that the city remembers the past through the remaking of its cityscape.

The Dilemma of 'Authenti(c)-city'

Entering the old city of Xi'an, one is overwhelmed by the large amount of neo-Tang-style construction in the city. In the 1990s, Xi'an City Planning Bureau started the Tang revitalization project with two streets and the Shaanxi History Museum. By the 2000s, Tang-style buildings were everywhere in the city. Mr. Li, an architect in his mid-fifties, used the term 'flooding' to describe the scale and critical situation of the neo-Tang expansion in Xi'an. He criticized how the Tang revitalization plan had replaced many old neighbourhoods with neo-Tang buildings. According to the city's Tang Imperial City Renaissance Plan, Xi'an City aimed at reconstructing the whole city layout based on the map of Tang Chang'an with the same roads and grid system (see Map 2).

By using the means of urban planning, Xi'an City engages actively in the revitalization of Tang Chang'an. Who made the decision where and what to rebuild? Where did the city get the inspiration of neo-Tang style? What do different social actors think about the buildings and the streets that have been revitalized? This section explores the emergence of the neo-Tang phenomenon in Xi'an and unfolds the dilemma between the revitalization project and speedy urban growth. Is it possible to maintain the balance between urban development and heritage preservation and achieve authenticity in a city setting?

In the 1990s, the city government invited a team of professionals composed of architects, urban planners, conservationists, and historians to discuss a suitable way to underline Xi'an's historical characteristics and to draw up a standardized neo-Tang representative design (Fayolle Lussac, Høyem and Clément 2007). Mr. Wu, an urban planner and former student of one of the invited architects, told me that the diverse opinions of the professionals split the group in two. While one camp evoked and designed the 'grand Tang-style' architectural proposal and suggested a larger-scale plan called Tang Imperial City Renaissance Plan, the other group proposed a subtler revitalization focused on preservation. How the professionals chose to side with or the other group was based on the individual educational background and political concerns, but also on social networks, such as the school attended or previous teacher. In the end, the government adopted the grand plan proposed by the first group because – so I was told – it was led by Zhang Jinqiu, a famous architect and wife of Han Ji, then-Secretary of Xi'an City Planning Bureau. Due to Zhang's *guanxi* with city government, her proposal was chosen and included in the Shaanxi Provincial Government's 11th Five Year Plan. Together with her husband and other professionals on their side, they introduced the neo-Tang architectural style that has continued to transform the cityscape for over 20 years – even after Han's retirement. The opposing professionals were still upset about the government's decision and referred to Zhang as a *goupi zhuanjia* (dog-fart expert) because she ruined the historical townscape.

Zhang acted as the backbone of neo-Tang architecture in Xi'an. Based on limited historical sources, archaeological remains, and mural paintings from Mogao Cave in Dunhuang, she developed a draft of the design. However, since all the Tang palaces and temples in Xi'an no longer existed, the team had to visit Japan to get inspirations from historical buildings, such as Heian Palace, which had copied the Chang'an-style architecture and been well preserved. Mr. Wu described this act as 'pitiful': Xi'an was copying copies of itself. The resulting neo-Tang architecture of Zhang's plan attempts to depict royal grandness through such features as gigantic rooftops, unique columns, roof decorations, and various patterns like interlocking brackets (*dougong*) and vertical and horizontal pillars. Because Tang buildings were mostly made of wood, the neo-Tang structures in Xi'an were textured and painted in a dark brownish red.

Once the design was accepted by the city government, it was rapidly replicated in Xi'an. Zhang designed the new building of the Shaanxi History Museum with this kind of design in the late 1990s. Afterwards, she was in charge of the West Street project, transforming most of the traditional neighbourhoods of the city centre. Other historical sites, such as the Tang West Market, Tang Paradise, and Daming Palace then requested her to design their main buildings. When Xi'an hosted the International Horticultural Exposition in 2011, Zhang was invited to design a neo-Tang Chang'an Tower characterizing the 'architectural culture' of Xi'an. Even Chengdu, the capital city of Sichuan Province, reconstructed a shopping street called Tang feng jie (Tang-style Street) identical to Xi'an's West Street.

Those who had opposed Zhang's plan deemed that the changing cityscape destroys Xi'an's actual characteristics. In their opinion, West Street used to convey Xi'an's ancient city image with original two-floor Ming-style buildings before the transformation. They blamed Zhang for demolishing those buildings and replacing them with gigantic neo-Tang constructions. Moreover, Zhang's 'Tang Imperial City' plan transformed West Street and its neighbourhood into a commercial district. Historians criticized the project and pointed out that the imperial city had been only an administrative area, and that commercial activities had taken place outside it. Moreover, the neo-Tang buildings could not depict the original picture and functions of the imperial palaces: they were too tall and portrayed only certain features of the original architecture. Mr. Lei, an architect in his early-forties, expressed disappointment about the project and said: 'before the demolition, I paid many visits to West Street to take some photos as memories... too bad that there was no digital camera at that time and films were very expensive, otherwise, I would have taken more photos!' Mr. Wu, the urban planner added, 'look at West Street now... I cannot bear it any-more because it looks so fake! As a Xi'an local, I am ashamed of that street! When foreigners visit Xi'an, I always felt embarrassed to show them that street!'

The urban planners and architects who opposed the neo-Tang plans cared about preserving an 'authentic' cityscape. They were mostly born and raised in Xi'an and were alumni of Xi'an University of Architecture and Technology. One might ask whether their opinion was more or less representative than Zhang's of that held by local people without specialized architectural training. How did such people view the neo-Tang revitalization projects? When I visited the Chang'an Tower in the Xi'an Expo-garden, Mr. Wei, a visitor from Xi'an, shouted excitedly as he read the information sign about the tower: 'Oh! Maestro Zhang (Zhang *dashi*) designed this tower! No wonder it looks so spectacular! She managed to mix Tang and modern architectural elements and the tower looks so modern'. Apparently, Zhang gained very good feedback and respect from at least some locals. But, local opinions on neo-Tang architecture were diverse and depended on the age, educational background, and personal attachment to the city as well as on the particular neo-Tang project in question.

The most controversial revitalization project in Xi'an was probably Tang Paradise Theme Park (Datang Furong Yuan). Opened in 2005 with its Ziyun Palace designed by Zhang Jinqiu, the theme park features Tang imperial culture in twelve themes: emperors, literature, folklore, gastronomy, women, tea culture, religion, technology, diplomacy, education, and music.[39] French and American tourists I met expressed that they felt irritated when visiting the site. One of them said angrily: 'Do not go to the Park of Tang [Tang Paradise]. It is all fake'. Yet, many local visitors were of a different opinion. Ms. Yao, a history student in her early twenties, told me that her family visited the theme park once a year to spend a day back in history and experience royal life. Mr. Qin, a restorer in his late fifties, said: 'it is best to visit Tang Paradise in summer because it served as a summer palace in the Tang Dynasty'. When he had visitors from other places, he showed them the park every time. Xi'an locals emphasized that the place was not purely a theme park because it was recorded in historical material. However, when I asked Ms. Yao to identity the original historical site on the map or describe that archaeological site in detail, she could not – she concluded that the site must be hidden for preservation. Appreciation was not distinct from an awareness of marketization: Ms. Li, a sales planner for Tang Paradise in her late twenties, told me that visitors were usually attracted to the site because of the bombastic advertisements and the commercialization of Tang culture. They did not have a clear understanding about the architecture and were satisfied to take photos as memories.

---

[39] See the description of 2007 on Tang Paradise's website http://www.tangparadise.cn/article.php?id=9. Last accessed 24 February, 2015.

The city's effort in building grand neo-Tang buildings has normalized locals' perception of how Tang Chang'an used to look. To many Xi'an residents, the neo-Tang transformation is considered harmless. For them, the reconstruction highlights the city's uniqueness. As far as they are concerned, the historical sites decorated with neo-Tang style are authentic. They also like the neo-Tang style because it gives them the feeling that Xi'an is modern and developed. Bruno Fayolle Lussac has already explained some of the reasons that the selective recreations of the neo-Tang style can be taken as historically authentic, albeit with more general reference to heritage:

> The concept of cultural heritage covers a different reality in the traditional Chinese culture: that of an essentially immaterial cultural heritage corresponding to a historical past founded on memory and its transformation (...) that rebuilding in an architectural style similar to the original has the same value (...) the object can be a building, but the subject is the memory (2007: 198).

In Xi'an the heritage sites and architecture depicting can be taken as real and authentic by locals as long as they are associated with social meanings and memories. For this reason, the reconstructed structures are popular among most locals and Chinese tourists. However, views differ about the desirability of changing the cityscape. Some informants insisted that the neo-Tang cityscape made Xi'an special; others favoured the Mingqing architectural style because it was the 'original' townscape as they knew it. When Mr. Lu, a company manager in his mid-thirties, showed me around West Street, he told me he felt saddened because the city government had removed all the original well-preserved shop houses. Now, he said, Xi'an just looks like any other big city in China and no longer matches its 'ancient city' image.

The case of Xi'an shows that the different social actors are still seeking and negotiating the meanings of authenticity. On the one hand, some professionals, who were concerned with historical preservation, were well-informed with international standards on authenticity and opposed the large-scale revitalization projects in order to protect as many original buildings as possible. On the other hand, a different group of architects – endorsed by the city government – kept replicating the neo-Tang design and transforming Xi'an into a much grander version of Tang Chang'an. The general public consisted of contested views, but on the whole, what mattered for them was their experience of a place and its symbolic meanings. For each group, 'authenti(c)-city' depends on how the social actors conceptualize the value of history and heritage.

'His'- story? 'Her'-it-age?

Before I departed from Xi'an, as a farewell present, my seniors from the Terracotta Army Museum invited me to watch a Tang music and dance show called 'The Song of the Everlasting Sorrow'. The performance utilized the real Huaqing Palace and Mount Li as the background. The story, featuring the love life of a Tang beauty, Concubine Yang, illustrated how she fell in love with the emperor and had to sacrifice her life for the continuity of Tang China. Combining stage effects, dazzling Tang costumes, and glamorous dances, the show created a dreamy and romantic atmosphere.

This show was not the only instance of Xi'an heritage to focus on women or their historical roles. There were many tangible and intangible references to women. For instance, Huaqing Palace placed a giant statue of Concubine Yang at the main entrance. The daily Tang parades organized at tourist attractions were mainly performed by female actresses. While the other parts of this chapter have discussed the characteristics of history expressed through everyday knowledge, selective glorification, and changing cityscape, this section turns to elucidate how female figures have been treated in the historical narrations of Xi'an brought about by the city government's plan, the market need, and the ordinary people's projection of the past.

The term 'history' has been criticized since the 1960s (Andermahr and Pellicer-Ortín 2013), as scholars have questioned the possibility of objectivity. Among the criticisms levelled at 'history' is that it cannot achieve its purported neutrality and wholeness when female actors are invisible (Ashby and Ohrn 1995). Feminist scholars have asserted that traditional approaches within the discipline have been only 'his-story'; that is, they have narrated the past from a wholly male perspective, and in the following ways. First, traditional approaches present one-sided accounts in favour of conquerors and emperors with a strong intention to lionize their figures. Second, historians from the past were mostly males who recorded history from their point of view resulting in the negligence of female lives and biographies. Third, even the present is dominated by male leaders, who choose a selective historical narrative to maintain their power. Therefore, history is regarded as a problematic field for its tendencies to glorify patriarchal societies.

However, with reference to Xi'an's historical narrative and heritage site displays, females are present. They are celebrated as national heroines and as romantic figures. Hence, I propose that a focus on 'her-it-age', as a supplement to 'history', also serves to provide a missing female perspective. Heritage and historical sites in Xi'an capture the essence of cosmopolitanism and modernity with their stress on female presence and roles.

If we understand heritage as 'her-it-age' we see how heritagization serves as a process for turning traditions and sites stigmatized as 'backwards' or 'useless' and making them 'representative' and 'fashionable'. If the first syllable (her-) references gender, the middle -it- recalls a prefix meaning 'trendy' and 'fashionable'. The final syllable, of course, conveys the sense of a particular era. Can we take it then, that heritagization – trendy and modern – is also a contemporary process that underlines female significance. I think it could be: the provincial and city governments both endorse the idea of gender equality in Tang Chang'an. They point out that not only were females free to dress as they wanted, they were also highly educated and could work as government officials. Many celebrated heritage sites in Xi'an carry a historical connotation of female impact, such as the Banpo Neolithic Site Museum, Qian Imperial Mausoleum, Huaqing Palace, Concubine Yang's tomb, Daming Palace, and Small Wild Goose Pagoda. Besides, almost all museums exhibit the lifestyle and social status of females during the Han and Tang dynasties. For instance, the seven-storey Han History Museum spares the whole third floor for the display of Han female costumes. The Daming Palace Museum presents the beauty standard of the Tang Dynasty by displaying artefacts related to make-up and hair styles. Tang Paradise even built a three-level Tang Females Museum, which exhibits Tang dresses and wax figures of influential female figures such as Empress Wu and Princess Taiping, to show that females also received high education and obtained power. The Xi'an City History Museum puts an enormous replica of a Tang female horse rider at the main entrance. Every tour guide stops by and explains the relic's portrayal of the open society in the Tang Dynasty: females could dress like men, participate in sports, and take up important political positions. The following section describes how the idea of 'her-it-age' bridges the past and the present in the contemporary society in Xi'an.

The fascination towards her-it-age is not limited to the exhibitions of museums and heritage sites. It is also expressed in everyday life. Upon my arrival in Xi'an in September 2013, one of the most popular topics was the excavation of a Tang tomb. The news gave updates on a daily basis, while people gossiped about the discovery and the archaeologists' interpretation. Hundreds of Tang tomb excavations take place every year in Shaanxi, but none of them has been so widely discussed by the public as this one which belonged to Shangguan Waner, the first female prime minister in Chinese history. The Shaanxi Provincial Archaeological Institute even organized a talk specifically on the excavation of the tomb and more than 500 people attended the event. All of my informants could recite her biography. It surprised me to see an archaeological excavation becoming the centre of public attention simply because of its association with a female historical figure. Informants felt proud when they mentioned Shangguan Waner because she was intelligent and ambitious, but more importantly, because her case showed the openness of the Tang Dynasty to educate and allow females to be appointed to such high official ranks.

During interviews, when I asked informants to name three famous historical figures who influenced Xi'an's history, everyone named the first emperor (Qin Shihuang), followed by Empress Wu, the first female empress. The third name varied and included Concubine Yang, Emperor Wu from the Han Dynasty, the Tang monk Xuanzang, and Han Princess Wang Zhaojun. Half of the names mentioned were female figures. Their stories were narrated only partly through museums and heritage sites, but had mainly spread through oral history, classical or popular literature, and traditional operas. Princess Wang's story, for example, is the subject of many poems and local operas. Princess Wang volunteered to marry a Hun to make peace, and played the *pipa* (a Chinese plucked instrument) on her way to the Huns, expressing love for her home country. (My informants compared me to Princess Wang as I can play the same instrument and I pursue my studies in the Far West). Actually, during the Han Dynasty, hundreds of princesses married into neighbouring kingdoms to maintain peaceful relationships and their stories are praised nowadays by locals for the sacrifice to the nation that such marriages entailed.

Interestingly, some informants even mentioned historical figures unrelated to Xi'an, believing they were connected to the city. Ms. Xiao, a human resources specialist in her mid-twenties, told me: 'Xi'an nurtured many great women in history'. She then quoted a Chinese poem about Mulan, a famous and now Disneyfied character, who dressed up as a man to join the army in place of her aged father. She said:

> The classical poem wrote about how Mulan prepared for war. She first went to the East Market to buy a horse and then to the West Market in Chang'an to buy a horsewhip.[40] The West Market still exists in Xi'an. I grew up in Xi'an and passed by there every day.

In fact, Mulan did not originate from Chang'an and the poem describes the markets of another city.

The local craving for her-it-age is also reflected through changing kinship perceptions. Traditionally, Chinese families prefer to have sons over daughters (Feng 1967; Chao 1983; Stacey 1983; Brandtstädter and Santos 2009). Yet, during my stay in Xi'an, I observed a tendency among locals to

---

[40] Ms. Xiao recited the original Mulan poem (木兰辞) and the lines about the East and West markets were: 东市买骏马，　西市买长鞭。 (She went to the East Market to buy a strong horse, to the West Market to buy a horsewhip).

prefer and long for daughters. Some older informants even wanted to adopt me as a fictive daughter because they only had a son. Mr. Xue, a government official in his late fifties, told me one day merrily that he attended his fictive daughter's wedding. He shared with me that he always wanted a daughter but he only had a son. Therefore, he 'adopted' a daughter from his good friend and treated her even better than his own son. The most extreme case was Mr. Hong, a businessman and father of five sons and one daughter. Despite the One Child Policy, he paid the penalty imposed by the government for each extra child he had with the aim of having a daughter. Mr. Hong spoiled the daughter and gave her everything she wanted. His friends said that they were jealous and if they had the money, they would do the same. Indeed, recent ethnographies about families in China show the growing preference for daughters and the rising role of women (Whyte 2003; Zhang Q. F. 2004; Zhang 2007; Shi 2009). In Xi'an, however, history has an added effect. When I asked locals why they preferred to have daughters, many quoted a Tang poem written by Bai Juyi about Concubine Yang. The poem describes how – since Yang's selection to the palace – Chang'an people have favoured daughters. When Yang married into the royal family, she changed the destiny of her whole family.[41] Mr. Xue said: 'Here in Xi'an, it does not matter if one gets a daughter or a son. History has shown us that women were successful too!' Informants expressed pride because they believed they had inherited the open mind-set of gender equality from the Tang Dynasty.

As shown from the heritage sites' displays and everyday life, the idea of her-it-age supplemented the one-sided his-story discourse. Even though the government departments are still dominated by male officials, the city stresses female strength and historical roles. The invocation of women both romanticizes the past and shows the openness of Tang society. Museums and site administrations invoked her-it-age, even in his-story, by indicating the sites' correlation with female historical characters and pointing out how artefacts reflected the social world of females in the past. Moreover, sometimes it is said that Xi'an City Planning Bureau chose the Tang Imperial City Renaissance Plan proposed by Zhang Jinqiu because of its gender. That is, as a dominant female architect in Shaanxi, Zhang Jinqiu's plan can be said to also resonate with the historical significance of females. Yet even as her-it-age in Xi'an displays female roles and perspectives, these

---

[41] They quoted these two sentences from 'The Song of the Everlasting Regret': (长恨歌): 姊妹弟兄皆列土，可憐光彩生門戶。遂令天下父母心，不重生男重生女。Ying (2008) translated these as, 'All her sisters and brothers had royal land granted. Imperial but pitiful glory on the Yang family was bestowed. On the mindset of all parents her success was a strong influence. Baby girls instead of baby boys became the popular preference'.

are celebrated to serve the nationalistic discourse. The 'important' female figures are those who sacrificed themselves for the country (Concubine Yang, Wang Zhaojun, Princess Taiping) or otherwise served the greater good of the nation (Mulan, Empress Wu, Shangguan Waner). Her-it-age does not empower women so much as emphasize the greatness of imperial China (or serve commercial purposes). Still, the broad societal obsession with her-it-age again reflects a dramatic convergence of political and popular efforts to reformulate history and the local Xi'an identity.

'Re-membering' the Past

This chapter illustrated Xi'an's process of remembering the past at different levels through the state's selective historical narrative focused on three dynasties, the city's revitalization plan, and individuals' memories of history. These remembrances are engraved in the urban spaces of the city through public places and heritage sites. History becomes alive again. Remembering is transformed to 're-membering' as the past is turned into a member of the present society. Historical knowledge is regenerated and reinterpreted. By glorifying the historical figures as national heroes, the city and its inhabitants regain and recapture the connection between the past and the present. 'Re-membering' draws attention to connections with history of which people might not be any longer aware. Through narrating history, revitalizing the past eras, and referring intensely back to history in social life, the re-membering and remembering of a distant past push history into everyday life and make it seem alive.

Hayden White's concept of the 'emplotment' of history can serve as a tool to analyse the process of 're-membering'. White defined emplotment as 'the assembly of a series of historical events into a narrative with a plot' (1978: 223). That is, historians take events and make a story out of them. White pointed out that a historian finds facts, and also presents them. The historian arranges events in a certain order to answer a set of questions, decides which events to include and exclude, and stresses some events while subordinating others (White 2001). Hence, history writing is never objective (White 1973). According to White, there are four types of historical emplotment, namely romance, satire, comedy, and tragedy (White 1992). Romance is to write history as a drama of victories, such as a hero's triumph over evil. Satire refers to the opposite of romance where people are captives in the world until they die. Comedy celebrates history as a harmony between the natural and the social world. Lastly, tragedy is when a hero has to face the limitations of the world and fails. When White called historiographical objectivity into question, however, he mainly considered the work of professional historians. My Xi'an observations suggest that history is also emplotted through national narrative, the remaking of cityscape, and individuals' memories.

Xi'an's emplotment can be said to mainly involve romance and comedy, as the city aims to glorify its imperial past. Historical figures are lionized and portrayed as heroes. The state celebrates China as mighty and influential. Thus, locals dream to be the people of Qin because they imagined it to be very strong and glorious. They ignored the brutal acts of the emperor and the facts that commoners in the Qin Dynasty were impoverished. The Tang Dynasty too was emplotted as a romance of an open and harmonious society. Only very few elites are aware of the extremely hierarchical nature of the Tang world. The inhabitants of Chang'an lived in different areas of the city based on their background, profession, and class. All emplotters take only the useful parts of the past and piece them together in narrative form. This explains why the mental time lines I solicited were so fragmented, fixing with any degree of precision only on the Qin, Han, and Tang dynasties with details that had been implanted by state and city projects.

Even though ordinary people were not conscious of emplotment, academics and professionals do recognize it. Mr. Tao, an urban planner, blamed Xi'an City for misusing history in four ways, which include 'selective history', 'revitalized history', 'ignored history', and 'historical massacre'. In his opinion, the city engaged in a series of revitalization projects to glorify (and capitalize from) a selective history, and sometimes developed a site even without acknowledging its historical significance. Although numerable scholars have observed the global phenomenon of using heritage sites as 'economic resources' (Harrison and Hitchcock 2005; Leask and Fyall 2006; Ruggles and Silverman 2009; Smith, Messenger and Soderland 2010; Silva and Chapagain 2013), the commodification of history in Xi'an seems extreme. Many professionals, like Mr. Tao, recognize the commercialization as well as the politicization of history. They see that the political and commercial aspects of imperial heritage align very well. The story of Chinese historical greatness is flavoured by the government authorities, as well as by the market. However, the past is commodified to suit the imagination and romanticization of the locals too.

By emplotting history and highlighting certain dynasties, the Chinese state reinforces its political discourse of China as a civilized and strong nation. Through spotlighting Xi'an's history and imperial heritage, the Xi'an city government creates an image of the 'city of China'. Their image satisfies national and local audiences alike. Although the city's revitalization projects have distorted locals' perception about authenticity, the 'new' cityscape has enhanced an already strong local identity. Even this new history is taken into, expressed, and remembered in the acts and relations of everyday life. Therefore, imperial his-story and her-it-age play an important role in boosting nationalism and strengthening ideology. But, they also help contribute to social life in Xi'an as the past is not only remembered, but 'remembered'.

Chapter 5
The City of Connectivity – Silk Road Heritage

Shaanxi Province's rich imperial history makes its provincial history museum, Shaanxi History Museum, one of the most famous and renowned museums in China. Here, visitors can appreciate some of the best collections of ancient artefacts, from delicate bronzeware to the finest glass bowl, all excavated in the province. The purpose of the entrance hall is to give visitors a first impression of the history of Xi'an and the province. This museum does not exhibit a gigantic bronze vessel (to represent the advanced Bronze Age), nor a terracotta warrior, nor even a tri-colour figure to display the beauty of Tang culture. Instead, a giant stone lion in the centre of the hall catches tourists' attention. Many foreign tourists were puzzled; they doubted whether lions existed in ancient China.

According to Ms. Lin, who worked as a museum guide, the stone lion dates to the Tang Dynasty and it used to stand in front of the tomb of Empress Wu's mother. Because of its exquisite craftsmanship and style, it was known as the 'Best Lion in the East' (dongfang diyi shi). She said that both the motif and the technique of the stone carving did not originate in China, but were imported from Afghanistan. Moreover, this was exactly the reason the museum had decided to display the stone lion in the entrance hall. The carving reflects Shaanxi history and culture, and was also a product of Eastern and Western cultural exchange. The lion conveys the glory of China's imperial past, but more importantly, it highlights the elements of cultural interaction with Central Asia and the Middle East along the Silk Road.

Increasingly since 2008, Xi'an City has attempted to feature such aspects of cultural exchange and the Silk Road through different kinds of displays. Before 2008, the city focused on its imperial heritage sites, but since 2008, the city's development policy has leaned toward the Silk Road discourse. By 2013 the focus was clarified as Xi'an City Tourism Board mentioned that new aspects of development would include natural and Silk Road heritage and Xi'an City Planning Bureau turned to cooperate with the

Xi'an City Urban Landscape Office to conduct various projects with the Silk Road theme. Why was there such a turn in 2008? What led to the rise of the Silk Road discourse? How does the city celebrate the Silk Road?

Xi'an City promoted the Silk Road discourse in 2008 due to political, economic, and institutional changes. Politically, Xi'an, located in western China, is regarded by other provinces as backward and less developed. Therefore, on top of uplifting its historical imperial status, the city is also keen to create a cosmopolitan image by boasting of its international connections during the Silk Road era.

But there are other reasons too. One has to do with changing patterns in domestic tourism. Specifically, through the early 2000s, Chinese tourists preferred popular attractions that represented Chinese greatness. They joined package tours and stayed within a group. But increasingly, Chinese tourists seek the adventure and excitement of other touristic forms such as backpacking and road trips (Winter, Teo and Chang 2009). These tourists tend to visit less popular sites alongside mainstream attractions, and they are drawn to exploring natural heritage sites and cultural routes. Xi'an City Tourism Board has thus sought to allure the new types of tourists by promoting elements of the natural environment (such as Mount Hua, Mount Li, and the Gobi Desert), as well as the Silk Road. Increasing the diversity of tourist attractions may also help resolve the city's problem of drawing too many short-term tourists who stay no more than two days because they come mainly for the terracotta army and may even completely leave the city aside.

Furthermore, a personnel change impacted directly the adaptation of the pro-Silk Road policy. In April 2006, Mr. Zhao Rong was appointed as the new secretary of Shaanxi Provincial Bureau of Cultural Heritage. Born and raised in Xi'an, he obtained his Masters degree from North West University with a major in historical geography and archaeology. When interviewed by local news reporters in June 2008, he mentioned that he aimed to upgrade as many historical sites in Shaanxi Province as possible to become world-class representations of China during his period in office. With that aim, he devoted himself to the Silk Road World Heritage serial nomination, striving to see its finalisation during his administrative period. Indeed, he has continuously been a member of the 'internal advisory committee'[42] of the Silk Roads nomination since 2006. By making use of his

---

[42] The 'internal advisory committee' for the Silk Roads World Heritage nomination was formed in 2006 during the UNESCO Stakeholders Consultation Workshop on the Silk Road World Heritage Nomination with participation by representatives from China, Kazakhstan, Kyrgyzstan, Tajikistan, Turkmenistan, and Uzbekistan. The internal advisory committee is composed by a government official, an archaeologist, and a heritage expert from each of the above-mentioned countries to monitor and assess the condition and progress of heritage nomination within each country and to facilitate the trans-boundary nomination. See 'The Silk

influence and network, he convinced other provincial and municipal government departments to support Shaanxi Provincial Bureau of Cultural Heritage's work on the World Heritage bid.

This chapter, 'The City of Connectivity', draws attention to the connection between China and its neighbouring countries through the Silk Road. It might appear that the Silk Road emphasis contradicts the focus on the famous dynasties in Chinese history described in the previous chapters. However, the two discourses are interrelated. In fact, the Silk Road discourse even supplements the imperial discourse. As James Millward (2009) pointed out, 'whereas outside China the cross-cultural exchanges of "the Silk Road" can serve as a heart-warming counter-argument to the "clash of civilizations" world view, Chinese silk-roadism is more parochial and nationalistic' (p. 55). Hence, the notion of Silk Road is subsumed by national self-glorification.

Previous research on the Silk Road in China included in-depth studies on the Silk Road's impact on human civilization (Dani 1992; Umesao and Sugimura 1992; Han 2006), history (Bentley 1993; Beckwith 2009; Liu 2010), arts (Boardman 1994), and religion (Sugiyama 1992; Foltz 2000; Zarcone 2002; Elverskog 2010). As for studies related to the socio-cultural dimension, Sinologists and historians delved into people's lives along the Silk Road and on the administrative and military aspects of Chinese rule in western regions (Leslie and Gardiner 1982; Di Cosmo 1994, 2002). Unlike those researches, this chapter focuses on the current political and societal role of the modern Silk Road with an emphasis on the inscription of the Silk Roads as a World Heritage property. The first part of the chapter investigates the politics of the Silk Roads listing. How were decisions made with the site selection? What were the politics involved in the process of the Silk Roads nomination? What kind of sites did the Chinese state tend to pick and why? The second part looks into the Silk Road through Chinese eyes. How does the Chinese state shape and disseminate the concept of the Silk Road to the public? How do local Xi'an people perceive the Silk Road? How do they react and relate to the Silk Road heritage sites and newly constructed related sites? By displaying the meanings of the Silk Road to the international organizations, national and regional governments, different site administrations, experts, professionals, and local inhabitants, this chapter analyses the Chinese version of the Silk Road.

Road Heritage Corridors Tourism Strategy Workshop' of 2013, http://en.unesco.org/silkroad/node/8434. Last accessed 1 May 2016.

The Silk Roads as World Heritage

The term 'Silk Road' sprang from Seidenstraße, coined by the German geographer Baron Ferdinand von Richthofen in 1887 (Drège and Bührer 1989). The term has been taken into Chinese with a literal translation, and is either called *sichouzhilu* or by its abbreviation, *silu*. It is challenging to trace the Silk Road's historical references. Roman sources, for example, only recorded the territories that its legions had conquered (Elisseeff 2000). Compared to the scarce information provided by the Greeks and Romans, China's amount of documentation about the Silk Road is enormous and dates back to the Han Dynasty (202 BCE – 220 CE)[43] (Zufferey 2008). The official historical records used the term *Xiyu*, literally translated as 'Western region' (Hill 2009), to point to the Silk Road area. However, historians contend that the term is not clear because it could have referred to the region of today's Xinjiang, Central Asia in the further west, or even Europe on the other side of the Silk Road (Millward 2009).

But what is the Silk Road? Academics have suggested various definitions, such as, 'a metaphor of transnationalism' (Millward 2009: 70), 'a dialogue of cultures' (Elisseeff 1992; 2000), and 'a major trade and exchange route connecting Eurasia passing through many countries and communities' (Sugiyama 1992; Liu 2010). Despite the diverse under-standings, scholars agree that the Silk Road was not a single road with a fixed route, but rather a network composed of many parallel roads and branches (Foltz 2000). David Christian defined the Silk Road as multiple: 'long and middle-distanced land routes by which goods, ideas, and people were exchanged between major regions of Afro-Eurasia' (2000: 3). UNESCO has always used the plural form, 'Silk Roads' (UNESCO 1988). Apart from foregrounding the roads' function as trading routes, UNESCO has also drawn attention to their cultural aspects, stressing that 'the ancient Silk Road was the greatest route in the history of mankind (...) that symbolized the multiple benefits arising from cultural exchange' (UNESCO 2013). From now on, I use the plural form 'Silk Roads' when I refer to the World Heritage nomination, and the singular form to describe the general idea and historical route.

Even though Xi'an only joined the nomination process in 2008, the Silk Roads World Heritage nomination planning can be traced to 1988. At

---

[43] The official historical documentation from the Han Dynasty includes *Shiji* written by Sima Qian in 109 BCE (Watson 1993), *Hanshu* (History of the Former Han) composed by Ban Gu in 111 CE (Chen and Zhang 2009), and *Houhanshu* (History of the Later Han) compiled by Fan Ye in the fifth century (Hill 2009). There is also an unofficial historical record from the Han Dynasty, *Shanhaijin* (Classic of Mountains and Seas), that existed since the fourth century BCE (Wang 2006).

that time, the UNESCO World Heritage Centre launched the Silk Roads project 'Integral Study of the Silk Roads: Roads of Dialogue'. The project, which ran until 1997, gathered scientists, academics, and the media worldwide to conduct a vast program of research (Elisseeff 2000) with the purpose to 'highlight the complex cultural interactions arising from the encounters between East and West and helping to shape the rich common heritage of the Eurasian peoples' (UNESCO 1988: 1). The Silk Roads project mapped out five different routes composing the network of Silk Roads: the desert route from Xi'an to Kashgar in China; the maritime route from Venice to Osaka; the steppe route in Central Asia; the nomad's route in Mongolia; and the Buddhist route in Nepal (UNESCO 1988). In 1990, as part of the project, China Central Television filmed a documentary entitled *Desert Routes of the Silk Road from Xi'an to Kashgar, China* (UNESCO 1990). For nearly a decade, many meetings and workshops were held to engage the related countries in collaboration. However, the trans-boundary World Heritage nomination plan only became more concrete after the UNESCO Stakeholders Consultation Workshop on the Silk Roads World Heritage Nomination held in Xinjiang in August 2006. At that time, six countries (China, Kazakhstan, Kyrgyzstan, Tajikistan, Turkmenistan, and Uzbekistan) came together to develop a systematic approach to the identification and nomination of the cultural route (UNESCO 2013). They started to draft the Tentative List for evaluation and set the goal to co-nominate the cultural route in 2010 at the 34th Session of the World Heritage Committee in Brazil.

At the end of the initial Silk Roads project, China submitted the Tentative List for the Chinese section of the Silk Road (UNESCO 1997). However, the further preparation of the Silk Roads nomination proved to be very difficult. In 2011, the six States Parties decided to split into two heritage routes for the nomination process to reduce the heavy workload of communication and negotiation between the countries. China, Kazakhstan, and Kyrgyzstan worked together on the Silk Roads network of the Tianshan corridor, while the others focused on the Penjikent-Samarkand-Poykent corridor. Cooperation on the Tianshan corridor went smoothly and in April 2013 (see UNESCO 2014b), China, Kazakhstan, and Kyrgyzstan submitted the nomination file with the finalized Tentative List to the World Heritage Centre. In October 2013, the advisory board visited the respective countries to evaluate the nominated properties (UNESCO 2014a). Then, in June 2014 during the 38th Session of the World Heritage Committee in Doha, the serial nomination 'Silk Roads: The Routes Network of Chang'an-Tianshan Corridor' was successfully listed.

The change in title from the original proposal of 'Silk Roads: Initial Section of the Silk Roads, the Routes Network of Tianshan Corridor' was made based on the suggestion of ICOMOS (UNESCO 2014c: 243). The Silk Roads heritage route fulfils four out of six selection criteria for World Heritage cultural sites (criteria ii, iii, v, and vi), exhibiting a long-lasting interchange of human values (UNESCO 2014c). For criterion vi, the nomination document especially mentions the significance of Zhang Qian, a Chinese diplomat from the Western Han Dynasty in opening up the Silk Road, who initiated the formation of the cultural route in the Eurasian continent (UNESCO 2014c). The descriptions of the criteria and the Silk Roads reflect the dominance of China in the process of the nomination as it illustrates the Chinese story of the Silk Road, emphasizes Chinese historical impact on the heritage route, and neglects the contributions by the other countries. At the end, 22 out of the 33 sites listed are located in China, while Kazakhstan has eight and Kyrgyzstan three (see Appendix 2 for the full list of sites). According to the Chinese officials in charge of the nomination, this imbalance was caused by the varied devotion and effort spent by the different countries during the process. While China has prepared the Tentative List since 1997, the other two countries did not submit any candidate sites until 2013.

The effort of the UNESCO World Heritage Centre contributes to the trans-boundary nomination. For over 26 years, the centre worked closely with the States Parties, supported the research and preparation of the nomination, and facilitated the collaboration between different countries.[44] Although the international organizations, such as World Heritage Centre, ICOMOS, and the International Union for the Conservation of Nature (IUCN), are heavily involved in the preparation, processing, and evaluation of nomination files, they have no real power to force countries to nominate heritage properties, nor to control which sites are nominated. In the end, the States Parties select the sites they intend to nominate, compose and submit the Tentative List, and decide when to present the nomination file. This means, as Silverman (2010) asserts, the process of heritagization is highly political and contested. In the politics of World Heritage making, negotiations and conflicts over the meaning and management of heritage sites take place across international, national, and regional levels. The next part displays the politics involved during the nomination period and describes how different levels of the government and market forces influenced the decision making.

---

[44] 'Ershiliu nian shengyi lu' (The 26 years of heritage nomination journey). *Renmin Ribao*, 21 June 2014. Available online, http://society.people.com.cn/n/2014/0621/c1008-25179680.html. Last accessed 16 December 2014.

The Politics of the Silk Roads Nomination

Despite the ten-year project initiated by UNESCO in 1988 and the long-time interest of UNESCO towards the Silk Road, it is hard to comprehend why the six countries started serious discussion of the nomination only in 2006. The sudden interest was no coincidence. The countries might have realized economic benefits brought from the Silk Roads nomination through tourism development, but economic benefit alone was not strong enough to drive the countries to invest so much time and effort, and to work together, on such a large-scale project. Another argument is the international tendency. In 2000 at the 24th Session of the World Heritage Committee in Cairns, Australia, a decision was made that every State Party could only nominate one World Heritage property per year in order to slow down the rapid growth of World Heritage sites.[45] This decision resulted in a huge drawback for many nations, which had planned to nominate many properties. One strategy to work around the new quotas is what Mr. Tao, an architect interested in heritage management in Xi'an, described as 'doggie-bag nomination' (*dabao shenyi*). This is a lively description of serial nomination, in which countries include as many sites as they can manage under a given theme. For example, 'City Walls of the Ming and Qing Dynasties' was entered as a single nomination, though it included four walls from different cities (UNESCO 2008b). A second strategy involves the nomination of sites through trans-boundary projects which are not counted in the respective nomination quotas of any of the involved states. The Silk Roads project captured both of these strategies and hence gained increased attention from especially China, which has many sites that it wants to advance to nomination. Furthermore, China aimed to advocate and promote political and economic exchange with its neighbouring countries. The co-nomination can enhance the establishment of a partnership with Central Asia and reinforce Chinese influence. Therefore, China took the lead to push the other countries to work on the Silk Roads nomination.

But then, why did it still take eight years until the successful inscription of the Silk Roads? The preparation lasted for so long due to both external and internal politics. Externally, the countries involved and the

---

[45] The matter of nomination quotas was discussed again in 2004 during the 28th Session of the World Heritage Committee in Suzhou, and the committee agreed to loosen the quota so that each State Party could nominate one Cultural Heritage item and one Natural Heritage item each year. In the 31st Session of the World Heritage Committee in 2007, the nomination quota was again changed so that each State Party could nominate a total of two heritage properties of any kind per year. Most recently in the 35th Session of the World Heritage Committee in 2011, the quota was again adjusted to allow each State Party to nominate one Cultural Heritage item and one Natural Heritage item or Cultural Landscape annually.

international bodies had to maintain close communication and cooperation. The secretary of Shaanxi Provincial Bureau of Cultural Heritage, Mr. Zhao Rong, said that the cooperation was rather problematic because it was the first time the six countries had worked together on a transnational nomination, and there were many misunderstandings and difficulties, especially at the beginning. Four years alone were devoted to maintaining cross-national coordination. The six countries split into two teams for two Silk Roads nominations. Internally, too, each state was slowed by political concerns regarding the heritage listing. For example, the Central State Administration of China had to coordinate the preparation of different provinces. At the beginning in 2006, China initially only planned to involve three provinces (Xinjiang, Gansu, and Shaanxi) in the Silk Road project, but over time Henan, Qinghai, and Ningxia provinces also joined (UNESCO 2008a). Each province had to suggest a list of sites related to the Silk Road for the national Tentative List. Based on the cases in Shaanxi Province, the following part will illustrate the internal political concerns during the site selection process.

As an important political and economic hub during the Silk Road era, many traces of the Silk Road still remain in today's Xi'an. According to Ms. Chen, one of the Chinese representatives on the internal advisory committee and an architect specialized in ancient Chinese architecture, the architecture of many sites in Xi'an reflect some degree of linkage to the Silk Road. This large variety of sites complicated the nomination process because the provincial and city governments had to select the 'most representative' sites. During the preparation period, the Shaanxi government proposed several pre-tentative lists in which a total of twenty sites were identified. Fourteen of these belonged to the Xi'an city area. In the end, only seven sites succeeded as World Heritage sites. How did the other thirteen sites get eliminated, and who made the decisions?

The whole short-listing process was highly opaque to the public. Instead of announcing and introducing each selected site, the government diverted public attention to the question of whether the Silk Roads nomination would be successful. After the success, the provincial government stressed the victory and the fact that Shaanxi Province had seven items inscribed, topping all other provinces in China.[46] By emphasizing that Shaanxi Province was the real 'winner' in the Silk Roads nomination, the government managed to distract attention from the politics involved in the nomination process. During a formal interview with Mr. Zhao, the secretary

---

[46] Five of the sites in Shaanxi Province are within the city of Xi'an: Big Wild Goose Pagoda, Small Wild Goose Pagoda, Xingjiao Temple, Daming Palace, and Weiyang Palace. The other two sites are Zhang Qian's Tomb and Bin County Cave Temple.

of Shaanxi Provincial Bureau of Cultural Heritage, I challenged him about the drastic reduction from more than twenty items nominated to only seven at the end. He frowned and answered briefly: '[The reduction] was only a re-consideration and a re-arrangement'.

As a researcher, I found it challenging to uncover the internal reasons for the addition or removal of the sites. Through formal interviews but mostly informal interactions and gossip with government officials, heritage experts, professionals from different sectors, and people working on sites, I gathered different pieces of information, which I will attempt to put together to show a clearer picture in the next part. In order to display a holistic view of the changes made and the different stages of site selection, Plate 4 demonstrates the five phases of the pre-tentative lists making for comparison and analysis. The five phases of list making were in 2006, 2008, 2012, 2013, and 2014. It was the last of these lists which was approved during the 38th Session of the World Heritage Committee in June 2014. The first list in 2006, which proposed eleven sites, was announced by the secretary of Shaanxi Provincial Bureau of Cultural Heritage as a result of the consultation workshop organized by the UNESCO World Heritage Centre. In 2008, China amended the registered Tentative List submitted in 1997 with 12 sites from Shaanxi Province. In 2012, the government circulated another list with 19 sites. Then in early 2013, after several inter-level government meetings, the provincial government eliminated 10 sites from phase three. In June 2014, the cultural route with the finalized Tentative List was inscribed on the World Heritage List.

By comparing the different versions of pre-tentative lists (Plate 5), we notice the renaming of some sites. Albeit some of these name changes were minor such as changing from 'Tomb of Zhang Qian' to 'Zhang Qian's Tomb', others implied a deeper meaning. For instance, Shaanxi Provincial Bureau of Cultural Heritage purposefully renamed 'Daming Palace' to 'Daming Palace in Chang'an City of Tang Dynasty' at the last phase in order to highlight the Tang-era Chang'an City and to pave the way for future extensions for sites related to it. As for the nomination of the Chang'an City of the Han Dynasty, the site was narrowed down from the whole city remains ('Site of the Chang'an City of Han Dynasty') to a smaller architectural complex ('Weiyang Palace, Chang'an City of the Western Han Dynasty'). This change featured China's strong imperial background and spotlighted China's leadership role in Silk Road history. While the proposed area for Han Chang'an City shrank, the property zone of Xingjiao Temple expanded. Shaanxi Provincial Bureau of Cultural Heritage extended the property from Xuanzang's Pagoda to the Xingjiao Temple pagodas which also include Xuanzang's two students' pagodas.

Phase One September 2006 (Sina 2006)	Phase Two March 2008 (UNESCO 2008)	Phase Three March 2012 (Daqin 2012)	Phase Four Jan 2013 (Hsb 2013)	Phase Five June 2014 (UNESCO 2014b)
In Xi'an City				
Site of the Chang'an city of Han Dynasty	Site of the Chang'an City of Han Dynasty	Site of the Chang'an City of Han Dynasty	Site of the Chang'an City of Han Dynasty	Weiyang Palace, Chang'an City of the Western Han Dynasty
Daming Palace	*	Daming Palace	Daming Palace in Chang'an City of Tang Dynasty	Daming Palace in Chang'an City of Tang Dynasty
	Site of the Chang'an City of Tang Dynasty*			
The Dagoba of Kumarajiva	The Dagoba of Kumarajiva	The Dagoba of Kumarajiva		
Big Wild Goose Pagoda	*	Big Wild Goose Pagoda	Big Wild Goose Pagoda	Big Wild Goose Pagoda
Small Wild Goose Pagoda	*	Small Wild Goose Pagoda	Small Wild Goose Pagoda	Small Wild Gose Pagoda
Xi'an Mosque	Xi'an Mosque	Xi'an Mosque		
	Xingjiao Temple Pagoda (Xuan Zang's Dagoba)	Xingjiao Temple Pagoda (Xuan Zang's Dagoba)	Xingjiao Temple Pagodas	Xingjiao Temple Pagodas
	Daqin Monastery Pagoda	Daqin Monastery		
	*	Site of the Mingde Gate of Tang Dynasty		
	*	Site of the Yanping Gate of Tang Dynasty		
	*	Site of the Hanguang Gate of Tang Dynasty		
	*	Site of the Xingqing Palace of Tang Dynasty		
	*	Site of the Temple of Heaven of Tang Dynasty		
	*	Site of the West Market of Tang Dynasty		
Within the Shaanxi Province				
Famen Temple	The Underground Chamber of Famen Temple			
Zhao Imperial Mausoeum	Zhao Imperial Mausoleum	Zhao Imperial Mausoleum		
Mao Imperial Mausoleum of Han Dynasty and Tomb of Huo Qubing	Mao Imperial Mausoleum of Han Dynasty and Tomb of Huo Qubing	Mao Imperial Mausoleum of Han Dynasty and Tomb of Huo Qubing		
Qian Imperial Mausoleum	Qian Imperial Mausoleum	Qian Imperial Mausoleum	Qian Imperial Mausoleum	
Tomb of ZhangQian	Tomb of Zhang Qian	Tomb of Zhang Qian	Tomb of Zhang Qian	Zhang Qian Tomb
	Great Buddha Temple Grottoes in Bin County	Great Buddha Temple Grottoes in Bin County	Bin County Cave Temple	Bin County Cave Temple

Plate 4. The five phases of pre-tentative list making for the Silk Roads nomination.

The following part analyses the reasons provided by different social actors on the selection, addition, and elimination of sites. The decision making reflects a number of political concerns in the process of heritagization. Only one withdrawal was initiated by a site itself. This was the Qian Imperial Mausoleum, the resting place of Emperor Gaozhong and Empress Wu Zetian built between 684 and 706 CE (Valder 2002; Eckfeld 2005). Government officials refused to provide more information during official interviews; however, during an informal conversation in a car ride, Mr. Yuan, a high-positioned official from Shaanxi Provincial Institute of Cultural Heritage told me more. At the beginning, he was also reticent to discuss the matter, but then said: 'the Qian Mausoleum quitted the nomination because it was unhappy with the delay of the nomination. But more importantly, it did not find the nomination beneficial for its future development'. When I pushed, it became clear that the site, as one of the most visited places in Shaanxi Province, would not gain much by adding the brand of World Heritage; instead, it would face limitations because of the additional regulations, preservation requirements, and limits on visitors. Nor would the title of World Heritage result in any extra financial support. Mr. Yuan found it a pity that the Qian Imperial Mausoleum withdrew but respected its choice. All other additions and removals were determined by third parties based on six different motives to be outlined in the following.

A Serial Nomination within a Serial Nomination

Three important sites of the Tang Dynasty, namely Daming Palace, Big Wild Goose Pagoda, and Small Wild Goose Pagoda, disappeared from the second list of 2008. They would later reappear, but in the meantime Shaanxi Provincial Bureau of Cultural Heritage replaced them with an item called 'Site of the Tang Chang'an City' (UNESCO 2008a). I attempted to find out which 'site' the list actually referred to, as most of the Tang city lies underneath present-day Xi'an, and it would seem impossible to cover its whole by size alone. Geographical coordinates were provided, but these were misleading[47], and no more detail was stated in the Tentative List. When I reviewed the internal documents provided by the Xi'an government, I learned that the term 'site' was misleading. In fact, the nomination was meant to include all the items marked by a star in Plate 4 (Xi'an City Office of Cultural Heritage 2008). This was meant to be a serial nomination within a serial nomination!

Why did Shaanxi compose a serial nomination within a serial nomination? In short, the obscurity allowed both the province and China to hide its ambitions. An official answer I got from a government official suggests as much. He said, 'the six countries did not yet collaborate intensively at the beginning stage'. Even though there was no specific limitation on the number of items within a serial nomination, the States Parties attempted to keep a balance between the countries, and may well have objected to the detailed listing of the several specific sites encompassed by the broader reference to Chang'an. In addition, strong inter-provincial rivalry exists within China as each province strives to inscribe more World Heritage properties to show its status. In the Silk Road case, the six provinces involved, namely Henan, Shaanxi, Ningxia, Gansu, Qinghai, and Xinjiang, secretly competed with each other, each aiming for the most sites

---

[47] The location of the 'Site of Tang Chang'an City' was given as N 34 17-18 30, E 108 56 30-58 30 (UNESCO 2008a). This refers to an area more than twenty kilometres from Xi'an City and from the Tang Chang'an City. Also, the area given is only 3.7 kilometres wide and 2.8 kilometres long – about the size of the old city of Xi'an surrounded by its Ming wall, but only one-fifth the size of Tang Chang'an. Further, only minor Tang heritage sites are located within the area. Coupled with the documentation in other internal documents, it would seem that these coordinates were mistakenly assigned to the nominated entry.

on the list. Thus in 2008 for the initial Tentative List, Shaanxi Province attempted to conceal the actual number of sites it meant to advance. That also explains why Shaanxi Province was so proud of its 'victory' over other provinces.

The Lack of Attractiveness

The list made in 2013 removed nine items from the former one, including Dagoba of Kumarajiva and Daqin Monastery Pagoda, which were both listed on the registered Tentative List in 2008. They represent the earliest religious architecture imported through the Silk Road. Mr. Wei, a heritage site administrator, told me that Daqin Monastery Pagoda has undergone a long-term preservation project since 1998 conducted by the provincial government because it suffered from earthquakes and flooding and was in a very bad condition. The government never explained the removal of these two buildings from the list. When I asked a government official, his first reaction to my answer without a thought was: 'that was because those sites did not have a strong link to the Silk Road!' The government officials tend to use such a standard justification for every removed item. However, what kind of linkage to the Silk Road did they seek? Dagoba of Kumarajiva symbolizes the earliest form of Buddhism imported to China, while Daqin Monastery Pagoda proved the presence of Nestorian Christians in Tang Chang'an. How were these not strong links to the Silk Road? As I looked further into the matter, it would appear that these sites do not fit in with other aspects of the developmental discourse of heritage sites in China.

Partly, these were economical. Mr. Cao, a heritage developer, commented on the two sites as being very small, not easily accessible with public transportation, and consequently, not very likely to be developed into popular tourist attractions. Both of the religious sites require the visitors to hike up a mountain after a bus ride. In addition, both sites are totally absent from all travelling brochures. Only religious studies scholars in Xi'an know about them. An official from the Shaanxi Provincial Institute of Cultural Heritage, Mr. Yuan, laughed sarcastically when I asked about them: 'those two sites? Maybe after the success of the inscription this time, we will consider to add them into the extension, they still have a chance. But not in the first round'. He insisted that Xi'an should only nominate the sites that would surely be selected in good condition with rich value in the first round and believed that the chance for sites like the dagoba and monastery would be higher in the second or third extension. Mr. Yuan was partly right, in that successful nominations must be found 'desirable' according to various external criteria. The ICOMOS evaluation report, after all, pointed out that the Silk Roads nomination for the Tianshan Corridor lacked a desired cultural richness as the nominated sites reflected mostly the power and wealth of towns and cities (UNESCO 2014a). But it would seem that the dagoba and pagoda might be desirable in the same eyes precisely because they show ancient religious diversity. Yet in China, nominated forms of 'heritage' are first of all restricted by their local conceptualization as potential goldmines – development projects that bring in tourists or revenue.

The Matter of Readiness

The Tang Temple of Heaven, Mingde Gate, Yan'an Gate, Hanyuan Gate, West Market, and Xingqing Palace also belonged to the Tang Chang'an mini-serial. However, these sites appeared only shortly on the list announced in 2012 and were removed in 2013. Let me focus on the cases of the Temple of Heaven and Mingde Gate. The former one is one of the very few well-preserved sites from the Tang period, which served as a ritual venue for the emperors to worship heaven. Mainly composed of earth, the temple had four round raised platforms with a base that measured fifty-four metres wide and eight metres tall. The temple building is unfortunately no longer there, but together with the Temple of Heaven in Beijing, this is one of only two such complexes remaining. Mingde Gate, one of the most important city gates in Tang Chang'an, is located in the south of the city, welcoming the most important people, such as political representatives from other countries. In Tang Chang'an, most of the city gates had only one or three openings, but Mingde Gate had five, which reflects its significance.

I first visited the Temple of Heaven with an architecture student because of her strong recommendation. Located in the southern part of the city area inside a university campus, it felt as if it was completely isolated from the urban area. I would not have found the site on my own, and the locals called the site 'the forgotten cultural heritage of the city' (*bei yiwang de yizhi*). The site was very well-preserved with four earth platforms and the staircases to the Temple of Heaven. The student who accompanied me kept reminding me of the importance of the site and compared it with the Temple of Heaven in Beijing: 'Not only Beijing has a Temple of Heaven, our Temple of Heaven is much more ancient and used to have a bigger scale'. Due to its rareness and well-preserved state, the Temple of Heaven caught the attention of Xi'an's City Office of Cultural Heritage in 2004. Later, the project was outsourced to a famous developer – Qujiang Corporation – which manages and develops many other heritage sites in Xi'an (see chapter 6). However, when Qujiang handed in the first draft of its plan, it put off many heritage experts as well as urban planners because real estate development dominated the whole plan with high rises even planned within the core area. The controversial draft drew attention from different government departments. After intense negotiations with State Administration of Cultural Heritage, the Xi'an city government, City Office of Cultural Heritage, and Xi'an City Planning Bureau, the developer finally gave in and made alterations to the plan, including a reduction in the number of high rises. The new plan for the Temple of Heaven conforms with UNESCO's requirements on property and buffer zones and imposes height restrictions in the area around the heritage property. In 2013, the authorities and the developer finally compromised for the final version and the restrictions for the buffer zone to a 12-metre zone, an 18-metre zone, and a 24-metre zone, but it was too late to complete the park in time for the World Heritage submission.

Mingde Gate underwent a similar process. I attempted to visit it in October 2013, but it was not easy for me to find the site. Even residents living just 200 metres away had no idea of its existence. Only those who had lived around that area for a long time were familiar with the place, but they did not know about its archaeological value, and described the site as a 'garbage dump' and a haven for homeless people. They told me that a number of government officials had visited the place a month before me and that after their visit, the area had been walled off, but they reported no knowledge of the reason. When I asked them if the government might be planning to develop the area as a heritage project, and whether they might face removal, they laughed and said the chance was very low for 'such a site with nothing inside'. However, just a few months after my visit, the whole neighbourhood was removed. Mr. Zhu, an urban planner who worked for the Mingde Gate project, told me that the government authority worked with a 'better' developer than Qujiang that was much more willing to take advice from the heritage experts from the City Office of Cultural Heritage and Xi'an City Planning Bureau. They also set up a research project to investigate the best way to balance the heritage site and its uses. After proposing three different drafts and improving each time, they came up with a plan that combined the historical site with residential, art, and commercial areas. In the end, they adopted the model of *jie-cheng-jiao* (street-city-countryside) to revive Mingde Gate as part of Tang Chang'an City and to highlight the contrast within and outside the city wall. On top of the aim of being nominated as a World Heritage site, the draft plan also proposed to solve the urban problem of the lack of greenery in southern Xi'an.

The two sites both intended to be nominated in 2014, however, due to the complicated negotiation between the government departments and the developers, they had to craft and compromise the developmental plans multiple times. As a result, the sites missed the deadline to be included in the finalized version of the Tentative List. The sites were simply not ready for the first nomination period. Actually, when I left Xi'an in September 2014, their condition was unchanged and no construction works had been carried out yet.

The Question of Authenticity

When it comes to heritage nomination, there are two international key concepts that the Chinese government does not dare to stretch too far: authenticity and integrity. Here they must follow the parameters of the concepts as stated in the Convention Concerning the Protection of the World Cultural and Natural Heritage (UNESCO 1972). There is only very limited tolerance for World Heritage sites that deviate on either point. Famen Temple is a good example of such. No other site was so desperately campaigned for inclusion on the Tentative List. Out of the twenty proposed items, Famen Temple was the only one in Baoji City. The deputy mayor of Baoji announced in 2008 when the experts visited the site for the first time: 'Baoji City has only this one property on the list, so, we cannot mess it up!' Indeed, the historical and aesthetic value of Famen Temple and its strong link to the Silk Road (manifest in its underground palace with a collection of Tang relics discovered after the collapse of the temple pagoda in 1981) increased the temple's likelihood of being listed. Still, nothing was certain in the years leading up to the submission of the Tentative List.

It started well. On the afternoon of 15 April 2008, some government officials accompanied a heritage assessment team to the temple to evaluate its condition for the nomination. During the visit, a local official gave a presentation about the current stage of the site's preservation and introduced the future plan. The assessment team was content. An official from State Administration of Cultural Heritage noted that since the underground palace of the temple was very well preserved, the temple only needed to collect the archival and material data in order to display the authenticity and integrity of the site to emphasize its historical value and the linkage with the Silk Road. More importantly, the state administration suggested the temple to enhance its environment so as to cultivate the 'cultural atmosphere' of the area, meaning that the temple had to change the signs, rubbish bins, information boards and other facilities. Despite those minor amendments, the chance of nominating Famen Temple seemed very promising.

However, the 'enhancement' of the site did not go as expected. Famen Temple and the Baoji city government decided to cooperate with Qujiang Corporation to develop the temple into a popular tourist attraction. To this end, Famen Temple was subjected to numerous administrative and physical changes. The temple area was expanded twenty times and the entrance fee increased by ten times. The construction of a new modern pagoda within the temple area triggered intensive resentment from the public and the doubt of the provincial government about putting the site onto the list. The modern building is controversial because of its physical appearance, and people were also unhappy with Qujiang's decision to relocate the sacred relics (*śarīra*)[48] from the underground palace of the original Famen Temple to the newly constructed building. In the eyes of many visitors and the government authority, the relocation of the sacred object, the construction of a modern building, and the commercialization development destroyed the authenticity and integrity of the site. An official from Shaanxi Provincial Bureau of Cultural Heritage told me that Famen Temple had 'crossed the line' (*tai guofen*) and that experts could not tolerate it anymore. More on the politics of Famen Temple's heritage development will be discussed in chapter 6, but suffice it to say that Famen Temple was eliminated from the Tentative List.

While the Famen Temple case demonstrates the negative consequences of disregarding authenticity, the case of Daming Palace shows that considering authenticity leads to success. During the aforementioned interview with Secretary Zhao, he said that the success of Daming Palace meant especially much to Xi'an, since it symbolized international recognition of a 'Chinese' way of preservation. He asserted:

> In the field of cultural heritage preservation, the world adopts a Western concept. Europe introduced the Venice Charter, Japan also created the Nara Document on authenticity. However, as a country that owns so many cultural heritage sites, what has China contributed to the world? After so many years of experience, the Daming Palace heritage project demonstrates a Chinese way of cultural heritage preservation.

He highlighted that the Chinese way of conservation referred mainly to the methods of showcasing and utilizing heritage sites by using modern material to cover the original remains. The main entrance gate of the palace, Danfeng Gate, for example, used a neo-Tang-style reconstruction to cover the original archaeological site and managed to manifest the original look as well as to achieve simultaneous conservation.

In fact, Mr. Zhao valued the successful inscription of Daming Palace so much because it had faced the initial opposition of ICOMOS. In 2005, ICOMOS held its 15th General Assembly in Xi'an. Michael Petzet, then-president of ICOMOS, refused to support the site's nomination. According to a German restorer who had accompanied the president's visit to Daming Palace, 'Petzet refused after seeing the plans and the condition of the site

---

[48] *Śarīra* is a generic term referring to Buddhist sacred relics. Famen Temple holds the bone of the Buddha's middle finger.

with the construction of many fake palace buildings'. That was a strong blow to the Shaanxi provincial government.

After Petzet's objections, the government demolished the replicated palace then under construction. It was to look very much like the Forbidden City. They conducted a thorough research on the historical background of the palace, and re-considered the ways to display its authenticity. Mr. Zhao admitted that Petzet was doubtful of the condition and plans for Daming Palace in 2005, but – what he stressed to me – was that during another meeting in 2012 Petzet saw the changes made to the site, changed his mind, and expressed his satisfaction with the Chinese efforts. Mr. Zhao also boasted that when Mr. Sok An (Chair of the 37th Session of the World Heritage Committee and Deputy Prime Minister of Cambodia) visited Daming Palace in June 2013, he even jokingly invited the Chinese to restore Angkor Wat. Since Daming Palace respected international advice, it succeeded in being included in the nomination.

The Preference for Buddhism

Chang'an was known for its cultural diversity, in terms of both the ethnicity and the religious beliefs of its inhabitants. 'Under the Tang, the city was also a major religious center, not only for Buddhism and Taoism but also for several religions which were relatively recent arrivals in China: Zoroastrianism, Nestorianism and Manichaeism' (UNESCO 2006). Peter Hopkirk described how in Chang'an, 'Nestorians, Manicheans, Zoroastrians, Hindus, and Jews were freely permitted to build and worship in their own churches, temples and synagogues' (2006: 28). Even ancient Islamic sources, such as the books written by Ibn al-Nadim in the tenth century already mentioned Chinese traditions of practising 'dualism and *shaminiyah* (faith)' (Elverskog 2010: 93), proving vivid cultural exchange between China and the Islamic World. Yet the items categorized as 'religious sites' in the final Silk Roads serial inscription were much more homogenous, evincing a clear preference for proclaiming the region's Buddhist past.

The four religious sites from Shaanxi Province (Xingjiao Temple, Big Wild Goose Pagoda, Small Wild Goose Pagoda, and Bin County Cave Temple) are all Buddhist sites. Indeed all the religious sites nominated by China are Buddhist sites. And though Islam and Manicheanism are occasionally represented across the Road's sites, Nestorianism has no visible recognition. Michael Clarke pointed out the greater importance of China's selective approach in which 'the Islamic past is downgraded in favour of highlighting the Buddhist and pre-Buddhist antiquity [of] Han and Tang period sites' (2009: 179). By putting stress on Buddhist heritage sites, a

'Chinese' vision of the Silk Road, in which China plays a leading role, is reinforced across the trans-boundary project.

Yet this vision was also not inevitable. The nomination only became Buddhism-dominated at the final stage. At earlier phases, the pre-tentative lists included the Xi'an Mosque (also known as the Great Mosque) and the Nestorian Daqin Monastery Pagoda. These had been on the list since 2006 and 2008 respectively. They were removed late in the process, and for unclearly documented reasons.

The Xi'an Mosque was delisted in 2013. Its architecture mixes Chinese and Islamic elements: the mosque looks like a Chinese temple (with neither domes nor minarets), but is decorated with Arabic lettering and other Islamic decorations. Xi'an's Hui community describes the chain of important mosques, joined together by Tianshan, as the 'Muslim Dragon' of Central Asia. The head of this dragon is the Xi'an Mosque and the tail is the Dungan Mosque in Karakul, Kyrgyzstan. Surely Xi'an's mosque was an important component of Silk Road heritage across Central Asia. But Mr. Yuan, an official from the Shaanxi Provincial Institute of Cultural Heritage, exclaimed that (after examining the themes and criteria required for the Silk Roads heritage nomination) the committee found the mosque not as qualified as other sites.

When I looked at the nomination files, I found that the Xi'an Mosque had been awarded the highest value (five stars), and fulfilled both the standards of 'authenticity' and 'integrity'. The mosque's only weak point was that it needed to improve its state of preservation (UNESCO 2008a: 536). Big Wild Goose Pagoda was assessed with exactly the same value and result. Why then was the mosque eliminated while the pagoda remained on the list?

Here, at the late stage of nomination, China's ethnic politics entered the equation. It was an open secret. Officials were frank, and also advised me to pursue the matter no further. One official from Shaanxi Provincial Bureau of Religious Affairs declared that the mosque could not go forward because Muslims 'do not have culture and they are violent, rude and uncivilized'. Ethnicity is a very sensitive topic in Xi'an especially on heritage making issues. Mr. Yang, a well-respected scholar on the architecture of the Muslim Quarter, commented that he never had high expectations that the Xi'an government would support the site's nomination. He told me that the heritage nomination process is very complicated and political, and advised me not to delve too much into such complexities. As a Hui himself, he felt justified in adding: 'after all, the mosque belongs to the Hui people [and we are] not representative for Xi'an'. Other Xi'an locals also explained

to me that the mosque could not fit into the 'Han-Tang' discourse fostered
by the government in recent years.

Thus, the government's elimination of the mosque and Nestorian
monastery in the last stage of the nomination process served to highlight
Buddhist heritage and bolster a Chinese version of the Silk Road. The final
decisions meshed well with larger-scale national and local goals, but also
included subtler assessments of cultural heritage and ownership with which
even local minorities somehow agreed.

The Means of Resistance

Plate 4 does not record all the changes in the list's composition. In some
cases, like that of Xingjiao Temple, the burial place of Xuanzang, the
support for nomination by one or another key party was in constant
fluctuation, but kept invisible. Xingjiao Temple, for example, appeared to
have a secure position on the list since 2012. Yet the relationship between
the temple's administration and the government was often hostile. It was not
clear until the last moment if Xingjiao Temple would (or even wanted) to
remain on the list. In the end, the temple was included and even managed to
expand its original proposal of inclusion to cover not just one pagoda, but all
three pagodas.

On my first visit in August 2013, the person in charge of the temple,
who had worked there for over thirty years, felt very pessimistic about the
World Heritage nomination. He said, 'Who cares if we are on the World
Heritage List or not? Of course it would be nice, but it is not our decision
(…) if we have to make the changes they [the Xi'an city government,
Chang'an district government, and Qujiang Corporation] want us to, we
would rather not become a World Heritage site'. A hostile relationship
between the temple and the government started in 2012 and reached its peak
by 2013. The temple refused to accept the developmental plan proposed by
Qujiang Corporation, which was supported by the government. The plan
suggested developing the temple into a cultural scenic area, and would
require the monks to move out. The monks were outraged. They protested
outside the temple and even demolished some of the construction works
undertaken by the developer.

A monk from the temple told me that after unsuccessful negotiation
with the city and district governments and the developer, the chief monk and
the temple administration had decided to withdraw from the nomination to
avoid further development of the temple complex in 2013. The withdrawal
went unrecorded. It upset the city and provincial government because they
valued the site's association with Xuanzang, celebrated in the Chinese
narration of the Silk Road story. Meanwhile, the temple utilized its religious

status and network to gain support from the Buddhist community and from academics to resist the government imposed developmental plan. This mobilization and the temple's announced withdrawal of its nomination worked; the temple leveraged support for its value as heritage and forestalled an undesirable development project. Probably, Qujiang Corporation's fall from favour with the government (to be discussed in chapter 6) also helped the temple's nomination.

Although the government authorities use the official justification of lack of connection to the Silk Road to explain each delisted item, I have displayed in the last sections some other political concerns made by various levels of government and other heritage actors. The government authorities define the understanding of authenticity, integrity, values, and 'linkage to the Silk Road' to determine what to keep and expel from the Tentative List. The politics of Silk Road heritage demonstrated the internal criteria of site selection. From the government agencies' point of view, the sites have to contain high historical and aesthetic values, but more importantly, they have to support Chinese national history and have rich potential for further development. The selection of sites shows Chinese and Xi'an's political and economic logic. On the one hand, the Silk Road nomination is a commercial strategy to boost tourism development. On the other hand, the selected sites have to manifest the consistency of the Chinese story of the Silk Road, in which China acts as the centre and initiator of the cultural route.

The Myths of the Chinese Silk Road

As outlined through the preference for Buddhist sites over those of other religions, the narration of the Silk Road in China is highly nationalized. The selection of Silk Road heritage sites in Xi'an does not contradict the state's Qin-Han-Tang imperial discourse, but rather reinforces it. In other words, the notion of the Silk Road in Xi'an was used to spotlight the strength and openness of the Han and Tang dynasties. The Chinese story puts stress on elements such as the silk trade and Buddhism to construct the Silk Road as a unidirectional trade route, dispersing Chinese culture outward with little or no 'exchange' or 'influence' coming into China from elsewhere. During my stay in Xi'an, I constantly faced Sinicized Silk Road elements displayed in public, circulated through media, or discussed by informants. The version of the Silk Road in China varied a lot from the Western one promoted, at least ostensibly, through projects like that run by UNESCO from 1988–97. To me, these elements were the myth of the Chinese Silk Road, which were created by the state through education, public display, and mass media. This part dismantles the myth of the Chinese version of the Silk Road, in order to understand how the state has constructed the popular understanding of the Silk Road in China.

First, when did the Silk Road start? My informants usually begin their tale with the mission of Zhang Qian given by Emperor Wu between 139 and 125 BCE to propose an alliance with the tribes in the 'Western lands' (Christian 2000; Foltz 2000). Most Xi'an natives strongly believe the Silk Road started in the Western Han Dynasty (206 BCE–220 CE). However, there is mounting archaeological evidence of an earlier beginning, such as the discovery of silk in Egypt from around 1000 BCE (Wilford 1993) and the excavation of chariots from Shang archaeological sites (ca. 1570–1054 BCE), which can show the influence from Indo-European people (Beckwith 2009). Other scholars even assert that the name Silk Road falsifies the time frame of the route, which would be more appropriately called the 'Spice Road', the 'Glass Road', the 'Horse-Tea Road', or even the 'Ceramic Road' (Shirin 1992) after goods that were exchanged even earlier than silk. However, Chinese discourse considers none of these options. Because silk was produced in China, its very incorporation into the naming of the trans-boundary trade routes supports a Sino-centric narration of a cultural route.

Second, where did the Silk Road begin? This very question is a Chinese one. Unlike the Western understanding of the Silk Road as a network with many nodes, the Chinese histories insist on finding a starting point. Identifying the head of the route fortifies the narration of a unidirectional east-west flow. Since 2008, most tourist brochures, display boards, and websites have featured Xi'an as the starting point of the Silk Road. Many international scholars have agreed that Chang'an was the starting point of the Silk Road from the east (Barthold 1956; Bonavia 2007). More recently, a number of Chinese historians have argued that Luoyang, the eastern capital of the Tang Dynasty, should be considered the real starting point. The debate remains open and important. In May 2014, reportage on an Italian opera performance that took place in the Tang West Market in Xi'an was described as a 'performance of the starting and ending point of the Silk Road' (i.e. Xi'an was the starting point and Italy was the endpoint).[49]

Third, where in Xi'an did the Silk Road begin? Let's assume, first, that Xi'an was the eastern starting point of the Silk Road. Then, this question appears with a surprising urgency. When walking around the western part of Xi'an, one finds various monuments and stones claiming to mark the starting

---

[49] 'Sichouzhilu qidian he zhongdian de Zhongguo qinqiang he Yidali geju tongtai yanchu' (The performance of the starting and ending points of the Silk Road: Chinese Qinqiang music and Italian opera). *Xinhua Net*, 25 May 2014. Available online, http://www.xinhuanet.com/world/2014-05/25/c_1110847259.htm. Last accessed 20 January 2019.

spot of the Silk Road. For example, the large sculpture *Sichou Qundiao*, erected in 1988, was meant to mark the starting point of the Silk Road in Tang Chang'an, as it was located close to the West Gate, where the traders from the Silk Road entered the city. There are also numerous signs. A sign-board at the entrance of the Tang West Market proclaims:

> [The Tang West Market] was the world business and trade centre, cultural communication centre, as well as fashion and entertainment centre at that time. As the starting point of the famous Silk Road in Sui and Tang dynasties, the grandness and prosperous market of the Tang West Market supported the world trading system and witnessed the most glorious and flourishing age of Zhenguan and Kaiyuan reign period.

A sign in the Daming Palace Museum, purporting to be the preface of the Daming Palace Silk Road Inscription Thematic Exhibition, reads:

> Being a dominating building in the northern part of Chang'an City, Daming Palace was the official royal palace [in which] the Tang emperors live[d] and handle[d] state affairs, and [it was] regarded as the heart of the Tang Empire, symbol of the nation, and the starting point of the Silk Road.

A sign in the Shaanxi History Museum in the Silk Roads exhibition focused on Weiyang Palace of Chang'an City of the Western Han Dynasty also marks the beginning of the Silk Road:

> [The site of Weiyang Palace] is a site of [an] imperial palace that represents Chang'an City of [the] Han Dynasty, the east[ern] origination of the Silk Road in its flourishing period. It witnesses the civilization and ritual culture of an empire in the East when its agricultural civilization reached its crest.[50]

In addition to claiming the sites as the starting point of the Silk Road, all the descriptions tried to link to the greater imperial prosperity of the Han and Tang eras and highlight their economic and political contributions. According to Mr. Wen, a professor of history at North West University, it is pointless to argue which site in Xi'an was the starting point of the Silk Road. However the act of different sites attempting to declare as the starting point demonstrates the rise of the Silk Road discourse in Xi'an.

Fourth, who was the father of the Silk Road? Xi'an people generally would say either Zhang Qian or Xuanzang. Zhang Qian, as mentioned before, is undoubtedly the main character of the most prevailing story on the Silk Road in China. A life-size wax figure of Zhang Qian was placed in the middle of the Silk Road's exhibition hall in Shaanxi History Museum.

---

[50] I have reproduced the English translations of the sign. They were accurate translations of the Chinese versions they accompanied.

Besides, the Chinese state decided to nominate his tomb along with the Silk Roads serial nomination in order to feature this heroic figure. The other 'father of the Silk Road', Xuanzang, was an eminent Buddhist monk and scholar, who travelled from Chang'an to India and translated many important Buddhist texts (Wriggins 1996). This figure was popularized because of a fictionalized legend about his life known as *Journey to the West*. In the city of Xi'an, he is celebrated in many ways. For example, Xi'an City built two museums narrating his story as well as a memorial plaza with his statue at the south end of Big Wild Goose Pagoda. Among the five sites in Xi'an on the Silk Road list, two relate directly to him: Big Wild Goose Pagoda, where he worked after his return back to Chang'an, and Xingjiao Temple, where he was buried. Many other heroes of the Silk Road could be celebrated too, including William of Rubrouck (UNESCO 2013: 493), Satuq Bughra Khan (Hamada 2002), Mawlana Yusuf Sakaki (Pantusov' 2002), Lalla Mamiya (Boissevain-souid 2002), Rabban Bar Sauma (Elisseeff 1992), and the famous Italian traveller who was the only one in documented history who completed the whole Silk Road journey – Marco Polo. Yet their significance is downplayed by the Chinese state and except for Marco Polo, the other historical figures are not even mentioned in the Chinese version of the Silk Road.

Fifth, who were the foreigners along the Silk Road? The diversity of the foreigners residing in Chang'an was huge, and the ethnicities represented include Turks, Iranians, Arabs, Sogdians, Mongolians, Armenians, Indians, Koreans, Malays, and Japanese (Hopkirk 2006). Foreigners were active in every known occupation: merchants, missionaries, pilgrims, envoys, dancers, musicians, acrobats, scribes, gem dealers, wine sellers, students, scholars, adventurers, courtiers, and courtesans. Yet museums or exhibitions in Xi'an usually portray foreigners only as traders or acrobats. The museums choose to feature foreigners from these two occupations because they want to label the foreigners as 'barbarians'. While Han and Tang Chinese male figures are depicted as clean-shaven and fully dressed, the foreign male figures are indicated by their hairiness and topless features. The displays illustrated a biased picture of the foreigners, as if only Chinese were educated, civilized, and respected. Daming Palace is the only exception, exhibiting a large number of pottery figures of properly dressed foreign ambassadors, who 'revered' the Chinese emperor every year by giving their countries' treasures as gifts. This display highlights Tang Chang'an's political power and shows how Tang China 'civilized' Central Asian countries.

These five myths reveal a Chinese version of the Silk Road where China played a central role in promoting its civilization and prosperity. The emphasis on Zhang Qian's story as coinciding with the origin of the Silk Road ignores the contributions made by thousands of other travellers on the route, and especially neglects traders' efforts to build up the whole network. The other myths position China as the (most) civilized centre of the Silk Road's substantial developments. It conveys a powerful China, but also an open China.

Although the narration of the Silk Road is highly nationalized, in comparison to other imperial-focused histories, it constructs a new image of a cosmopolitan China. Silk Road China testifies to the greatness of the Tang Empire in that it attracted all kinds of foreigners. In this, Xi'an's museums are explicit. The Daming Palace Museum, for instance, exhibits a recon-struction of the Tang imperial court, which showcases the presence of a multitude of ambassadors from other countries. Other museums narrate how the 'splendid', 'rich', and 'open' Tang society attracted scholars from abroad to learn about the world and Chinese culture. Kobo-Daishi, a Japanese monk, who introduced Buddhism from Chang'an to Japan, is a famous example. Consequently, the Silk Road in the Chinese national discourse only 'highlights aspects of Chinese past that resonate with today's vision of "rising China" playing a major role on the world stage' (Millward 2009: 55). The Silk Road, contrary to its Western understanding of acting as a transnational bridge linking different regions, was conceived in Chinese terms to reinforce the national discourse.

Silk Road on the Ground

Along with the Silk Roads nomination and the increasing use of the Silk Road in the political agenda, the notion of Silk Road became more visible on the ground during my fieldwork. Since March 2014, the term Silk Road appeared every day in the newspapers in different contexts. The papers carry reports on the Silk Roads nomination, descriptions of the related sites, advertisements for Silk Road tourism, articles on culture and lifestyle along the route, and updates on Sino-Central Asian economic cooperation. The mass media was obsessed with Silk Road topics and even labelled the opening of the new international air routes and expansion of the airport as the start of the 'Air Silk Road'. Furthermore, from 2008 to 2014, the government built two Silk Road museums, Silk Road Street, and Silk Road Market, and has future plans for an international Silk Road museum, Silk Road plaza, and various Silk Road parks. Both the Shaanxi History Museum and Xi'an City Museum changed the script for the tour guides to give more emphasis to the Silk Road. Eye-catching spots, such as at bus stops, in busses, or on bridges, advertised slogans about the heritage bid. Tourist sites added display boards describing the history of the heritage route and its relation to Xi'an. Public venues organized special exhibitions and events on the theme. The provincial and municipal governments tried to promote the idea of the Silk Road in every way in the course of the World Heritage candidacy. However, how did the general public comprehend the Silk Road? Was their version of the Silk Road in line with the state's discourse? How much were they informed about the heritage nomination? This part discusses the notion of the Silk Road on the ground and explores its meaning to the general public in Xi'an.

Despite the high visibility of the Silk Road in everyday life in Xi'an, most residents did not feel enthusiastic about the idea. Unlike the imperial history of Xi'an, which was discussed all the time over dining tables, the topic of the Silk Road did not come up naturally in conversations. When I informed Mr. Li, a local architect, about the advisory board report on the Silk Roads nomination approved by ICOMOS in late May 2014, he asked immediately: 'how about the Grand Canal nomination? Did you read that report?' He explained that the Grand Canal nomination is more significant for China because it was a massive construction built solely by China throughout many dynasties. The general public did not seem to be very enthusiastic about the Silk Road heritage bid. For example, when I asked informants to name the five sites listed in Xi'an, most of them failed to name any. Some people named the Wild Goose pagodas and Daming Palace simply because they were important landmarks. Some even failed to identify the sites when I showed them the photos. None of them could explain the linkage of the sites to the Silk Road and suggested me to ask historians instead. Locals were aware of the nomination, but they did not seem to have any personal attachments to it.

To many, the idea of the Silk Road seemed exotic and adventurous. 'If you want to experience the Silk Road, you have to visit Silk Road Street in the Tang West Market', noted Ms. Zhang, a religious studies student. The Tang West Market opened the Silk Road Museum in 2010 and Silk Road Street in 2013.[51] Silk Road Street is divided into three parts: South and East Asia, Central Asia, and Europe. The street is consisted of restaurants that serve foreign cuisines and shops selling products representing the afore-mentioned regions, occasionally with salespersons dressing in different ethnic and national costumes. It is decorated by full-size reconstructions of historical landmarks of different countries (see Plate 5). Apart from the

---

[51] The museum's opening was even announced in economic and industrial fora. See Guo, T. 'Quanguo shoujia yizhilei minbang datang xishi bowuguan jijiang kaiguan' (First private historical remains museum in China opened in Xi'an at the Tang West Market). *China Economy Net*, 9 March 2010. Available online, http://district.ce.cn/zg/201003/09/t20100309_21085216.shtml. Last accessed 1 May 2016.

commercial Silk Road Street offering foreign goods and tastes, the Tang West Market regularly organizes multi-cultural events – such as a German Oktoberfest, intangible cultural heritage festival and world food festival – to boost the market's international image and to underscore its connection to the Silk Road. Instead of the nominated heritage sites, it was the theme-park-like Silk Road Street that first came to the mind of many informants when I asked them about the Silk Road.

Plate 5. Salespersons dressed in Korean costumes in front of a reconstructed building in Silk Road Street.

Other sites that locals associate with the Silk Road include Famen Temple, Big Wild Goose Pagoda, Daming Palace, and Green Dragon Temple. Mr. Cai said: 'even though Famen Temple looks horrible now with its new modern building, its religious and historical values are undeniable'. He thought that no matter how commercialized the temple had become, the national treasure stored in the underground palace could not be belittled. Many of my informants assumed that Famen Temple would be successfully inscribed and were disappointed to hear that it could not sustain its place on the Tentative List. Interestingly, locals regard Green Dragon Temple as the site that can fully convey the meaning of the Silk Road. The temple, built in the Sui Dynasty in 622 CE, represents the connection to Japan in the Tang Dynasty because Kukai (posthumously known as Kobo-Daishi) came to the temple to learn about Buddhism and then took the religion back to Japan. Mr. Zhao, who was a tour guide before his retirement, said that every time he had guests visiting Xi'an, he showed them the terracotta army and Green Dragon Temple. He also reminded me that I should not miss the chance to visit the Japanese garden attached to the temple in spring when the sakura trees blossom. Many other informants shared the same view as Mr. Zhao and confirmed the temple's contribution to the cultural exchange of the Silk Road.

Plate 6. Reconstructed building in Silk Road Street.

However, besides their associations with these sites, what else did the residents think about the Silk Road? How did they interpret the term Silk Road? This part explores the meaning of the Silk Road to Xi'an's inhabitants. Some of these meanings resemble those of the national Silk Road discourse. When Xi'an people imagined the Silk Road, they narrated the flourishing moment of Tang Chang'an. In their mind-set, the Silk Road represented an extension of the city's imperial discourse. They believed that the Tang Empire brought the cultural route to its peak. Locals did not mention how the Silk Road promoted intercultural exchange, but romanticized the greatness and openness of Tang Chang'an, which attracted foreigners from all over the world and was tolerant in allowing them to stay. In this sense, locals' perception of the Silk Road aligns with the government's narrative.

But not all aspects of local imaginings align with the national discourse. For example, the national discourse as embodied in Zhang Qian's story, imagines the Silk Road as always going westwards into Central Asia. Yet I found out that when Xi'an locals imagine the influence of the Silk Road, they look eastwards. They emphasize Chang'an's influence on eastern neighbours, Japan and Korea, in various ways. It is for this reason that they see Green Dragon Temple as a 'Silk Road site'. Many informants mentioned that ancient cities in Japan, such as Nara and Kyoto, copied the layout of Tang Chang'an, and stressed the striking similarity between the Xi'an dialect and Japanese. Locals told me that because their dialect was the official language of the Tang Dynasty, some language elements were exported to Japan during that time. They named a few words that sound similar such as *qiao er* (Xi. birds) and *chô-rui* (Jap.)[52], and *mada* (Xi. problem) and *mondai* (Jap.), as well as the common practice of adding *desi* at the end of sentences to indicate 'is that right?'. This, they claimed, was the equivalent of the Japanese *desu* (see also Hu and Wang 2010: 155). Moreover, informants never mentioned the influence of the Silk Road on any countries in Central Asia. Mr. Zhang, a restorer, emphasized how Japanese and Korean ambassadors came to the Tang Dynasty to show respect to the Chinese emperor. He complained that the world had since turned around, and that the Korean government no longer respects China; South Korea, he said, even felt insulted when China sent the Deputy Minister of Defence to visit. He said: 'in the Tang Dynasty, that would be impossible. Korea would have been so honoured if any [even] low-ranked Chinese official visited their country!' Other informants expressed puzzlement that South Korea and especially Japan had become so much more developed than China when their culture had originated from Xi'an.

Yet for the perceived importance of eastward cultural influences, locals considered the economic aspects of the Silk Road to overrule its cultural and historical importance, both past and present. They thought the Silk Road was primarily a trade route, rather than a cultural bridge. For example, Mr. Li, a guard at Small Wild Goose Pagoda, introduced the pagoda to me proudly as a Silk Roads World Heritage candidate. However, when I asked him for the historical connection, he said: 'good question, the

---

[52] There is a slight difference in meaning; the Japanese *chô-rui* refers to birds as a technical biological order.

Silk Road was only for trade. I have no idea why they put it into the list'. The president of the Shaanxi Provincial Chamber of Commerce, Ms. Ji, also remarked that 'traders were the main characters of the Silk Road'. Such a focus on trade and traders misshapes the Silk Road into a purely economic route. At the same time, traded can be marshalled to explain why Xi'an locals look eastwards when assessing the route's importance. After all, Japan and Korea are richer than the Central Asian countries. During a dinner gathering, Ms. Dou, a professor of economics, openly commented that she did not understand why the government had nominated the Silk Roads as *cultural* heritage. She opined that the nomination was solely an aspect of economic strategy. Mr. Li, a professor of cultural studies, agreed. He argued that China was using the World Heritage nomination as a chance to co-operate with the Central Asian countries and that under the guise of cultural cooperation the countries had already signed contracts on the building of factories and the manufacture of clothing. He joked that the Silk Road should be called the Cotton Road because of the contemporary importance of the clothing industry.

After the successful inscription of the Silk Roads on the World Heritage List in June 2014, Xi'an did not organize any grand celebrations. The Shaanxi provincial government hanged a red banner on the Bell Tower for a month to announce the news, and Daming Palace (the only site to do so) organized an event, a 'Silk Road treasure hunt', to educate the public about the new status. There was plenty of dissemination of the news: in the newspapers, on television, and in public transportation, but no one was excited about the success, not even government officials. I argue that this lack of excitement was because the imperial Chinese discourse still dominates the people's mind-set. The Silk Road, as a story of trans-boundary relations, is only a supplement to the dominant historical imagination. It too is taken to show, primarily, the imperial power of the Han and Tang dynasties. As for the specific qualities of the Silk Road as a trade route, locals had only limited knowledge about its historical importance or cultural significance. Thus, though the World Heritage listing was celebrated by national and provincial administrative bodies, there was little attention given at the local level to this national 'victory'.

From the Ancient Silk Road to the Modern Silk Road Economic Belt

As several informants suspected, the Chinese government did look to revitalizing the Silk Road as a trade route for its national economic development plan. Xi Jinping, President of China, coined the term 'Silk

Road Economic Belt' (*sichouzhilu jingjidai*) during his visit to Kazakhstan in September 2013. He proclaimed that building up the Silk Road Economic Belt is a joint mission for Eurasia. The Silk Road Economic Belt would intensify cooperation between the different Eurasian countries and promote economic development. He suggested achieving this goal through policy making, strengthening the transport network, and enhancing trade and exchange between the countries. Only half a month after he made that statement, thirteen cities from eight countries (including China, Italy, Belarus, and Kazakhstan) gathered in Xi'an to declare their commitment to joining this economic belt. The Shaanxi provincial and Xi'an municipal governments viewed the proposal of the Silk Road Economic Belt as a golden opportunity to come under the spotlight of China, or even the world. Consequently, the term was excessively utilized in the mass media, development plans, and government slogans. So too came the term *yidaiyilu* (land and sea Silk Roads).

Thus, even as the World Heritage nomination was under review, many 'new Silk Road'-related events, conferences, and talks took place in Xi'an. The Xi'an government set short- and long-term plans to accomplish the goals of the economic belt, including strengthening communication with the national level, intensifying logistics facilities, improving networks with Central Asia, encouraging more businessmen to invest in Central Asia, organizing training programs for Central Asians, and popularizing the idea of the economic belt. The plans aimed at using the economic belt as an opportunity to transform Xi'an into a national Free Trade Zone, like Shanghai, to promote more open trade and transportation. However, none of these plans set up by the government mentioned any cultural aspects of the Silk Road. Different districts in Xi'an made the corresponding plans. Specifically, Gaoxin District proposed to establish a 'Silk Road sample area' (*sichouzhilu chuanxin shifanqu*); Jingkai District intensified the industrial development for larger scale productions; and Qujiang District planned to make use of its cultural resources to create a 'Silk Road cultural highland' (*sichouzhilu wenhua gaoyuan*) with a high concentration of museums, heritage parks, and hotels. The ancient notion of the Silk Road that associated economic, social, and cultural exchange was transformed into plans for 'purely' economic cooperation and tourism projects between China and Central Asia. Xi'an aimed to use the Silk Road as a new platform for international cooperation, which would then turn the ancient capital into a modern cosmopolitan city.

In terms of heritage development, historical site administrations, and heritage developers in Xi'an took this chance to develop tourism and to promote the Silk Road in all directions. In these projects, there was some vision of cultural exchange to be facilitated through the integration of culture, tourism, and trade. The Tang West Market Cultural Corporation, for example, foresaw the potential of the Silk Road in 2008 and began to plan secretly the Four Silk Projects of Silk Net, Silk Embassy, Silk Expo, and Silk Street.[53] Silk Street, described above, was opened to the public in September 2013. The other projects are still in development: Silk Net envisions a series of online platforms to promote trade and cultural exchange. The Silk Embassy will finance the opening of Silk Road museums in 40 countries along the Silk Road. The Silk Expo, inspired by World Expositions, will organize regular international trade fairs. In mid-March 2014, the corporation added the Silk School as a fifth project which would support and fund research on the connections between the ancient and modern Silk Roads with the publication of books and regular scholar exchange programs along the Silk Road.

Still, the major focus remains on an attempt to draw a vision of historical continuity and developmental evolution in the parallel ancient and new roads. For example, the Silk Road Museum located in Han City River Park opened in summer 2014 has a permanent exhibition which divides the Silk Road into two phases (see Plate 7). The first phase, the ancient Silk Road, showcases a huge model of a desert with camels in a brown dusty tone. The second phase, the Silk Road Economic Belt, features colourful neon lights and elements, giving the impression of high technology and advancement. The contrast shown through the museum exhibition reflects exactly the ambition of the government to turn the ancient Silk Road not only into a tourism attraction, but to 'revitalize' it into a modern technological economic route.

---

[53] 'Gongjian sichouzhilu jingjidai "sisi" yantaohui zhaokai' (The Silk Road Economic Belt Conference has started). *Shaanxi Daily*, 28 February 2014. Available online, http://www.sxdaily.com.cn/n/2014/0228/c266-5369848.html. Last accessed, 16 December 2014.

Plate 7. Model in the Silk Road Museum displaying the ancient Silk Road and the Silk Road economic belt.

A Chinese official once leaked the following statement during a conversation: 'the Silk Roads heritage nomination is only the harbinger for the Silk Road economic development'. It revealed China's intention of developing the Silk Road for economic reasons. As addressed by James Millward, 'the Silk Road idea resonated positively with developments in the post-Deng, post-Soviet era of openness and economic reforms, and especially the region's renewed communications with Central Asia and increased autonomy from Beijing in dealing with foreign tourists, governments, NGOs, trade partners and investors' (2009: 65). Although China submitted the Tentative List of the Silk Road for the Chinese section in 1997, it seems that it may have waited patiently for the other countries because it saw potential economic benefit from cultural cooperation with Central Asia. Certainly outside observers have pointed to a number of international and internal developments that would have made westward development desirable for China. For example, the United States' policy Pivot to Asia has seen the US work closely with Japan, Taiwan, South Korea, the Philippines, Australia, and India since 2010. Strong American relationships with these countries, it is said, have encouraged China to look to its western neighbours for partnerships. And, as economic growth remains key to Chinese national security, orientations like those of the Silk Road Economic Belt are important because they promote China's global economic development. By establishing good relationships with Central Asian countries, proclaiming cultural similarities, and engaging in economic co-operation, China might offset, or at least balance, the relations those countries forge with Russia and to build up China's own 'Asian' partners against those cultivated by the US in East and South East Asia.[54]

During the operation of the ancient Silk Road, Chinese silk manu-facturers and traders kept secret their technology for over 1,000 years. So well-kept was this knowledge that Pliny the Elder, a Roman scholar, wrote in his encyclopaedia on the natural history of China that silk grew on trees: the Chinese, he wrote, 'combed off leaves their delicate down' (Tucker 2015: 202). China's contemporary commitment to 'silk roads' belies a similar determination to pursue self-interest (and self-aggrandizement), regardless of rhetorical gestures towards international cooperation or cultural exchange. On the surface, it would seem that China supports UNESCO's doctrines of promoting cultural diversity and maintaining respect and mutual understanding by cooperating with Kazakhstan and Kyrgyzstan in its serial nomination of the Silk Road as World Heritage. In fact, China's nominations, discourse, and development of heritage sites more clearly aggrandizes national history while belittling other countries, including its 'partners'. Nor is there much room for alternative visions of the Silk Road to appear within China. After a talk I gave at a language centre in Xi'an about the heritage politics of China, for example, a man in his early thirties raised his hand and asked me if the Central Asian countries are very poor, and specifically, if India has highways. His question mirrored the poor understanding that ordinary people have about Central Asia, and indeed, other countries generally. As I considered his question, the man clarified that he was asking me this because the state and the media conveyed such an impression of thoroughly uneven development between China and its neighbours. This image is found in and through heritage sites too: Central Asian countries are depicted as under-developed and backwards, while China always appears as strong and civilized. By listing 'the most' heritage sites, China furthers the image that it has long provided development aids and brought civilization to Central Asia. In all phases of China's 'proactive'

---

[54] Speculation about China's geo-political strategies is widespread in Western media. This presentation summarizes those made by Lo C., 'The Economics and Politics of China's New Silk Road'. *South China Morning Post*, 30 June 2015. Available online, http://www.scmp.com/comment/insight-opinion/article/1829384/economics-and-politics-chinas-new-silk-road. Last accessed 1 May 2016.

involvement in the World Heritage nomination process, it has consolidated a Sino-centric story of the Silk Road and reaffirmed its leading role in international affairs, past and present.

Chapter 6
The City of Copies – Modelized Heritage

In June 2012, the God of Fortune Temple in Xi'an was successfully listed on the stock market, meaning that everyone could buy and sell shares of the temple. However, this act offended the believers as well as the national government. Two weeks before the listing, the State Administration of Religious Affairs warned the company from continuing with the bid. It maintained that all religious venues in China have to minimize commercialized activities, and therefore, selling the venue on the stock market would be unacceptable.[55] This was not the first temple to make such an attempt. Two other temples in China had previously tried to be listed on the stock market – Shaolin Temple which was inscribed on the UNESCO World Heritage List in 2010 with the serial entry of the 'Historic Monuments of Dengfeng' (UNESCO 2010), and Famen Temple. Both temples had failed because of the strong opposition from the State Administration of Religious Affairs. The God of Fortune Temple was not so easily deterred, and it succeeded using another 'doggie-bag strategy' (*dabao shangshi*). According to local economists (Zhao 2011; Chen 2012), the temple succeeded by not listing itself directly, but under the name of a company called Xi'an Qujiang Cultural Tourism Co., Ltd. This company included stocks from not only the temple, but also other historical sites, such as Xi'an City Wall, Daming Palace, and Big Wild Goose Pagoda (Chen 2012). Moreover, in order to prevent the national government from intervening on account of the commercialization of religious venues, the company changed the temple's name (and status). Within the company's records, it was officially no longer the God of Fortune Temple but the Birthplace of God of Fortune Cultural Scenic Area.[56] Two weeks before the

---

[55] Caisheng miao yu jie ke shangshi zhu weiguan ST changxing zhongzhu huo shouzhu (The plan of selling the God of Fortune Temple on the stock market has been questioned). *Tencent Finance*, 14 June 2012. Available online, http://finance.qq.com/a/20120614/002045.htm. Last accessed 1 May 2016.

[56] 'Caisheng miao yu'.

listing on the stock market, the company removed all god statues and ritual objects from the premises of the 'scenic area', and cancelled all 'temple' events, so as to further distance its relationship with religion. This incident shows the rising power of heritage developers and companies in Xi'an. They increasingly risk confronting the central government in order to commercialize and even privatize heritage sites for greater economic benefits.

    Among the general public, some people criticized attempts to list historical sites on the stock market as encouraging an undesirable privatization and monopolization of the sites. Nevertheless, the city government celebrated the 2012 success of the Xi'an Qujiang Cultural Tourism Co., Ltd., and regarded it as a milestone of heritage development in Xi'an. The listing had been planned carefully for seven years by Xi'an Qujiang Cultural Industry Investment (Group) Co. – the same Qujiang Corporation mentioned in previous chapters.[57] In fact, this event was only a small part of Qujiang Corporation's activities in Xi'an. Since the 1990s, the company's influence had made the term 'Qujiang' synonymous with heritage projects and urban transformation. The company changed the cityscape and the attitude of people towards cultural heritage through its Qujiang Model (Qujiang moshi) of heritage site management and development that aimed to increase the city's economic growth through combining tourism industry and real estate market development. In the name of cultural and heritage development, the final goal of the model was to maximize the profit made from the heritage sites.[58] Because of the potential economic gain, the Xi'an city government, Shaanxi provincial government, and other nearby city and provincial governments all thought highly of the model and invested billions of CNY to make it happen.[59] According to my informants, Nanjing and some cities in Yunnan and Hunan provinces have applied the model to their sites too. The Qujiang Model became a representation of modern Xi'an and elevated Xi'an's position from a poor and backward city to a metropolis with rich cultural resources and economic potential.

---

[57] 'Caishengmiao A gu shangshi beihou: Xi'an Qujiang 7 nian zhiqian yi kaishi muhua letan' (Behind the scenes of the God of Fortune Temple: Qujiang has planned the stock market action for seven years). *Tencent Finance*, 11 June 2012. Available online, http://finance.qq.com/a/20120611/006998.htm. Last accessed 1 May 2016.

[58] This orientation towards profit was made clear in online presentations such as, 'General Description of Qujiang New District'. http://www.qujiang.com.cn/zjqj/xqgl.htm. Last accessed 15 June 2015.

[59] The corporation embraced this image with its presentation of 2010 achievements on its website. http://www.qujiang.com.cn/English/nr.jsp?urltype=news.NewsContentUrl& wbnewsid=4792&wbtreeid=1150. Last accessed 15 June 2015.

Due to the success of the first heritage project in Qujiang District in Xi'an, Qujiang Corporation established a model of heritage park designs and management system and duplicated it at a rapid pace between 2009 and 2013 at various sites. The idea of applying a model on heritage sites might be new, but similar urban development practices have been observed by Aihwa Ong (2011), which she described as 'modeling city'. She explained that 'a number of Asian cities have come to stand as replicable models of urban futurity (…) and have become centers to be invoked, envied, and emulated as exemplary sites of a new urban normativity' (ibid.: 4). She pointed out that Singapore, Hong Kong, and Shanghai have been the standard model cities being copied by other developing Asian cities. The other cities import urban projects and innovations, such as industrial estates, upscale residential enclaves, and even water resource management systems. Although 'modeling city' is conceptualized as a global technology (Ong and Collier 2005), Ong argued that urban modeling is not only a technology for building garden cities or knowledge hubs elsewhere but can also become a political tool for changing the built form and social environment (Ong and Roy 2011). In the case of Xi'an, the modeling process did not take place in terms of the city but on the smaller scale of the area around heritage sites.

Different from the three kinds of heritage mentioned in the previous chapters (archaeological, imperial, and Silk Road heritage), modelized heritage demonstrates the function of heritage as a revenue generator to push the economic value of the heritage sites to the limit. This chapter illuminates the expansion of the heritage model in Xi'an and discusses its political-economic role. How did Qujiang Corporation come to power? What are the features of the sites under the Qujiang Model? How do different social actors perceive the effects brought by the model? And, how do the different associations of Qujiang – as district, company, and heritage development model – come together? The first part of this chapter introduces the back-ground and the rise of Qujiang Corporation. The second part analyses the expansion of the model and looks into particular sites managed by Qujiang Corporation, others inspired by the Qujiang Model, and some that are definitively anti-Qujiang in their conception. Lastly, the third part looks at how different social actors react to the model and how it influenced Xi'an natives' attitudes towards heritage and their living environment.

The Rise of Qujiang

In the Tang Dynasty, the summer palace and imperial garden were located in the area of today's Qujiang District. By the 1960s, the Xi'an city government had classified the area as a rural district (Fayolle Lussac, Høyem and Clément 2007). Qujiang District Administrative Committee began to draft development and heritage projects in the 1990s, but the district, located 6.5 kilometres south-east of the city's centre, retained its rural status until 2002. In April 1998, with the approval of the Xi'an city government, Qujiang District Administrative Committee founded the state-owned Xi'an Qujiang Cultural Industry Investment (Group) Co., Ltd.[60] The corporation devoted itself intensively to the district's cultural industry and heritage development and made vital changes in both. The district transformed from a rural area composed mostly of farmlands to a major heritage attraction, cultural destination, tourist zone and the most-desired residential area of Xi'an. The corporation and the district administrative committee walled and renewed historical sites and archaeological remains, erected neo-Tang-style buildings to create new tourist attractions, and constructed cultural facilities including cinemas, art galleries, concert halls, theatres, museums, and an international convention centre.[61]

The corporation is a wholly state-owned enterprise, meaning that the only stockholder is the government and that it undertakes commercial activities and earns profits on behalf of the government. Qujiang's stock is held by (the so re-named) Qujiang New District Administrative Committee and the Xi'an city government. The managing director and the five members of the directorate are appointed by the Xi'an city government (China Info 2016: 52). Due to the close relationship with the government, the corporation enjoyed a lot of advantages and could easily gain control over land use and heritage management. As a consequence, the size of the corporation expanded rapidly. In the 2000s, it started to establish subsidiary companies. By 2016, the corporation had ten subsidiaries, including the Xi'an Qujiang Cultural Tourism Co., Ltd. and the Xi'an Qujiang Lintong Tourism Investment Co., Ltd. The former one is in charge of tourism and heritage development and founded a further ten subsidiaries. Plate 8 shows the structure and interrelations between the core company and its subsidiaries. The bold letters indicate companies directly related to heritage projects and management. To give some sense of its size at the time of my fieldwork: as of 30 June 2015, the corporation (all the companies listed in Plate 8) had in total 8,769 employees (China Info 2016: 49).

[60] An article penned in 2010 documented the company's early history on its website. 'Qujiang wenhua lvyou jituan jianjie' (Brief introduction of Qujiang Culture and Tourism Corporation). http://www.qjculture.com/cyqj/ShowArticle.asp?ArticleID=60. Last accessed 29 September 2016.
[61] Progress was reported, and discussed, nationally. See Chang, X. M., 'Shaanxi Qujiang wenhua kaifa moshi: qujing tong "xiu" haishi tong "xiu"' (The cultural development model of Qujiang in Shaanxi Province: Would it bring us benefits or worries?). *People Daily*, 3 September 2010. Available online, http://cpc.people.com.cn/GB/64093/82429/83083/12623567.html. Last accessed 1 May 2016.

The CEO of Qujiang Corporation, Duan Xiannian, once said: 'since Xi'an is located neither at the border nor along the sea, it has to rely on culture' (Duan 2011: 78). Accordingly, Qujiang uses 'culture' as a catch-phrase to carry out its developmental projects and to transform Xi'an into an international hub. The Qujiang concept of culture is a fairly broad one (Jaivin 2010), appearing with an over-emphasis in advertisements for projects spanning cultural heritage, cultural resources, cultural branding, cultural industry, and cultural production.[62] Taken together, such advertise-ments make it clear that the corporation aims to commercialize 'culture' and to translate 'culture' into business. Nor does it perceive a separation between the kinds of business it undertakes, but stresses, for example, that the development of cultural industry involves all forms of business activities involving the cultural aspects of the city, including heritage management, tourism, events organization, and creative industries. Qujiang District was even designated in August 2007 as a National Cultural Industry Sample Area (guojiaji wenhua chanye shifan yuanqu) by the central government, and the corporation received a large amount of financial support to promote cultural industry development in the district.[63] For example, it created a Centre Cultural Business District (CCBD) in an area of 176 hectares in September 2012 which it described as a place where 'the city and the environment, business and culture, tradition and innovation' interweave to create a 'modern city image'.[64] In September 2013, twenty large-scale construction projects were carried out in the CCBD with themes such as modern tourism economy, urban commercial culture, international convention industry, and international events organization.[65]

---

[62] 'General Description of Qujiang New District'.

[63] Details again appeared in the press: 'Shaanxi shengzhang tan wenhua chanye fazhan kending Qujiang chanyeyuan moshi' (The governor of Shaanxi province talks about the development of cultural industria and confirms the Qujiang model). *Shaanxi Daily*, 8 August 2013; 'Quanguo wenhua yichan chuanyi chanye peixunban Xi'an kaiban' (National Cultural Heritage Creative Workshop starts in Xi'an). *Shaanxi Daily*, 30 October 2013. Available online, http://xian.qq.com/a/20130808/013445.htm; and http://www.sxdaily.com.cn/n/2013/1030/c266-5259015.html. Last accessed 1 May 2016.

[64] 'Xi'an Center Culture Business District'. http://www.bdp.com/en/projects/p-z/xian-centre-culture-business-district-ccbd/. Last accessed 15 June 2015.

[65] See Timeline of 2013. http://www.qujiang.com.cn/info/1347/6060.htm. Last accessed 15 June 2015.

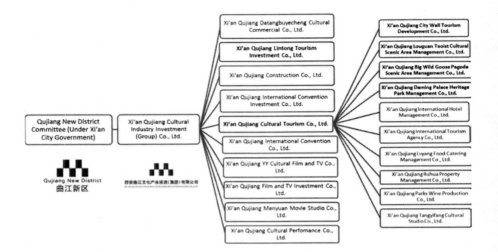

Plate 8. Structure of Qujiang Corporation.

The year 2002 can be considered a watershed for Qujiang District because it saw the opening of the biggest musical water fountain in Asia at the northern square of Big Wild Goose Pagoda.[66] From that point on, the corporation launched a series of large-scale plans to develop all the heritage sites located in the district. Tourism was enhanced demonstratively. The number of visitors to Qujiang District increased drastically from 1.2 million in 2002 to 51.46 million people in 2013 (Xi'an City Tourism Board 2013a). Land prices rose alongside the opening of heritage parks and popularized tourist destinations. The corporation and the government profited. Statistics show that the price of land in Qujiang District skyrocketed from 300,000–500,000 CNY per Chinese acre[67] before Qujiang's development to 3,000,000–6,000,000 per acre in just three years' time (Chang 2010). The Xi'an city government increased the area of Qujiang District from 20.57 square kilometres to 40.97 square kilometres, so as to enable more real estate and heritage development (Sina Stock Finance 2011: 15). The district's transformation from a quiet rural region to a popular district for tourists, and then even a high-class residential area, is what is certainly praised under the phrase 'Qujiang Model'.

---

[66] The organization tracked its own history with informational summaries and timelines. See Timeline of 2002. http://www.qujiang.com.cn/info/1347/5924.htm. Last accessed 15 June 2015.

[67] One Chinese acre equals approximately 666.67 square metres.

The heritage development plan of Big Wild Goose Pagoda and its surrounding area is regarded as the blueprint of the Qujiang Model. The model uses one or more historical sites as the centre of development to generate economic gain through intensified tourism and ultimately to bolster the surrounding real estate market. In short, the Qujiang Model relies on a three-zone concept, which could be described as consisting of a 'core zone', a 'buffer zone', and a 'high-rise zone'. If the first two zones are reminiscent of the 'core' and 'buffer' zones indicated by UNESCO's idea of 'heritage property', the third zone of the Qujiang Model visually distinguishes heritage development projects in Xi'an. But the Quijiang Model is also intentionally commercial: the 'core zone' of the heritage site is meant to attract visitors, while the buffer zone is replete with shopping malls, hotels, and restaurants to further boost traffic (and spending) in the area. The attempt to generate higher levels of spending continues into the high-rise zone, where residential buildings for the middle and upper classes replace former lower-class living areas. Plate 9 shows a photo from a bird's-eye view over Qujiang District, in which the concentric three-zone model becomes clearly visible.

Based on the blueprint of projects undertaken in Qujiang District, Qujiang Corporation has applied its model to many other heritage sites in Xi'an, Shaanxi, and other cities across China, contributing to the emergence of modelized heritage. The modelized heritage sites follow the same design and principal as the Big Wild Goose Pagoda development plan. Many researchers have studied the impact of commercialization and tourism development on heritage sites and nearby communities (Teo and Yeoh 1997; Terkenli 2002; Gotham 2005; Lyon and Wells 2012; Zhu and Li 2013), but few reported cases seem to have nearly the extensive effects as those under the Qujiang Model. This model is exceptional in terms of its power and influence beyond local communities to affect whole cityscapes. Certainly it has been described as China's 'most ambitious hyper-heritage develop-ment'.[68] The next part will illustrate how in copying its own model, the Qujiang corporation expanded its control over Shaanxi Province.

---

[68] Editorial comment preceding the online publication of Jaivin (2010). Available online, http://www.chinaheritagequarterly.org/articles.php?searchterm=024_qujiang.inc&issue=024. Last accessed 1 May 2016.

Plate 9. Bird's-eye view over Qujiang District (the 'blueprint' of the Qujiang Model) from the Qujiang sightseeing hot air balloon.

'Xi'an City, Qujiang Province'

Mr. Zhong, a professor from Xi'an North West University, described the impact of Qujiang Corporation as a 'Qujiang storm' (*Qujiang fengbu*) that commercialized every possible historical site and commodified every cultural element as it swept across the landscape. He blamed the model for destroying the authenticity of heritage sites and the diverse cultural background of Xi'an because it had replaced the original sites with reconstructions (see also Chang 2010). Other locals too used the metaphor 'Qujiang storm' to describe how Qujiang Corporation turned many historical places into seemingly homogenous Tang-themed parks. When Mr. Zhu, a restorer in his early forties, talked about the influence of Qujiang on the city, he could not help but comment: 'Xi'an city no longer belongs to Shaanxi Province, but [to] Qujiang Province'. The power of Qujiang Corporation went far beyond the district and historical sites. Among the 125 square kilometres of land under its management, 64 per cent is located outside Qujiang District (Zhang 2014). The corporation planned to execute major heritage and urban transformation projects, such as the erection of a 'meta-wall' around the ancient city wall (Feighery 2008), the 'restoration' of

Daming Palace into a heritage park, and the creation of a holiday resort near the Mausoleum of the First Qin Emperor in Lintong District.[69]

   After 2003, the city government continued to favour the Qujiang Model and allowed the corporation to conduct numerous projects. Map 5 shows the expansion of the Qujiang Model from the initial light dot marking Big Wild Goose Pagoda to all the dark dots. Between 2005 and 2010, the corporation applied its model to seven other attractions in Qujiang District, namely Tang City Wall Remains Archaeological Park, Tang Paradise, Qujiang Lake Archaeological Park, Love Cave Archaeological Park, and Mausoleum of the Second Qin Emperor Archaeological Park. In the 'buffer zone' of all these sites, the company built neo-Tang-style buildings to house shopping malls, bar streets, and other commercial areas. In just ten years, Qujiang District became one of the most visited areas in Xi'an, and drew even more visitors than the terracotta army (Xi'an City Tourism Board 2013b). The corporation's own outlay was astounding, amounting to the investment of billions of CNY in each site. The first phase of the Famen Temple project cost 3.2 billion CNY, Tang Paradise 1.4 billion, and the construction of Daming Palace Heritage Park 12 billion (Zhang 2014).

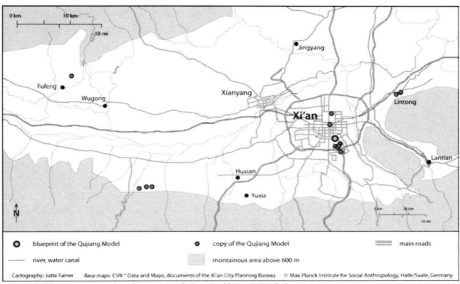

Map 5. The sphere of influence of the Qujiang Model.

---

[69] 'Shaanxi Qujiang wenhua kaifa moshi'.

The relations between government and company grew ever tighter. Duan Xiannian[70], the CEO of the corporation, served also as deputy city mayor. In 2013, he announced proudly (in his first role) that the city government had decided to let the company operate all the important heritage development plans within Xi'an.[71] Thereafter, other historical sites such as Daming Palace, City Wall, Louguan Tai Temple, and Famen Temple came under the corporation's control to become modelized Qujiang sites.

Not all site management is the same. In practice, Qujiang Corporation outsources the management of sites under its control to Xi'an Qujiang Cultural Tourism Co., Ltd., and in many cases a new private company is established for each Qujiang site. For example, Xi'an Qujiang Lintong Tourism Investment Co., Ltd. is in charge of developing the Lintong holiday resort and heritage project, while Xi'an Qujiang City Wall Tourism Development Co., Ltd. is responsible for the management of the city wall.

Still, the similarities are overwhelming. The corporation (through its subsidiaries) turned most of Qujiang sites into 'cultural scenic areas' (*wenhua jingqu*) because this designation enabled the acquisition and use of space for commercial activities. The cultural scenic areas are much larger than the original historical sites (by a factor of about 20 in Xi'an), and they are no longer bounded by national and regional laws and regulations concerning preservation. Those regulations apply only to the heritage property within the cultural scenic area, while the developer is given wide latitude to boost commercialization in the rest of the area. The company should not destroy the cultural landscape or violate some rules, like building height, but otherwise the government levies few restrictions. Qujiang Corporation has

---

[70] I observed that people never used Duan's full name in any conversations. When I embarked on my fieldwork in August 2013, locals would rather use terms such as 'one of the deputy mayors', 'the big boss', 'a highly ranked official', and even 'you-know-who' to describe him. Once, when I voiced his name in a question to an informant in Qujiang District, the man suddenly became very uncomfortable, looked around, and whispered quietly: 'You never know when and where he is in Xi'an, or whether his supporters are around. So, you should never say his name so openly, especially here in Qujiang District, directly within his boundaries'. After this encounter, I could not help but think of Duan as Lord Voldemort, the villain of the Harry Potter novel series, who is also referred to as 'you-know-who'. In the novels, people avoided saying his name because they feared his dark power. Only after the fall of Qujiang did people dare to utter Duan's name, but then in the formula 'Boss Duan' (Duan *laoban*). The hesitation to talk about Duan in public hints at the tremendous power that he was believed to have over everyday life and the changing city. But unlike Voldemort, there was no consensus about whether Duan's power was for good or bad, either before or after his fall. Below, I review his achievements.

[71] 'Guanshang heti de zhengzhi jingji luoji' (The political economic logic of the Guanshang unification). *Nandu Daily*, 21 April 2013. Available online, http://www.nandu.com/nis/201304/21/41604.html?bsh_bid=221582004. Last accessed 1 May 2016.

profited from this freedom. As the majority of Chinese tourists already prefer the diversity of attractions associated with cultural scenic areas, the corporation uses the new status to increase entrance fees to heritage sites and produce lucrative entertainment and tourism packages.

Yet for the apparent commonalities brought about in site development by the desire to generate tourist revenue, it is possible and important to distinguish between three types of Quijiang site. The first are the modelized Qujiang sites managed, invested in, and planned by Qujiang Corporation or its subsidiaries. Second are Qujiang-inspired sites; these are not related to the corporation, but administered and planned by other developmental agencies in Xi'an which borrowed and modified parts of the Qujiang Model. Third are anti-Qujiang sites which have risked fighting against the Qujiang storm in defence of 'history', 'religion', and 'heritage'. The following selected case studies from the three types will demonstrate the political and economic concerns in the making of heritage as well as the sites' expectations and views of the Qujiang Model.

Modelized Qujiang Sites

Aihwa Ong pointed out that the key to modelized cities is the use of blueprints, plans, or built forms of one standard city (2011: 15). The copies do not have to be faithful duplicates of the original, but they should capture its aspects, styles, or essences. Indeed, beyond the distinctive similarities in how the sites are constructed to enhance tourism and revenue, each site has its own selling point. For example, Famen Temple stresses Buddhist belief, Louguan Tai Temple promotes Taoist culture, and Daming Palace represents the imperial culture of the Tang Dynasty. The Qujiang sites are highly structured and strictly monitored by Qujiang Corporation. A closer look at the sites also reveals nuances in the 'success' of the Quijiang Model.

Famen Temple

Before 2007, Famen Temple was managed by a committee led by the Baoji city government, aiming to promote the temple and put it on the World Heritage List through the Silk Roads nomination. However, due to the lack of financial capital to complete its development plan, some government officials from Shaanxi Province recommended the committee to include Qujiang Corporation in the project in 2007. As described in chapter 5, Qujiang's involvement ushered in a series of major changes: a cultural scenic area was registered, zoning off an area twenty times larger than the original Famen Temple zone (in which the authentic temple complex remains), and more than 50 20-metre-tall golden Buddha statues, gigantic neo-Tang buildings, and a museum were erected within the new scenic area. Besides, the entrance fee of the site rose from 28 CNY to 120 CNY.

The change that most captivated public opinion, however, was the relocation of sacred relics. Qujiang Corporation did not just move the relics, it constructed a contemporary pagoda (in the form of two hands joined in a Buddhist gesture) in which to exhibit the finger-bone. To reach the pagoda, visitors have to walk two kilometres from the main entrance through the cultural scenic area. Or, they can pay 30 CNY one-way to ride a shuttle. Religious experts and the general public were furious. Locals delineated the act as a 'kidnap of the Buddha' (*xie fu nian cai*), clearly perceiving that Qujiang had seized on the sacred relics as a way to introduce new and higher charges for site visitors.

As mentioned too in chapter 5, Famen Temple had public support when it opposed plans to move resident monks out of the temple zone. Yet despite broad support, the monks' protests, and even the engagement of university students who utilized social media in defence of the monks, Quijiang Corporation persisted. The monks lost control over temple adminis-tration. Their number decreased from 260 in 2007 to 70 in 2010.[72] They could not bear the commercial activities overtaking the temple area, and after 2007, they lost their voice in all decision making regarding the development of the temple. From 2007, Qujiang Corporation put donation boxes every five metres and in front of each statue in the cultural scenic area and the temple zone. All the 'donations' (except, after intensive negotiation by the monks, that from the one located in the original temple) went to the pockets of the company. The monks who remained at the temple were hostile toward the corporation, and rarely ventured into the cultural scenic area.

Ms. Qi, a former staff member of the temple, told me that Famen Temple's management level was unorganized and unsystematic. There were, she said, too many stakeholders attempting to administrata the cultural scenic area at the same time: Qujiang Corporation, the national government, Shaanxi Province, Baoji City, the Famen Temple Committee, Fufeng County, Famen Village, the Famen Temple Museum, and the monks. As the other stakeholders did not communicate with each other, Qujiang came to dominate. According to Mr. Tao, an urban planner: 'Famen Temple is the worst example and the biggest failure of Qujiang'. He saw in it a double failure. First, the development and commercialization of the temple into a

---

[72] 'Famensi jituan fouding "shangshi jihua" 50 yi shouru bei zhi bushi' (Famen Temple Corporation denies the "stock market plan": People question about the revenue of 50 million CNY). *Phoenix New Media*, 20 June 2012. http://fo.ifeng.com/news/detail_2012_06/20/15435823_0.shtml. Last accessed, 1 May 2016.

tourist destination had neglected its protection as heritage (and led to its elimination from the Silk Roads World Heritage nomination). Second, it was a failure for the Qujiang Model. Though the corporation invested 3.2 billion CNY to beautify the cultural scenic area during the first phase of development completed in May 2009, it failed to maintain a steady flow of tourists.[73] The number of visitors soared from 400,000 to 1,400,000 in 2008, but then dropped significantly after news of the 'kidnap of the Buddha' circulated. Land price in the surrounding area did not rise. Instead of profit, the Famen Temple project resulted in 15 billion CNY of debt. Qujiang Corporation attempted to introduce a second phase of development, altering its original formula of 'culture + tourism = real estate' (*wenhua + lvyou = fangdichan*).[74] Its new formula was 'culture + religion = real estate for the dead' (*wenhua + zhongjiao = siren de fangdichan*). Instead of creating a residential area around the heritage site, the corporation proposed to develop the area into a cemetery and sell the graves at a high price.[75] This plan was heavily condemned by heritage and religious experts for exploiting religion for economic gain, and because of the high debt from the first developmental efforts, the corporation could not begin the second phase (estimated with a cost of 4.5 billion CNY).[76]

The City Wall

The most recent project that Qujiang Corporation had conducted, as of my fieldwork, was Xi'an City Wall. This case exemplifies how the company achieved its goals by, in part, ignoring governmental and international regulations. The city wall, with its erection dated to 1370–78 (Ming Dynasty), was inscribed in the first cohort of national heritage sites in 1961 (State Administration of Cultural Heritage 2014b). Hence its management has to follow national heritage protection laws, and no changes can be made to its structure without permission from State Administration of Cultural Heritage (National People's Congress of People's Republic of China 1982) (see

---

[73] ibid.

[74] 'Yin Xingjiaosi yishi zhiyi Famensi jingqu wei daibiao de Qujiang moshi' (The incident of Xingjiao Temple make people doubt about Qujiang Model). *Takungpao*, 21 June 2013. Available online, http://bodhi.takungpao.com/topnews/2013-06/1705153.html. Last accessed 1 May 2016.

[75] The plan was widely known. 'Qujiang moshi zai shengnei buduan fuzhi 1500 nian Hancheng gucheng bei chai' (Qujiang Model kept being duplicated within Shaanxi Province, the 1500-year-old city of Han was destroyed). *Daqin Net*, 15 May 2013. Available online, http://xian.qq.com/a/20130515/006922.htm. Last accessed 1 May 2016.

[76] 'Famensi jiyu shangshi muhou xuanji' (The intention of putting Famen Temple on the stock market). *News Business Daily*, 18 June 2012. Available online, http://www.nbd.com.cn/articles/2012-06-18/661477.html. Last accessed 1 May 2016.

chapter 2). The preservation of the city wall is conducted by Shaanxi Provincial Bureau of Cultural Heritage. In 2009, both the Xi'an city government and Shaanxi provincial government ratified the Xi'an City Wall Protection Ordinance to monitor the construction, restoration, and commercial activities in the heritage area.[77] Besides, as a World Heritage candidate listed under 'City Walls of the Ming and Qing Dynasties' in 2008 (UNESCO 2008b), any physical changes of the heritage property have potential consequences on the heritage nomination.

The Xi'an city government granted the right of management to Qujiang Corporation in 2010 and the corporation founded a daughter company named Qujiang Xi'an City Wall Tourism Development Co., Ltd. to promote the site's tourism development, including tourism event organization, souvenirs retail services, and facility construction.[78] It carried out different development projects and made various changes to the heritage property openly and in secret. Publicly, it finished South Gate Park and beautified the areas along the city wall.[79] However, in the same year, newspapers reported that the corporation secretly emptied the core of the northern wall close to the North Gate to build a four-storey structure inside the city wall for the Qujiang City Wall Company's office spaces, canteen, restaurant, and entertainment room.[80] Before that, it was reported that Qujiang City Wall Company made other changes to the physical condition of the wall without informing any national or provincial heritage preservation government units, such as the installation of an elevator inside the wall and the opening of a Starbucks café, which involved the demolition of a corner of the city wall. All these acts violated the regulations made by the city and provincial government and even national laws. Were the destruction to be discovered by international organizations such as ICOMOS, it would almost certainly hinder the World Heritage nomination process for the city wall. Yet none of the government levels punished the company for its acts, underscoring the power of Qujiang and its model in the city.

---

[77] 'Xi'an chengqiang de baohu' (The preservation of the Xi'an city wall). http://www.xacitywall.com/index.php?m=content&c=index&a=show&catid=76&id=147. Last accessed 1 May 2016.

[78] The daughter company was described online under 'Qujiang Xi'an City Wall Tourism Development Limited', http://special.zhaopin.com/xa/2010/qjcq072233/index.htm. Last accessed 1 May 2016.

[79] 'The Opening of the City Wall South Gate Square'. http://www.qujiang.com.cn/info/1052/6309.htm. Last accessed 15 June 2015.

[80] 'Xi'an guchengqiang bei taokong jian bangonglou canting pailianchang yiying juquan' (Part of the Xi'an City Wall was rebuilt in secret into an office building with canteen and entertainment rooms). *China Daily Net*, 9 February. Available online, http://news.qq.com/a/20150209/063070.htm. Last accessed 1 May 2016.

Qujiang-Inspired Sites

Qujiang Corporation only chose to manage sites with high potential revenue, leaving other developers to pursue heritage projects at many other sites. However, these other developers and site administrators were often inspired by the company and copied its model in whole or part. The following two sites – one administered by a city government department and one by a private cultural corporation – demonstrate the indirect influence of the Qujiang Model.

Han Chenghu Cultural Scenic Area

Han Chenghu Cultural Scenic Area, located in the north-western part of Xi'an, was built along the city wall and moat that protected Han Chang'an. Under the supervision of Xi'an City Water Resources Bureau, the park was completed in 2010. The 12.54-square-kilometre park consists of the original city wall, the reconstruction of the city moat, a Han-style pagoda, a giant statue of Emperor Wu, and many sculptures that depict royal life during the Han Dynasty. The park borrowed the layout concept from Daming Palace Heritage Park managed by Qujiang Corporation by building an on-site museum and placing many modern sculptures throughout the park. A museum of Han history is housed in the seven-storey Danfeng Pagoda. Moreover, similar to Big Wild Goose Pagoda, Xi'an City Water Resources Bureau constructed a gigantic musical fountain which performs every evening at the eastern square of the park. Locals appreciated and approved the government's decision of the building of the park. They were glad that the government made use of the wall, tried to display it to tourists, and finally drew attention to Han heritage.

Mr. Huang, an official from Xi'an City Water Resources Bureau in charge of the development of the park, proudly showed me around and told me about his plans for future development. He drove me to the western end, which was not developed yet, and said he planned to build a performance venue for Han music and dance shows. He said he got this idea from Huaqing Palace and Tang Paradise. Since both Huaqing Palace and Tang Paradise are Qujiang sites, I asked him if Qujiang Corporation was involved in the Han Chenghu project. He disclaimed the relationship with Qujiang immediately and emphasized that the bureau belonged to the government and did not aim to make any profit. Then, he criticized Qujiang Corporation for manipulating heritage sites and the environment. Yet, when we climbed to the top of the pagoda, he pointed at the surrounding areas in the south and east and revealed his own bureau's plan to demolish and remove neighbourhoods and villages and to replace them with high-rise buildings. The park was also filled with apartment and real estate advertisements. This park too clearly sought to duplicate the formula 'culture + tourism = real estate'.

Tang West Market

The Tang West Market Cultural Corporation manages and conducts the Tang West Market heritage project. The original Tang-era market was a busy place of exchange for Chang'an and foreign people. Now, archaeological remains of the original market are protected and displayed in an on-site museum, while a 'reconstructed' market stands above ground. The appearance of the market area looks very similar to Qujiang District, but on a smaller scale. Some of the project should be seen as reflecting a desire for accuracy: the Tang West Market Cultural Corporation consulted historians and experts in designing the layout of the market. However, other aspects of the project clearly borrow from the Qujiang Model. The corporation invited Zhang Jinqiu, the same architect who designed Ziyun Palace in Tang Paradise, to design its main neo-Tang-style market building (see chapter 4), and it clearly borrowed the idea of combining tourism and heritage to build up the real estate market. The cultural part of the market consists of a history museum with archaeological remains, an art museum, Silk Road Street, and some antiquity markets. When locals thought of the Tang West Market, they mostly associated it with shopping, cinemas, and good exotic restaurants. Due to the development and convenient geographical location of the Tang West Market, the residential buildings around the site are very popular.

Despite the influences of the Qujiang Model, the Tang West Market developed a very different management style. As a state-owned-enterprise, Qujiang relied heavily on government support to accomplish its projects. In contrast, the private Tang West Market used the power of the local business community.[81] It encouraged locals to invest in the market area by setting up business there. It supported small businesses and gave them a place and opportunity to build a business community. Though Qujiang's financial support came mainly from the trust of national banks and the municipal government (China Info 2016: 87), the Tang West Market relied on businessmen's involvements. Historians even complimented its business model for fidelity to Tang-era practices.

---

[81] The website for the Tang West Market describes its business orientation. http://www.dtxs.cn/index.php?m=content&c=index&a=lists&catid=22. Last accessed 1 May 2016.

Anti-Qujiang Sites

As indicated in the above examples, there were alternatives to the Qujiang Model and the model itself sometimes failed. Especially after the incidences surrounding Famen Temple in 2010, the reputation of the Qujiang Model dropped significantly. The administration at some sites became loathe to accept Qujiang's large-scale approach to development, whether direct or indirect, and the risk it poses to the original sites. Of such anti-Qujiang sites, mostly temples, Xingjiao Temple resisted most furiously.

Xingjiao Temple

Despite the disastrous outcome of the plans to develop Famen Temple, Qujiang pursued the economic potential of other important religious monuments. Xingjiao Temple, the resting place of Xuanzang (see chapter 5), was one site coveted by the company. The temple contains the cultural and historical resources to attract tourists. But – so the monks told me – Xuanzang's final wish was to be buried in Xingjiao Temple away from the city, so that he could enjoy quietness and peace, and because of this wish, Xingjiao Temple had only ever been a very small temple accommodating no more than 15 monks. The temple only had basic facilities and a small well that provided enough water for the limited number of monks. Without getting the temple's agreement, Qujiang Corporation made a secret decision with the Chang'an district and Xi'an city governments to develop the site into a Buddhist cultural scenic area. One morning in April 2012, the monks woke up to find construction workers ready to build walls around the temple. They resisted, and they succeeded.

Qujiang Corporation had planned to transform the temple into a cultural scenic area. Under secret agreement, the area had been rezoned to cover the whole hill on which the temple stands.[82] Villages along the way to the temple were to be cleared and the temple area was to be restructured. The monks were to be relocated outside the temple area. According to the master plan, 4,000 square metres within the temple zone were to be demolished and only 2,000 square metres would remain untouched.[83] The monks were upset.

---

[82] 'Fengyu Xingjiaosi: Qujiang Zhongguoshi shengyi heimu' (The Storm of Xingjiao Temple: Revealing the intension of Qujiang's heritage nomination plan). *Takungpao*, 23 May 2013. Available online, http://bodhi.takungpao.com/topnews/2013-05/1630435.html. Last accessed 1 May 2016.

[83] 'Wenhua zuo dijia shinian zhang shipei Xingjiaosi chaiqian shijian kaowen Qujiang moshi' (Using culture to boost real estate development: the land price rose ten times in ten years with the Qujiang Model). *Xinhua Net*, 16 April 2013. http://news.xinhuanet.com/ fortune/2013-04/16/c_124586182.htm. Last accessed 1 May 2016.

They complained that the Xingjiao Temple plan was an exact copy of the Famen Temple Cultural Scenic Area. The head of the monks told me:

> The biggest fear of our monks is that Xingjiao Temple will become a second Famen Temple surrounded by a heavy commercial atmosphere. Using the excuse of heritage development and the Silk Roads World Heritage nomination, Qujiang Corporation executed its power over us and wanted to force us to follow its business plan. The Qujiang Model is a huge disaster for Buddhist temples.

Xingjiao Temple employed different measures and actions to resist Qujiang's power. In April 2012, when the construction workers blocked the road to the temple, all the monks from the temple came out to stop further construction work. Some of them attempted to push down the wall that had been built. The highest official from Chang'an District as well as Duan Xiannian (in his role as deputy mayor of Xi'an) showed up to inspect the working process. They warned the monks not to disturb the construction work or they would bear the consequences of a failed World Heritage nomination. Duan set a deadline for the construction work to finish, and the new scenic area to open, by late April.[84] Facing the time pressure, the monks asked the public and academics for help. According to local newspapers, there were two kinds of experts, those hired by the government and Qujiang Corporation to make pro-Qujiang and pro-development statements, and the ones who supported the monks.[85] In the end, some professors from the departments of religious studies and history, the Buddhist community, and university students made use of mass and social media to draw public attention to the incident. Additionally, Xingjiao Temple eliminated its 10 CNY entrance fee for 2013 to show their will to fight against commercialization. It offered free incense sticks for worshippers to contrast with the situation at the Qujiang religious sites, where incense sticks cost hundreds of CNY. It even declared in the press that it would withdraw from the Silk Roads World Heritage nomination in order to be free from Qujiang's plan (see chapter 5).[86] Initially, Qujiang Corporation persisted. It continued with its plan until mid-2014, but Xingjiao Temple eventually prevailed, foreshadowing the fall of Qujiang.

These case studies demonstrate the power of Qujiang over heritage and urban developmental projects. Due to the company's close relationship to the city government, it was assigned the most important heritage projects and was empowered to carry out large-scale changes, without considering the consequences on the state of historical buildings and the local com-

---

[84] ibid.

[85] 'Fengyu Xingjiaosi: Qujiang Zhongguoshi shengyi heimu'.

[86] 'Yin Xingjiaosi yishi zhiyi Famensi jingqu wei daibiao de Qujiang moshi'.

munities in or nearby the project areas. The Qujiang Model transformed historical sites to renovated and reconstructed cultural scenic areas. Ignoring national laws and provincial warnings, the corporation continued to modelize and commercialize more sites. Other government departments and developers also used the model as a blueprint. Anti-Qujiang sites had a hard time fighting against the corporation, which allied with the government. The power of Qujiang in Xi'an reflects the significance of the economic aspect of heritage and how it determines the politics of heritage in China.

2014: The Fall of Qujiang

Locals regarded the period between 2008 and 2012 as the Qujiang Era, marking the corporation's impact on Xi'an's contemporary history. The era started when Duan Xiannian, the CEO of the corporation, was appointed as the deputy mayor of Xi'an (Yao 2010). He became very well-known in China for his business model and was frequently invited to share his entrepreneurial experience with newspapers and magazines across the country. In 2009, he was selected China's Person of the Year (Zhonghua wenhua renwu) for his contribution to cultural heritage and economic development.[87] Yet, after 2010, the popularity of Qujiang slowly deteriorated. After the Famen Temple project resulted in huge debts, Qujiang returned all its administrative power back to Baoji city government in June 2013. Then, as the resistance of Xingjiao Temple against the company and its model caught local and national attention, even professors in Beijing criticized Qujiang. People no longer trusted the company and started to doubt the effect of the model. They condemned the model for destroying the 'authenticity' of the sites and the originality of religions. More negative news were publicized and reported. The power of Qujiang finally failed in 2014. Duan was dismissed from his position as the deputy mayor of Xi'an by the Shaanxi provincial government.[88] Locals marked the time thereafter as 'post-Qujiang' to indicate a new page of the city's history.

---

[87] Media coverage by Phoenix television is still available: 'Duanxiannian huode 2009 zhonghua wenhua renwu timing' (Duan Xiannian nominated for 2009 person of the year). http://phtv.ifeng.com/hotspot/2009zhihuidongfang/zuixin/201001/0107_8925_1502051.shtml. Last accessed 28 February 2019.

[88] News of Duan's dismissal was widely available. 'Xi'an fushizhang churen Huaqiaocheng zhongjingli cheng kaichuang Qujiang moshi' (Deputy Mayor of Xi'an become CEO of Huaqiaocheng to further develop Qujiang Model). *Daqin Net*, 21 February 2014. http://xian.qq.com/a/20140221/009407.htm. Last accessed 1 May 2016. Some of Qujiang's fall, however, was also related to changes in national government. When President Xi Jinping came to power in 2013, he carried out massive anti-corruption campaigns, and many government officials were fired. His intents were announced as early as 15 November 2012.

After 2014, Duan moved from Xi'an to the southern city of Shenzhen to work as a project manager for the Huaqiao Cheng real estate project. The power and scale of Qujiang Corporation shrank significantly. Mr. Wu told me that in the past, the government approved all the heritage project proposals submitted by Qujiang Corporation. Many times, the company even started construction work before receiving approval because the right was sure to be granted. However, after the fall of Qujiang, the company's proposals were examined carefully and were mostly rejected. All the on-going projects had to stop and be re-assessed by the city and provincial governments. No government officials dared to support the Qujiang Model because they might end up like Duan – losing their positions and being 'deported' to the south. Qujiang turned from a monopoly of urban and heritage development into an ordinary tourism agency, managing a few hotels and organizing tours for tourists within Xi'an and Shaanxi Province. Even for this business, it was monitored strictly by the municipal and provincial government departments. According to Shaanxi Provincial Tourism Administration, Qujiang Corporation was punished in 2014 for some minor legal violations and even had to pay a fine – neither of which would have happened under Duan's watch.[89] Qujiang lost all its privileges with tourism and heritage development, not to mention its influence over city planning.

I speculate that both internal and external forces resulted in the fall of Qujiang. Internally, the relationship between the corporation and the city government deteriorated. Mr. Yu, an official from Shaanxi Provincial Bureau of Cultural Heritage, told me that Qujiang Corporation conducted heritage projects or made changes to many heritage properties without informing any government departments. For example, it cleared the land and developed a nationally protected Qin mausoleum as a part of the Lintong national holiday resort project without obtaining any permission from the national or provincial governments. These illegal heritage projects offended departments within the city, provincial, and national governments. The relationship between Qujiang Corporation and the city government also worsened due to the corporation's disrespectful attitude towards the government. According to Mr. Hu, a high-level manager of Qujiang, the city government was dissatisfied because the company did not give enough credit

---

See 'China's New Party Chief Xi Jinping's Speech', http://www.bbc.com/news/world-asia-china-20338586. Retrieved 1 May 2016.

[89] 'Guanyu dui Xi'an Qujiang guoji lvxingshe weigui xingwei chufa de tongzhi' (Notice about the punishment of the illegal activities of Qujiang International Travel Agency). Available online, http://www.sxta.gov.cn/proscenium/content/2014-08-06/10218.html. Last accessed 1 May 2016.

to the city government's support and investment. Mr. Hu said that Qujiang rather used the government as a shield when its projects or sites were criticized by the public. Eventually, he said, the city government decided to end its relationship with the company. After Duan's dismissal, it completely cut-off its friendly contacts with the corporation.

Besides the souring relationship with government, the Qujiang sites failed economically. Only the heritage projects carried out within Qujiang District truly succeeded in bringing in crowds of visitors or boosting the real estate market. In fact, most of the Qujiang projects were in huge debt. Qujiang Corporation made use of its connection with the government to get funding and loans from state-owned banks for every project, but as its debt increased, even these banks refused to provide loans. Thus, many projects were left unfinished and sites remained under construction. For instance, during my fieldwork, the staircase to the original temple at Louguan Tai Taoist Cultural Scenic Area was blocked with an 'under construction' sign, and visitors could only visit the newly built temple buildings in the cultural scenic area. Lacking capital, the corporation could not realize its projects and thus lost further credibility.

After the Famen Temple incident, public resentment towards the Qujiang Model also accumulated. Beyond their specific protests over the Famen and Xingjiao temples, the Buddhist community, academics, professionals, and university students organized anti-Qujiang events and spread information about the intention and actions undertaken by Quijiang. Moreover, local communities that were relocated for heritage and other gentrification projects were also unhappy. The projects failed to bring in tourists and raise land prices, so their on-site compensation and new apart-ments were not worth as much as they wanted (see chapter 8). Yet, the company's failure has also produced a sense of loss in the community. In August 2014, the Terracotta Army Museum invited me to give a talk about my research. Mr. Song, the head of department, asked me not to talk about certain taboo topics in my presentation including politics, economy, and anything related to Qujiang Corporation or Duan Xiannian. He said that if I talked about any of those topics, I would put him at risk of dismissal. After I prepared the presentation material and the PowerPoint slides, he wanted to proofread them. In the end, he asked me to omit a photo of Famen Temple. Mr. Song explained that it was geographically not located in Xi'an and more importantly, it was a politically sensitive Qujiang site. After the fall of Qujiang, government departments tended to avoid all topics related to Qujiang because it implied a failed model and a wrong decision of the Xi'an city government.

Local Views of Qujiang

Mrs. Lau, whose son-in-law worked for the headquarters of Qujiang Corporation, told me:

> In the past, as a family member of a Qujiang Corporation employee, we could get free tickets to sites managed by the company, such as Tang Paradise, Big Wild Goose Pagoda, and Famen Temple, any-time. We organized family trips regularly to those sites. I felt very proud that my son-in-law worked for the corporation. However, since last year [mid-2013], it changed totally. We could only get a limited quota of tickets annually. Now [June 2014], it gets even worse and it is impossible for us to get any tickets. Working at Qujiang is just like working in any other travel agencies or hotels.

In this section, we look more closely at how locals perceive the fall of Qujiang. Has the company's failure been a loss not only for Qujiang employees and their families, but also the general public in Xi'an?

Local views about the Qujiang Model varied a lot depending on individual education, social background, and interests. The more educated my informants were, the more likely they were to criticize the Qujiang Model. Urban planners, conservationists, architects, and other academics were especially critical. But, people who lived in Qujiang District tended not to criticize the model. Generally, people's views of Qujiang were nuanced. They tended not to harshly criticize the company's activities from its peak nor those undertaken in Qujiang District. It was the development of religious sites that received a lot of negative feedback, and even that was most strongly voiced by members of the mass media and other professional communities.

Qujiang as a Dream

Xi'an natives generally thought of their city as comparatively backward and marked by a relatively low living standard. The city was not 'modern' enough in their eyes. The emergence of the Qujiang Model gave them hope for improvement. Many people told me very proudly that the model showed how fast Xi'an had developed. They stressed how Qujiang District had been changed. Almost overnight, it went from farmland to a pleasant urban environment with a new business centre, the walkable Qujiang Lake Archaeological Park, and parks and public squares open for exercising, dancing, and Taichi. They liked that tourists visited the music fountain, and that youngsters could go out night shopping. The new district was well-planned and well-maintained, and people were grateful. 'We enjoy exercising around the Qujiang area because even the air is better here. Even when other districts in Xi'an are covered by smog, Qujiang always has a lower air pollution index', said Ms. Lin, a resident of Qujiang District. Locals claimed that the city would become very boring without the district.

Indeed, many Xi'an residents dreamed of owning an apartment in Qujiang District. Mr. Sun said: 'living in the Qujiang area is like having Big Wild Goose Pagoda and the Tang Paradise palace in your own garden because you can see them from your balcony'. Many young people worked hard with the goal of living in the district. When Mr. Li, a tour guide working at Qujiang Corporation, showed me around the district, he said: 'although I work here every day, it is impossible for me to get an apartment here. Everyone in Xi'an wants to buy an apartment here and that is also my dream'. Locals could not afford the apartments in Qujiang District because they cost at least 30 per cent more than apartments in other parts of Xi'an.

Of course, the corporation never meant for it to be otherwise: Duan Xiannian once said openly in an interview that he did not build up Qujiang District to benefit Xi'an residents, but to attract foreign investors to buy apartments there. It was Qujiang's plan to construct a high-class residential area unaffordable for ordinary people. He said: 'every city has its own CBD and high- class residential area where only rich people live. So I see no problem with the intention to create [one in] Qujiang District. New York has one, and Beijing has one. Every city has this pattern' (cited in Yao 2010). He admitted that most of the people who bought the apartments in Qujiang were rich mine owners from northern Shaanxi Province. He added that if Xi'an locals were rich enough, they could also buy those apartments in Qujiang District.

While many Xi'an locals still admired the Qujiang Model, a large number of people were not sure about their opinions. Even during my fieldwork, some changed from supporting the model to disagreeing with it, or the other way round. Mr. Chuan, a restorer in his late thirties, first complained that Qujiang destroyed historical sites in Xi'an and recommended me journal articles about the drawbacks of the model when we met in 2013. However, after the fall of Qujiang, when we walked around Huaqing Palace Square in Lintong District, he told me that it was a pity that the corporation lost its power. It had, after all, enhanced social solidarity by making large plazas for people to exercise, dance, and gather in the evening, and he wished that the Qujiang era had not come so definitively to an end before doing more good in the district in which he lived. Likewise, Ms. Qin, a primary school teacher who lived in Lintong, condemned the corporation as a murder of history and authenticity during an interview in December 2013, but in July 2014, she had changed her attitude. By that time, the corporation had started to influence her neighbourhood and she had hoped that her living quality would improve and that her living area would be transformed into another Qujiang District. She was, therefore, disappointed that the company's fall meant that her neighbourhood's transformation was stalled.

Qujiang as a Nightmare

Though people hoped to move into apartments in Qujiang District, they knew that no matter how hard they worked, they were unlikely to ever achieve this dream. For many, the immediate reality was even a nightmare: land prices rose unevenly around Qujiang sites, some locals received low compensation for their land or apartments that were of little value. For example, locals who lived around the God of Fortune Temple described the Qujiang Model and its influence as a disaster. Before the project, the villagers were economically independent and each household brought in an annual income of more than 2,000 CNY from farming cash crops, such as kiwis and strawberries (Chen 2012). When they lost their land in the construction of the cultural scenic area, the villagers became increasingly dependent on tourism development. Ms. Yao, a local woman in her thirties, told me that she considered herself and the other younger people as the lucky ones because the cultural scenic area administration offered them the opportunity to work as salespersons. Mr. Cai, a farmer in his forties, was not that fortunate. In order to earn a living, he used his motorcycle to transport visitors from one site to another. He said that farmers only received a compensation of 650 CNY annually from Qujiang Corporation. They had no more land and could not go on with their original mode of production. Mr. Cai joked sarcastically that the God of Fortune did not bring fortune to his village, but poverty instead.

Still, most criticism of Qujiang did not concern its economic influence on local lives and livelihoods. Rather, it was directed at the company's treatment of heritage sites, religion, and history per se. Mr. Yan, an urban planner, commented: 'Qujiang is a devil!' He blamed Qujiang for manipulating tourism and real estate development, which resulted in the destruction of the authenticity of heritage sites. Mr. Tao, an architect, exclaimed that the Qujiang Model exploited history, land, and heritage. He pointed out that the destruction caused at the Qujiang sites was irreversible. Mr. Chen, a historian, emphasized the drawbacks of the commercialization of historical sites. He said, most of the time, visitors to the sites focus too much on entertainment and recreational activities, missing the site's historical importance. Moreover, he disliked that Qujiang Corporation had constructed so many 'archaeological parks' around insignificant historical monuments or even legends, confusing visitors by presenting a misleading history (see chapter 4).

Sometimes, the development in the 'buffer zones' obscured locals' awareness of the heritage sites. Ms. Jian, an agriculture student who grew up and lived in the southern part of Xi'an, did not go to the northern part of the city very often. She could only list the historical sites located in the south. During an interview I asked her about Daming Palace, and she said – surprisingly – 'I have never been there and I never knew that the palace actually exists! I always thought it was the name of a furniture wholesale market or a shopping mall!' Indeed, Xi'an's new furniture wholesaling and retailing market is located right next to the heritage park, drawing local people's attention away from Daming Palace itself. Mr. Liang, a businessman in his late twenties, also could no longer 'see' the heritage in his midst. He said he felt devastated to see such change: 'Xi'an has no more heritage sites, but only shopping malls, karaoke centres, and massage houses'.

The public most attacked the Qujiang Model for its manipulation of religion. There were many complaints: Qujiang Corporation charged high entrance fees, increased the price of incense sticks from 5 CNY up to 500 CNY; at Famen Temple the cultural scenic area was filled with stands selling other ritual objects at high prices. According to Ms. Qi, a former staff member at Famen Temple, the company had even hired people to dress like monks and perform fortune-telling and other rituals. The intent to manipulate people's religious belief so that they would buy expensive incense sticks or blessed objects for good health and fortune was rejected. Many informants shared personal experiences of fraud at various cultural scenic areas. For example, when Ms. Luo and her husband visited Famen Temple, the freshly married couple was approached by a friendly 'monk' who gave them blessings. He asked them to make a wish in front of the Buddha statue, and as they did, he slipped two notes into their hands, each bearing the figure '4,800'. When they asked what it meant, the monk compelled them to pay the written sum lest their wishes not come true. Ms. Lou felt like she was being cheated, but at the same time was afraid, so they paid the monk all the cash they had and the rest with a credit card. She said that she was lucky that the monk did not ask for more – she knew other people who had been told to pay more – but she swore that she would never again go to a temple or trust a monk. Buddhist and religious studies experts also found the company's engagement with religious sites unacceptable. They thought that the placement of fake monks especially constituted religious manipulation and that their acts polluted the nature of the religions.

I too had encounters with fake monks during my fieldwork in Xi'an. Actually, I even interviewed one through a connection with some Qujiang tour guides. Mr. Fu worked as a fortune teller in Louguan Tai Taoist Cultural Scenic Area. He told me that he did not believe in any religion. He was hired by Qujiang and had to take some training courses with necessary religious vocabularies as well as psychology. The latter, he said, was important; it helped him grasp what people usually pray for. I asked if he felt like he was cheating tourists, but he answered that he did it for his living and claimed that it had nothing to do with religion. Tourists, he thought, should be clear about that too. Yet, when I observed Mr. Fu at work, I saw that he did mislead tourists; he told them what to buy from the temple to keep their family safe, to make their wishes come true.

Branding the City

In 2011, the China Chamber of International Commerce selected Xi'an as one of China's top ten 'branded cities' (*pingpai chengshi*). Such cities package their uniqueness, present this well to others, and leave a strong impression on visitors. The selection committee – comprised of city branding experts, economists, entrepreneurs, and media professionals – evaluated numerous Chinese cities in terms of their creativity, productivity, way of branding, and branding impact. Xi'an was chosen alongside cities like Qingdao, Shenzhen, and Beijing.[90] Local television coverage reported that in the eyes of the committee, Xi'an's 'brand' made a unique use of its historical and cultural resources to increase its popularity and attractiveness.[91] In the same year, Xi'an won the Urban Life Accomplishment Model Award because of its outstanding urban resettlement projects. According to the statistics that year, Xi'an was the fourth most popular tourist destination and the third most cultural city in China.[92]

Titles and awards like these show that Xi'an was succeeding in improving its image across China, and particularly had the state's approval.

---

[90] 'Zhongguo shida pingpai chengshi qiexiao Qingdao Shenzhen Suzhou pai qiansan' (The ten branded cities in China: first three are Qingdao, Shenzhen and Suzhou). *Zhongguo Xinwen Wang*, 11 August 2011. Available online, http://city.sina.com.cn/focus/t/2011-08-11/101421118.html. Last accessed 1 May 2016.
[91] 'Xi'an rushuan "Zhongguo shida pingpai chengshi"' (Xi'an selected as one of the ten branded cities in China). *Xi'an TV*, 15 August 2011. Available online, http://www.xantv.cn/newschannel/zhiboxian/detail_2011_08/15/12421_0.shtml. Last accessed 3 March 2016.
[92] 'Xi'an Chosen as Top Ten Branded City'. *China West*, 14 August 2011. Available online, http://news.cnwest.com/content/2011-08/14/content_5046103.htm. Last accessed 1 May 2016.

This meant a lot to Xi'an residents. Ms. Su, a lecturer at Shaanxi Normal University, commented on the branded city award: 'being regarded as a branded city shows how great Xi'an has become. Xi'an is a city that the citizens should feel proud of and a city that people from other places should feel envious about'. Due to the increasing recognition from the central authorities, Xi'an locals are not only proud of the city's imperial past, as demonstrated in chapters 3 and 4, but they also see the rise of Xi'an to become a more modern, important, and international city because of its heritage and urban development.

Previous studies point out that historical sites awarded the designation of UNESCO World Heritage are more attractive and visited than other similar sites. This recognition has resulted in a heritage boom in many countries (Fyall, Garrod and Leask 2003; Ryan and Silvanto 2009; Yaniv, Arie and Raviv 2010), as the inscription of new World Heritage sites attracts tourists from all over the world. However, this chapter shows that 'World Heritage' is not the only heritage brand available. Heritage may also be used to brand a city on principles other than those of meticulous preservation, authenticity, and 'value' in representing or transmitting cultural and historic knowledge. In the Qujiang case, nationalism and the commercialization of tourism and real estate were key aspects of the envisioned brand.

The durability of a branded city, however, cannot be achieved through a marketing strategy alone. John Hannigan (1998) has analysed other post-industrial cities that became sites of entertainment through heritage and retail development. Such fantasy cities, he concluded, are usually aggressively branded, but even an appealing brand cannot overcome or even mask all social problems. Similarly, Jonathan Gabay, founder of Brand Forensics, has argued that 'city branding is not just about the logo'; it is about 'intricate details' like clean and orderly streets, and the pride of local residents.[93] The brand needs locals to be its 'brand ambassadors'. As my fieldwork concluded, it seemed that locals were losing pride in the Qujiang brand because their benefits from it were diminishing. Besides, there had always been other 'brands' in the making that people could openly prefer as Qujiang's fate changed. Although the corporation dominated the urban and heritage development for over a decade, its influence did not spread to every corner of the city. The next chapter turns to look at the community heritage districts that escaped Qujiang's branding and demonstrates other local efforts in preserving urban heritage.

---

[93] See 'Future of Cities: Brand of Gold'. *The Guardian* 1 October 2008. Available online, http://www.theguardian.com/society/2008/oct/01/city.urban.branding. Last accessed 1 May 2016.

Chapter 7
The City of Communities – Urban Heritage

Although many foreign tourists looked forward to seeing the well-known heritage site of the terracotta army before coming to Xi'an, many told me that although they found the warriors great, it was their experience in the Muslim Quarter that was unforgettable. An engineer from France said: 'after I discovered the Muslim Quarter on the first day of my stay in Xi'an, I went there every evening for food and the atmosphere!' She was impressed by the harmonious society of the Muslim Quarter because in France, she said, Islam and Muslims were stigmatized as 'terrorists'. In Xi'an, she learnt about the friendly side of Muslim culture and people. She was astounded, too, to see people from different ethnicities and religions living peacefully together. A German restorer, who worked in Xi'an for the Sino-German project, told me: 'for my work, I have to stay in a small temple in a suburb three hours from the centre, but I always take the chance to come to Xi'an on the weekends and visit the Muslim Quarter to experience the genuine way of life in China. To me, it is the most interesting place in Xi'an'. She liked the food culture a lot and proudly told me that she tried every single kind of food sold in the quarter during her stay; but more importantly, she enjoyed observing the busy community life in the Muslim Quarter with the many social activities going on. Unlike the terracotta army, which people did not visit more than once, tourists kept revisiting the Muslim Quarter. Foreign tourists underlined the liveliness and harmony of the community, which are absent from heritage sites and national monuments.

The Muslim Quarter represents a vision of heritage that is characterized by what Michael Herzfeld (1991) described as 'social time'. In contrast to the 'monumental time', or 'bureaucratic measure of history that is calibrated in well-defined periods' experienced by visitors to many heritage sites, the Muslim Quarter invites its visitors to experience heritage as 'social time' pertaining to 'unpredictable events and the reality' (ibid.: 10). The sites mentioned in the previous chapters present heritage as 'frozen' in a certain era. They demonstrate the process of monumentalization through state-initiated programs, such as the construction of archaeological parks, the selective historical narrative, and the revitalization projects. In contrast, the sites in this chapter run on 'social time'. Here, dynamic everyday life and social events take place and locals have developed personal attachment, family ties, and communities.

In 1982, the national government inscribed Xi'an into the first cohort of 'national historic cities' with 23 other cities in China (China Culture Information Net 1982).[94] This designation drew attention to a new dimension of heritage understanding. For the first time, China put the focus on heritage sites with a 'social time' aspect – not monumentalized sites, but traditional living quarters. Xi'an, like the other 'historic cities', is required to follow the Cultural Relics Protection Law enacted in 1982 (see chapter 2). In 1989, the national government passed the National Law on Urban and Rural Planning to further standardize the criteria in all historic cities (National People's Congress of the People's Republic of China 1989). In 2005, the Ministry of Construction ratified the Code of Conservation Planning for Historic Cities to strengthen the conservation of historic quarters in these cities (Ministry of Construction of the People's Republic of China 2005). Lastly in 2008, the Central State Administration of China passed the Historic Cities, Historic Towns, and Historic Villages Protection Regulations (Central People's Government of the People's Republic of China 2008) to monitor the preservation of historic cities at different levels. The making of these laws shows the increasing effort put by the state to maintain the historic cities. Yet, the question arises as to how 'historic cities' are distinguished from cities with heritage sites?

One of the criteria for a historic city is that encompasses at least two 'historic conservation areas' (*lishi jiequ*, lit. historic street quarters) (Central People's Government of the People's Republic of China 2008). This requirement underlines the importance of what is considered a holistic architectural landscape (i.e. 'a quarter') distinct from other adjacent areas. More exact requirements are set out by national law (Ministry of Construction of the People's Republic of China 2005). A historic conservation area must include a total area of at least 10,000 square metres in which at least 60 per cent is of authentic historic buildings. For designation, the national government also considers the style, colour, and height of the architectural landscape and its state of preservation. More importantly, the law also regulates social aspects and states that the shop owners in each area must practice a unified and traditional business activity, so as to maintain an

---

[94] China Culture Information Net. 'Diyipi lishi wenhua mingcheng' (The first batch of national historic cities in China). Available online, http://www.ccnt.com.cn/culture/famouscity/ famous-city/city1/city100.htm. Last accessed 2 February 2016.

energetic urban social life. Xi'an has three historic conservation areas: the Muslim Quarter (officially called Beiyuanmen lishi wenhua jiequ), the Calligraphy Quarter (Sanxue jie lishi wenhua jiequ), and the Qixian Zhuang Quarter (Qixian Zhuang lishi jiequ) (Cao 2010). Map 6 displays the location and size of these three quarters.

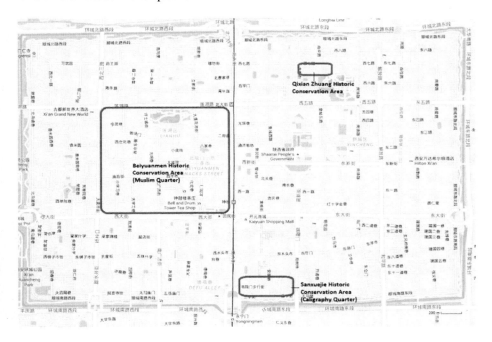

Map 6. Location and size of the three historic conservation areas in Xi'an. (Source: https://goo.gl/maps/oDAoXS56xZNGRtPHA).

Urban planners whom I interviewed emphasized the importance of the preservation of these quarters because they portray the living side of Xi'an's history. They embraced a similar distinction to Herzfeld's 'monumental' and 'social' times. Mr. You, an experienced heritage site and archaeological park planner, said:

> The historical remains are undoubtedly very impressive, however, they represent only the time that has already passed by, meaning these heritage sites are dead. In contrast, the notion of historic city, as opposed to heritage, highlights the dynamics and complexity of urban settings. In addition, the architectural forms are still occupied and lived in, unlike the heritage sites that cannot be used for living.

Ms. Lin, an architect specialized in the preservation of traditional houses, also pointed to a binary relationship between heritage and the historic city.

She said that in order to grasp a full understanding of heritage development in Xi'an, one should not ignore Xi'an's historic city title.

In the 1980s, Xi'an was still composed of many traditional districts similar to the Muslim Quarter. With the urban renewal development programs of the early 1990s, however, all but three were demolished or gentrified. This chapter shifts the focus from state- and investor-oriented heritage projects to community-based heritage sites that are shared by everyone. It introduces and compares two of the traditional quarters, the Calligraphy Quarter and the Muslim Quarter, and thereby presents a case of bottom-up social heritagization, instead of the top-down political and economic forms. It also explores the difficulties that the communities encountered due to urbanization and modernization and their counter-strategies. Although most urban renewal and heritage projects in China are carried out by the state, the historic quarters in Xi'an demonstrate the limited, yet, existing, space for local communities to negotiate change with the government.

The Calligraphy Quarter

The Calligraphy Quarter is located in the southern part of the urban centre within the city wall (see Map 6). Its total area is 148,000 square metres (Xi'an City Planning Bureau 2014b). Since a scholar built Guanzhong College and settled down in the area in the Ming Dynasty, the Calligraphy Quarter has been known locally as College Gate (Shuyuan men). The quarter encompasses numerous heritage sites including Guanzhong College, which represents education and literacy, and is now used as a government building; the Forest of Steles Museum; and the Buddhist Baoqing Pagoda. Nowadays, the Calligraphy Quarter mainly functions as a commercial district selling calligraphy-related products. The main architectural style of the shop houses and residential vernacular buildings is a Mingqing style of two-storey structures made of grey brick. Since the quarter originated in the Ming Dynasty, the district and city governments implemented laws and standard-ization criteria to monitor the height and style of the buildings. The closer the buildings are to the Forest of Steles, the more unified they look. For example, the houses at the beginning of the quarter near the South Gate use different kinds of bricks, decorative motifs, and windows, but the houses located close to the Forest of Steles all use the same material and paint.

The 570-metre-long-pedestrian street and many alleys jointly form the district. City dwellers reside in the vernacular houses hidden in the alleys or on the upper floors of their shop houses along the main street. Following the guidelines of the national law, the whole quarter practices a common business activity, selling calligraphy products and Chinese traditional art works. There are three different kinds of shops and businesses. First, there are traditional shop houses; these are mostly two-storey-buildings in which the first floor serves as the shop and the second floor is used for living and storage of goods. This arrangement originated from family businesses so that owners could live close to their shops. These shops are located along the main street selling items related to calligraphy and antiquity. The second type of shops consists of the booths on the main streets, managed under the Beilin district government. The stand keepers have to pay a monthly rent. The stands, provided by the district government, are designed in neo-Tang style and painted in dark woody-red – the 'imperial heritage colour' – in response to the Tang Imperial City Renaissance Plan initiated by the Xi'an city government in 2014 (as discussed in chapter 4). The booths usually sell a range of cheap goods to tourists, such as music instruments, postcards, ancient coins, and paper cuts.

During my fieldwork, I first cultivated relationships with the stand owners as a way of joining the community. Sometimes, when informants had to go to the hospital or appointments in other parts of the city, I looked after their stands for a few hours, during which I could socialize with other stand owners and interact with the customers. Stand owners mostly rent apartments and live within the Calligraphy Quarter in the small alleys because they stored the goods at home and had to carry them to the stands every day. The third type of shops comprises those located in the alleys, selling books, paintings and calligraphy materials, as well as services such as framing and stamp-making. They rely highly on professional customers because their products are too specialized for tourists and they cannot compete with the shops on the main street due to lower customer exposure.

Although the quarter serves as a representation of old Xi'an, I realized that most shop owners did not come from Xi'an. Only shops located in the alleys were operated by locals. Mr. Peng, for example, owner of a book store in a small alley, inherited the house and business from his father-in-law. The shops and stands along the main streets were rented by businessmen from other provinces, namely Zhejiang and Henan. Many of these shop owners told me that they came to the Calligraphy Quarter to continue their family business from back home. Ms. Zhang, a primary school teacher in her early twenties from Henan, spent every summer holiday at her parents' stand to help them sell calligraphy brushes and materials. Ms. Li, a tourism studies researcher who investigated the recent tourism development of the district, found out that the Calligraphy Quarter is mostly used by calligraphy lovers, artists, and tourists. Locals also go there, but only when they have to buy calligraphy materials or artwork.

Every year, the Calligraphy Quarter gets extraordinarily busy and crowded two weeks before Lunar New Year. Famous calligraphers from the whole province set up temporary stands along the main street to sell their own calligraphies of couplets or *feichun* written on red or golden paper.[95] Some calligraphers write on the tables they bring along, but others who produce large calligraphy works, simply spread paper on the floor for writing. Customers can buy finished work or order a personalized work with specific characters or phases. Normally, factory-produced couplets sold in the supermarket cost 20 CNY but the couplets sold in the Calligraphy Quarter cost upwards of 1,000 CNY. If customers requested a personalized calligraphy work, calligraphers charged them between 200 CNY and 500 CNY per character (a couplet contains usually 14 to 22 characters and a *feichun* of four characters). Despite the high price, many locals came to the quarter to buy them during this time of year.

The Muslim Quarter

The Muslim Quarter is located in the western part of the urban centre within the city wall (see Map 6). The whole Muslim Quarter encompasses more than 1.2 square kilometres but the official conserved area is 0.5 square kilometres, including six main streets and some residential areas (Xi'an City Planning Bureau 2014b). Mr. Yang, a Muslim expert of architecture, told me that in the Tang period, the Muslim Quarter was located close to the West Market; it was where Muslim traders from the Silk Road gathered and resided. However, after the fall of the Tang Dynasty, the traders moved into the shrinking city's centre, reaching the present location of the Muslim Quarter in the Yuan and Ming dynasties. Now, the quarter is a dense complex of narrow streets full of businesses catering to the local community and visitors with a population of over 50,000 people (China Statistics 2005).

Like the Calligraphy Quarter, the Muslim Quarter is also composed of Mingqing-style buildings with their specific roofs and grey bricks. A few mosques in the quarter date back to the Tang Dynasty, such as the most ancient Daxuexi Alley Mosque, built in 705, and Great Mosque, built in 724. Their architecture displays both Islamic and Chinese elements (see chapter 5 for more detail). Originally belonging to part of the Tang Chang'an palace, the buildings were only used as mosques from the Ming Dynasty on, during which they were renovated to their current look. The mosques were inscribed into different levels of heritage management under various govern-

---

[95] Traditionally, Chinese people decorate doors with two giant couplets and use *feichun* (wishes written on red papers) to embellish the interior of the house during the Chinese New Year period to bring good luck.

ment levels. Xi'an Hui criticized the inconsistent preservation plan adopted by the government departments; lack of internal communication, they said, had resulted in the different states of the mosques. Mr. Ma, a Hui architect, suggested that the government departments and levels should consult history experts and standardize their way of restoring the heritage sites in the district. For instance, the praying hall of Daxuexi Alley Mosque, as a provincially ranked heritage site dating back to the Ming Dynasty, was rebuilt and enlarged, without informing any governmental departments. Another provincially ranked heritage site, Xiaopiyuan Mosque, also made similar changes to the praying hall's size and roof colours without any interference from any government departments. In contrast, Great Mosque, a nationally ranked heritage site co-managed under the national and provincial governments, was in a much better shape and all the small details, such as the restoration of architectural features, were very well-monitored. It preserves original forms of Tang, Ming, and Qing architecture. According to the locals, the district no longer looked the same as when it was first assessed by the national government as an urban historic conservation area in 1982.

In terms of historical sites in the quarter, several mosques are listed as nationally ranked heritage sites and the Great Mosque was even a World Heritage candidate from 1997 to 2012 for the Silk Roads nomination (see chapter 5). Moreover, a few of the vernacular houses in the quarter won the UNESCO Asia-Pacific Award for Cultural Heritage Conservation in 2002 for their community commitment to urban heritage preservation. The UNESCO award certificate states that the houses 'serve as a model for local residents to follow in carrying out future work in Xi'an's Drum-Tower Muslim Quarter and in urban neighbourhoods all around China' and praises the quarter as an 'outstanding urban fabric' (Song 2012: 124).[96] The biggest difference between the shop houses in the Calligraphy Quarter and the Muslim Quarter is their layout. Whereas the shop is located on the ground floor and the living area on the second in the Calligraphy Quarter, the shop houses in the Muslim Quarter have historically been single-storey buildings (Feighery 2008). So, the shop is set at the front while the family lives in the back. Although the main entrance of the shop appears to be very narrow, the living area extends very deep, containing up to three courtyards and gardens. Mr. An's house, one of the UNESCO awardees, for example has two inner courtyards.

---

[96] The announcement of the 2002 UNESCO Asia-Pacific Cultural Heritage Conservation Awards Winners was made available through UNESCO's Bangkok office website, http://mailbot.unescobkk.org/555/. Last accessed 1 May 2016.

Similar to the Calligraphy Quarter, there are different kinds of shops including the traditional shop houses as described above and hawkers. In the core area, 85 per cent of the businesses are restaurants and snack stands and the rest of the shops sell souvenirs to tourists. Unlike the city-organized neo-Tang-style stands in the Calligraphy Quarter, the hawkers in the Muslim Quarter own their stands and design them according to their own wishes with colourful signs, photos of food, and blinking neon lights. According to the local Muslims, the quarter is at its most genuine in the early day before the massive flow of tourists. Then, it is very quiet and peaceful. From midday the quarter becomes increasingly crowded as old restaurants fill with visitors trying their signature dish and other visitors stop to buy drinks and snacks from hawkers.

As for the ethnic composition, approximately 70 per cent of the inhabitants, around 30,000 people, belong to the Hui minority. The remaining 30 per cent include Han, Uyghur, Kazakh, Yi, and other ethnic minorities (Gillette 2000). The Han people in the quarter ran most of the souvenir shops, selling dried fruits, postcards, and products with 'ethnic minority' characteristics, as well as the coffee and bubble tea cafés. The Hui, however, form the richest group in the quarter because they own the properties and land. Some continue to operate family businesses and restaurants, but many have rented their land to Han businessmen. There are also many Hui migrants from Gansu and Ningxia provinces. They are, however, mostly rather poor and could not pay the high rent for shop houses (or even stands which cost from 3,000 to 18,000 CNY per month depending on the location). These migrant Hui either work for the Han shop owners, rent the stands at less popular locations, or become motorcycle drivers transporting people around the district. For instance, I got to know Mr. Feng as I requested him to show me around the quarter with his motorbike and tell me the stories of the oldest and best-preserved buildings and mosques. Throughout the conversation, I learnt about his background as a migrant worker from Gansu. He felt grateful that Xi'an has a Muslim Quarter because he could integrate easily into the community. Eventually, his whole family also moved from their hometown to settle down in Xi'an with him.

The most crowded period in the Muslim Quarter happens to be only four weeks apart from the one of the Calligraphy Quarter, also related to the Chinese Lunar New Year. Although Hui do not celebrate Han Chinese festivals, those in Xi'an profit from the festival. On the fifteenth day after Lunar New Year, Han Chinese welcome the first full moon by celebrating Yuanxiao Festival. In Xi'an, people enjoy eating big round sweet rice dumplings called *yuanxiao,* which represent the moon and the sweetness of the coming successful year. At this time, many restaurants and stands in the

Muslim Quarter produce these dumplings. Interestingly, even outside the Muslim Quarter, hawkers or shops selling *yuanxiao* dumplings all put on signs indicating that they are produced by Muslims. During the spring festival, my informants reminded me again and again to buy the dumplings in the Muslim Quarter because they tasted the best and were made in the most traditional way. When asked why they preferred to buy the dumplings from Hui, even though *yuanxiao* is not a tradition of the Hui-Muslims, local Han Chinese mentioned aspects such as hygiene, quality, and tradition.

Comparison between the Two Quarters

Despite the commonalities of the two quarters in terms of architectural styles and conservation regulations, the social and commercial life in the two communities is different. The following section will compare the two quarters in terms of the relationship between the communities and the heritage sites, the urban life of the local residents, and their willingness to conserve. Mr. Tao, an urban planner in his late thirties, remarked that all the three official historic conservation areas in Xi'an were destroyed to a certain extent in the 1990s because of the modernization policy of the national and provincial governments. The Qixian Zhuang Quarter is, in his view, not preserved at all since not a single building remained. As for the Calligraphy Quarter, he mentioned that the municipal government only preserved a small area around the Forest of Steles with a historical townscape. Although the general public regards the Muslim Quarter as the best-preserved area, having dodged many urban regeneration and revitalization projects initiated by the municipal government, Mr. Tao revealed that the district government tore down many shop houses with only some houses and streets behind the Drum Tower remaining well-preserved. All the traditional quarters encountered different degrees of destruction and remaking and received different treatments of preservation, which resulted in their current condition.

Outsiders, including Xi'an people who do not live in the respective quarters, perceive the places differently from Mr. Tao and other professionals. This general public considers the Muslim Quarter the most traditional and oldest quarter in Xi'an. More importantly, they think that it represents the city's food culture. Like history, the local cuisine is said to characterize Chinese culture because it originated during the Tang Dynasty or even earlier. When I requested people to mark the oldest houses and structures in the quarter on a map, they only circled famous restaurants and indicated them as the most 'traditional' places. They judged the authenticity of the shop houses based on the food being served. Many Han locals told me passionately about how the food was prepared, how the bread was made, and how Muslims butchered goats. The history of the houses or mosques and their architectural elements meant little to non-Hui who did not live in the quarter, but they did know where to get the best food and which brands were the oldest in the quarter.

The Calligraphy Quarter gives outsiders a completely different image from that of the lively Muslim Quarter. My informants claimed that the present quarter conveys a sense of backwardness. Mr. Zhang, a student in his late twenties, told me that the quarter gave him a sad, desolated, and empty feeling (*xiaotiao*). Ms. Qian also said that her father, who practiced calligraphy, went to the quarter regularly with his friends, but that she and her friends seldom set foot there. The quarter, she said, suited only old people. Everything seemed to have slowed down a beat. Indeed, I rarely found young local Xi'an residents hanging out there. I asked my young informants if the district was nevertheless representative of Xi'an's cultural side – did it matter, I asked, that calligraphy is a traditional art? Yes, they agreed, the quarter provided a good educational venue for children and it enabled artists to exchange thoughts and create new works. But that was about it. Mr. Zhang thought that the quarter could not represent Xi'an because Mingqing-style buildings could not depict the city's Han and Tang imperial past. Here, architecture was drawn on as a non-negligible aspect of authenticity, though it was ignored in the case of the Muslim Quarter.

Relationship between the Communities and the Nearby Heritage Sites

To insiders of these quarters, the neighbourhoods are not only sites from the past, but also social venues and places of memory, economic resources, and everyday living. Their core historical sites are distinct. The Calligraphy Quarter expanded based on three main historical sites: a Buddhist pagoda, Guanzhong College, and the Forest of Steles. The core of the Muslim Quarter is composed of a few ancient mosques, which still serve as places of worship and are visited by locals and tourists on a regular basis.

In the Calligraphy Quarter, the Ming-era building of Guanzhong College kept its educational function and was used as the campus for Shaanxi Teachers University until the early 2000s when the university moved to a new campus in the university district. The Forest of Steles can be described as the current core of the quarter, attracting thousands of visitors. It has existed since the Tang Dynasty as a Confucian temple, an examination venue, and the earliest form of museum, storing an exquisite collection of steles, including rare paintings, calligraphies, and official documents. Ms. Wen, a tourism studies scholar in her thirties, said that although the Xi'an city government had tried to bring more tourists to the Calligraphy Quarter with various renewal projects and urban redevelopment plans, the Forest of Steles Museum is still the main tourist attraction. Even the booths selling tourist souvenirs rely heavily on the museum.

In the 1980s, and even early 1990s, before Xi'an became a popular tourist destination, the Forest of Steles used to be open to the public for a very low entrance fee. Ms. Chen, a housewife in her early forties, recalled that she liked to go to the Forest of Steles when she was young to observe how people attempted to reproduce the calligraphy works from the steles on paper. They would first brush a thin layer of ink onto a stele and then cover the inked area with a piece of blank paper, 'printing' the image. There were many people who came with their own tools, papers, and ink to make these prints and some businessmen even took the opportunity to sell inks and papers outside the site. Thus, the Calligraphy Quarter was formed as a hub for artists and businessmen selling traditional Chinese art materials.

As time passed and Xi'an became more popular among tourists, the Forest of Steles forbade visitors from copying the steles. Only artisans hired by the museum were allowed to do so. Additionally, the museum increased the entrance fee from three CNY to 80 CNY. Today, if visitors want to get a print of their favoured stele, they have to buy the ones produced by the official artisans from the museum shop at the cost of around 230 CNY. However, shop and stand owners in the Calligraphy Quarter make use of their connections to museum employees; they secretly copy the prints and sell them at a much lower price. Mr. Zhang, a stand owner selling calligraphy brushes and prints in his mid-thirties, went in to the Forest of Steles multiple times per day. Sometimes, he went to collect freshly printed works for his own stand; sometimes he was called to bring brushes to the museum shop because they had run out. Thus perhaps what is most visible about the role of heritage sites in the Calligraphy Quarter is the strong economic collaboration between the central touristic site and other community members.

In the Muslim Quarter, business is important to the quarter's inhabitants (as described above), but mosques are at the centre of local life in a particular way. Muslims do build up their social and economic life based on the location of the mosques, but not because they see the mosques as prestigious heritage sites. The Hui from the Muslim Quarter do not see the historical mosques so much as 'heritage' or 'cultural relics', but as functioning religious venues where they can also socialize. Old and retired men even spend whole days sitting and chatting in the mosque yards. Nor are the old mosques of much greater value in the everyday lives of my informants; they attend whichever mosques are closest or that are attended by their friends. The mosques too are resistant to overt change for tourists; tourists can visit most mosques for free as long as they dress and behave appropriately, but prayer halls are restricted to believers. Only the Great Mosque charges an entrance fee of 25 CNY, and that is not for 'tourists' but for 'non-Muslims' (defined ethnically or religiously).

Urban Life

Mr. Yang, an author in his late forties, who devoted himself to the promotion of Xi'an's local traditional urban life, stated during an interview: 'without the Muslim Quarter, Xi'an [would be] just a dead city'. Indeed, both quarters are unique: the Calligraphy Quarter preserves traditional art and the Muslim Quarter represents the lifestyle of an ethnic minority. However, each quarter has a different rhythm and pattern in terms of the members' urban life. Comparatively speaking, the Calligraphy Quarter is more orderly. The shopkeepers usually start their days between nine and ten o'clock in the morning. Since they own their businesses, they enjoy flexible opening hours. Mr. Feng, a stand owner of pottery music instruments in his early sixties, told me that he could come to work whenever he wanted, sometimes at eight, sometimes even at ten thirty. In contrast, the food-oriented shops and stands in the Muslim Quarter only start their business around lunch time. Ms. Luo, a stand owner in her mid-sixties who sold sweet sticky rice cakes, said she came to her stand every day at noon and worked until around two o'clock in the morning, depending on when the last piece of cake was sold. Ms. Luo's stand was among one of the oldest in the district. She had taken over her husband's family business; her son and husband made the cakes, and her son came to help sell from time-to-time.

In comparison, the stands in the Calligraphy Quarter depend on relations beyond those of the family. Still, members help each other what is felt to be a family-like network. For example, Mr. and Ms. Li, owners of an antiquity stand, prepared enough food for all the stand-sellers during lunch time and sold the lunches at a low price. The arrangement had come about because everyone liked their cooking, and Mrs. Li was proud that they had eventually taken up the 'duty' of preparing lunch for the whole quarter. Sometimes, I took care of Mrs. Li's stand while she cooked, and I too experienced the strong sense of community support between the stand owners. Even though each stand sells different goods, the owners know the prices and catalogue of each other's products very well. For example, the first time Mrs. Li asked me to take care of her antiquity stand, which sold all kinds of artefacts (coins, various pots, and vessels), Ms. Lau from the neighbouring embroidery stand assisted me in bargaining and negotiating prices with customers. Such networks could not form among hawkers in the Muslim Quarter, it seems, because of the higher customer flow. In the

Muslim Quarter, hawkers were constantly serving customers and had less time and ability to help neighbouring stands. Each stand could rely only on its 'employees', which is to say the family that owned it.

Community support in the Muslim Quarter was configured otherwise. Shops, restaurants, and hawkers collaborated with an efficient division of labour based on specialization. Each shop and stand serves only one specific kind of food: Shop A is famous for and only serves cold noodles, Shop B makes only mutton soup, and Shop C provides only dumplings. Yet, after eating there for a few times, I discovered that customers could actually order food of all choices from any restaurant. If one ordered cold noodles in Shop B, the shop would send a waiter across the road to Shop A. Similarly, shops would procure additional food and drinks for their customers from stand-sellers. Though this worked for the restaurants, stands did not reciprocate; they sold only their own products.

Outside of work life, the social life of the members from the two quarters also has different characteristics. The social life in the Calligraphy Quarter begins in the evening around six o'clock and continues until all the shops close. After the stand keepers store their goods, other hawkers occupy the street selling snacks. People bring their mahjong tables out to the street to play with their neighbours, and the public area close to Wenchang Gate is filled with at least thirty mahjong tables that attract crowds of spectators. Groups of people gather at other public squares along the city wall to do evening sports and dance until eleven o'clock in the evening. Mr. Wang, an artist in his early twenties, who moved to the Calligraphy Quarter after his graduation from an art school in Xi'an, said he enjoyed living in the quarter because it was located close to the Forest of Steles, from where he could get inspiration. Also, he found it practical to get supplies for his art work, such as papers and inks in the district. Most importantly, he thought that the social life in the quarter portrays the lifestyle of the 'old Xi'an', before the city was so modernized and lost close community relationships.

Still, it is the lifestyle of the Muslim Quarter that is still seen as older. The Hui residents of the Muslim Quarter describe their urban life as 'Silk Road style' inflected with a mixture of Chinese and Western elements from different historical periods. The two most common examples used by my informants are both from Xi'an Hui cuisines. *Roujiamo*, a very typical Xi'anese 'hamburger' with mutton or beef inside a small bun, was regarded as proof of East-West interaction. Also, *liangpi*, a Xi'anese dish of cold noodles, was said to have a Silk Road touch in its sauce. Mr. Ma, a Hui resident in the district in his early seventies, told me excitedly that Han people usually put soya sauce on cold noodles, but the *liangpi* in Xi'an uses sesame paste instead, which shows the influence of Middle East cuisines.

Thus, one district claims a 'Silk Road' lifestyle while the other claims an 'old Xi'an' style.

Willingness to Conserve

One of the obvious differences between the Calligraphy and the Muslim quarters lies in the willingness to conserve the shop houses. In the Calligraphy Quarter, the local inhabitants did not regard the shop houses as historical or valuable. To them, the buildings were not, and did not look, old. Indeed, many were not old because they had been (re)built in the city's renewal projects of the 1990s. Therefore, there was no need to preserve them. They believed the only monuments that needed preservation were the Forest of Steles and Guanzhong College, and that responsibility for each belonged to the provincial government.

By contrast, the view of conservation in the Muslim Quarter varies. In the core area, where commercial activities take place, the buildings are better preserved. Since the old houses were owned by rich families, their descendants felt an obligation to preserve them as family heritage. A few families even took efforts that were recognized and confirmed by the UNESCO Asia-Pacific Award for Cultural Heritage Conservation. Still, there are only six complete and well-preserved houses in the quarter. The city government turned one of them, Gao's Grand Courtyard, into a museum, while the remaining five are still occupied. Residents told me about some of the difficulties they encountered when preserving the old family houses, among which is the lack of financial support. Mr. An, a descendent of one of the UNESCO-award-winning houses, said that it would have been financially very hard to conserve the house with his own money and effort. He and his family were very thankful that they could benefit from a co-operation program between Xi'an Technological University of Architecture and Technology and Norwegian University of Science and Technology, Trondheim, which provided technical, manual, and financial support. During my visit, Mr. An proudly showed off his house as the best preserved house in the whole district that still kept the oldest parts and building techniques. He told me that the researchers from the respective universities restored the open house museum based on his house, as the other houses in the district have all been renovated too many times and lost part of their original forms and details.

Yet, at the outskirts of the core area of the Muslim Quarter, local residents took positions more similar to those in the Calligraphy Quarter. They too had little willingness to conserve their houses. Since the 1980s, most of the traditional single-storey buildings outside the core area of the Muslim Quarter have been replaced by multi-storey houses (Feighery 2008).

Through the 1990s, local Hui had engaged enthusiastically in private rebuilding projects to improve their living standards (Gillette 2000: 63). Mr. Bo, a Hui in his late forties who is deeply interested in the architecture of the quarter, pointed out that most residents do not have a strong incentive to preserve their houses. He said that local residents felt 'traditional houses are just old architecture and old houses without much value. Hence, many would rather take the chance to build a bigger, newer, and prettier modern building than to spend time and money to restore the old ones if they have the choice'. Indeed, Maris Gillette remarked that inhabitants who resided close to the Great Mosque were the most optimistic about renewal and the slowest to realize its drawbacks to community life in the 1990s (2000: 59). By the time of my fieldwork in 2013, the situation had changed. Contrary to Mr. Bo's pronouncements, I found out that at least the groups living close to the old mosques had become the protectors of the traditional quarter and were taking the lead to preserve their shop houses. Informants living outside the core area, however, did view the old houses as 'useless'. They even secretly made contact with some urban planners and government officials to evaluate their houses and discuss the possibility for the government to expropriate them in exchange for new apartments and compensation. An expert on Hui architecture, Mr. Yang, told me that residents in the Muslim Quarter renovated their houses individually and chose features or decoration they preferred without considering the historical and original content, and that it was this practice that produced the eclectic combination of architectural styles from different eras.

Historic Quarters in Change

It is important to note that although the municipal, provincial and national governments put in place regulations to monitor local rebuilding activities in these 'historic areas', inhabitants had little incentive or desire to uphold them. Moreover, as the heritage preservation department of the municipal government did not conduct regular and strict inspections at the quarters, residents were not punished for changes they made to the physical structure of their houses. This means that despite official pronouncements, there was little community or governmental effort to direct or control 'internally' motivated directions of architectural or social change (or continuity) in either district. In contrast, external forces of change were supported by the city government. These were in the form of commercialization and urban renewal projects.

Commercialization

In some Muslim communities around the world, commercial activities are dictated by the religious practices of business owners. In Damascus, for example, restaurants are closed from dawn to dusk during Ramadan (Salamandra 2004: 94). This is not the case in Xi'an's Muslim Quarter. Here restaurants remain open even when their owners are fasting. My informants explained, 'life must go on, we are relying on the food industry here, so we need to continue our business. We do not stop working because of our religion. As long as we do not eat ourselves, cooking for others is no problem'.

The on-going food business during Ramadan highlights the commercialized nature of business in Xi'an's historic areas. As I embarked on my fieldwork, I found it challenging to enter both districts as field sites because of this commercialization. Shop owners were not interested in talking to me except as a customer or business partner. I had to devise different tactics to get to know shop owners as community members. In the Muslim Quarter, I built a network focused on 'heritage' through academics and NGO connections; and, I learned to approach business owners in the morning when they were more relaxed. In the Calligraphy Quarter, as mentioned above, the business atmosphere was friendlier and less stressed, and I was able to befriend some shop owners and stall-owners. Here, a snowball methodology was applied as my initial informants were keen to introduce more contacts and shops to me.

Although the national government states that the historic areas should keep their traditional businesses, both the Muslim and Calligraphy quarters are now rather filled with touristic souvenir shops. Out of the 300 shops in the Calligraphy Quarter, more than two-thirds sell souvenirs and low quality calligraphy to tourists, and only one-third sell tools for calligraphy, copies from the steles, paintings, and stamps for professionals and amateurs. In the Muslim Quarter, the whole core area is tourism-oriented, selling typical snacks, drinks, and souvenirs.

The changes in shop-type have an impact on the everyday lives of residents. Residents' own consumption practices have changed. Ms. An, who lived next to Great Mosque, said that she no longer ate and bought food from the core area. She preferred 'genuine' Hui restaurants in outlying areas where the food was cheaper and of better quality. Quality of life and public hygiene are also impacted. The Muslim Quarter during public holidays is so crowded that people can hardly move. Piles of garbage accumulate along the streets: plastic containers, paper plates, and bamboo sticks. Residents, other Xi'an people, and visitors all regard the Muslim Quarter as very dirty and 'uncivilized'. The residents blame the visitors for creating the rubbish and polluting the quarter. They take their own reputation for cleanliness very seriously; they believe that customers come to them for high quality and clean food. Indeed, Xi'an Hui declared again and again that their religion emphasized a lot of personal and environmental hygiene. As Muslims, they necessarily engaged in frequent hand washing and vegetable rinsing. They put up signs to remind tourists to keep the district hygienic.

Few people considered alternatives to commercialization or imagined controlling the changes it produced. Many local residents thought that commercialization (and tourism development) was 'normal' and un-avoidable. They saw this as especially true for the Calligraphy and Muslim quarters because they were both created by traders and businessmen. Business was 'in the blood' of the people in these districts from the time of the Silk Road. But at least a large group of residents in the Muslim Quarter who were not involved in business found the effects of tourist-oriented commercialization disturbing.

Even efforts to draw tourists' attention to the historic and contem-porary life-ways of the quarters are likely to enhance commercialization in the same directions. Mr. Dei, an editor of a book series on the Muslim Quarter, for example, told me that the goal of his series was to draw attention to the historical buildings and social life of the Hui. However, when he showed me one of the books (Song 2012), I noted that a full quarter (54 out of 215 pages) was devoted to describing local foodways. Mr. Dei said that this was a marketing strategy; the book would sell better because it began with food topics and introduced culinary specialties. Mr. Xiong, an activist and artist who founded his own company producing hand-drawn maps, specifically made a map for the Muslim Quarter with indications of the best and most traditional restaurants and their kinds of food. Of course, his map also contained annotations about the heritage sites, in the hope that people would also pay a visit to them, but it was food that he expected to attract most attention. If it is food and its consumption in the quarter that is marketed to tourists, how can the commercialization of food and restaurants be stopped? How can the demands of food-industry tourism not be the drivers of undesirable social change among residents?

Urban Renewal Projects

Both quarters encountered waves of urban renewal projects conducted by the district and city governments, aiming to preserve, revitalize, or modernize the quarters. Before 1980, the city only conducted small-scale urban heritage projects on particular heritage sites and only paid attention to certain buildings. For example, the Drum Tower was among the earliest restoration projects the Xi'an City Planning Bureau carried out (Høyem 2007). After

1982, when Xi'an was designated a 'historic city', the city government started to preserve the historical and cultural townscape of certain quarters, including the main streets of the Calligraphy and Muslim quarters. In 2002, the Xi'an city government announced the Xi'an Historic City Protection Ordinance and introduced a revitalization project concerning 'one district, two traditional areas, four lines, and thirty-three spots', in which the two traditional areas referred to the Calligraphy and Muslim quarters. The ordinance set restrictions, such as for building heights and architectural style (Legislative Affairs Office of the State Council P. R. China 2002).

For the Calligraphy Quarter, the Beilin district government announced a renewal project in 1990 to improve the city image for tourists and promote sustainable cultural tourism development. It demolished all the shop houses along the main street and replaced them with new buildings in barely one year's time. It claimed to rebuild the quarter in order to unify the architectural style. In 1992, the Xi'an city government conducted a revitalization project in the Calligraphy Quarter, including the standardization of all houses along the street to Mingqing style and named the quarter College Gate Cultural Street. However, this project only covered the core area and the main street of the district, while the outer area remained undeveloped. In 2003, echoing the city government's Tang Imperial City Renaissance Plan, the Beilin district government started to redevelop its tourist attractions. In May 2004, the Beilin district government conducted an urban renewal project, covering an area of over 17,000 square metres, involving not only the main street but also the surrounding area.[97] The project aimed to build up a historic district image through the standardization of the booths along the main street in neo-Tang style and the renovation of shop houses. The whole renewal project was finished and the district became a pedestrian zone in late April 2005.[98] The government plans, however, were generally weak in distinguishing between whether they were meant to preserve the original architecture of a 'historic district' or to produce a 'revitalized district' (with replicas). And, as Ms. Wang (a heritage studies lecturer in her late thirties) complained, all the urban renewal projects ignored the relationship between architecture and community members.

---

[97] 'Woqu quanli tuijing shuyuanmen sanxuejie jiejing zhengzhi Gongzuo' (The district government puts effort to improve the street view of the Calligraphy Quarter). Beilin District website. http://www.beilin.gov.cn/ptl/def/def/index_4_4998_ci_trid_28129-resid_4297831. html. Last accessed 1 May 2016.

[98] 'Shuyuanmen lishi wenhua shanbudao kaijie yishi longzhong juxing' (The opening of the walking zone of the Calligraphy Quarter). Beilin District website. http://www.beilin. gov.cn/ptl/def/def/index_4_4998_ci_trid_15277-resid_4297831.html. Last accessed 1 May 2016.

Nevertheless, some of the government's efforts in the Calligraphy and Muslim quarters were influenced by their identification as Mingqing-style historic districts (Xi'an Municipal Government 1980). In the Muslim Quarter, Xi'an City Planning Bureau imposed height control and executed preservation programs for the mosques, temples, and local houses. The density of buildings in the core area was reduced from 64 per cent to 50 per cent (Wang and Liu 2010). Government schemes too made reference to 'preserving the Hui ethnic characteristics' of the quarter, and as part of its efforts to preserve traditional business, it encouraged local shopkeepers to form a business network and it provided them with business advice (Xi'an Municipal Government 2008).

Owing to the Silk Roads World Heritage nomination, the government paid even more attention to the development of the Muslim Quarter as it hosts one of the World Heritage candidates – Great Mosque. The Xi'an Municipal Government General Plan 2008–20 (Xi'an Municipal Government 2008) underpins the goal to reduce population density in the area based on the so-called Demolish More, Build Less Policy. In 2004, the Muslim Quarter also fell into the Tang Imperial City Renaissance Plan, which planned to rebuild a large amount of original shop houses (Feighery 2011). These renewal projects were not executed, partly due to community opposition (see below), but also because the government encountered difficulties in finding private investors (Gillette 2000: 55). Since the district was densely populated, the revenue from the renewal projects would not be as high as in other parts of Xi'an due to the potential compensation that the developer has to pay (see chapter 8), and as a consequence, no real estate companies were willing to take over the project.

Social Strategies against Change

Though commercialization is now felt to be unavoidable and even natural, the transformation of Xi'an from an ancient capital to a domestic and international tourist destination has not gone uncontested. When the government sought to impose urban renewal 'plans' (not just regulations) on the Muslim Quarter in the 1990s, locals were worried about losing their community life, extended families, mosques, and businesses. Mr. Liu, a local resident in his mid-sixties, told me: 'everyone in the community felt anxious about the renewal plan of Lianhu District back then[99], as we saw that it would potentially harm the community. We stuck together and did not compromise with the government in order to protect our community and defend

---

[99] The Muslim Quarter belongs to Lianhu District while the Calligraphy Quarter belongs to Beilin District in Xi'an.

our interest'. The Muslim community was determined to resist the government-led urban renewal plans. As a result, no overarching 'renewal project' took place until 2004. In 2004, the city government sought to regenerate the quarter within the context of a revitalization project for the whole city, but this larger project was cancelled as well. By the time I conducted my fieldwork, most informants were not willing to talk about the decades-old project. Ms. Yuan, a hawker in her late fifties, said: 'as long as it is peaceful now, we do not want to comment on that'. Therefore, I only collected a limited amount of data from previous ethnographies and some informants, who were open to talking about the incidents. In Jonathan Lipman's (2004) ethnography, he recorded how some Xi'an Hui used their personal network with academics and urban planners to negotiate with the local government, without involving the central authorities (p. 35). A group of diverse participants, including residents of the district, small business entrepreneurs, academics, school teachers, and religious professionals, founded the Xi'an Islamic Cultural Study Society. The members collected opinions from local residents about the renewal projects through questionnaires, group meetings, and home visits. Then, they transmitted the results to the locals and the city and provincial governments (Lipman 2004: 37). After viewing the research results, the government withdrew the renewal plan.

In contrast, when the Calligraphy Quarter faced renewal projects imposed by the government, most residents welcomed the change. Mr. Peng, an eighty-year-old book shop owner, who lived in the Calligraphy Quarter above his store, told me that he observed the whole renewal process. He recalled that people willingly moved out of the quarter at the government's order. According to Mr. Huang, a high-level government official of the provincial cultural heritage preservation department, the government had initially planned to preserve the original buildings of the district in the 1990s. It suggested a plan to the community and tried to collect money from the shops, but no one was interested. The local residents were enthusiastic about modernization and wanted to move into new high-rise apartments. Because they refused to support the government's preservation plan, the old buildings were demolished in the first urban renewal project.

In fact, the disinterest in preservation in the Calligraphy Quarter is typical for the many Han-dominated quarters of Xi'an. What is less typical, according to Ms. Zhang, an urban planner in her late forties, is that the quarter was consulted by the government. The many other traditional quarters within the city wall with well-preserved original Mingqing-style buildings did not even have a chance to negotiate with the government. Residents elsewhere had no way to dodge the government projects, even if they had wanted to resist them. In the eyes of many urban planners and academics, the Muslim Quarter presented the only successful case of resistance.

Both the desire to resist and the success in doing so seems related first of all, to the nature of the Muslim Quarter. In this district, the majority of residents share a common religion and ethnicity which strengthens their sense of belonging to the quarter. To them, the quarter is more than a place to work and live; it signifies the boundary between Hui and Han. The Hui in Xi'an do not have a great sense of belonging to the city; it is the Muslim Quarter that they regard as 'home'. While their religion and ethnicity separate them from the majority of the society, it fortifies the formation of a strong community.

Second, the fate of the Muslim Quarter must be understood in connection to the 'ethnic issue' as one of the most sensitive topics in Chinese politics. In the late 1950s, China conducted a survey investigating the number and types of all ethnicities in China (*minzu shibie*) and classified over 200 ethnic minority groups into only 56 official ones (Schein 2000a). In order to build up one harmonious China, the state tried to use both soft and hard power to include the minorities. Some of the soft methods are the exemption from the one-child policy and lower requirements for university entries (Wu 1990). In Xi'an, the city government was exceptionally cautious about how to include the Hui as the biggest minority group (Lipman 1998; Gillette 2000). As Xi'an is the most politically important city in western China, the government was concerned that if it provoked the hostility of the Hui in Xi'an, it might trigger riots by other minorities in the west, especially the Uyghurs in Xinjiang. It is with this concern, most probably, that the city preferred to appease the Hui community and cancel the renewal projects (Feighery 2008). In turn, (and informants admitted as much), the Hui made use of their ethnic advantage to express resentment about government plans – an unacceptable option for the 'loyal' Han Chinese communities.

In addition, the Muslim Quarter received support from the wider public in its resistance. This support confirmed the historical value of the original architecture and helped the community take further action. In recent years, non-Hui residents of Xi'an have supported the Muslim Quarter, including by seeking to demonstrate its uniqueness as particular to Xi'an. Mr. Song, a Han Chinese and owner of a publishing company, for example, has initiated a documentary series about the lifestyle of the Muslim Quarter. He recruited a group of young journalists to conduct the project, and between 2012–14, they had already finished six books (available for sale in all book shops in Xi'an). The journalists enjoyed conducting interviews with the residents and experts of the quarter and documenting the area's oral

history. Mr. Chen, a team member in his early thirties, told me that they
planned to rent a space in the Muslim Quarter and open a book shop of their
own that would also function as a touristic information centre addressing not
only food culture, but also the traditional shop houses and historical
mosques. Members of the Hui community would be hired as local guides to
give community tours. Mr. Chen said: 'Community tours are the trend in the
world now and it is the best way to show visitors an insider's view of a
quarter. These tours are very successful in many Jewish quarters in Europe,
therefore we would like to copy the idea and apply it to the Muslim Quarter'.
With these efforts and cooperation with non-Hui, the Muslim Quarter is
promoted as socially and historically important, making it especially difficult
for the government to leverage change without community consent.

The two districts reflect the interaction and dilemma between history
and modernity at the local level. The renewal projects and commercialization
process in the quarters had the potential to bring numerous benefits and
modernization to the local communities, but in return, the individuals and
communities had to give up their original social conditions and community
values. Although commercialization in the Muslim Quarter also disturbed
part of the communities, it was still considered tolerable compared to the
renewal projects. Residents have mixed feelings towards the commercialization. In part, they welcome tourists to appreciate their food culture
because it demonstrates their 'open' Silk Road characteristics. For example,
Mr. Hui (in his thirties), told me that even though Muslims did not like to eat
yuanxiao, that the dumplings are sold in the Muslim Quarter during Chinese
New Year reflects the Hui ethnic nature: harmonious and willing to integrate
into the Han Chinese society. It was mostly the consequences brought by
tourism development that local Hui people disliked. The communities of the
two quarters in Xi'an chose different paths due to the varied sense of
belonging and perception of heritage of the members. While the residents of
the Calligraphy Quarter preferred modernization and did not attempt to
preserve the quarter and the houses, the Xi'an Hui community demanded
that any urban renewal plans should leave room for them to maintain their
solidarity and community interests.

Social Resilience with Chinese Characteristics

The comparison between the two quarters displays the urban social life and
city characteristics of old Xi'an. Social changes have taken place, but each
district has kept various features of 'traditional' quarters which can be seen
by the informed visitor in the mode of economy, community ties, relationship to heritage sites, and social life. It is these elements which make community heritage 'alive' and distinct from 'frozen' historical monuments.

Furthermore, the two quarters demonstrate different reactions towards external imposed changes, such as tourism development and government-led urban transformation. I call the social attitude of the Calligraphy Quarter 'social silence', since the community chose not to preserve their shop houses and organized no resisting events. Hence, the district government replaced all the original houses along the main street, removed the inhabitants from the Mingqing-style houses. The shops are also occupied by migrants from other provinces for business opportunities. Mr. Sun, a booth owner in his mid-thirties from Shanxi Province, said: 'here in the Calligraphy Quarter, people speak all different kinds of dialects, except the local Shaanxi dialect'. Except for the Forest of Steles and some shops in the alleys, which dodged the renewal projects, the quarter has been rebuilt since 1990. Although the urban social life was very lively with strong family-like community ties, when facing changes, the members were not willing to stick together to preserve their community life. Whereas the Calligraphy Quarter demon-strated 'social silence', the Muslim Quarter portrayed 'social resilience' with Chinese characteristics.

Studies on social resilience look at how social entities resolve threats that accumulated over time or caused by unpredictable hazards.[100] There are three kinds of social resilience studies (Keck and Sakdapolrak 2013). The first type is centred on natural hazards and disasters and investigates how social groups respond to those sudden threats (Tobin and Whiteford 2002; Rockstrom 2004; Tompkins 2005; Braun and Aßheuer 2011; Howe 2011; McGee 2011). The second type addresses long-term stress associated with natural resource management, resource scarcity, and environmental variability (Adger 2000; Berkes and Folke 2000; Bradley and Grainger 2004; Langridge, Christian-Smith and Lohse 2006; Endfield 2007; Hayward 2008). Both types also explore how local communities use indigenous knowledge to tackle ecological problems. The last type of social resilience studies – and most relevant to Xi'an – focuses on urban settings and analyses local communities' tactics to deal with different kinds of social change and development which endanger the sustainability of the community. These include policy and institutional change (Thomas and Twyman 2005; Marshall 2007; Marshall and Marshall 2007), regional economic trans-formation (Evans 2008), tourism (Orchiston, Prayagand and Brown 2016),

---

[100] The concept of social resilience emerged in the 2000s from the notion of resilience, which was originally applied in the fields of ecology and biology where it meant the ability of a system to maintain a steady ecological state (Holling 1986, 1995; Common 1995; Gunderson et al. 1997; Adger and Kelly 2001). By the 2000s, social scientists started to use this term and to define social resilience as 'the ability of groups or communities to self-organize in the face of social, political or environmental stresses and disturbances' (Adger 2000: 347).

infrastructural development (Perz et al. 2010), and urban social-spatial transformation (Bouzarovki, Salukvadze and Gentile 2011; Zingel et al. 2011). In other words, social resilience can be understood as a combination of 'coping strategies' and 'adaptive capacity' in times of change (Keck and Sakdapolrak 2013).

According to Markus Keck and Patrick Sakdapolrak (2013), social entities usually apply strategies to increase three types of capacity: coping, adaptive, and transformative. The Muslim Quarter enhances social resilience and the related capacities in the follow ways. First, the community maximizes its coping capacities, meaning the ability of social actors to overcome adversities, by gathering experts within the quarter to cope with problems and find solutions. They formed an intellectual group to collect supporting data and convinced the government that the quarter contained their heritage, which was inseparable from their everyday life. Second, Muslim Quarter community members used adaptive capacities related to the ability to learn from past experiences and adjust to future challenges. The Muslim Quarter built on past experiences from other quarters in Xi'an, reflected on the reasons for observed failures, and tried to draw up its own strategies. Last but not least, the community developed transformative capacity, which is the ability to craft institutions to support the community' sustainability. The quarter reached out to different institutes and associations and managed to recruit more and more people to help, not only experts of Islamic studies or famous Hui, but also Han activists and foreign scholars. In terms of Keck and Sakdapolrak's (2013) theory of achieving social resilience, the Muslim Quarter managed to utilize all the mentioned capacities to fulfil social resilience against urban renewal projects. Although the quarter became very commercialized in the past years and tourists visited the quarter mainly for food, the majority of Xi'an Hui, especially those who lived in the core area and the educated ones, stayed together to preserve the urban life and houses in their home quarter.

The contrast between the Calligraphy and Muslim quarters shows how differently two communities react towards change, and it shows how the Muslim Quarter community members utilized various strategies to achieve social resilience. It also displays the role of the Chinese government in the process of change. In the face of commercialization and urban renewal projects, the Calligraphy Quarter has always been cooperative; at most, community members have demanded more compensation. As a Han-dominated community, they are expected to be loyal and to support the government's projects. On the other hand, even though the Muslim Quarter has shown that they have proactively used different strategies and reached out for support in order to preserve their social life, it was the state that enabled them and gave them room to do so due to the political sensitivity of ethnic policies in China.

Modernization and progress were unquestionable for both the state and the local residents, but the way to accomplish these goals differed. Even if the central authorities were not involved directly in the negotiation process, the state was omnipresent. The case of the Calligraphy Quarter shows that residents and mediators (including urban planners and academics) had internalized the state's ideology of modernization. The Muslim Quarter shows an interplay between the state, the community, and other agents to find common ground between preservation and modernization. Although some scholars propose that the concept of social resilience is too optimistic because there is only a limited participation capacity that does not allow everyone, especially locals, to take part in the decision making process (Voss 2008; Bohle et al. 2009; Davidson 2010), the case study of the Muslim Quarter demonstrates a kind of 'social resilience' with Chinese character-istics through which it was feasible for the community to make a change.

Chapter 8
The City of Construction – New Heritage

Shaanxi Province is called the 'kneeling archer' after its geographical shape (see Map 1). The name has been embraced by locals who say that, economically, Shaanxi Province is such a warrior: waiting patiently for the right time to attack just as Shaanxi has waited for its economic boom. Along with the provincial government's modernization effort since the late 1990s, GDP has risen, the living standard has improved, and the popularity of Xi'an has soared. Locals also say, 'the kneeling warrior is about to stand up' to acknowledge the government's effort and express hope for the future. At the same time, this metaphor also reflects the close relationship between history and modernity in their mind-set, as they use an archaeological icon to describe the rise of a modern era. Indeed, both history and modernization dominate the urban development process of Xi'an and these two components cannot be separated from each other.

Xi'an's modernization began relatively late compared to other Chinese cities. China's other big cities underwent a process of urbanization and modernization in the 1980s under Deng's development policy (Chan and Hu 2003). The national government standardized the planning of Chinese cities through a 'blueprint planning model' (Stares and Zhi 1996: 420), common guidelines, and urbanization policies (Chan and Xu 1985; Zhang Li 2003; Zhou and Ma 2003; Zhu 2003; Henderson 2005; Yusuf and Saich 2008). With the goal of modernization, cities were redeveloped and designed in similar ways to facilitate the economic priorities of the central state. This approach has been criticized by Chinese social scientists (e.g. Yeh and Wu 1995; Hsu 1996; Wu 1999; Ma 2002) because the state neglected elements that defined the unique characteristics of the cities and regarded them as 'backwards'. By the late 1990s, the national government slowly changed its focus and increasingly granted municipalities the right to prepare and approve their own urban plans, regulate development, and issue land use permits (Ning 1998; Abramson, Leaf and Ying 2002; Wu 2002; Gaubatz 2005). Because state funding for urban development did not reach Xi'an until the 1990s, certain historical features in the urban centre escaped the first round of modernization and were subject to local discretion in subsequent planning.

As the modernization wave hit Xi'an in the late 1990s, the city replaced most old neighbourhoods and some historical monuments with high rises, wide roads, huge public squares, and construction sites. Even though national policies would have allowed Xi'an to keep more of its historical characteristics, the regional government and inhabitants demanded modernization. At the same time, the emerging heritage boom made local authorities see value in the historical sites. Hence, Xi'an planning was characterized most by its efforts to balance between modernization and historical preservation, between becoming a modern leading city and an ancient capital.

It might appear that modernization and heritage preservation would contradict each other. However, Alexander Reichl pointed out that 'when it is politically advantageous to do so, pro-growth forces are drawing on the past to build the city's future' (1997: 531). As we have seen in previous chapters, in Xi'an historical preservation became a strategy for economic growth and heritage development was shaped as a form of modernity. Indeed, heritage became something that could be created (cf. Zhang Liang 2003). As the former deputy mayor Duan Xiannian asserted, 'what we are creating now will be cultural heritage in 100 years!' Consequently, the city government underwent the making of three kinds of 'heritage'. In less than fifteen years' time, intensive construction and reconstruction, of heritage sites, high rises, and transportation networks created a brand-new cityscape for Xi'an.

Residents constantly compared the city's past with its present and emphasized that Xi'an used to be small, dense, and full of slums[101] until the early 2000s. Once, I crossed a dangerously busy road with Mr. Chu, an environmental activist in his early thirties, and he recalled how his parents let him cross the same road on his way to school from the age of seven. He said that all the roads in Xi'an had been very narrow, fitting at most two cars side-by-side, but in the past ten years, roads were widened, and now had six lanes on average. Others told me about the changes of the main roads around the Bell Tower. Ms. Ye, an engineer in her early thirties, said that when she was young, the traffic around the Bell Tower was not congested at all, and

---

[101] The term for slums (*chengzhongcun*) literally refers to villages within cities. These are quarters where low-class people or migrant workers reside. Usually composed of self-built houses with simple building material, the slums are stigmatized as crowded, dirty, and hubs for criminal activities, such as robbery and drug dealing. More about slums in Xi'an will be discussed in the second part of this chapter.

that people could cross the road easily. On hot summer days, she had chased after the street-rinsing-cars at the ring road with other children to cool down. Now, pedestrians were prohibited from crossing the road and there was a newly built (but confusing to locals) underpass under the Bell Tower. Urbanization had taken place so quickly that people already held nostalgic feelings for the vanishing older districts, narrow streets, and lifestyle of fifteen years previously.

This chapter discusses the dilemmas produced between the dual infatuation with history and craving for modernization held by both Xi'an's residents and the government. The first part of this chapter addresses the city's strategy for merging history into the urban landscape and the use of heritage as a form of modernity. What does 'modern' mean to local residents? Do they prefer the historical or the modern side of the city? What do they think about the old and new heritage sites? The second part delves into the new construction and infrastructure that is meant to become 'heritage'. It draws attention to the consequences of the urbanization and construction projects, such as gentrification, the formation of slums, and the creation of ghost towns.

A New Old Xi'an

Christa Salamandra (2004) used the idea of a 'new old Damascus' to describe the modern phenomenon in Damascus of 'returning to the old' as the old city and tradition have been commercialized as popular culture. She looked into how 'authenticity' is constructed in an urban context. Similar to Damascus, Xi'an's history and tradition faces intensive commercialization. Xi'an might still be old in local inhabitants' memories, but in fact, it has changed drastically in the past two decades. History and pop culture interplay with each other on an everyday basis. For instance, café culture started to dominate today's Xi'an, replacing traditional tea houses. Youngsters prefer to hang out in the cosy ambience of cafés and have adopted the Western taste for coffee. Yet, interestingly, I found the decoration of some cafés was rather 'traditional'. Ms. Yao, a linguistics student proudly said: 'Xi'an's ancient city image is displayed everywhere in the city. Even Starbucks at Big Wild Goose Pagoda attempts to decorate its interior with Tang pottery figures and Qin terracotta warriors'. The cafés display the interface between tradition and modernity. In the past, locals liked to visit the Forest of Steles for cultural events in their free time, but now, they prefer to visit the International Convention Centre, especially when it organizes international trade conventions. Many of my informants treated these conventions as an international experience to get in touch with the rest of the world and consume foreign products. Initiated by the government's modernization schemes and globalization, not only the city-scape but also the lifestyles and traditions of the locals altered.

People interpreted the 'new old Xi'an' differently. Some found it exciting that the city finally started to become modernized, but others viewed the changes pessimistically as a destruction of their original town-scape and tradition. Some saw continuity, albeit in distinct stages, of a disregard for the 'real' past. Mr. Wu, an urban planner in his mid-forties, segmented four stages of heritage-handling in modern China: 'the dumping stage' in the 1950s when the state treated heritage as rubbish or a burden to any kind of development; 'the revolutionary stage' during the Cultural Revolution (1966–76) during which the Four Olds were eliminated and historical buildings were destroyed (see also Morton 1995: 216); 'the developmental stage' from the 1980s when China prioritized development over anything else; and lastly, 'the manipulative stage' of the present when the state realized the political and economic potential of historical sites and saw heritage as a tool for politics, ideology, and economy. Mr. Wu saw this last stage as having the strongest impact on Xi'an. Ms. Zhang, a sociology postgraduate student would have agreed. She exclaimed, 'we have no more real heritage in Xi'an. Everything is new!' and opined that the government's statement that it was creating future cultural heritage was ridiculous. The government, she said, had destroyed many original and 'authentic' heritage sites that cannot be replaced. But what was 'authentic' heritage? According to my observation, the changes in Xi'an meant that there was old heritage with new meanings and new heritage with old meanings.

Old Heritage with New Meanings

Similar to Salamandra's Damascus (2004), the 'new old Xi'an' has been changed by commercialization. But the changes are not only the large-scale ones documented in previous chapters. Many changes have gone almost unnoticed by locals who also assume that the commodification of historical and even religious sites is more or less normal progress and necessary for the improvement of the city. For example, Xingshan Temple, a Buddhist temple located in the heart of urban Xi'an, initiated a fund-raising program by engraving donors' names in the temple's bricks, roof tiles, and columns. The collected money was to go towards building an extension complex, which would eventually result in the demolition of the original entrance gate and two ancient temple buildings close to the entrance – all dating to the Ming Dynasty. Though academics did not support the extension plans, local residents and believers viewed expansion and rebuilding of a temple as normal.

As the city expands, many heritage sites are reused or commercialized, losing their previous meanings and functions. The city walls in Xi'an serve as another example. Walls (*cheng*) have been a central structure of cities in China as mirrored by its Chinese character (城). The left part (土 *tu*) means earth and symbolizes the city wall because of the building material (Chan 1994: 1). In imperial times, China's urban population was concentrated within walled cities and a settlement without a wall was not considered a proper city (Chang 1977: 75). Xi'an's Ming city wall preserved its function as the border of the urban centre until the late 1990s. Rapid urbanization then changed its function to the boundary of the city's first ring, but no walls enclosed the second or third rings.[102] Thus Xi'an City Wall has become a tourist destination, offering a wide range of activities. Visitors can cycle on top of the wall, take photos with soldiers, and enjoy the hourly 'rite of soldiers' performances. Mr. Yao, one of the performers dressed as a soldier, told me that he was very proud of his job because he could revitalize the important rituals from the past. On the ground, the meaning of entering the city wall changed too. Ms. Jiang, an aerospace engineer in her early thirties, recalled that when she was a child, she felt very special entering through the gate of the city wall, as if she entered a different world, coming from a rural outside space into the crowded city. Xi'an people even used the historical word *jincheng,* which literally means 'to enter the city', to describe the action of going through the city wall gate. However, Ms. Jiang said: 'Now that Xi'an is so crowded everywhere, I do not have any special feelings when I *jincheng* anymore'.

Xi'an's two other ancient city walls long ago lost their original function of protecting the city. The Han Chang'an city wall remains represent the most ancient type of city wall. Yet, according to Ms. Ma, a restorer in her early forties, the wall was poorly conserved because people could climb up and down freely and plants grew along the wall, destroying the earth structure. A part of the wall functions as the border of Han Chenghu Cultural Scenic Area, but a large part was also torn down for the surrounding urban transformation projects. The Tang Chang'an city wall is the longest city wall in Xi'an, but many parts were removed because of urban development. Only scattered remains in the south and in the west are left. The western remains were turned into a park and the southern remains became an archaeological park in Qujiang District with an open air restaurant and one end connected to a bar street.

---

[102] '"Sanhuan" huo cheng' (The proposal of the construction of the third ring). *Xi'an Daily*, 14 January 2015. Available online, http://epaper.xiancn.com/xarb/html/2015-01/14/content_346113.htm. Last accessed 1 May 2016.

By giving heritage sites a new commercial function, they may survive the rapid urbanization. But, their meanings change. Most importantly, they can come to convey a sense of modernity. The fact that people remember their recently past state means that the malleability of the sites to fit present social and economic needs becomes one of the sites' characteristics.

'New Heritage' with Old Meanings

According to City Tourism Plan 2013–20 (Xi'an City Tourism Board 2013a), the city is to become a world-class archaeological park city by 2020 and boast the highest number of large-scale archaeological parks around the globe. Such a goal means there is no end in sight for the creation of 'new heritage'. It can be found in several forms – all hark back to the past and insist that they convey the meanings, culture, or essence of that past.

Some new heritage sites are relatively contained. Such is the case of Tang Paradise, the first Tang-period historical theme park in China, which opened in 2005. (People rumoured that a similar Han theme park was on the way). The park is meant to recreate the city's Tang-era and its culture. It is composed of many artificial attractions such as bridges, pavilions, pagodas, and the eye-catching Ziyun Palace, which contains museums and performance venues. The park offers different kinds of music, dance, acrobatics performances, and a daily parade as the highlight. All workers in Tang Paradise have to dress in Tang style. The park also organizes festivals and events with Chinese cultural or historical themes, such as 'A Day back to Tang' and 'Lantern Festival'. To many who worked there, the clear invention of heritage did not appeal. Ms. Li, an intern at the park in her twenties, was highly disappointed. She was a heritage studies major and had an internship as an assistant in the Ziyun Palace Museum. She had hoped to learn about heritage management skills. Yet, she had a hard time accepting Tang Paradise as a heritage site. She felt that there was nothing special about the museum's collection, and that its management did not care about exhibitions because it was only meant to be part of the theme park, which itself concentrated on entertainment and tourism, but not on history.

But, as the city government has attempted to integrate historical features into the urban cityscape, and in accord with the Tang Imperial Renaissance Plan (see chapter 4), elements of new heritage have spread everywhere. For example, many residential buildings in Xi'an are now decorated with an extra pavilion or Chinese rooftop (see Plate 10). Although the decorations are not very big, usually covering only one-third of the roof, when many buildings share this pattern, it is easily noticeable. The standardized rooftops create a unified skyline for Xi'an, not only in the city centre, but also along the road from the airport. Mr. Li, an urban planner, said: 'adding the neo-Tang roofs to the condominiums is one of the easiest ways to balance between modernization and the history of the city. It is a powerful reminder for the visitors about the city's own history'. Yet an easy solution that satisfied urban planners was not all that satisfying to others. Ms. Yuan, an architect and expert in Chinese traditional architecture, found the city's revitalization and universal application of one or two Tang features in modern construction to be ridiculous. The result she said did not evoke but misrepresented Tang architecture. Tang architecture was rather characterized by the grandness of rooftops five times bigger than the buildings they covered; tiny pavilions on condominium rooftops evince the opposite proportions. Such a 'cheap' solution, she said, was a waste of resources that could have been used to preserve the real old architecture.

Plate 10. High rises in Xi'an decorated with a neo-Tang style rooftop.

A third form of new heritage is less architectural than referential. For example, restaurants, theatres, and shopping malls – even when they have no architectural pretensions to the past – tend to be named after historical places, people, or eras. Names like Chang'an, Daqin (Great Qin), Shengtang (Prosperous Tang), Qin Han Tang, and so on are popular. The most popular shopping mall located next to the Bell Tower is Kaiyuan Mall, referencing the Kaiyuan shengshi (713–41 CE) during which, under the rule of Emperor Li Longji, Tang China reached its peak economically, diplomatically, and militarily (Wang 1988).

Some forms of new heritage are even hybrids of the other forms, resulting in particular confusions about what they are meant to be. The Never Sleeping City of Great Tang (Datang buyecheng), for example, is a complex full of shopping malls and restaurants. It is in Qujiang District, and with its neo-Tang construction and decorative sculptures from historical figures, it is sometimes taken as a theme-park-like area in itself. To the extent that it means to convey something about the Tang, it could be said to aim at displaying the cosmopolitan side of the Tang Dynasty. People who lived nearby told me that the Never Sleeping City was convenient because they could go to its restaurants even in the middle of the night. However, visitors did not like the place so much. Mr. Zhou from Chengdu said: 'the name of the commercial district has no taste at all and to be frank, I thought initially that it was [meant to be] a red light district of the Tang Dynasty!'

The government has also reassigned old place names to educate people about the city's history. For example, though Mingde Gate no longer exists, the bus stop nearest the empty land which it once occupied is called 'Mingde Gate'. This name might equally be seen as old heritage, left to remind people of the site's historical importance. Naming as a form of new heritage is more evident in the names given to new metro stops. The Ming city wall had 18 gates in total, but not many locals could name them all; moreover, as locals had long preferred to use alternate names like 'North Gate' and 'South Gate', the original names of the gates had been forgotten. Hence, the Xi'an metro project decided to name its new stations after the gates' original names; Yongning men (Gate of Forever Peace) marked South Gate and Anyuan men (Gate of Settling the West) marked North Gate. This invention was well-received: locals appreciated the new names and accompanying decorative elements of each station as a general education and reminder of the city's history.

The Making of Renqi

Whether old or new, heritage sites need *renqi*, the breath and energy of human beings. Without this human element, space (and heritage) is unappealing if not actually destroyed, as Zhang (2006) found with her study of Kunming. In Kunming, people felt that *renqi* was destroyed when the older street markets were replaced with underground shopping malls because the new spaces could not gather visitors. In Xi'an, by contrast, my informants tended to emphasize how *renqi* was being generated at various heritage sites and in their surroundings.

Mr. Wu and Mr. Yuan, engineering students at Jiaotong University, brought me once to a famous local restaurant. The place was crowded and we could not find seats, so we ordered take-away. The two men suggested that we eat at the empty café across the street. I hesitated because we did not intend to consume anything from that café, but would only use their tables and chairs. However, both informants confirmed that the act would be fine and said: 'the café should feel thankful that we sit there, because we bring them *renqi*!' Indeed, the waitresses did just let us sit there, and slowly our presence attracted new customers. During the meal, Mr. Wu explained:

> The same concept works for Big Wild Goose Pagoda and its surrounding area. Qujiang Corporation did not mind offering free archaeological parks and a daily water fountain show, because they would bring more people to visit its expensive tourist attractions, such as Big Wild Goose Pagoda and Tang Paradise. Creating *renqi* is the best way to advertise a district or a heritage site.

Mr. You, an urban planner, shared the same logic and viewed that the free recreational space together with the commercial activities created *renqi* in Qujiang District. He reasoned: 'historically speaking, Big Wild Goose Pagoda and the area around had strong *renqi* back in the Tang Dynasty as it was a central religious and social venue. So, the crowdedness in today's Qujiang revitalizes its past'. Nowadays, the free heritage parks act as a common ground for socializing. Mrs. Feng, a housewife in her mid-fifties, living in the centre of the city, enjoyed going for a walk in Qujiang District every evening. This was, she said, because she could feel *renqi* everywhere: many other people go to the park for leisure activities and sports. Mr. Lai, a sociology postgraduate, regarded the park around Big Wild Goose Pagoda as the ideal place to observe genuine urban social life in Xi'an.

A site that cannot draw *renqi* suffers in a downward spiral. Daming Palace Heritage Park and Han Chang'an City National Archaeological Park, for example, lack *renqi*. The Daming Palace project was criticized even by its original residents for being too spacious and unattractive. Even locals residing close to these two sites preferred to take a thirty-minute bus ride to Qujiang District for an evening walk. A number of reasons contributed to the parks' failure to attract the visitors who generate *renqi*. First, the sites' locations in the north, isolated from other famous heritage sites and busy commercial districts, reduced their popularity. Second, they failed to balance the spatial arrangement between the commercial area and the park. Both sites give visitors an empty feeling; they are too spacious. Without infrastructure, shops, and facilities. Qujiang District successfully generated *renqi* because of its favourable location and strategic combination of free parks, heritage sites, and the making of the fountain as an eye-catcher.

Mr. Yang, an engineer working at various heritage sites, said that he needed to consider many aspects in order to design the layout of the heritage sites. On top of the basic facilities such as water and electricity supplies, he also had to concern the pragmatic matter such as double checking land use permits and land ownership so that the building of the heritage parks would not violate any laws. Moreover, before any construction, he had to conduct field evaluations to assess the historical resources, architectural landscape, and cultural characteristics of the site to ensure the historical correctness of the site. Lastly, he had to anticipate the *renqi* factor to develop the site into one that people would want to go again and again. *renqi* is critical to urban design, just as people's perception of authenticity in myriad registers is important to heritage construction. Yet these subjective considerations are relatively unimportant to planners and developers. Similarly, compared to other construction and urbanization projects, heritage development is just the tip of the iceberg. The next section addresses the massive demolition and construction across Xi'an.

China or Chai-na?

The Chinese term *chai* (拆) characterizes the Chinese state's idea of urban development. Travelling around cities in China, one often sees the character for *chai* written in red on walls or buildings, indicating that the marked areas have to be demolished. The question '*Chai na?*' comes up repeatedly in daily conversations among local residents, meaning, 'where has demolition taken place?' or 'where will demolition take place?' Demolition, as part of urban development scheme, has penetrated into urban social life in China. Xi'an, the biggest city in north-west China, faces the same challenge. In 1995, with the goal of 'improving the quality of life', the city conducted a demolition-rebuilding program affecting 85 per cent of the inner city area (Fayolle Lussac, Høyem and Clément 2007). Old urban districts were removed, buildings were torn down, and roads were widened.

Under the modernization discourse of the national government, cities in China have engaged in the process of demolition and transformation. Old buildings and abandoned houses were labelled as obstacles for future development, which resulted in the removal of many neighbourhoods and slums. Xi'an, regardless of its status as an ancient capital, follows the national developmental discourse. The city government does not only conduct demolition projects in the name of modernization and a better future, but also claims to do so for heritage preservation. The largest demolition project in Xi'an between 2004 and 2014 was the Daming Palace project. It involved the removal of more than 10,000 households from an area of 56 square kilometres (Zhang 2014).

Demolition is undertaken in the names of modernity and heritage. But what happens after the demolition of neighbourhoods? How is social life affected by demolition? How do different social actors perceive the large-scale demolition and construction projects? The next two subsections will display the major forces of demolition and urban transformation in Xi'an.

The City under 'Excavation'

In the 1970s, the Shaanxi provincial government approved Xi'an city government's plan to build a metro line. The plan envisioned tearing down the Ming city wall, just as had been done in Beijing. The plan was not carried out for lack of capital[103], but in 1994 Xi'an City Planning Bureau included the project in the Third Xi'an Master Plan 1995–2010 with a projection of four metro lines with a total length of 73.17 kilometres (State Council 1999). In September 2006, Xi'an received approval from the national government to carry out the construction. In 2012, Xi'an City Planning Bureau published the Xi'an City Public Transportation Network Plan, which envisioned a massive extension: the building of 15 metro lines across 586.7 kilometres.[104] During my fieldwork between 2013 and 2014, construction sites were everywhere, and most of them occupied the main roads. Almost half of the demolition projects conducted in urban Xi'an were related to the metro construction. Shops and residential areas were turned into construction sites too.[105]

The first metro line (Line Two) opened to the public on 16 September 2011, after five years of construction. The metro construction was extremely difficult as the construction team constantly ran into archaeological remains. Since present Xi'an lies above Tang Chang'an, the metro construction was almost like an archaeological excavation. The government tried to achieve both historical preservation and the construction at the same time. Each time the construction workers discovered archaeological artefacts, they had to report to management. Then construction paused while the metro construction committee and government officials from Shaanxi Provincial Bureau of

---

[103] 'Xingyuner Xi'an chengqiang' (The luck of the Xi'an City Wall). *China Weekly*, 18 May 2012. Available online, http://www.chinaweekly.cn/bencandy.php?fid=63&id=6052. Last accessed 1 May 2016.

[104] The plan was readily accessible: 'Xi'an shi chengshi guidao jiaotongxianwang guihua (xiupian) guihua fangan' (Xi'an city transportation and underground network planning). https://web.archive.org/web/20130208205107/http://www.xaghj.gov.cn/content.jsp?urltype=news.NewsContentUrl&wbtreeid=1037&wbnewsid=2899. Last accessed 28 February 2019.

[105] Progress reports, statistics, and other information were posted throughout 2013 on Huashang Net in articles like 'Xi'an ditie kaijian' (The construction of Xi'an underground has started). http://news.hsw.cn/node_3656.htm. Last accessed 1 May 2016.

Cultural Heritage, Xi'an City Planning Bureau, City Construction and Housing Bureau and the City Office of Cultural Heritage met at Qujiang Hotel to discuss the next steps. Mr. Zhong, a staff member from Qujiang Hotel, reported that these meetings were held regularly and in secret. The mass media was not alerted as decisions were made about whether to conduct excavations or continue construction. It seems decisions most often favoured construction: Mr. Li, a curator of a state-owned museum in Xi'an, said: 'of course we, as historical relics conservers and protectors, ha[d] to attend these meetings deciding the destiny of the national archaeological treasures of the country, but we ha[d] no say in them'. He reported that the meeting parties generally decided against extensive excavations in the area and only preserved single excavated items. Archaeology had to happen on the spot. As Mr. Fang, a construction site worker informed me: 'if you want to get to know about archaeology in Xi'an, you have to talk to us and come and watch us work, because we are the first ones who get to see the artefacts and we discover cultural relics almost every day'. Still, the regular meetings, constant interruptions and even limited archaeological preservation work resulted in the relatively slow progress of the construction.

Line One opened in 2013. Then, in early 2014, the development of the metro changed completely. The city government announced its plan to speed-up construction and open new lines from April.[106] The extended line of Line Two started to operate in 2014.[107] Line Three opened in November 2016 after months of delay and Line Four started in 2018 according to plan. Lines Five, Six, Nine, and Fourteen are planned to open between 2019–21 (National Development and Reform Committee 2016). Mr. Chao, the manager of Qujiang Hotel, told me that the metro committee had decided to prioritize the completion of the metro network over archaeological findings because the delays and cost of preservation was too great a financial burden. He said: 'from now on, they will just smash all remains found underground with the machines and concentrate on the metro construction'. Such a decision promised to reduce construction time from five years per line to one year per line. Mr. Li explained, 'Archaeological artefacts have to sacrifice for city development. What can we do? We cannot avoid it. When facing city development, heritage preservation plays only a tiny part'. Perhaps Mr. Li had such an emotionless reaction and pro-government view because he

---

[106] 'Xi'an ditie 5,6 hao xian he 1 hao xian 2 qi huopi jihua 2019 tongche' (Xi'an underground line 1, 5, and 6 are expected to be finished in 2019). *Xinhua Net*, 16 April 2015. http://www.sn.xinhuanet.com/news1/2015-04/16/c_1114996859.htm. Last accessed 1 May 2016.

[107] Plan and progress were publicly available on the website of the Xi'an Metro under 'Important Dates of the Construction of Xi'an Metro'. http://www.xametro.gov.cn/dashiji.phtml. Last accessed 1 May 2016.

was a government official as well as being a curator. However, many other urban planners, architects, restorers, and archaeologists in Xi'an felt the same way – they could do nothing and chose to remain silent and give way to city development.

Even though no one openly opposed the metro construction, a group of urban planners and architects attempted to find ways to save as many artefacts as possible. Ms. Lin, a freshly graduated architect, told me that she and her colleagues had sent a recommendation to the government to learn how other ancient cities (like Athens and Rome) had managed to build a their metros while preserving artefacts; they had also provided a concrete suggestion for an underground museum. They had received no response, and she assumed this meant the government was not interested. She assumed it would take too much money and effort to design the museum and maintain the safety measures. By the time I last interviewed her in late August 2014, she had given up hope and said: 'it would be a miracle if they adopt our plan'.

Obviously, the pro-developmental city government and metro committee benefited from the decision of neglecting the archaeological content. At the local level, a group of construction workers and the antiquity market also profited from the decision. One construction worker told me how he saved artefacts and sold them. I also learnt about this black market in antiquities from some of its patrons. Even staff from the nearby Qujiang Hotel bought freshly discovered artefacts from the metro construction workers. A chef in his mid-forties showed me proudly a jade necklace and his colleague showed me another jade ornament. I questioned the authenticity of the relics, but they affirmed the jades were real. When they realized I knew government officials and provincial restorers (who greeted me on their way into the hotel), the two men begged me not to disclose their stories. They knew that the sale of artefacts was illegal.

Even after Line One opened, the congestion problem around the Bell Tower was not solved. Car owners complained that the road remained over-crowded. People were afraid to use the metro! Ms. Liang, a housewife in her mid-forties, said: 'I do not dare to use the metro because I know the government risked everything to dig it. They might have disturbed some ancient tombs. What if our ancestors or the previous emperors' spirits got angry because of the destruction of their tombs? They could use their power to destroy the metro'. Other informants also expressed anxiety and fear about the safety of the metro on precisely the same grounds. Though developers had considered the costs of 'archaeological' preservation, they had not considered how 'artefacts' were connected to the dead, ancestors, or cemeteries – all of which living people respect, whether or not they value 'heritage'. The metro construction demonstrates the dilemma between archaeological preservation and modernization at all levels.

The Glorification of Gentrification

On the morning of 22 July 2009, the family of Mr. Tang was busy preparing for his funeral in their village in Lintong District. Following village tradition, his family started to build a bamboo shelter as the funeral venue. However, a few police officers interrupted the construction. The village was expected to be demolished in the near future for a Qujiang heritage project, so no new building activities were to be allowed. This was so. Mr. Liu, a villager, said that after the start of construction on the Qujiang Lintong National Resort, the district government sent an 'anti-construction monitor team' to all villages within the project area to prevent them from transporting construction materials and building new houses. But the construction for Mr. Tang's funeral was meant just for temporary use. The family protested that the restriction on new building should not apply; the officers ignored their claim and insisted that they stop. The quarrel turned to a fight and led to the death of one of the officers.

And that was the end. An event that could have sparked widespread social concern, legal action, or protests on any number of points was quickly forgotten. At first, there were calls for Qujiang Corporation to clarify the matter. But the company refused to take any responsibilities, reasoning that the incident had taken place outside of the planned heritage park area. The village was located only in the extended area for real estate market development and would be gentrified to become high rises. Then, the city and district governments forbad the local newspapers from reporting further on the incident. It pointed to conflict between traditions and urban development and could make the public rethink the urban renewal project (Yao 2010). And, it might hinder other heritage and urban transformation projects.

I argue that the government was so quick to cover-up a homicide because it is deeply attached to glorifying gentrification and specifically because it endorses the Qujiang three-zone model which uses heritage sites as hubs of gentrification (see chapter 6). 'Gentrification' entails numerous relationships with the state, global capital markets, and large development corporations, as revealed in studies by urban scholars including social geographers, sociologists, and anthropologists (Gale 1986; Zukin 1987; Wittberg 1992; Bridge 1995; Smith 1996; Gotham 2005; Smith and Graves 2005). Gentrification is generally defined as 'the transformation of a working-class or vacant area of the central city into middle-class residential or commercial use' (Lees, Slater and Wyly 2008: xv). Yet, in practice, each case of gentrification is distinct depending on the geographical, institutional, and historical background of the city (Lees 2000). Most case studies follow the archetypal pattern in which low(er) income residential areas are upgraded (Smith 1996), but understanding how class, space, and social change are interrelated requires 'geographically sensitive research that pays close attention to both temporal and spatial context' (Smith and Graves 2005: 416). In some cases, 'low' is already relatively 'high'. For example, Loretta Lees (2003) proposed the concept of 'super-gentrification' to describe the transformation of middle-class residential areas into a high-class district in New York. For this reason, Eric Clark has defined gentrification as 'a process involving a change in population of land-users such that the new users are of higher socio-economic status than the previous users, together with an associated change in the built environment through a reinvestment in fixed capital' (2005: 25). In other words, the qualities and valuation of both space and people change with gentrification.

In Xi'an, there is a wide range of transformation that can be glossed as gentrification. Here, there is inner city displacement as well as suburban development, and in both locations it is motivated by a combination of generalized 'urban development' and a specific desire to increase tourism. For this reason, it is necessary to give special weight to what Kevin Gotham called 'tourism gentrification', that is 'the transformation of a middle class neighbourhood into a relatively affluent and exclusive enclave marked by a proliferation of gentrification that took place for tourism corporate entertainment and tourism venues' (2005: 1099). Under touristic gentri-fication, the changing value of space and people is seen 'an altered relation-ship between culture and economics in the production and consumption of urban space' (ibid.: 1115).

In most cases of gentrification, the former occupants of the space that becomes gentrified are considered victims. They are normally from lower income groups and are removed from their neighbourhoods with unfair treatment, low compensation, and unfavourable relocations (Zukin 1987; Smith 1996; Atkinson and Bridge 2005). It is easy to see how they, or others viewing their plight, might contest the desirability of gentrification. In Xi'an, however, there are few 'objective' reasons to oppose gentrification. The Chinese government has set very strict laws to safeguard the legal rights of both the demolition and relocation parties. Since 2011, it is the government that has assumed responsibility for authorizing demolition and setting compensation levels, but its packages have been generous.[108] During the

---

[108] Before 2011, following the Urban Housing Demolition and Relocation Management Regulations (CECC 2001), the entity conducting demolition was required to provide compensation and resettlement for the subjects of demolition. Moreover, it could only

Daming Palace project, the city government and Qujiang Corporation spent a total of 12 billion of which 9 billion were said to have gone towards the compensation and relocation of the original residents (Zhang 2014). In addition to a cash payment, residents also received three to eight apartments (according to the size of their original land) as compensation. Mr. Yang, an urban planner, told me that everywhere in China compensation normally includes at least two apartments. Thus while relocation is considered a generally favourable option everywhere, it was particularly so in Xi'an.

As a consequence, the gentrification wave has unleashed desire, rather than resistance, in the local population. Farmers and urban dwellers waited patiently to move to brand new apartments in modern condominiums. While gentrification in some countries means that people lose their assets (along with their home) overnight (Atkinson and Bridge 2005), in Xi'an, demolition and urban renewal projects resulted in the 'becoming rich overnight' phenomenon – so enormous was their compensation. In previous chapters, I have mentioned the disappointment expressed by people who were displaced from, or still lived near, less-successful heritage sites. Their disappointment should not be overshadowed, but here is the place to investigate how it was perceived by their co-citizens.

Indeed, from time to time, when I passed by the Shaanxi provincial government building, I saw groups of farmers protesting. They carried signs with slogans such as 'give me back my farmland' and seemingly protested against the demolition of their homes. I never approached them directly, as it would have put my permission to stay at risk (a Hong Kong citizen should not be seen to support political protests in the mainland), but I did ask my other contacts about these protestors. Many people regarded them as 'greedy farmers'; they told me that the protests were only a strategy to negotiate for higher compensation. Mr. Wang, a civil servant in his late thirties, commented once as we passed by a group of protestors: 'these farmers are not very sincere with their goal of demonstration to save their homeland because once the government compromises to give them more money, they would happily end their protest. More compensation is all they want'.

Indeed, the overall social discourse focused on the possibility that there was too much compensation, rather than too little. Many Xi'an residents criticized the phenomenon of 'getting rich overnight'. Mr. Zhang, a

---

conduct demolition with a valid 'housing demolition and relocation permit' obtained from the regional government authorities (Article 4). From 2011, the national government replaced the aforementioned regulation with the Regulations on the Expropriation and Compensation of Buildings on State-Owned Land (Law of China 2011). Under these regulations, the city and county governments are responsible for expropriation and compensation. They are to create a building expropriation department which organizes and implements the expropriation and compensation (Articles 4 and 22).

restorer in his mid-thirties, said: 'it is indeed true that many people become very rich overnight, unfortunately, these people from slums or farmlands are not very educated. They do not know how to spend their money, and worst of all, they also do not educate their younger generation properly'. He pointed out that usually the second generation of these compensation holders would be very lazy because they had no worries about money. Mr. Wei, whose father owned a piece of land in Han Chang'an City Archaeological Park and received six apartments as compensation, told me: 'I worked in Shenzhen, but then I came back to Xi'an because my father told me about the news that the government finally decided to develop our land and we would get new apartments. I gave up my job in Shenzhen immediately and flew back to Xi'an!' On top of the material compensation, Mr. Wei also got a job offer from the government as a construction worker. He was very satisfied because he and his family did not need to work hard anymore. They earned enough money by receiving rent from the other five apartments. He added: 'in the past, girls were interested in men from the city [with an urban *hukou*] because they are richer, but now, the society has changed. Many girls want marry us, the farmers, because we are becoming rich from our previous farmland while we do not need to work hard'. Mr. Wei's comment represents the view of many farmers.

However, only people who held a land use grant[109] benefited from the compensation policies. Those who merely lived in the areas to be gentrified received no compensation. Mr. Zhou, a taxi driver in his late forties, complained that he had been forced to move out of his former low-rent apartment in Qujiang District, but that it had been very difficult for him to find another affordable apartment since he did not receive any compensation. Ms. Su, the director of an orphanage for prisoners' children, also told me that the orphanage almost had to close because of the Daming Palace project. The orphanage had been considered a tenant of the building it occupied, and therefore did not receive any compensation or offers for resettlement. Ms. Su said:

> The former location at the Daming Palace area was perfect because it was cheap and spacious for our children to have a good environment to grow up in. We had a hard time finding a new place in Xi'an with such low rent because, as an NGO, we do not have a lot of money. At the same time, we would like to stay close to the city so that our donors can reach us easily.

In the end, they rented another place in rural Xi'an, reachable only by car.

---

[109] In China, all urban land belongs to the state while rural land can be owned by the state or by collectives. Individuals need to obtain a land use grant in order to use land for residential, business, or other purposes. The land use grant for residential purpose lasts 70 years.

In the process of Xi'an's gentrification there are many winners. The government, development agencies, and landowners are all, generally speaking, satisfied with the process. But even Xi'an has victims. Those who own no official grant to use the property at the outset of the process are the victims of the transformation projects. They do not even have the right to express their resentment towards the changes.

Plate 11. Signboard in Daming Palace Heritage Park.

Since the city government supports the heritage and urban transformation projects to modernize the city, Xi'an transmitted a one-sided view of gentrification focusing on its positive impacts. For instance, Daming Palace Heritage Park designed a series of 'before and after' signboards with photos of the places before the construction of the park and short descriptions, allowing visitors to compare the differences. The 'before' photographs show dirty public toilets, garbage dumps, and shared public water taps to highlight a poor and 'backward' lifestyle. Plate 11 shows a corner of the former Daming Palace area used as a garbage dump. Furthermore, the Daming Palace Museum hosts a permanent exhibition on the neighbourhood removal and gentrification process. It displays a model of one of the demolished houses and a public water tap, again conveying the impression that the former lifestyle in the area was marked by poor hygiene and that it was 'uncivilized' and 'undisciplined'. The museum hanged more than sixty red flags given by the local communities to the government and the demolition team to show their gratitude for bringing them civilization (referring to the improvement of hygiene) and a better life (see Plate 12). Despite such widespread focus on 'overnight wealth', were people who have lived in the communities really thankful for demolition? Did they regard their former houses and the public water taps as 'backward'? As we already know from the orphanage case, the answer is no.

When I visited the heritage park with former residents from the area, they told me that it was a pity that they had moved out for the construction of such a park. Ms. Ma said: 'our house might not look very good with its low ceiling and small windows, but my grandfather built it himself with his bare hands'. The house, she said, symbolized the hard work and dedication of the elder generation. There was much that was good about these houses. Because they were very dark inside, people spent a lot of time outside socializing with their neighbours, which resulted in very close ties between the households. When her mother was busy, her neighbours always babysat her. They shared food together and helped each other. These relations no longer took place after people moved to the new high rises. Mr. and Mrs. Jin, a retired couple in their sixties, were excited to see the reproduction of the house in the museum because it reminded them of the harmonious life with the community. They did not obey the cues to remember their former life as 'backward'. The reconstruction made them feel rather nostalgic for the good old days. Just as Ms. Ma had noticed changes between neighbours, Mrs. Jin said that the relocation had caused a change in kinship. Her family had received more than one apartment – which accounted for the number of family members – but they were in different locations. Now that all family members did not live together anymore, it was more difficult to share the care of the elderly members.

Although the content of the heritage park and museum exhibition did not contradict local memories, they only glorified gentrification. They celebrated the urban renewal project. But this was a one-sided story. Locals may be satisfied with comfortable and well-equipped apartments, but they still miss many aspects of the community and social life in the slums.

Plate 12. A museum reconstruction of a house in the Daming Palace area before the construction of the heritage park.

A yet more subtle element of the glorification of gentrification in Xi'an is that the government and developers posture their work as providing a service to the people who are about to be dislocated. As deputy mayor, Duan Xiannian is said to have claimed that the government, as well as Qujiang Corporation, were 'non-profit' organizations. All the demolition and renewal projects, he said, were carried out for the sake of Xi'an's social and future development (Yao 2010). Indeed, such was the meaning conveyed by government departments when they provided newspapers with statistics concerning the cost, areas, numbers of affected households, and amount of compensation involved in demolition and gentrification. All of this outlay was for the future. No one, it seemed, could dare suggest that there might be profits to be made in the present.

Remaking the Urban Landscape

When I first arrived in Xi'an, locals used historical icons such as the Bell Tower, the gates of the city wall, or Wild Goose Pagoda as meeting points. These landmarks have existed for centuries and characterize the city. However, as I stayed longer, I realized that people preferred to meet in front of shopping malls. They chose to meet at Kaiyuan Mall instead of the Bell Tower and Qin Han Tang Mall replaced Big Wild Goose Pagoda. Some people even decided to meet up in brand-new business districts such as Xiaozhai.[110] Modern edifices substituted the historical landmarks not only physically in the urban space, but also socially in people's everyday life. The urban landscape of Xi'an has altered as condominiums mushroomed at a rapid speed. In the past, Xi'an people could enjoy a good view of the whole city from the city wall and could even see the shadows of the Qin Mountains. Nowadays, people have to visit the 245-metre television tower to view a panorama of the city. Who is responsible for these changes?

Though the various players have been introduced across preceding chapters, it is perhaps useful one more time to underscore their roles. In the process of remaking the urban landscape, the regional government plays undoubtedly the key role, as it approves all projects. Next to it, the developers, real estate companies, and urban planners all have a hand in final shape of projects. The provincial or city government usually contracts the project to semi-state or private companies. These developers pay the government some fee in exchange for the right to sell or rent spaces in the edifices they construct (Gillette 2000). The developers then hire urban planners and architects to design the projects. For heritage projects, the urban planners have to propose a layout and plan for the 'heritage zone', 'buffer zone', and 'high-rise zone' (see chapter 6).

Thus though the government signs off on projects, it is private developers who define the function and image of whole areas. Depending on the developers, the urban planners they hire may have a high degree of freedom to design and determine the final plan, but other developers, like Qujiang Corporation, uses the planners to execute their ideas rather than to create new ones. For instance, according to Mr. Shen, the chief planner of the Mingde Gate project, the planners and the developer negotiated intensively and repeatedly about the development of all three zones. The development agency initially planned to build a five-star hotel in the buffer zone and to build a high-class residential area, but this was opposed by the planners. In the end, the developer and the planners agreed to build an artist studio in the 'buffer zone' and middle-class residential area with a few blocks of lower quality buildings in which the original residents would resettle. The Mingde Gate project exemplifies the possibility for urban planners to use their professional knowledge to intervene in development

---

[110] Xiaozhai, three kilometres south of the city wall, is regarded as the most popular commercial area in Xi'an. Many banks, shopping malls, and office buildings are located there. Specifically, the Seg International Shopping Mall, the Xi'an International Convention Centre, and the Parkson International Shopping Mall are the most popular malls in Xi'an.

projects. But, the degree of negotiation between these social actors varies in each case.

So too discretion is exercised by government officials as they accept proposals submitted by developers. Mr. Shi, an official from Shaanxi Provincial Bureau of Housing and Urban-Rural Construction, acknowledged that the government (almost always) approves plans that put forward urbanization projects. The state prioritizes modernization. He envisioned too that urbanization is inevitable in Xi'an, as the city continues to attract more and more outsiders to work and settle down. Mr. Shi himself, however, believed that massive urbanization would necessarily increase social problems. Therefore, when he was in charge of urban transformation projects, he encouraged his colleagues not to commit mistakes made in other Chinese cities; massive urbanization and real estate marketization should not be undertaken blindly, he said.

Thus, Xi'an's transformation is also a moment of great learning and discretion for those professionals who take up the responsibility. In Xi'an there are three major urban changes under discussion: the fate of villages within the city, the appearance of ghost towns, and invisible boundaries.

Villages within the City

Reinforced by the *hukou* system, which classifies each individual as either an urban or rural citizen, Chinese people generally believe that cities symbolize modernity and good life while villages represent backwardness. Due to the rapid urbanization and the influx of migrant workers in Xi'an, 'villages' within the city have emerged in the past two decades, where lower-class workers or people with rural *hukou* reside. Many Xi'an people regarded these *chengzhongcun* as true slums – dirty and dangerous. Mr. Cheng, whose father worked as the chairman of the provincial railway construction workers' association, told me that when he was little, his father prohibited him from entering the *chengzhongcun* that was just fifty metres away from their government-allocated apartment because many criminals lived there. Four years previously, that slum had been cleared and turned into two big shopping malls, which became a place where Mr. Cheng and his friends met regularly. He felt grateful for the city's effort to get rid of the slums and he agreed with the government's gentrification discourse, believing that urban regeneration projects bring civilization and a better quality of life. But Mr. Cheng's view, as that of the son of a government official, only represented part of the Xi'an population.

As illustrated in the previous part, inhabitants from the *chengzhongcun* within the Daming Palace area perceived the slums differently. They saw them not as places of criminality, but as places with strong community relationships. Mr. Yang, an urban planner who lived in a slum in the south of Xi'an, understood the arguments of both sides. On the whole, these places were less than desirable: He told me not to visit any *chengzhongcun* alone, accompanied me when I visited places in his neighbourhood, and advised me to wear only a simple pullover and jeans (I might catch the attention of robbers if I went there too well-dressed). He said: 'if you pay attention to your belongings and stay low-toned, *chengzhongcun* are not dangerous at all'. His family was overjoyed at the impending demolition of the neighbourhood because they dreamed of moving to new modern apartments. Yet, he admitted that he would miss the community ties and the lively social life, with hawkers and restaurants staying open into the middle of the night.

For the most part, as detailed above, little consideration has been given to the fate of those who live in, but do not own property in, the villages within the city. There are many there who are socially vulnerable: those with rural *hukou* as well as those who simply have too little income to find accommodation in more expensive areas of the city. Moreover, the 'villages' with their extended social networks and late-hour establishments address many of their inhabitants' needs that are not well-met by more 'modern' urban arrangements. How will they cope? So far, only a few urban planners seem to care.

Ghost Towns

The city government changed the urban landscape by turning kilometres of low-rise *chengzhongcun* and farmland to high-rise residential areas, but the population of Xi'an did not grow that significantly. Thus the city is now pock-marked with 'ghost towns'. The street view of the one-hour bus ride from the Xi'an airport to the city centre is dominated by endless construction sites and empty high rises. When I passed by these areas at night, I never saw more than five apartments with lights switched on in each building. Yet, the city and the developers did not see this as a problem and were keen to invest in more such projects. When Mr. Huang, an official from Xi'an City Water Resources Bureau and project manager of the Han Chenghu project in his early sixties, showed me around the heritage project he was in charge of, he pointed at the land in the east of the park and said: 'the neighbourhoods on this piece of land will all be removed soon for the building of high rises. This is getting exciting and I do not want to retire because I want to see the result of this development'. In fact, that area in the west and north of the park had already been filled with empty ghost towns, but Mr. Huang remained optimistic that the new high rises he intended to build would be sold out.

According to Mr. Chen, a manager of Qujiang Corporation, the apartments in these ghost towns were designed for rich people. The developers and Xi'an City targeted businessmen for their sale and would rather leave the apartments empty than reduce the price to accommodate ordinary people. In Qujiang District, for example, the owners of apartments were mainly businessmen from northern Shaanxi Province. In fact, Duan once answered a question about 'ghost towns' by saying that the buildings in Qujiang District only appeared to be unoccupied, but many apartments had been sold as investment or holiday flats.

Some of these apartments were bought more deliberately as a status symbol than as an investment. In late August 2014, I was invited to work as an interpreter for Ms. Cheng and Mr. Müller's wedding. This bi-national couple planned to spend their life in the groom's hometown in Germany where they had met when Ms. Cheng studied abroad. Despite these plans, Ms. Cheng's parents bought her a two-storey apartment in Qujiang District to show off both their wealth and love for their daughter. Many relatives and friends were impressed. Similarly, Mr. Zhao, a businessman from Baoji City and father of two daughters in their twenties, bought two extra apartments with his own savings in 2013 and planned to give them as dowry when his daughters married in a few years' time. Both of the apartments were located at the northern part of the city in the 'ghost towns'.

However, these purchased apartments almost certainly account for only a small amount of the number of 'apparently' empty ones. Without public statistics, the 'problems' with which they may be associated are hardly possible to discuss. But, of primary importance would seem to be the very obvious one: what does it mean for urban life, to say nothing of the value of real estate, when a city's neighbourhoods are empty because the buildings are owned by people who do not live in them?

The Invisible Boundaries within the City

The demolition and gentrification movement also resulted in the fortification of invisible boundaries within the city. In the city plan of the 1980s, Xi'an City Planning Bureau divided the city into different functional sectors: east for light industry, north for transportation, south for culture and education, and west for heavy industry (Yin, Shen and Zhao 2005). Until now, the south is still considered a cultural district because most of the universities, museums, and heritage sites are located there. For example, Gaoxin District in south-western Xi'an became a hub for scientific research institutes and Qujiang District is of course famous for cultural development. Ms. Qian, a research assistant working in Gaoxin District laughed when I suggested that she should move there to shorten her two-hour commute. The price of apartments in the 'cultural' south was too high for 'cultured' workers!

Xi'an people who live in the west or north are stigmatized as lower class and 'uncivilized'. Because they were undeveloped until the late 1990s (see chapter 6), they had attracted 'illegal' migrants who settled and formed slums over several decades. As late as 2010, the area around Daming Palace attracted refugees from Henan. Even after the construction of the heritage park, my informants asked me not to go there too often because the area remained disorderly (za), as many Henanese migrants had been allocated to buildings nearby. Thus, the northern and western parts of the city represent the lower-class area with heavy industrial workers living in the west and unwanted refugees residing in the north.

What about the city centre? The social status of living in the centre has dropped drastically in the past ten years. In the past when Xi'an had not expanded yet, people preferred to live within the city wall because of the centre's vivid social life. I remember visiting a photo exhibition showing 'old Xi'an' with Ms. Yu, an aerospace engineer working for the military, and she lingered beside a photo of the city wall and recalled:

> I remember climbing up and down the city wall when I was little. Our family was quite well off and that was why we could live in the city centre. I moved to Gaoxin District a few years ago because I have a decent government job. However, frankly speaking, I would have never envisioned areas like Gaoxin or Qujiang becoming middle- and upper-class residential areas because they were unwanted farmland ten years ago.

Along with the rise of the districts in the south and the urban expansion, the centre lost its previous status. Houses within the city wall were regarded as old-fashioned and under-equipped, lacking facilities such as elevators, central heating, and piped hot water.

Urban expansion changed, but also reinforced, the invisible boundaries between high and low-class districts in the city. Because of the modernization and heritage project advocated by the city and provincial governments, not only the urban landscape was remade, but also people's perception about urban space and social life have changed.

The Dilemma between Pride and Shame

When I embarked on my fieldwork in Xi'an, I was surprised by local residents' sense of direction, regardless of their age, occupation, or gender. Every time I got lost in the city and sought help from people, they showed me the way by using cardinal directions. For example, if I searched for a nearby supermarket, the answer would be: 'go north for twenty metres and then turn west'. No one said go straight or turn left. Mr. Liu, a shop owner in his mid-sixties, said:

> Xi'an has preserved the grid system from the Tang Dynasty and the present city setting is exactly the same as Tang Chang'an. It is impossible to get lost in Xi'an because all the streets face either north, south, east, or west. If you follow one direction, you will eventually reach a main street. It is part of ancient wisdom to build a city this way and all ancient cities in China share this feature. However, only Xi'an manages to preserve the city layout so well.

The obsessive use of cardinal direction mirrors the efforts of locals to preserve the historical meanings of the city layout and their pride in the city's history. Locals have developed emotional attachment especially for certain heritage sites, such as the Bell Tower and the Wild Goose pagodas, which have served as landmarks for decades. Mr. Deng, a dentist in his late thirties, said: 'I live in Gaoxin District surrounded by high rises, and I easily forget the historical background of Xi'an, but every time when I go to the city centre, the Bell Tower reminds me that Xi'an is indeed an ancient city!' As observed by Mr. Shao, a postgraduate student of anthropology from Xi'an, the sense of belonging has suddenly grown very strong in the past five years and people have become more proud of the city. Could it be because people have started to appreciate their city's history? Or does it rather relate to the modernization process undertaken by the city?

In the pursuit of modernization, heritage development has become a symbol of modernity because of its economic potential in the context of a global heritage boom. Locals no longer regarded historical sites as useless 'garbage' hindering the city's urban development, but rather saw it as a cultural-economic resource. In the modernization process, heritage sites are reconfigured from space-occupying remains to economic possibilities, and this rising value of heritage contributes to strengthening the sense of belonging to a common city identity.

Xi'an shows the far-reaching appeal of modernization in China. The city could have exercised the freedom given by the national government to local planning department in the late 1990s to pursue preservation or revitalization. Xi'an City still chose to prioritize modernization, seeing this as the best path for increasing the city's national status and boosting its economic development. Relatively little concern has been publicly directed to the social changes that will and have inevitably come with demolition, construction, and changing real estate values.

Most locals craved modernization so that the 'kneeling archer' could finally stand up against other big cities like Shanghai and Beijing. They took pride in the city's metro construction, the fast growth of urbanization, and the modernizing aspects of heritage projects. Still, some of my informants, and especially those with higher levels of education, reacted with infuriation to the scale of Xi'an's development. They felt proud of the city's ancient history, but ashamed at the city's exploitation of the past. Mr. Ou, a teacher in his late forties, said:

> I feel embarrassed to show Xi'an to my friends from other countries, especially the area around West Street and the Bell Tower because that area was re-planned and filled with neo-Tang-style structures. This cityscape only shows the short-sighted and narrow-minded philosophy of urban planning of the city government.

Mr. Gu, a hotel marketing manager in his mid-twenties, also found it shameful to see the ancient city being covered by smog produced by construction sites and the busy traffic. He lamented:

> It is a pity that nothing that we create now can be compared to our wise ancestors' great heritage sites. If the Qin, Han, Tang emperors would time-travel to present day Xi'an, I am sure they would not be impressed by any of our present construction. Every time I show my foreign friends around Xi'an, I beg them to tolerate the inconvenience brought by the development of modern China and try to concentrate on the original and authentic historical sites.

Some people, especially the younger ones, are afraid to imagine how the future will be if modernization continues at this speed. Mr. Dai, a cartoonist in his early thirties who raised a campaign to 'Save Xi'an Culture', joked: 'the Bell Tower has already stood in the heart of Xi'an for 600 years, but who knows if the government will plan to demolish it one day and turn it into a shopping mall or massage centre'. They paint pictures of valuable culture and heritage traded in for worthless kitsch and vulgar consumer indulgences.

Though Xi'an has pursued modernization like other Chinese cities, it can be said that its residents and the city government have still not pursued a rigorous over-valuation of modernization at the expense of heritage. In this respect the city is different from other locations in China, like Kunming, where Zhang (2006) demonstrated the operation of a hegemonic belief in the values of modernization and development and the presence of very little affection for heritage. In Xi'an, however, people have long appreciated archaeology and history; as I showed in chapters 3 and 4, for several decades bright and talented youngsters have been drawn to heritage-related careers while older adults remain amateur archaeologists and historians. The new heritage boom has complicated these relations: 'heritage' is now conceived, valued, and developed partly in distinction from actual physical remains, and decisions about the fate of remains is determined not only by the value of the past but by the economic potential of the sites and the land in and on which they rest.

Chapter 9
Conclusion: The City of Cosmopolitanism

In summer 2008, Beijing, the capital of China, hosted one of the world's most eye-catching events – the Olympic Games. Through the organization of the Olympics, China showed the world its characteristics and uniqueness. Five authentic terracotta warriors from the Terracotta Army Museum were transported from Xi'an to Beijing for display during the Olympics. Moreover, the event organizers designed a giant puppet performance, featuring a 9-metre-tall terracotta warrior marionette and a Chinese girl marionette. The terracotta warrior represented ancient China while the Chinese girl in a modern dress symbolized modern China. In the performance, the terracotta warrior and the Chinese girl chased a blue butterfly, which depicted the pursuit of a beautiful shared future. By using the image of the terracotta warrior from Xi'an, this performance displayed a sense of 'Chineseness' and highlighted the interaction between history and modernity in present-day China.

Of course this is just one example in a centuries-long tradition of drawing on Xi'an's culture to define China's international identity. In recent years, the terracotta warriors have been commonly used in international events or travelling brochures to represent China. But Xi'an's role as an international symbol is much older, though by now very subtle. The English 'China', after all, is derived from 'Qin', referencing the dynasty and its emperor (Kam 2008). The award of the World Heritage title to the terracotta army is, from this perspective, long overdue. The award, however, tied as it is with broader national and global heritage industries, most obviously promotes China's splendid ancient civilization to build a good reputation for modern China, and particularly one that shapes China as an international, strong, open, and world-class nation. I argue that Xi'an's historical remembrance and heritage politics now serve as a tool to construct a cosmopolitan identity and image for the city and even the nation.

Cosmopolitanism can be understood as 'the manifold expressions of an international culture, expressed by the commercial elites before the shaping of national identities' (Sifneos 2005: 98). Evridiki Sifneos (2005) examined the degree of cosmopolitanism in two ancient Greek cities and characterized cosmopolitanism as a public worldview of a place that is open to influence from the outside world through economic exchanges and immigration of different ethnic groups. Ulf Hannerz understood true cosmopolitanism as 'the willingness to engage with the other' and the 'intellectual and aesthetic stance of openness towards divergent cultural experiences' (1990: 239). Scholars have conceptualized various types of cosmopolitanism in different urban settings, such as 'vernacular cosmopolitanism' (Bhabha 2001), a form a cosmopolitanism that was brought about by migrant workers and postcolonial subalterns; 'indigenous cosmopolitanism' (Goodale 2006), the ability of a local community to transcend political and social commitments through ethnic and linguistic boundaries; 'imagined cosmopolitanism' (Schein 2001), the pursuit of cosmopolitanism through the consumption of foreign and high-class products; 'rooted cosmopolitanism' (Appiah 1996, 2005), where people have a strong attachment to their home but enjoy the presence and influences of divergent people from other places; and 'market cosmopolitanism' (Diawara 1998; Scheld 2007), which highlights the economic aspect related to the urban market and consumer behaviour.

From this ethnography of Xi'an, we can see a 'historically rooted cosmopolitanism'. Inhabitants believe that their city was once cosmopolitan, and they are seeking to revitalize and reconstruct that cosmopolitan era from the past. Locals have a strong attachment to their city, and they are proud of its history, which they want to bring back to the present. This makes Xi'an's residents stand somewhere between the English-language scholarly discourse on 'true' cosmopolitanism and more official and widespread Chinese versions.

A Chinese View of Cosmopolitanism

There are more cynical views about how 'cosmopolitanism', derived as it may be from Greek concepts, functions globally as another 'form of westernization, favouring liberal goals of individual rights over collective and socio-economic goals' (Martell 2011: 619). And, at least many scholars point out that there are likely other meaningful roots and associations to the term in the Chinese context. Some Chinese researchers, for example, purport that the Chinese understanding of cosmopolitanism (*shijie zhuyi*) originates from the Confucian worldview of *tianxia,* meaning heaven and earth (Callahan 2007; Bell 2009; Chun 2009; Zhao 2009), and as such refers to a kind of soft power to shape official nationalism, state sovereignty, and territorial integrity (Swain 2013: 36). In any case, the Chinese usage does not deny the important role of the Chinese state, however 'international' it may act. Zhao Tingyang (2009) translated *tianxia* in its contemporary uses as 'worldliness' and interpreted it as referring to a utopian social order during the era of globalization, related to physical, philosophical, and political global governance. Elena Barabantseva (2009) suggested that the worldwide opening of Confucius Institutes to promote Chinese culture, as well as Beijing's bid to host the Olympics Games, both exemplify how the state uses international events and connections to shape nationalism. The feverish listing of World Heritage might also be seen as a good example of *tianxia*.

In Xi'an, however, despite wide talk of 'heritage', world and otherwise, no one ever used the term *tianxia* to refer to the city. Neither Xi'an, nor its historical antecedents, nor other major Chinese cities were described as 'cosmopolitan'. Instead, my informants described Han Chang'an, Tang Chang'an, modern Beijing and Shanghai as *guoji da dushi* (international city) or *guoji da duhui* (international metropolis). These cities were 'international' because they had established international connections and trade activities with foreign countries. Locals also used terms, such as *guojihua* (internationalization), *duoyuan wenhua* (multi-cultural), *kaifang* (open), and *duo mingzhu* (multi-ethnic) to describe these cities. Yet, as these emic expressions capture several dimensions of the Western understanding of cosmopolitanism, I will describe the city as 'cosmopolitan'. Zhu Shiguan (2010) asserted that Xi'an became 'cosmopolitan', that is *guoji da duhui*, through the advancement of infrastructure (e.g. transportation, water supply, and inter-governmental communication) to keep up with the rest of the world politically and economically. By unfolding the emic view of cosmopolitanism, this chapter demonstrates the pursuit of cosmopolitanism as the ultimate goal of Xi'an's heritage and urban transformation projects, and looks into how locals and different social actors perceive and perform cosmopolitanism in their everyday life.

The emic view of cosmopolitanism, as seen through vocabulary and practice, puts stress on four orientations: internationalism, multi-culturalism, modernization, and historical rootedness. Certainly, the historical cities are claimed to have been 'cosmopolitan', almost by accident rather than intention. Its geographic location, as Zhu (2010) pointed out, gave ancient Chang'an a developmental advantage. It could be developed into a big city because it lay at the confluence of two rivers – one flowing from north to south and the other from north to east (p. 339). Indeed, Tang Chang'an became the world's biggest city during the peak of the Silk Road era, and the trade road as well as diplomacy brought foreigners. Historians are therefore certain about the status of Chang'an as a cosmopolitan city in the Tang

Dynasty (Han 2006; Hopkirk 2006; Beckwith 2009; Zhu 2010). Christopher
Beckwith remarked:

> [Chang'an] enjoyed the most cosmopolitan period in its entire
> history. The city was the largest, most populous and wealthiest
> anywhere in the world at that time, with perhaps a million residents,
> including a large population of foreigners either residing per-
> manently or visiting in various capacities (2009: 126).

Since Han and Tang Chang'an was known as an international metropolis,
offering a rich cosmopolitan and multi-ethnic lifestyle, the descriptor *guoji
da duhui* for Xi'an is omnipresent nowadays too. It comes up in the
government's plans and slogans, in companies' advertisements, and in
interviews with my correspondents. Pheng Cheah argued that since the turn
of the twenty-first century, the concept of cosmopolitanism has 'changed
from an intellectual ethos to a vision of an institutionally embedded global
political consciousness in modernity' (2006: 486). Perhaps this is so for
some places and people. In Xi'an though, cosmopolitanism is neither an
intellectual ethos nor a global consciousness. It is more simply the pursuit to
revitalize the historical past with a focus on present and future economic
prosperity.

By placing stress on the relationship between modern development
and the recent heritage projects carried out in the city, this thesis presented
the political, economic, and social changes that have occurred in Xi'an, and
examined the role and perception of concepts such as heritage, history, and
modernity among different social actors. To the Chinese state, heritage and
history are a means to boost nationalism and popularize the official historical
narration. To the provincial and municipal governments, heritage is used as a
tool to implement policies and execute modernization to improve the
reputation of the city. To the real estate developers, heritage sites are
goldmines to expand their revenue. Locals relate heritage to their collective
memories or everyday manifestation. Officials and locals share the
conviction that modernization and the revitalization of the glorious past are
desirable goals. The need for modernization and the celebration of the past
both serve as the key elements to pursue a historically rooted
cosmopolitanism. Heritage, hence, acts as a vehicle for different social actors
to create a cosmopolitan identity through heritage projects, policy making,
and collective imagination.

Chapters 3 and 4 demonstrated the city and provincial governments'
increasing interest in archaeology and history. On top of the city
government's efforts of expanding the scale and number of heritage parks, it
also fills its cityscape with neo-Tang buildings. The Tang Imperial City
Renaissance Plan states that Xi'an should engage in the protection, recon-

struction, interpretation, and (re)presentation of elements of the Tang Dynasty to accomplish the cultural rejuvenation of urban space (Feighery 2011). These two chapters presented the socio-political use of heritage in Xi'an to build up an image of a great China and to remind the city's residents and visitors of Xi'an's cosmopolitan status in the past. Chapter 5 showed the transition from the focus on imperial heritage to Silk Road heritage as a way for the city and provincial governments to pave the way for the making of cosmopolitanism. Margaret Swain proposed that cosmopolitanism is used as 'a political project to constitute nationalism' (2009: 35); others see it as a way to maintain national solidarity (Tyfield and Urry 2010). Consequently, the city increasingly put stress on Silk Road heritage after 2008, on top of promoting its imperial heritage. Silk Road heritage not only serves as a political tool to assure China's central role on the international stage, but also brings in an economic aspect as the idea of the Silk Road is popularized as the Silk Road Economic Belt, emphasizing China's business cooperation with Central Asia.

Chapter 7 investigated how the community members of two urban quarters perceive heritage and shed light on the local understanding of modernization and cosmopolitanism. Cosmopolitanism became a claim for the respective local communities to preserve or not to preserve their quarters. In the Calligraphy Quarter, the local residents chose not to preserve the old shop houses because they did not want to stay within the quarter but live a 'cosmopolitan' life outside in new modern high rises. To them, cosmopolitanism correlates more with economic development and modernization. In the Muslim Quarter, most locals perceived cosmopolitanism as multi-ethnic and used it to fight against the government's renewal projects. Xi'an Hui believe that the quarter enriches the cultural diversity of the city, which helps to achieve cosmopolitanism. They regard the history of the quarter as a proof of cosmopolitanism because the historical sites in the quarter demonstrate mixed elements from Chinese and Western culture and the locals believed that they still sustained a 'Silk Road lifestyle' from the Tang Dynasty.

Chapters 6 and 8 showed how the city and provincial governments achieve cosmopolitanism through economic development and modernization. Chapter 6 described the creation and expansion of the Qujiang Model, a combination of cultural tourism and real estate development. The tourism industry is seen too as a revival of the local circulation of foreigners (and foreign capital) during the Tang Dynasty. Chapter 8 focused on the construction of new heritage sites, as well as new infrastructure to increase the status of Xi'an in order to become a real international metropolis in today's China. This concluding chapter brings together all the chapters to explain the logic of heritagization and the philosophy of urban transformation in Xi'an on three different levels, 1) individual, 2) municipal and provincial, and 3) national.

Connecting World Cities

The research group 'The Global Political Economy of Cultural Heritage' included the study of three World Heritage cities: Istanbul, Melaka, and Xi'an. Based on the framework of earlier research conducted in Kyoto by the head of the research group, Christoph Brumann (2009, 2012a, 2012b), the three projects endeavoured to explore the dynamics of urban heritage making and the articulation of UNESCO World Heritage with local situations. In February 2013, August 2013, and March 2014, members of the group met for seminars in each other's field sites.

Although the location and size of the three cities differ, they share some commonalities. From the perspective of World Heritage, Istanbul experienced its first fame in 1985, when the Historic Areas of Istanbul, including the Archaeological Park, the Theodosian Land Walls, the Sülemaniye Mosque and associated conservation area, and the Zeyrek Mosque and associated conservation area on the Historical Peninsula, were inscribed on the list. Melaka was inscribed in 2008 together with George Town as the Historic Cities of the Straits of Melaka. Perhaps most importantly, the three field sites are not only World Heritage cities full of historical sites, they are also world cities.

Each of the three cities played an important role in history, and was at one time a centre of political and economic power, connected to other such centres across the world. While Istanbul now advertises itself as 'Eurasia's centre' linking Europe and Asia, Melaka focuses on its historical status as an international hub along the maritime Silk Road, accommodating traders travelling through the Indian Ocean and the South China Sea. Like Xi'an, Melaka lost its world city status through the centuries, and it has tried to get it back, at least on the world tourism map, through heritage development. All three cities celebrate their multi-ethnic and multi-religious cosmopolitan pasts and serve as important historical cities to promote nation-building nowadays.

Like Xi'an, Istanbul and Melaka also had to face the tension between heritage preservation and urban transformation. In Istanbul, massive urban transformation projects were carried out, resulting in the demolition of many traditional neighbourhoods, such as Süleymaniye and Ayvansaray. Similarly, urban transformation projects also took place in the buffer zone of Melaka and changed the historical townscape. In terms of the role of heritage, the Turkish, Malaysian, and Chinese governments emphasize selective heritage to recuperate pasts that support the national discourse. Xi'an's past is meant to be distinctively 'Chinese' (and Tang); Istanbul's celebrated past is clearly neo-Ottoman (and Muslim), while Melaka's glorified past emphasizes the Malay sultanate. In Melaka, as in Xi'an, the past is also 'coloured in' with an official heritage colour. The rise of cultural tourism as well as the combination of tourism and real estate development is also noticeable in all three cities.

Nevertheless, heritagization had distinct qualities in each of the three cities. I found that the degree of commercialization was by far the strongest in Xi'an. The number, size, scale, and speed with which standardized Qujiang heritage sites were emplaced in Xi'an were unmatched. It took less than a decade to turn vast acres of farmland, slums, and older neighbourhoods into archaeological parks and real estate project areas, while existing historical sites were standardized and expanded in size by twenty times. Equally distinct, and not observed in the other two cities, was the locals' own relationship with history. Xi'an's residents had a strong consciousness of the city's history, displayed in their worldview, behaviours, and habits. They referred to historical figures as ancestors and quoted them as friends. Thus, though the effort to balance modernization and heritagization may characterize all World Heritage projects, in Xi'an this balancing effort is tangible in the everyday lives of people as constitutive of social life. History has penetrated into society in such a way, that the desire for revitalizing Xi'an's cosmopolitan identity aligns with all other goals of the national, provincial, and city governments.

'Once a Cosmopolitan City, Forever a Cosmopolitan City'

In November 2013, a Chinese social media platform, Xinhua Net, organized a 'personages of Chinese provinces poll'. All internet users were invited to vote for a figure from their own province to represent the regional characteristics. The result astounded the mass media.[111] People in Shaanxi Province did not pick China's current president, Xi Jinping, who was born in Shaanxi. They selected the historical figure Qin Shihuang. (There were even some votes for the terracotta warriors who were anonymous soldiers during the Qin Dynasty.) Why was there such a preference for the First Qin Emperor and the Qin Dynasty?

---

[111] 'Zhongguo gesheng xingxiang daxing minyi diaocha: Qinshihuang dangshuan Shaanxi daiyanren' (Personage of Chinese provinces poll: the first Qin Emperor was chosen to be the representative of Shaanxi). *Shaanxi Daily*, 22 November 2013. Available online, http://www.sxdaily.com.cn/n/2013/1122/c324-5275688.html. Last accessed 1 May 2016.

People in Shaanxi Province believe that China was stronger and more significant in the Qin Dynasty than it is now. In Xi'an, residents identify themselves more with the history than the present of the city. Indeed, the previous chapters, especially chapters 3 and 4, showed the strong archaeological and historical awareness among the local people. History and archaeology contribute to the social life, memories, and the constitution of local identity. How do Xi'an natives remember, or even romanticize the past? How does the city's past influence the present, and maybe the future?

During daily conversations, locals constantly referred back to history and the glorious eras. They yearned for the past and believed that Xi'an was much more international and open in the Han and Tang dynasties than it is nowadays. Mr. Zhu, a university student, thought that there were many more foreigners in Tang Chang'an because the city promoted intercultural exchange and he imagined that if he had been born in Tang Chang'an, it would have been much easier for him to learn a foreign language. My informants also mentioned other aspects of cosmopolitanism. Ms. Ma, a cosmetics salesgirl in her mid-twenties, said that if she could time travel, she would pay a visit to Tang Chang'an to experience a harmonious society, where everyone was treated equally without any gender inequality or racial discrimination. My female informants especially stressed the aspect of dress as a key component in the openness of Tang society. Not only could women dress as men, but as Ms. Pan, a university student, said: 'Tang girls wore very low-cut and see-through dresses and showed a lot of their breasts, which is unacceptable in Xi'an nowadays. Therefore, compared to back then, our society has become more backward in terms of openness'.[112] These laments share one commonality: Informants believed that Tang Chang'an people enjoyed a true liberal and cosmopolitan society, which today's Xi'an can no longer sustain.

Xi'an residents' affection for the past can be described as nostalgia, but it does not quite fit common definitions of the term. For example, Michael Pickering and Emily Keightley stressed the irrecoverability of the past by defining nostalgia as a 'longing for what is lacking in a changed present and a yearning for what is now unattainable, simply because of the irreversibility of time' (2006: 920). And David Berliner (2012) distinguished nostalgia in terms of the ownership and experience of the desired past by

---

[112] This aspect resonates with other ethnographic studies on cosmopolitanism, which record how locals use dress and fashion as signifiers of cosmopolitan identity (Heath 1992; Mustafa 1997, 2006; Rabine 1997, 2002; Scheld 2007). The difference between those ethnographic studies and Xi'an is that my informants did not dress in a particular way to show their cosmopolitan taste, rather they emphasized how females in the Tang Dynasty could dress freely.

conceptualizing nostalgia as existing in two types, endo-nostalgia and exo-nostalgia. The former pertains to 'the past that one has lived personally, implying a sense of personal ownership of the past'; the latter refers to 'the past not experienced personally (…) common among Western tourists and UNESCO experts based in Paris, whose externalist discourses about cultural loss do not refer to their own historical past' (ibid.: 781).

In Xi'an, locals have something between endo- and exo- nostalgia. Though they did not live in the Tang era, for example, this past has never been foreign to them. They have not only learned about the city's past through historical genres, they have lived in an environment surrounded by the historical remains from those times. Although no one has any direct encounter or personal memories of the very distant past, they do have access to at least two or three generations of direct memories of these places, entangled with historical facts, interpretations, and imaginings. Thus history is not quite lost and irrecoverable, and people regard even the city's most distant historical eras as their own historical pasts.

The ex-endo-nostalgic past is constructed from fragmented information people receive from different channels. In the case of Xi'an, people projected a strong, harmonious, and cosmopolitan past of the Qin, Han, and Tang dynasties. Locals selected and pieced together historical facts to create an ideal past, which often contradicted the real Tang society. According to historians, Tang Chang'an was in fact not as open as locals believed. It was highly hierarchical, restricting the inhabitants to live in different areas of the city according to their social classes and professions. Only females from high social background, namely from the royal and noble families could wear fashionable dresses and participate in men's activities. Furthermore, the Tang society did not integrate the foreigners, who came to Tang Chang'an, as the foreign traders stayed mostly within the West Market; exchange students around the Daxuexi Alley close to the royal palace; and the ambassadors within the palace area. Thus, foreigners were active only in certain districts in Chang'an and the Tang society was not as international and harmonious as Xi'an locals now project.

Locals claimed that they are more open-minded compared to people from other parts of China due to their cosmopolitan history. Examples for this are the preference for daughters in many Xi'an families as discussed in chapter 4, the open attitude towards migrant workers similarly illustrated in chapter 4, and the ethnic diversity and harmony as shown in chapter 7. Xi'an people emphasized these social behaviours to demonstrate how they have inherited and internalized the city's cosmopolitan characteristics. They owed their openness towards foreigners, Muslims, and gender issues to the city's historical background. However, according to my observation, locals' open mindedness was not consistent. For example, sometimes, I heard laments and stereotypical comments about the Xi'an Hui in the Muslim Quarter. Chapter 4 also showed the hostile attitude towards outsiders, from Henan Province and Japan in particular, due to historical reasons. As a result, both the nostalgia and cosmopolitan identity of Xi'an natives are selective as they long for a certain past only and are partly tolerant to others.

Especially when it comes to the matter of cultural heritage preservation, locals and the government became more reluctant to cooperate with foreign institutions. The Terracotta Army Museum hires only Chinese, specifically Han Chinese, for archaeological and restoration works. Other archaeological institutes in Xi'an adopted the same policy. I was rejected by the Terracotta Army Museum as a volunteer at the beginning because as a Hong Kong Chinese, I was not considered a full Chinese citizen. Spokesmen from different cultural institutions told me that they do not permit foreigners to work with nationally ranked heritage sites and relics because they do not trust anyone with a foreign background. Ms. Spalek, a German restorer working in Shaanxi Provincial Archaeological Institute through the Sino-German cooperation project, told me that there was a strong division between foreign and local restorers and she had the feeling that none of her Chinese colleagues were interested in her restoration skills. Another German restorer, Ms. Reuter, who was assigned to work with the Terracotta Army Museum, complained that she barely saw the impressive site because she was not allowed to enter the archaeological pits and could only work in a room within the administration area piecing-together a broken warrior. Mr. Zhang, a senior restorer at the museum told me that foreign restorers had no chance to enter the pit, and so far, only foreign prime ministers or political leaders have been permitted to set foot there.

Such local practices to discourage foreign involvement align with the view of the central authorities. Moreover, people are conscious, and supportive, of these forms of discrimination. Mr. Guo, a public relations officer of a private company in his early sixties, reacted strongly when I questioned why the Chinese authorities chose not to cooperate with foreign institutes. If they did so, I said, they could surely speed up the excavation of the mausoleum of Qin Shihuang, which was said to be stalled due to the lack of appropriate technology. 'There is no rush to collaborate with other countries with more advanced technology', he said, continuing 'I would rather wait until our nation grows strong enough to carry out its own excavation. After all, it is our own cultural heritage, so we need to be the ones who excavate and preserve it'. Some of this reticence is pure nationalism; some, however, has historical roots. During a dinner with Mr. Hong and his friends, all businessmen aged between forty and seventy, I was warned to be careful with 'German archaeologists'. When I asked why, I was told that 'they' had stolen the mural paintings from the Mogao Cave in Dunhuang. Then the men provided many details on how foreign troops had dug out pieces of murals and transported them to Europe.[113] They feared a repetition of such unfortunate precedents.

The desire for a 'cosmopolitan' city, however, also contributes to the 'identity crisis' faced by Xi'an's residents in chapter 8. If a 'cosmopolitan city' is an 'international metropolis' in today's world, Xi'an desperately needs modernization. Though people were so proud of the city's imperial history that they wanted to resurrect much through heritagization, they were also ashamed that their city lacked so many signs of modern and economic development. During my stay in Xi'an, locals often asked me to compare their city with Hong Kong and Beijing. They considered Xi'an under-developed to such an extent that they might conceal their origins when they were in more developed cities. When I met Ms. Yi in Hong Kong, for example, she told me that she came from Beijing. In fact, she had only been in Beijing for two years on a Master's program. Similarly, Ms. Cha presented herself as being from Shanghai, where she studied.

Good infrastructure, high rises, and a convenient transportation network are the most important components for a modern international metropolis. Thus 'cosmopolitanism' also describes the struggle at every level in Xi'an to combine heritagization with modernization. As people often say: 'once a cosmopolitan city, forever a cosmopolitan city'. In practice, this means that historical recuperation may have to suffice with the imagination of an open and multi-ethnic life in Chang'an so that economic development can be pursued.

The Making of Cosmopolitanism

The struggle to be a cosmopolitan city takes place also beyond the parameters of heritagization and modernization that I have so far described. The status of 'international metropolis' is an official one. Therefore, and yet one more turn, the various levels of government play a key role in implementing the plans and policies that will determine whether or not Xi'an is granted the title its residents hold so dear.

According to Mr. Su, a lecturer at Xi'an Administration College, 183 out of 667 cities in China intend to become an international metropolis. The

---

[113] In 1907, the Hungarian-born British archaeologist Aurel Stein negotiated with the Chinese guard of the Mogao Cave to remove some of the manuscripts, paintings, and textiles. Since he has a German last name, some of my informants mistakenly assumed that he was from Germany. After Stein, the French, Japanese, and Russians also showed interest towards the paintings and manuscripts stored in the caves.

status of *guoji da dushi* needs to be approved by the national government, and there are a number of formal steps leading to this award. In May 2008, the Shaanxi provincial government proposed the Guanzhong-Tianshui Economic Development Plan 2009–20 to the Central State Administration of China, hoping to be granted the permission to be developed as an international metropolis. The plan was accepted by the national government in June 2009, making Xi'an one of only three cities in China that were approved as candidates for the title (Beijing and Shanghai were the other two).[114] Xi'an hence receives financial support from the national government to become a state-recognized international metropolis by 2020. The decision shows the national government's recognition of Xi'an's efforts and plans in the past years.

However, Xi'an has to fulfill a list of criteria set by the national government by 2020 in order to become an international metropolis. Some of the targets include having a population of 8–15 million people and reaching a minimum GDP of 10,000-12,000 USD. In 2009, Xi'an's GDP stood at 43,470 CNY (approximately 6,673 USD) per capita. The plan outlined that it would be necessary for Xi'an to attract branch offices of at least 250 international firms and to organize more than 150 international conferences (with participants from at least 80 countries) per year. In 2009, Xi'an had only 97 international branches and hosted 16 international conferences. Lastly, it was to bring its foreign population up to the required level for an international metropolis (5–20 per cent). In 2009, Xi'an's foreign population stood at only 0.08 per cent.[115]

Certainly the bid to become an international metropolis impacted on many other aspects of urban planning. The city and provincial governments had to strengthen Xi'an's economic development and increase its degree of internationalization. Many steps were already taken in the decade before the city advanced in its candidacy. For example, the Ordinance on the Improvement of Investments was announced in March 2001 to make Xi'an a desirable place for economic exchange and to attract more foreign investment.[116] Another plan for internationalization was drafted in 2005 as a White Paper on Xi'an City Development, addressing economic, cultural, and

---

[114] 'Guanyu Xi'an dazhao guoji dadushi de shikao he zhanwang' (About how Xi'an plans to be developed as a metropolis). *Xi'an Daily*, 22 January 2010. Available online, http://news.xiancn.com/content/2010-01/22/content_2037589.htm. Last accessed 1 May 2016.

[115] 'Guanyu Xi'an dazhao guoji dadushi de shikao he zhanwang'.

[116] 'Zhonggong Xi'an shiwei, Xi'anshi renmin zhengfu guanyu jinyibu zhengzhi he gaishan touzhi huanjing de jueding' (Xi'an city people's government's decision on the improvement and changes of the environment). Available online, http://www.fawuzaixian.com/wenku/view/id/236074. Last accessed 1 May 2016.

environmental aspects.[117] The Xianyang-Xi'an Economic Unification Treaty signed in 2002 proposed to combine Xi'an and Xianyang cities into one urban area.[118] Xi'an also 'collaborated' with three other big cities in southern Shaanxi (Shangluo, Ankang, and Hanzhong) to expand the scale of city and enhance urbanization and modernization. Shaanxi Provincial Bureau of Housing and Urban-Rural Construction proposed the Greater Xi'an Strategic Development Plan in 2009 to the national government. This plan envisioned industrialization, modernization, and the revitalization of the Silk Road (see chapter 2).

All these plans informed the urban planning and heritagization underway at the time of my fieldwork. Most visible, from my focal point, were 'branding' efforts. The increased prominence of the 'Silk Road' in heritage projects, to say the least, conveyed the city's cosmopolitan past and future. The Tang West Market, opened in 2010, advertises itself as an international site and highlights its connection to the Silk Road. It organizes international events and festivals to reconstruct Chang'an's international image. There were also many invocations of 'international' within heritagization. Qujiang Corporation changed its advertisement slogan to 'international metropolis, Qujiang dream' in 2013. South Gate Park, opened to the public in May 2014, was described as the 'international gate', insisting that the heritage site resumed its historic function of welcoming travellers from abroad.

National Rejuvenation: Fulfilling the 'China Dream' in Xi'an

By the time of my fieldwork, however, it was not enough that the various government bodies active in Xi'an were attempting to achieve the near-impossible goals of becoming a registered 'international metropolis', nor that they and the general population were struggling to continue and reinvigorate the imagined and desired cosmopolitan past while becoming modernized. There was also the 'China Dream' to fulfil. In May 2013, two months after Xi Jinping became the president of the People's Republic of China, he coined the term 'China Dream' (*Zhongguo meng*) as his political slogan (Xi 2014). As soon as Xi proposed the catchphrase, the term went viral in China, widely cited in everyday conversations and used to decorate

---

[117] 'Yangshi jingtou zujiao Xi'an fazhan nantu' (CCTV reports the blue print of Xi'an's development). *Xi'an Evening Daily*, 26 March 2005. Available online, http://www. xiancn.com/gb/wbpaper/2005-03/26/content_510715.htm. Last accessed 1 May 2016.

[118] 'Xixian jingji yitihua zhashi tuijing chengxiao xianxian' (The unification of the economic development of Xi'an and Xianyang). *People China Daily*, 22 January 2008. Available online, http://www.people.com.cn/GB/43063/107687/107820/108016/6807887.html. Last accessed 1 May 2016.

public space such as shopping malls, plazas, and tourist attractions (Plate 13). The magic of the slogan is its vagueness, which provides room for imagination. Ordinary people usually envision it as referring to the individual pursuit of a better life, including enjoying the freedom to travel and an increase in the general living standard. However, scholars point out that it has an undeniably nationalistic function to unite the people, to reflect China's position with foreign relations, and to make a greater and stronger China (Callahan 2013; Ren 2014; Liu 2015). Mr. Li, a professor at North West University, related the 'China Dream' to a collective hope for restoring China's lost national greatness, in short a national rejuvenation. Xi himself clarified the concept along exactly these lines during a 2013 museum-visit: 'I think the China Dream is the revitalization of ancient civilization and the great rejuvenation'.[119] The present regime has since then promoted the idea of national rejuvenation, connecting history to the present and future development.

Plate 13. 'China Dream' slogans in Xi'an, Quijang District.

---

[119] The president's comments were reported in the press. See 'Xi Jinping guanyu shixian zhonghua minzu weida fuxing de zhongguomeng lunxu' (The China Dream national rejuvenation theory by Xi Jinping). *Chinese Communist Party News*, 5 December 2013. Available online, http://theory.people.com.cn/n/2013/1205/c40555-23756883.html. Last accessed 1 May 2016.

Mr. Yan, a professor from Tsinghua University explains that the national government attempts to achieve national rejuvenation by revitalizing a few selected historical eras, when China was particularly strong, namely the Han Dynasty, Tang Dynasty, and the early period of the Qing Dynasty (Tsinghua University News 2014). He asserts that the idea of 'China Dream' underlines the role of history in modern China and relates to China's international politics, and specifically to how the rest of the world views China. He thinks that the goal of Chinese national rejuvenation is to repossess China's historical international standing as a well-respected country in the Han and Tang dynasties, both admired and feared by its neighbours.

In order to pursue the 'China Dream', the national government has, since 2013, emphasized both heritage and modern development. Whereas the heritage development reminds its citizens and visitors of the glorious past of the nation, the modernization progress keeps China's place as one of the world's top political and economic leaders. The twining of heritage and development can be seen in a series of multi-national economic development plans, such as the revitalization of the land and sea Silk Roads, that emphasize trading and economic exchange as the face and drivers of both culture and development (as discussed in chapter 5). The national understanding of cosmopolitanism, not unlike the local one in Xi'an, has hence become strongly historically-rooted and market-oriented.

Xi'an as the China Dream

Xi'an stands at the crossroads, it would seem, between old and new forms of cosmopolitanism. But how can we summarize the new form? Pauline Kleingeld (1999) theorized the history of cosmopolitanism from the vantage point of late eighteenth-century Germany. There were, she said, six varieties or ideal types of cosmopolitanism: (1) moral cosmopolitanism (2) political cosmopolitanism (3) cultural cosmopolitanism (4) market cosmopolitanism (5) a kind that was rooted in a strong notion of human rights; and (6) romantic cosmopolitanism (ibid.: 506).

In twenty-first-century China, the varieties of cosmopolitanism seem to have altered and narrowed down due to the strong role of the state. While the state celebrates political, market, and cultural cosmopolitanism, focusing on international diplomatic relations, stressing cultural pluralism, and establishing a global market, the cosmopolitanisms of morality and human rights are neglected. Margaret Swain has observed, too, that the cosmopolitanism discourse in China lacks the concept of a civil society (2013: 36). As for the sixth (romantic) type of cosmopolitanism, Germans of the eighteenth century may have imagined the possibility of a world 'united by faith and love' (Kleingeld 1999: 506), but Chinese people seem not to

imagine any such possibility. Rather, the Chinese romanticize cosmopolitanism as a time period, during which China had a leading role in the
world.

Cosmopolitan China, like cosmopolitan Xi'an, is strongly ethno-
nationalistic and inseparable from a historically great state. It is the 'great
China', promoted over several decades, that carries the glorious legacies of
the Qin, Han, and Tang dynasties. It is also an 'open China', as manifest
since 2008 in its attention to the revitalization of Silk Road heritage,
advocacy of international trade projects, and facilitation of cross-national
exchange programs. China 'opens', however, with the clear goals of building
its economic prosperity and improving its international reputation (cf. Zhang
W. 2012). In the process, China brokers a complex conversation about
'foreignness' between the past and present. On the one hand, it 'de-
foreignizes the past', trying to celebrate the cosmopolitan past and
integrating it into people's everyday life, values, and identity. On the other
hand, China undergoes 'foreignizes the present', introducing foreign
elements, bringing in more foreigners and international tourists, and
attracting transnational investment to increase internationalism.

Hence, Xi'an's heritage and modern developments mirror the political
economy of the whole nation. The city's policies reflect the goal of the
national government. Since Xi'an served as the eastern end of the ancient
Silk Road, it fits the political pursuit of national rejuvenation. National
rejuvenation involves a high degree of self-aggrandizement, which results in
the boosting of patriotism. The heritagization of archaeological remains and
historical buildings mainly serves politically as a means to constitute
nationalism. Xi'an's effort in heritage projects, its urge to modernize the
city, and its intensive involvement in World Heritage nominations all
constitute to the construction of a cosmopolitan image, reminding the world
of its previous international status. In the end, Xi'an aims at being an
economic centre in western China, a national technological and
transportation hub, and internationally, a world-class tourist destination,
celebrating Chinese civilization and culture (Tsinghua University News
2014).

Yet, as this book has amply demonstrated, Xi'an is not just a puppet
on the end of a national string. Nor can it be concluded, as do many studies
on contemporary China, that the goals of economic development dominate
all changes taking place in Xi'an (Wilkerson and Parkin 2013). Economic
prosperity is of vital concern in modernization and heritagization projects.
The state does occupy a powerful role in heritage making, and heritage does
act as a political tool to glorify a selective national history and to pursue the
China Dream. But in Xi'an there are other driving forces for the process of

heritagization. The developers, government officials, architects, consulting archaeologists are overwhelmingly of local origin, and they share with their co-residents emotional attachments, creative visions, social attitudes, and religious beliefs that motivate their professional activities. (They are also citizens of China, and share attachments, visions, attitudes and beliefs with co-nationals).

In the preceding chapters I have displayed the complexity of the making of heritage in urban China. I combined top-down and bottom-up perspectives and presented the opinions and views of a wide range of heritage actors. I showed the intertwinements and collisions between different levels and departments, as well as social actors with different interests and backgrounds. I documented conflicts on the ground, but I did not over-emphasize the 'dark side' of heritagization, neither of planning and projects in China. Though these worlds are full of tension, there is also much social cohesion; various social actors ally with and support each other without either obvious coercion or enticement. Though heritage projects and management are government-led, the case studies in Xi'an also demonstrate existing, if limited, space for locals, professionals, site administrations, and communities to shape emerging projects or change the course of existing ones. Such evidence appears with regard to the Qian Imperial Mausoleum (chapter 5), the Tang Temple of Heaven (chapter 5), Mingde Gate (chapter 5), Xingjiao Temple (chapter 6), Famen Temple (chapter 6), and the Muslim Quarter (chapter 7). Heritage actors utilized professional knowledge, the social media, and networking skills to develop strategies to negotiate with the government. Hence, this holistic study of Xi'an sheds light on the understanding of the complex, yet interlinked networks in the process of heritage making in an urban context.

Certainly heritagization and modern development in Xi'an elucidate the social politics of urban heritage and the uses of the past. The state instrumentalizes the past to fulfil the China Dream. The province brands its history to attract foreign tourists and investors. The city stages its glorious historical eras to increase its status within the nation and to boost the local identity. The local population yearns for the past because it gives them hope for the future. Perhaps, the past is not a foreign country at all in Xi'an. Perhaps, even the most commercialized forms of heritage show that the past is everywhere integral to society, deeply rooted in the identity, individually and collectively.

Appendices

Appendix 1

Neolithic	c. 8500 – c. 2070 BCE
Xia Dynasty	c. 2070 – c. 1600 BCE
Shang Dynasty	c.1600 – c. 1046 BCE
Zhou Dynasty	c.1046 – 256 BCE
Qin Dynasty	221 – 206 BCE
Han Dynasty	206 BCE – 220 CE
Three Kingdoms	220 – 208
Jin Dynasty	265 – 420
Northern and Southern dynasties	420 – 589
Sui Dynasty	581 – 618
Tang Dynasty	618 – 907
Five Dynasties and Ten Kingdoms	907 – 960
Song Dynasty	960 – 1279
Yuan Dynasty	1271 – 1368
Ming Dynasty	1368 – 1644
Qing Dynasty	1644 – 1911
Republic of China	1912 – 1949
The People's Republic of China	1949 – present

Appendix 2: All sites listed on the 'Routes Network of Chang'an-Tianshan Corridor' co-nominated by China, Kazakhstan, and Kyrgyzstan as World Heritage

China:
Luoyang City of the Eastern Han to Northern Wei dynasties, Luoyang, Henan Province
Dingding Gate, Luoyang City of the Sui and Tang dynasties, Luoyang, Henan Province
Longmen Grottoes (already inscribed on the World Heritage List in 2000), Luoyang, Henan Province
Hangu Pass, Lingbao, Henan Province
Shihao section of Xiaohan Route, Xin'an County, Henan Province
Weiyang Palace, Xi'an, Shaanxi Province
Daming Palace, Xi'an, Shaanxi Province

Giant Wild Goose Pagoda, Xi'an, Shaanxi Province
Small Wild Goose Pagoda, Xi'an, Shaanxi Province
Xingjiao Temple, Xi'an, Shaanxi Province
Bin County Cave Temple, Bin County, Shaanxi Province
Tomb of Zhang Qian, Chenggu County, Shaanxi Province
Maijishan Cave Temple Complex, Tianshui, Gansu Province
Bingling Cave Temple Complex, Yongjing County, Linxia Hui Autonomous
Prefecture, Gansu Province
Yumen Pass, Dunhuang, Gansu Province
Xuanquanzhi Posthouse, Dunhuang, Gansu Province
Magao Caves, Dunhuang, Gansu Province (already inscribed on the World
Heritage List in 1987)
Suoyang City Ruins, Anxi, Gansu Province
Qocho (Gaochang) City Ruins, Turpan, Xinjiang Uyghur Autonomous
Region
Yar City Site of Bashbaliq City (Jiaohe Ruins), Turpan, Xinjiang Uyghur
Autonomous Region
Beshbalik City Ruins, Jimsar County, Xinjiang Uyghur Autonomous Region
Kizil Gaha Beacon Tower, Kuqa, Xinjiang Uyghur Autonomous Region
Kizil Caves, Kuqa, Xinjiang Uyghur Autonomous Region
Subash Buddhist Temple Ruins, Kuqa, Xinjiang Uyghur Autonomous
Region

Kazakhstan:
Site of Kayalyk, Almaty Province
Karamergen, Almaty Province
Talgar, Almaty Province, Kazakhstan
Aktobe, Jambyl Province
Kulan, Jambyl Province
Akyrtas, Jambyl Province
Ornek, Jambyl Province
Kostobe, Jambyl Province

Kyrgyzstan:
Suyab (Site of Ak-Beshim), Chuy Province
City of Balasagun (Site of Burana), Chuy Province
City of Nevaket (Site of Krasnaya Rechka), Chuy Province

Bibliography

Abramson, D. 2001. Beijing's Preservation Policy and the Fate of Siheyuan. *Traditional Dwellings and Settlements Review* 13 (1): 7–22.

Abramson, D., M. Leaf, and T. Ying. 2002. Social Research and the Localization of Chinese Urban Planning Practice: Some Ideas from Quanzhou, Fujian. In J. R. Logan (ed.), *The New Chinese City*, pp. 167–180. Oxford: Blackwell.

Abu el Haj, N. 1998. Translating Truths: Nationalism, the Practice of Archaeology, and the Remaking of Past and Present in Contemporary Jerusalem. *American Ethnologist* 25 (2): 166–188.

——. 2001. *Facts on the Ground: Archaeological Practice and Territorial Self-Fashioning in Israeli Society*. Chicago: University of Chicago Press.

Adger, W. N. 2000. Social and Ecological Resilience: Are They Related? *Progress in Human Geography* 24 (3): 347–364.

Adger, W. N., and P. M. Kelly. 2001. *Living with Environmental Change: Social Vulnerability, Adaptation and Resilience in Vietnam*. New York: Routledge.

Allan, S. 2005. *The Formation of Chinese Civilization: an Archaeological Perspective*. New Haven: Yale University Press.

Anagnost, A. 1997. *National Past-Times: Narrative, Representation, and Power in Modern China*. Durham: Duke University Press.

Andermahr, S., and S. Pellicer-Ortín. 2013. *Trauma Narratives and Herstory*. New York: Palgrave Macmillan.

Antweiler, C. 2004. Urbanität und Ethnologie: aktuelle Theorietrends und die Methodik ethnologischer Stadtforschung. *Zeitschrift für Ethnologie* 129 (2): 285–307.

Appiah, K. A. 1996. Cosmopolitan Patriots. In J. Cohen (ed.), *For Love of Country: Debating the Limits of Patriotism – Martha Nussbaum and Respondents*, pp. 21–31. Boston: Beacon Press.

——. 2005. *The Ethics of Identity*. Princeton: Princeton University Press.

Arantes, A. A. 2007. Diversity, Heritage and Cultural Politics. *Theory, Culture and Society* 24 (7-8): 290–296.

Ashby, R., and D. G. Ohrn. 1995. *Herstory: Women who Changed the World*. New York: Viking.

Ashworth, G. J. 2011. Preservation, Conservation and Heritage: Approaches to the Past in the Present through the Built Environment. *Asian Anthropology* 10 (1): 1–18.

Ashworth, G. J., and B. Graham. 2005. *Senses of Place: Senses of Time*. Burlington: Ashgate.

Ashworth, G. J., and P. J. Larkham (eds.). 1994. *Building a New Heritage: Tourism, Culture and Identity in the New Europe*. London and New York: Routledge.

Atkinson, R., and G. Bridge. 2005. *Gentrification in a Global Context: The New Urban Colonialism*. London and New York: Routledge.

Auty, R. M. 1992. Industrial Policy Reform in China: Structural and Regional Imbalances. *Transactions of the Institute of British Geographers* 17 (4): 481–494.

Bakken, B. 2000. *The Exemplary Society: Human Improvement, Social Control and the Dangers of Modernity in China*. Oxford: Oxford University Press.

Barabantseva, E. 2009. Change vs. Order – Shijie Meets Tianxia in China's Interactions with the World. *BICC Working Paper* 11. Manchester: British Inter-University China Centre, University of Manchester.

Barthold, V. V. 1956. *Four Studies on Central Asia*. Leiden: Brill.

Bartu, A. 2001. Rethinking Heritage Politics in a Global Context: A View from Istanbul. In N. Al Sayyad (ed.), *Hybrid Urbanism*, pp. 131–155. London: Praeger.

Beckwith, C. 2009. *Empires of the Silk Road: A History of Central Eurasia from the Bronze Age to the Present*. Princeton: Princeton University Press.

Bell, D. 2009. War, Peace, and China's Soft Power: A Confucian Approach. *Diogenes* 56 (1): 26–40.

Benavides, O. H. 2005. *Making Ecuadorian Histories*. Austin: University of Texas Press.

Bentley, J. H. 1993. *Old World Encounters: Cross-Cultural Contacts and Exchanges in Pre-Modern Times*. New York: Oxford University Press.

Berkes, F., and C. Folke. 2000. *Linking Social and Ecological Systems Management Practices and Social Mechanisms for Building Resilience*. Cambridge: Cambridge University Press.

Berliner, D. 2012. Multiple Nostalgias: The Fabric of Heritage in Luang Prabang (Lao PDR). *Journal of the Royal Anthropological Institute* 18 (4): 769–786.

Bhabha, H. 2001. Unsatisfied: Notes on Vernacular Cosmopolitanism. In G. Castle (ed.), *Postcolonial Discourses: An Anthology*, pp. 38–53. Oxford: Blackwell.

Biener, A. S. 2001. Das deutsche Pachtgebiet Tsingtau in Schantung, 1897–1914. *Studien und Quellen zur Geschichte Schantungs und Tsingtaus* 6. Bonn: Selbstverlag Prof. Dr. W. Matzat.

Blumenfield, T., and H. Silverman (eds.). 2013. *Cultural Heritage Politics in China*. New York: Springer.

Boardman, J. 1994. *The Diffusion of Classical Art in Antiquity*. London: Thames and Hudson.

Bodde, D. 1986. The State and Empire of Ch'in. In D. Twitchett, and M. Loewe (eds.), *The Cambridge History of China: Volume I: The Ch'in and Han Empires, 221 B.C. – A.D. 220*, pp. 20–102. Cambridge: Cambridge University Press.

Bohle, H. G., B. Etzold, and M. Keck. 2009. Resilience as Agency. *IHDP – Update* 2: 8–13.

Boissevain-Souid, K. 2002. The Legend Lalla Mamiqa. In T. Zarcone (ed.), *Saints and Heroes on the Silk Road*, pp. 317–324. Paris: Maisonneuve.

Bonavia, J. 2007. *The Silk Road: From Xi'an to Kashgar*. Hong Kong: Odyssey.

Bouzarovki, S., J. Salukvadze, and M. Gentile. 2011. A Socially Resilient Urban Transition? The Contested Landscapes of Apartment Building Extensions in Two Post-Communist Cities. *Urban Studies* 48 (13): 2689–2714.

Bradley, D., and A. Grainger. 2004. Social Resilience as a Controlling Influence on Desertification in Senegal. *Land Degradation and Development* 15 (5): 451–470.

Brandtstädter, S., and G. Santos. 2009. *Chinese Kinship: Contemporary Anthropological Perspectives*. London: Routledge.

Braun, B., and T. Aßheuer. 2011. Floods in Megacity Environments: Vulnerability and Coping Strategies of Slum Dwellers in Dhaka/ Bangladesh. *Natural Hazards* 58 (2): 771–787.

Breglia, L. C. 2006. *Monumental Ambivalence: The Politics of Heritage*. Austin: University of Texas Press.

Bridge, G. 1995. The Space for Class? On Class Analysis in the Study of Gentrification. *Transactions of the Institute of British Geographers* 20 (2): 236–247.

Broun, E. 2004. Telling the Story of America. In B. M. Carbonell (ed.), *Museum Studies: An Anthology of Contexts*, pp. 296–301. Malden: Blackwell.

Brumann, C. 2009. Outside the Glass Case: The Social Life of Urban Heritage in Kyoto. *American Ethnologist* 36 (2): 276–299.

——. 2012a. *Tradition, Democracy, and the Townscape of Kyoto: Claiming a Right to the Past*. London: Routledge.

——. 2012b. Multilateral Ethnography: Entering the World Heritage Arena. *Working Paper* 136. Halle: Max Planck Institute for Social Anthropology.

——. 2014. Heritage Agnosticism: A Third Path for the Study of Cultural Heritage. *Social Anthropology* 22 (2): 173–188.

——. 2015. Vom Nutzen der Verbindungen: Die 'cultural routes' im UNESCO-Welterbegeschehen. In A. Ranft, and W. Schenkluhn (eds.), *Kulturstraßen als Konzept: 20 Jahre Straße der Romanik*, pp. 211–221. Regensburg: Schnell & Steiner.

Burke, P. 1987. *The Historical Anthropology of Early Modern Italy: Essays on Perception and Communication.* Cambridge: Cambridge University Press.

Callahan, W. A. 2007. Tianxia, Empire and the World: Soft Power and China's Foreign Policy Discourse in the 21st Century. *BICC Working Paper* 1. Manchester: British Inter-University China Centre, University of Manchester.

——. 2013. *China Dreams: 20 Visions of the Future.* Oxford: Oxford University Press.

Cao, T. 2010. Xi'an de lishi jiequ baohu – yi Qixian Zhuang lishi jiequ weili. (The restoration of Xi'an's historic conservation areas: using Qixian Zhuang Quarter as an example). *Tangdu Qikang* 26 (2): 101–103.

CECC. 2001. *Urban Housing Demolition and Relocation Management Regulations.* Available online, http://www.cecc.gov/resources/legal-provisions/urban-housing-demolition-and-relocation-management-regulations-cecc-full, last accessed 1 May 2016.

Central People's Government of the People's Republic of China. 2008. *Lishi wenhua mingcheng mingzheng mingcun baohu tiaoli.* (The regulations for the protection of historic and cultural cities, towns, and villages). Available online, http://www.gov.cn/zwgk/2008-04/29/content_957280.htm, last accessed 1 May 2016.

Chan, C. K-C., and P. Ngai. 2009. The Making of a New Working Class? A Study of Collective Actions of Migrant Workers in South China. *The China Quarterly* 198 (June): 287–303.

Chan, J., and P. Ngai. 2010. Suicide as Protest for the New Generation of Chinese Migrant Workers. *The Asia Pacific Journal* 8 (37/ 2). Online publication: https://apjjf.org/-Jenny-Chan/3408/article.html.

Chan, K. W. 1994. *Cities with Invisible Walls: Reinterpreting Urbanization in Post 1949 China.* Hong Kong and New York: Oxford University Press.

Chan, K. W., and X. Xu. 1985. Urban Population Growth and Urbanization in China since 1949: Reconstructing a Baseline. *The China Quarterly* 104 (December): 583–613.

Chan, K. W., and Y. Hu. 2003. Urbanization in China in the 1990s. *The China Review* 3 (2): 37–59.

Chan, L. M. 1972. The Burning of the Books in China, 213 B.C. *The Journal of Library History* 7 (2): 101–108.

Chang, K. 1986. *The Archaeology of Ancient China*. New Haven: Yale University Press.

Chang, K. C. 1983. *Art, Myth, and Ritual: The Path to Political Authority in Ancient China*. Cambridge: Harvard University Press.

Chang, S. 1977. The Morphology of Walled Capitals. In G. W. Skinner (ed.), *The City in Late Imperial China*, pp. 75–100. Stanford: Stanford University Press.

Chao, P. 1983. *Chinese Kinship*. London and Boston: K. Paul International.

Cheah, P. 2006. Cosmopolitanism. *Theory, Culture & Society* 23 (2–3): 286–296.

Chen, D. 2003. *The Third Front Construction: The Western Development in Pre-War Period*. Beijing: Central School of Communist Party Press.

Chen, L. 2012. *Shaanxi Caishengmiao muhua shangshi quanqian tepuo shehui dixian zhao zhiyi* (The listing of God of Fortune Temple on the stock market's social impact). *Tencent Finance*, 12 June 2012. Available online, http://finance.qq.com/a/20120612/002859.htm, last accessed 1 May 2016.

Chen, P., D. Wang, and X. Chen. 2009. *Xi'an: Dushi Xiangxiang yu Wenhua Jiyi* (Xi'an: The Urban Imagination and Cultural Memories). Beijing: Beijing Daxue Chubanshe.

Chen, Q., and A. Zhang. 2009. *Hanshu Yanjiu* (The Studies of the Book of Han). Beijing: Zhongguo Dabaike Quanshu Chubanshe.

Cheung, A. L. 2019. The Voices of the Voiceless: The Cantonese Opera Music Community in Guangzhou, China. *Asian Education and Development Studies*: 8 (4): 443–453.

Cheung, S. C-H. 1999. The Meanings of a Heritage Trail in Hong Kong. *Annals of Tourism Research* 26 (3): 570–588.

——. 2003. Remembering through Space: The Politics of Heritage in Hong Kong. *International Journal of Heritage Studies* 9 (1): 7–27.

Childe, V. G. 1946. Anthropology and Archaeology. *Southwestern Journal of Anthropology* 2 (3): 243–252.

China Info. 2016. *Xi'an Qujiang Cultural Industry Investment (Group) Co., Ltd. Annual Report 2016*. Available online, http://www.cninfo.

com.cn/finalpage/2016-01-22/1201935743.PDF?COLLCC=
3539081109&, last accessed 1 May 2016.

China Statistics. 2005. *Xi'an Statistical Yearbook – 2004*. Beijing: China
    Statistics Press.

Chinese Civilization Center. 2007. *China: Five Thousand Years of History
    and Civilization*. Hong Kong: City University of Hong Kong Press

Chris, R., H. Gu, and M. Fang. 2009. Destination Planning in China. In R.
    Chris, and H. Gu (eds.), *Tourism in China: Destination, Cultures
    and Communities*, pp. 11–37. New York: Routledge.

Christian, D. 2000. Silk Roads or Steppe Roads: The Silk Roads in World
    History. *Journal of World History* 11 (1): 1–26.

Chun, S. 2009. On Chinese cosmopolitanism (Tian Xia). *Culture Mandala:
    Bulletin of the Centre for East-West Cultural & Economic Studies* 8
    (2): 20–29.

Chung, S. P. 1996. Symmetry and Balance in the Layout of the Sui-Tang
    Palace-City of Chang'an. *Artibus Asiae* 56 (1/ 2): 5–17.

——. 1998. The Sui-Tang Eastern Palace in Chang'an: Toward a
    Reconstruction of its Plan. *Artibus Asiae* 58 (1/ 2): 5–31.

Clark, E. 2005. The Order and Simplicity of Gentrification – A Political
    Challenge. In L. Lees, T. Slater, and E. Wyly (eds.), *The
    Gentrification Reader*, pp.24–29. London: Routledge.

Clark, G. 1957. *Archaeology and Society*. London: Methuen.

Clarke, M. 2009. Glocality, Silk Roads, and New and Little Great Games in
    Xinjiang and Central Asia. In C. Mackerras, and M. Clarke (eds.),
    *China, Xinjiang and Central Asia: History, Transition and
    Crossborder Interaction into the 21st Century*, pp. 173–189.
    London: Routledge.

Clausen, S., and S. Thogersen (eds.). 1995. *The Making of a Chinese City:
    History and Historiography in Harbin*. Armonk: M. E. Sharp.

Clifford, J. 2004. Looking Several Ways: Anthropology and Native Heritage
    in Alaska. *Current Anthropology* 45 (1): 5–30.

Cochrane, S. 2000. Marketing Medicine and Advertising Dreams in China,
    1900–1950. In W-H. Yeh (ed.), *Becoming Chinese: Passages to
    Modernity and Beyond*, pp. 62–97. Berkeley: University of
    California Press.

Colwell-Chanthaphonh, C., and T. J. Ferguson (eds.). 2007. *The
    Collaborative Continuum: Archaeological Engagements with
    Descendent Communities*. Thousand Oaks, CA: AltaMira.

Common, M. 1995. *Sustainability and Policy: Limits to Economics*.
    Cambridge: Cambridge University Press.

Coombes, A. E. 2004. Museums and the Formation of National and Cultural Identities. In B. M. Carbonell (ed.), *Museum Studies. An Anthology of Contexts*, pp. 231–246. Malden: Blackwell.

Currier, J. 2008. Art and Power in the New China: An Exploration of Beijing's 798 District and its Implications for Contemporary Urbanism. *The Town Planning Review* 79 (2/ 3): 237–265.

Damir-Geisdorf, S. 2005. *Mental Maps – Raum – Erinnerung. Kulturwissenschaftliche Zugänge zum Verhältnis von Raum und Erinnerung.* Münster: LIT Verlag.

Dani, A. H. 1992. Significance of Silk Road to Human Civilization: Its Cultural Dimension. In T. Umesao, and T. Sugimura (eds.), *Significance of Silk Roads in the History of Human Civilizations*, pp. 21–26. Osaka: National Museum of Ethnology.

Davidson, D. J. 2010. The Applicability of the Concept of Resilience to Social Systems: Some Sources of Optimism and Nagging Doubts. *Society and Natural Resources* 23 (12): 1135–1149.

Davis, D. J. 2012. Qin Shihaung's Terracotta Warriors and Commemorating the Cultural State. In M. A. Matten (ed.), *Places of Memory in Modern China: History, Politics, and Identity*, pp. 17–50. Leiden and Koninklijke: Brill.

Davis, M. 1990. *City of Quartz: Excavating the Future in Los Angeles.* London: Verso.

Davis, D. S. 2000. *The Consumer Revolution in Urban China.* Berkeley: University of California Press.

De Giosa, P. 2016. *Heritage Below the Winds: The social life of the cityscape and UNESCO World Heritage in Melaka.* Ph.D. dissertation, Martin Luther University Halle-Wittenberg.

Dean, K. 2003. Local Communal Religion in Contemporary South-East China. *The China Quarterly* 174 (June): 338–358.

Demgenski, P. 2018. Living in the 'Past': The Effects of a Growing Heritage Discourse in Contemporary Urban China. In M. Marinelli, Y. Ding, and X. Zhang (eds.), *China: A Historical Geography of the Urban*, pp. 149–225. London: Palgrave.

Denton, K. 2005. Museums, Memorial Sites and Exhibitionary Culture in the People's Republic of China. *The China Quarterly* 183 (September): 565–586.

Di Cosmo, N. 1994. Ancient Inner Asian Nomads: Their Economic Basis and its Significance in Chinese History. *Journal of Asian Studies* 53 (4): 1092–1126.

———. 2002. *Ancient China and its Enemies: The Rise of Nomadic Power in East Asian History.* Cambridge: Cambridge University Press.

Diawara, M. 1998. Toward a Regional Imaginary in Africa. In F. Jameson, and M. Miyoshi (eds.), *The Cultures of Globalization*, pp. 103–124. Durham: Duke University Press.

Diaz-Andreu, M., and T. Champion (eds.). 1996. *Nationalism and Archaeology in Europe*. London: University College London Press.

Dirks, N. B. 1990. History as a Sign of the Modern. *Public Culture* 2 (2 Spring): 25–32.

Dombroski, K. 2008. The Whole Nine Villages: Local-Development through Mass Tourism in Tibetan China. In J. Connel, and B. Rugendyke (eds.), *Tourism at the Grassroots: Villagers and Visitors in the Asia-Pacific*, pp. 98–113. London: Routledge.

Dorsten, L., and Y. Li. 2011. Research in Ambiguous, Conflictual, and Changing Contexts: Studying Ethnic Populations in China, Xi'an to Urumqi. *The Qualitative Report* 16 (6): 1465–1476.

Drège, J. P., and E. M. Bührer. 1989. *The Silk Road Saga*. New York: Facts on File.

Du Cros, H., and Y-S. F. Lee. 2007. *Cultural Heritage Management in China: Preserving the Cities of the Pearl River Delta*. London and New York: Routledge.

Duan, X. N. 2011.The Way to Achieve Cultural Industrialized Heritage Preservation. *Architecture and Culture* 88 (7): 78–79.

Duara, P. 1995. *Rescuing History from the Nation: Questioning Narratives of Modern China*. Chicago and London: University of Chicago Press.

Duara, P. 2000. Of Authenticity and Woman: Personal Narratives of Middle Class Women in Modern China. In W-H. Yeh (ed.), *Becoming Chinese: Passages to Modernity and Beyond*, pp. 342–364. Berkeley: University of California Press.

——. 2009. *The Global and Regional in China's Nation Formation*. London: Routledge.

Eckfeld, T. 2005. *Imperial Tombs in Tang China, 618–907: The Politics of Paradise*. New York: Routledge.

Eisenstadt, S. 2000. Multiple Modernities. *Daedalus* 129 (1): 1–29.

Elisseeff, V. 1992. Silk Roads: Past and Future. In T. Umesao, and T. Sugimura (eds.), *Significance of Silk Roads in the History of Human Civilizations*, pp. 1–3. Osaka: National Museum of Ethnology.

——. 2000. *The Silk Roads: Highways of Culture and Commerce*. New York: Berghahn Books.

Elliott, M. C. 2001. *The Manchu Way: The Eight Banners and Ethnic Identity in Late Imperial China*. Stanford: Stanford University Press.

Elverskog, J. 2010. *Buddhism and Islam on the Silk Road*. Philadelphia: University of Pennsylvania Press.

Endfield, G. H. 2007. Archival Explorations of Climate Variability and Social Vulnerability in Colonial Mexico. *Climatic Change* 83 (2-3): 9–38.

Errington, S. 1998. *The Death of Authentic Primitive Art and Other Tales of Progress*. Berkeley: University of California Press.

Evans, G. R. 2008. Transformation from 'Carbon Valley' to a 'Post-Carbon Society' in a Climate Change Hot Spot: The Coalfields of the Hunter Valley, New South Wales, Australia. *Ecology and Society* 13 (1): 39–59.

Evasdottir, E. E. S. 2004. *Obedient Autonomy: Chinese Intellectuals and the Achievement of Orderly Life*. Vancouver: University of British Columbia Press.

Farrer, J. 2010. 'New Shanghailanders' or 'New Shanghainese': Western Expatriates' Narratives of Emplacement in Shanghai. *Journal of Ethnic and Migration Studies* 36 (8): 1211–1228.

Fayolle Lussac, B. 2007. State Listed Monuments and Stakes of Urban Development: The Case of the Great Archaeological Sites. In B. Fayolle Lussac, H. Høyem, and P. Clément (eds.), *Xi'an – An Ancient City in a Modern World: Evolution of the Urban Form 1949–2000*, pp. 196–202. Paris: Ed. Recherches.

Fayolle Lussac, B., H. Høyem, and P. Clément. 2007. *Xi'an – An Ancient City in a Modern World: Evolution of the Urban Form 1949–2000*. Paris: Ed. Recherches.

Feighery, W. G. 2008. Heritage Tourism in Xi'an: Constructing the Past in Contested Space. In J. Cochrane (ed.), *Asian Tourism: Growth and Change*, pp. 323–334. London: Elsevier.

Feighery, W. G. 2011. Contested Heritage in the Ancient City of Peace. *Historic Environment* 23 (1): 61–66.

Feng, H. 1967. *The Chinese Kinship System*. Cambridge: Harvard University Press.

Festa, P. E. 2006. Mahjong Politics in Contemporary China: Civility, Chineseness, and Mass Culture. *Positions: East Asia Cultures Critique* 14 (1): 7–36.

Feuchtwang, S. 2004. *Making Place: State Projects, Globalization, and Local Responses in China*. London: UCL Press.

Fiskesjö, M. 2015. Terracotta Conquest: The First Emperor's Clay Army's Blockbuster Tour of the World. *Studies in Global Asia* 1 (1): 162–183.

Flath, J. A. 2002. Managing Historical Capital in Shandong: Museum, Monument, and Memory in Provincial China. *The Public Historian* 24 (2): 41–59.

——. 2004. Setting Moon and Rising Nationalism: Lugou Bridge as Monument and Memory. *International Journal of Heritage Studies* 10 (2): 175–192.

Foltz, R. 2000. *Religions of the Silk Road: Overland Trade and Cultural Exchanges from Antiquity to the Fifteenth Century*. Basingstoke: Macmillan.

Fong, G., N. Qian, and H. T. Zurndorfer (eds.). 2004. *Beyond Tradition and Modernity: Gender, Genre and Cosmopolitanism in Late Qing China*. Leiden and Boston: Brill.

Fong, M. H. 1991. Antecedents of Sui-Tang Burial Practices in Shaanxi. *Artibus Asiae* 51 (3/ 4): 147–198.

Franquesa, J. 2013. On Keeping and Selling the Political Economy of Heritage-Making in Contemporary Spain. *Current Anthropology* 54 (3): 346–369.

Fresnais, J. 2001. *La Protection du Patrimoine en Rèpublique Populaire de Chine 1949–1999*. Paris: Ed. of the CTHS.

Fyall, A., B. Garrod, and A. Leask. 2003. *Managing Visitor Attractions: New Directions*. Oxford: Butterworth-Heinemann.

Gale, D. 1986. Demographic Research on Gentrification and Displacement. *Journal of Planning Literature* 1 (1): 14–29.

Gaubatz, P. 2005. Globalization and the Development of New Central Business Districts in Beijing, Shanghai and Guangzhou. In L. J. Ma, and F. Wu (eds.), *Restructuring the Chinese City: Changing Society, Economy and Space*, pp. 98–121. London: Routledge.

Ge, Q., and S. P. Zhang. 1998. Industrial Restructuring and the Choice of Key Industries in Xi'an. *Journal of the Shaanxi College of Economics and Business* 2: 51–56.

Ge, Z. 2011. *Preserving China: Reconstructing the Historical Narrative about 'China'*. Taibei City: Lianjing Press Limited.

Giddens, A. 1990. *The Consequences of Modernity*. Stanford: Stanford University Press.

Gillette, M. 2000. *Between Mecca and Beijing: Modernization and Consumption among Urban Chinese Muslims*. Stanford: Stanford University Press.

——. 2008. Violence, the State, and a Chinese Muslim Ritual Remembrance. *The Journal of Asian Studies* 67 (3): 1011–1037.

Gladney, D. C. 1998. Clashed Civilizations? Muslim and Chinese Identities in the PRC. In D. C. Gladney (ed.), *Making Majorities: Constituting the Nation in Japan, Korea, China, Malaysia, Fiji, Turkey, and the United States*, pp. 106–131. Stanford: Stanford University Press.

———. 2004. *Dislocating China: Reflections on Muslims, Minorities and other Subaltern Subjects*. London: C. Hurst & Co.

Goldin, P. R. 2005. The Rise and Fall of the Qin Empire. In V. H. Mair, N. Schatzman Steinhardt, and P. R. Goldin (eds.), *The Hawai'i Reader in Traditional Chinese Culture*, pp. 151–160. Hawai'i: University of Hawai'i Press.

Gong, Q., and P. Jackson. 2012. Consuming Anxiety: Parenting Practices in China after the Infant Formula Scandal. *Food, Culture and Society* 15 (4): 557–578.

Goodale, M. 2006. Reclaiming Modernity: Indigenous Cosmopolitanism and the Coming of the Second Revolution in Bolivia. *American Ethnologist* 33 (4): 634–649.

Goodman, D. 2002. Structuring Local Identity: Nation, Province and County in Shanxi during the 1990s. *China Quarterly* 172 (December): 837–862.

Gotham, K. F. 2005. Tourism Gentrification: The Case of New Orleans' Vieux Carré (French Quarter). *Urban Studies* 42 (7): 1099–1121.

Greenberg, C. 1993. Modernist Painting. In J. O'Brian (ed.), *Clement Greenberg: The Collected Essays and Criticism*, vol. 4, pp. 85–93. Chicago: University of Chicago Press.

Greenhalgh, S. 2003. Science, Modernity and the Making of China's One-Child Policy. *Population and Development Review* 29 (2): 163–196.

———. 2009. The Chinese Bio-Political: Facing the Twenty-First Century. *New Genetics and Society* 28 (3): 205–222.

Grimwade, G., and B. Carter. 2000. Managing Small Heritage Sites with Interpretation and Community Involvement. *International Journal of Heritage Studies* 6 (1): 33–48.

Gruber, S. 2007. Protecting China's Cultural Heritage Sites in Times of Rapid Change: Current Developments, Practice and Law. *Asia Pacific Journal of Environmental Law* 10 (3-4): 253–301.

Guang, L. 2003. Rural Taste, Urban Fashions: The Cultural Politics of Rural/Urban Difference in Contemporary China. *Positions* 11 (3): 613–646.

Guldin, G., and A. Southall. 1993. *Urban Anthropology in China*. Leiden, New York, and Köln: E. J. Brill.

Gunderson, L. H., C. S. Holling, L. Pritchard, and G. D. Peterson. 1997. Resilience in Ecosystems, Institutions and Societies. *Discussion Paper* 95. Stockholm: Beijer International Institute of Ecological Economics.

Guo, Q., and Q. Guo. 2001. The Formation and Early Development of Architecture in Northern China. *Construction History* 17: 3–16.

Gustafsson, B., and S. Li. 2000. Economic Transformation and the Gender Earning Gap in Urban China. *Journal of Population Economics* 13 (2): 305–329.

Halegua, A. 2008. Getting Paid: Processing the Labor Disputes of China's Migrant Workers. *Berkeley Journal of International Law* 26 (1): 256–283.

Hamada, M. 2002. The Mausoleum and the Cult of Satuq Bughra Khan at Artush. In T. Zarcone (ed.), *Saints and Heroes on the Silk Road*, pp. 63–88. Paris: Maisonneuve.

Han, X. 2006. *Sui Tang Chang'an he zhongya wenming* (Chang'an in the Sui and Tang Dynasty and Central Asian Civilization). Beijing: Zhongguo Shehui Kexue Chubanshe.

Han, Y., P. Du, J. Cao, and E. S. Posmentier. 2006. Multivariate Analysis of Heavy Metal Contamination in Urban Dusts in Xi'an, Central China. *Science of the Total Environment* 355 (1): 176–186.

Hannerz, U. 1980. *Exploring the City: Inquiries toward an Urban Anthropology*. New York: Columbia University Press.

——. 1990. Cosmopolitans and Locals in World Culture. *Theory, Culture and Society* 7 (2-2): 237–251.

Hannigan, J. 1998. *Fantasy City: Pleasure and Profit in the Postmodern Metropolis*. London and New York: Routledge.

Härke, H. 2000. *Archaeology, Ideology and Society: The German Experience*. Frankfurt am Main: Lang.

Harrell, S. 1995. Civilizing Projects and our Reaction to Them. In S. Harrell (ed.), *Cultural Encounters on China's Ethnic Frontiers*, pp. 3–36. Seattle: University of Washington Press.

——. 2013. China's Tangled Web of Heritage. In T. Blumenfield, and H. Silverman (eds.), *Cultural Heritage Politics in China*, pp. 285–294. New York: Springer.

Harris, P. 2009. *Three Hundred Tang Poems*. New York: Alfred A. Knopf.

Harrison, D., and M. Hitchcock (eds.). 2005. *The Politics of World Heritage: Negotiating Tourism and Conservation*. Tonawanda: Channel View Publications.

Harvey, D. 1989. *The Condition of Postmodernity*. London: Blackwell.

——. 2001. Heritage Pasts and Heritage Presents: Temporality, Meaning and the Scope of Heritage Studies. *International Journal of Heritage Studies* 7 (4): 319–338.

Hayward, B. 2008. Nowhere far from the Sea: Political Challenges of Coastal Adaptation to Climate Change in New Zealand. *Political Science* 60 (1): 47–59.

Heath, D. 1992. Fashion, Anti-Fashion and Heteroglossia in Urban Senegal. *American Ethnologist* 19 (2): 19–33.

Henderson, J. C. 2002. Heritage Attractions and Tourism Development in Asia: A Comparative Study of Hong Kong and Singapore. *The International Journal of Tourism Research* 4 (5): 337–344.

Henderson, J. V. 2005. Growth of China's Medium Size Cities. In G. Burtless, and J. R. Pack (eds.), *Brookings-Wharton Papers on Urban Affairs*, pp. 263–303. Washington D.C.: Brookings Institution Press.

Herzfeld, M. 1991. *A Place in History: Social and Monumental Time in a Cretan Town*. Princeton: Princeton University Press.

——. 2009. *Evicted from Eternity: The Restructuring of Modern Rome*. Chicago: University of Chicago Press.

Hiery, H. 1999. *Alltagsleben und Kulturaustausch: Deutsche und Chinesen in Tsingtau 1897–1914*. Wolfratshausen: Edition Minerva.

Hill, J. E. 2009. *Through the Jade Gate to Rome: A Study of the Silk Routes during the Later Han Dynasty, 1st to 2nd Centuries CE: An Annotated Translation of the Chronicle on the 'Western Regions' in the Hou Hanshu*. Charleston, South Carolina: BookSurge Publishing.

HKTDC. 2011. *Xian Economic and Social Development Report*. Available online, http://china-trade-research.hktdc.com/business-news/article/Fast-Facts/Xi-an-Shaanxi-City-Information/ff/en/1/1X000000/1X07322S.htm, last accessed 1 May 2016.

Hobsbawm, E. 1983. Introduction: Inventing Traditions. In E. Hobsbawm, and T. Ranger (eds.), *The Invention of Tradition*, pp. 1–14. Cambridge: Cambridge University Press.

Holling, C. S. 1986. The Resilience of Terrestrial Ecosystems: Local Surprise and Global Change. In W. C. Clark, and R. E. Munn (eds.), *Sustainable Development of the Biosphere*, pp. 292–317. Cambridge: Cambridge University Press.

——. 1995. What Barriers? What Bridges? In L. Gunderson, C. S. Holling, and S. S. Light (eds.), *Barriers and Bridges to the Renewal of Ecosystems and Institutions*, pp. 14–36. New York: Columbia University Press.

Holston, J. 1989. *The Modernist City: An Anthropological Critique of Brasilia*. Chicago: University of Chicago Press.

Honig, E. 1992. *Creating Chinese Ethnicity: Subei People in Shanghai, 1850–1980*. New Haven: Yale University Press.

Hopkirk, P. 2006. *Foreign Devils on the Silk Road: The Search for the Lost Treasures of Central Asia*. London: Murray.

Howe, P. D. 2011. Hurricane Preparedness as Anticipatory Adaptation: A Case Study of Community Businesses. *Global Environmental Change – Human and Policy Dimension* 21 (2): 711–720.

Høyem , H. 2007. Permanence and Change in the Muslim Drum Tower District. In B. Fayolle Lussac, H. Høyem, and P. Clément (eds.), *Xi'an – An Ancient City in a Modern World: Evolution of the Urban Form 1949–2000*, pp. 222–231. Paris: Ed. Recherches.

Hsu, M. L. 1996. China's Urban Development: A Case Study of Luoyang and Guiyang. *Urban Studies* 33 (6): 895–910.

Hu, J., and S. Q. Wang. 2010. *Bravo Shaanxi Dialect*. Xi'an: Xi'an Press.

Huang, F-T. 1999. *Qingdao: Chinesen unter deutscher Herrschaft 1897–1914*. Bochum: Projekt-Verlag.

ICOMOS. 1965. *International Charter for the Conservation and Restoration of Monuments and Sites (The Venice Charter 1964)*. Available online, http://www.icomos.org/charters/venice_e.pdf, last accessed 1 May 2016.

Ikels, C. 1996. *The Return of the God of Wealth: The Transition to a Market Economy in Urban China*. Stanford: Stanford University Press.

——. 2004. Serving the Ancestors, Serving the State: Filial Piety and Death Ritual in Contemporary Guangzhou. In C. Ikels (ed.), *Filial Piety: Practice and Discourse in Contemporary China*, pp. 88–105. Stanford: Stanford University Press.

Jacques, M. 2009. *When China Rules the World: The Rise of the Middle Kingdom and the End of the Western World*. London: Allen Lane.

Jaivin, L. 2010. Qujiang: Loved Up on History and Culture. *China Heritage Quarterly* November (24). Available online, http://www.chinaheritagequarterly.org/articles.php?searchterm=024_qujiang.inc&issue=024, last accessed 14 February 2019.

Jankowiak, W. R. 1993. *Sex, Death, and Hierarchy in a Chinese City: An Anthropological Account*. New York: Columbia University Press.

Jia, P. O. 2011. *Old Xi'an*. Beijing: Chinese Society Press.

Jing, X. F. 2014. *Kongjian Geli yu Wailai Renkou de Chengshi Rungru* (The Urban Integration of the Future Population and Space Planning). Beijing: Zhongguo Shehuikexue Chubanshe.

Johnson, G. E. 1993. The Political Economy of Chinese Urbanization: Guangdong and the Pearl River Delta Region. In G. Guldin, and A. Southall (eds.), *Urban Anthropology of China*, pp. 167–204. Leiden, New York and Köln: E. J. Brill.

Joy, C. 2007. Enchanting Town of Mud: Djenné, a World Heritage Site in Mali. In F. De Jong, and M. Rowlands (eds.), *Reclaiming Heritage: Alternative Imaginaries of Memory in West Africa*, pp. 145–160. Walnut Creek: Left Coast Press.

——. 2012. *The Politics of Heritage Management in Mali: From UNESCO to Djenné*. Walnut Creek: Left Coast Press.

Kam, L. 2008. *The Cambridge Companion to Modern Chinese Culture*. Cambridge: Cambridge University Press.

Kaplan, F. E. S. (ed.). 1994. *Museums and the Making of 'Ourselves': The Role of Objects in National Identity*. London: Leicester University Press.

Kaufman, E. N. 2004. The Architectural Museum from World's Fair to Restoration Village. In B. M. Carbonell (ed.), *Museum Studies: An Anthology of Contexts*, pp. 273–289. Malden: Blackwell.

Keck, M., and P. Sakdapolrak. 2013. What Is Social Resilience? Lessons Learned and Ways Forward. *Erdkunde* 67 (1): 5–19.

Kennedy, R. G. 2004. Some Thoughts about National Museums at the End of the Century. In B. M. Carbonell (ed.), *Museum Studies: An Anthology of Contexts*, pp. 302–306. Malden: Blackwell.

Kirby, W. C. 2000. Engineering China: Birth of the Developmental State, 1928–1937. In W-H. Yeh (ed.), *Becoming Chinese: Passages to Modernity and Beyond*, pp. 137–160. Berkeley: University of California Press.

Kjellgren, B. 2002. *The Shenzhen Experience or City of Good Cats: Memories, Dreams, Identities and Social Interaction in the Chinese Showcase*. Stockholm: Stockholm University, Department of Chinese Studies.

Kleingeld, P. 1999. Six Varieties of Cosmopolitanism in Late Eighteenth-Century Germany. *Journal of the History of Ideas* 60 (3): 505–524.

Knight, J., and L. Yueh. 2006. Job Mobility of Residents and Migrants in Urban China. In S. Li, and H. Sato (eds.), *Unemployment, Inequality and Poverty in Urban China*, pp. 637–660. London and New York: Routledge.

Lafrenz Samuels, K. 2009. Trajectories of Development: International Heritage Management of Archaeology in the Middle East and North Africa. *Archaeologies* 5 (1): 68–91.

Lagerkvist, A. 2010. The Future Is Here: Media, Memory, and Futurity in Shanghai. *Space and Culture* 13 (3): 220–238.

Langridge, R., J. Christian-Smith, and K. A. Lohse. 2006. Access and Resilience: Analyzing the Construction of Social Resilience to the

Threat of Water Scarcity. *Ecology and Society* 11 (2). Online publication: https://www.ecologyandsociety.org/vol11/iss2/art18/.

Latham, K., J. Klein, and S. E. Thompson (eds.). 2006. *Consuming China: Approaches to Cultural Change in Contemporary China*. London and New York: Routledge.

Law of China. 2011. *Regulations on the Expropriation and Compensation of Buildings on State-Owned Land*. Available online, http://www.lawinfochina.com/display.aspx?lib=law&id=8580&CGid,   last accessed 1 May 2016.

Leask, A., and A. Fyall (eds.). 2006. *Managing World Heritage Sites*. Burlington: Butterworth-Heinemann.

Lee, L. O-F. 2000. The Cultural Construction of Modernity in Urban Shanghai: Some Preliminary Explorations. In W-H. Yeh (ed.), *Becoming Chinese: Passages to Modernity and Beyond*, pp. 31–61. Berkeley: University of California Press.

Lees, L. 2000. A Reappraisal of Gentrification: Towards a 'Geography of Gentrification'. *Progress in Human Geography* 24 (3): 389–408.

——. 2003. Super-Gentrification: The Case of Brooklyn Heights, New York City. *Urban Studies* 40 (12): 2487–2509.

Lees, L., T. Slater, and E. K. Wyly. 2008. *Gentrification*. New York: Routledge.

Lefebvre, H. 1991. *The Production of Space*. (trans. Donald Nicholson-Smith). Oxford: Blackwell Publishers.

Legislative Affairs Office of the State Council P. R. China. 2002. *Xi'an lishi wenhua mingcheng baohu tiaoli* (Regulations of the protection of the historic city of Xi'an). Available online, http://fgk.chinalaw.gov.cn/article/dffg/200207/20020700313271.shtml,   last   accessed   2 February 2016.

Legislative Affairs Office of the State Council. 2004. *Zhonghua renmin gongheguo tudi guanli fa* (The land management law of the People's Republic of China). Available online, http://www.chinalaw.gov.cn/article/fgkd/xfg/fl/200409/20040900052441.shtml, last accessed 1 May 2016.

Leibold, J. 2006. Competing Narratives of Racial Unity in Republican China: From Yellow Emperor to Peking Man. *Modern China* 21 (2): 181–220.

Leslie, D. D., and K. H. J. Gardiner. 1982. Chinese Knowledge of Western Asia during the Han. *T'oung – Pao* 68 (4/ 5): 254–308.

Lewis, M. E. 2007. *The Early Chinese Empires: Qin and Han*. London: Belknap Press.

Li, N. 2010. Preserving Urban Landscapes as Public History: The Chinese Context. *Public Historian* 32 (4): 51–61.

Li, X., and L. Feng. 2010. Spatial Distribution of Hazardous Elements in Urban Topsoils surrounding Xi'an Industrial Areas: Controlling Factors and Contaminating Assessments. *Journal of Hazardous Materials* 174 (1-3): 662–669.

Li, Y. 2011. Minorities, Tourism and Ethnic Theme Parks: Employees' Perspectives from Yunnan, China. *Journal of Cultural Geography* 28 (2): 311–338.

———. 2013. Ethnic Tourism and Minority Identity: Lugu Lake, Yunnan, China. *Asia Pacific Journal of Tourism Research* 18 (7): 712–730.

Li, Y., and G. Wall. 2008. Ethnic Tourism and Entrepreneurship: Xishuangbanna, Yunnan, China. *Tourism Geographies: An International Journal of Tourism Space, Place and Environment* 10 (4): 522–544.

Liggett, H. 1995. City Sights, Sites of Memories and Dreams. In H. Liggett, and D. C. Perry (eds.), *Spatial Practices: Critical Explorations in Social/Spatial Theory*, pp. 243–273. Thousand Oaks, Calif.: Sage Publications.

Lilley, I. 2009. Strangers and Brothers? Heritage, Human Rights, and Cosmopolitan Archaeology in Oceania. In L. Meskell (ed.), *Cosmopolitan Archaeologies*, pp. 48–67. Durham: Duke University Press.

Lilley, I., and M. Williams. 2005. Archaeological and Indigenous Significance: A View from Australia. In C. Mathers, T. Darveill, and B. Little (eds.), *Heritage of Value, Archaeology of Renown: Reshaping Archaeological Assessment and Significance*, pp. 227–247. Gainesville: University of Florida Press.

Lipman, J. N. 1998. *Familiar Strangers: A History of Muslims in Northwest China*. Hong Kong: Hong Kong University Press.

———. 2004. White Hats, Oil Cakes and Common Blood. In R. Morris (ed.), *Governing China's Multiethnic Frontiers*, pp. 19–52. Seattle: University of Washington Press.

Liu, X. 2010. *The Silk Road in World History*. New York: Oxford University Press.

Liu, Y. 2015. *The China Dream: Great Power Thinking and Strategic Posture in the Post-American Era*. New York: CN Times Books.

Louis, F. 2005. The 'Palace Concert' and Tang Material Culture. *Notes in History of Arts* 24 (2): 42–29.

Low, S. M., and D. Lawrence-Zúñiga. 2003. *The Anthropology of Space and Place: Locating Culture*. Malden: Blackwell.

Low, S. M. 1996a. The Anthropology of Cities: Imagining and Theorizing the City. *Annual Review of Anthropology* 25: 383–409.

——. 1996b. Spatializing Culture: The Social Production and Social Construction of Public Space in Costa Rica. *American Ethnologist* 23 (4): 861–879.

——. 1999. *Theorizing the City: The New Urban Anthropology Reader.* New Brunswick: Rutgers University Press.

Lowenthal, D. 1985. *The Past is a Foreign Country.* Cambridge: Cambridge University Press.

——. 1998. *The Heritage Crusade and the Spoils of History.* Cambridge and New York: Cambridge University Press.

Lu, D. 2006. *Remaking Chinese Urban Form: Modernity, Scarcity and Space, 1949–2005.* London and New York: Routledge.

Lu, T. L-D. 2003. The Management of Cultural Heritage in Hong Kong. *Occasional Paper* 137. Hong Kong: Hong Kong Institute of Asia-Pacific Studies, Chinese University of Hong Kong.

——. 2006. *Preserving the Tamped Earth Dwellings in South China.* Unpublished manuscript.

——. 2008. Some Issues on the Management of Archaeological Sites in Mainland China. *Conservation and Management of Archaeological Sites* 10 (4): 353–366.

——. 2009. Heritage Conservation in Post-Colonial Hong Kong. *International Journal of Heritage Studies* 15 (2/ 3): 258–272.

——. 2014. *Museums in China: Power, Politics and Identities.* Oxford and New York: Routledge.

Lynch, D. C. 2006. *Rising China and Asian Democratization: Socialization to 'Global Culture' in the Political Transformations of Thailand, China, and Taiwan.* Stanford: Stanford University Press.

Lyon, S., and E. C. Wells. 2012. *Global Tourism: Cultural Heritage and Economic Encounters.* Lanham: AltaMira Press.

Ma, L. J. C. 2002. Urban Transformation in China 1949–2000: A Review and Research Agenda. *Environment and Planning* 34 (9): 1545–1569.

Mackerras, C., and M. Clarke (eds.). 2009. *China, Xinjiang and Central Asia: History, Transition and Crossborder Interaction into the 21st Century.* London: Routledge.

Mackerras, C. 2003. *China's Ethnic Minoirties and Globalizaion.* London: Routledge Curzon.

Mandelbaum, G. D., G. W. Lasker, and E. M. Albert. 1963. *The Teaching of Anthropology.* Menasha, Wis: American Anthropological Association.

Manoukian, S. 2012. *City of Knowledge in Twentieth Century Iran: Shiraz, History and Poetry*. Abingdon and New York: Routledge.

Marinelli, M. 2010. Internal and External Spaces: The Emotional Capital of Tianjin's Italian Concession. *Emotion, Space and Society* 3 (1): 62–70.

Marquart, V. 2015. *Monuments and Malls: Heritage Politics and Urban Strruggles in Istanbul*. Ph.D. dissertation, Martin Luther University Halle-Wittenberg.

Marshall, N. A. 2007. Can Policy Perception Influence Social Resilience to Policy Change? *Fisheries Research* 86 (2-3): 216–227.

Marshall, N. A., and P. A. Marshall. 2007. Conceptualizing and Operationalizing Social Resilience within Commercial Fisheries in Northern Australia. *Ecology and Society* 12 (1). Online publication: https://www.ecologyandsociety.org/vol12/iss1/art1/.

Martell, L. 2011. Cosmopolitanism and Global Politics. *Political Quarterly* 82 (4): 618–627.

Matten, M. A. (ed.). 2012. *Places of Memory in Modern China: History, Politics, and Identity*. Leiden and Boston: Brill.

McGee, T. K. 2011. Public Engagement in Neighborhood Level Wildfire Mitigation and Preparedness: Case Studies from Canada, the US and Australia. *Environmental Management* 92 (10): 2524–2532.

McGuire, R.H. 2008. *Archaeology as Political Action*. Berkeley and Los Angeles: University of California Press.

Mclaren, A. E. 2010. Revitalization of the Folk Epics of the Lower Yangzi Delta: An Example of China's Intangible Cultural Heritage. *International Journal of Intangible Cultural Heritage* 5: 30–43.

Meskell, L. M. 1998. *Archaeology under Fire: Nationalism, Politics and Heritage in the Eastern Mediterranean and Middle East*. London: Routledge.

——. 2005. Archaeological Ethnography: Conversations around Kruger National Park. *Archaeologies* 1 (1): 81–102.

Millward, J. A. 2009. Positioning Xinjiang in Eurasian and Chinese History: Differing Visions of the 'Silk Road'. In C. Mackerras, and M. Clarke (eds.), *China, Xinjiang and Central Asia: History, Transition and Crossborder Interaction into the 21st Century*, pp. 55–74. London: Routledge.

Ministry of Construction of the People's Republic of China. 2005. *Code of Conservation Planning for Historic Cities*. Beijing: Ministry of Construction of the People's Republic of China.

Morton, W. S. 1995. *China: Its History and Culture*. New York: McGraw-Hill.

Murphy, J. D. 1995. *Plunder and Preservation*. Hong Kong and New York: Oxford University Press.

Mustafa, H. 1997. *Practicing Beauty: Crisis, Value and the Challenge of Self-Mastery in Dakar, 1970–1994*. Ph.D. dissertation, Harvard University.

——. 2006. *La mode dakaroise*: Elegance, Transnationalism and an African Fashion Capital. In C. Breward, and D. Gilbert (eds.), *Fashion's World Cities*, pp. 177–200. New York and London: Berg.

Nas, P. J. M., and R. J. Sluis. 2002. In Search of Meaning: Urban Orientation Principles in Indonesia. In P. J. M. Nas (ed.), *The Indonesian Town Revisited*, pp. 130–146. Münster: LIT Verlag.

National Development and Reform Committee. 2016. *Guojia fanzhan gaige wei guanyu Xi'anshi chengshi guidao jiaotong dierqi jianshe guihua zhentiao fang'an (2013–2021 nian) de pifu* (The national approval of the transportation development and reform in urban Xi'an (2013–2021) plan). Available online, http://www.ndrc.gov.cn/zcfb/ zcfbghwb/201602/t20160218_774911.html, last accessed 27 January 2019.

National People's Congress of People's Republic of China. 1982. *Zhonghua renmin gongheguo wenwu baohu fa* (The cultural heritage protection law of the People's Republic of China). Available online, http:// www.npc.gov.cn/wxzl/gongbao/2000-12/06/content_5004416.htm, last accessed 1 May 2016.

National People's Congress of People's Republic of China. 1989. *Zhonghua renmin gongheguo chengshi guihua fa* (The urban planning law of the People's Republic of China). Available online, http:// www.npc.gov.cn/wxzl/gongbao/2000-12/05/content_5004524.htm, last accessed 1 May 2016.

Ning, Y. M. 1998. Xin Chengshihua jincheng- 90 niandai Zhongguo chengshihua dongle jizhi he tedian tantao (The new urbanization: The reflection of the urbanization in China in the 1990s). *Dili Xuebao* 53 (5): 470–477.

Nitzky, W. 2013. Community Empowerment at the Periphery? Participatory Approaches to Heritage Protection in Guizhou, China. In T. Blumenfield, and H. Silverman (eds.), *Cultural Heritage Politics in China*, pp. 205–234. New York: Springer.

Notar, B. 2006. *Displacing Desire: Travel and Popular Culture in China*. Honolulu: University of Hawai'i Press.

Nyiri, P. 2006. *Scenic Spots: Chinese Tourism, the State, and Cultural Authority*. Seattle: University of Washington Press.

Oakes, T. S. 1997. Ethnic Tourism in Rural Guizhou: Sense of Place and the Commerce of Authenticity. In M. Picard, and R. E. Wood (eds.), *Tourism, Ethnicity and the State in Asian and Pacific Societies*, pp. 35–70. Honolulu: University of Hawai'i Press.

———. 1998. *Tourism and Modernity in China*. London: Routledge.

———. 2006. The Village as Theme Park: Mimesis and Authenticity in Chinese Tourism. In T. Oakes, and L. Schein (eds.), *Translocal China: Linkages, Identities, and the Re-Imagining of Space*, pp.166–192. London: Routledge.

———. 2013. Heritage as Improvement: Cultural Display and Contested Governance in Rural China. *Modern China* 39 (4): 380–407.

Ong, A. 2005a. Anthropological Concepts for the Study of Nationalism. In P. Nyíri, and J. Breidenbach (eds.), *China Inside Out: Contemporary Chinese Nationalism and Transnationalism*, pp. 1–34. Budapest and New York: Central European University Press.

Ong, A., and A. Roy. 2011. *Worlding Cities: Asian Experiments and the Art of Being Global*. Chichester: Wiley-Blackwell.

Ong, A., and S. J. Collier (eds.). 2005. *Global Assemblages: Technology, Politics, and Ethics as Anthropological Problems*. Malden, MA: Blackwell.

Orchiston, C., G. Prayagand, C. Brown. 2016. Organizational Resilience in the Tourism Sector. *Annals of Tourism Research* 56 (13): 145–148.

Overmyer, D. L. 2003. Religion in China Today: Introduction. *The China Quarterly* 174: 307–316.

Pan, S. 2016. Local Histories and New Museological Approaches in China. In J. Gledhill (ed.), *World Anthropologies in Practice: Situated Perspectives, Global Knowledge*, pp. 117–130. London: Bloomsbury.

Pan, T. 2005. Historical Memory, Community-Building and Place-Making in Neighbourhood Shanghai. In J. C. L. Ma, and F. Wu (eds.), *Restructuring the Chinese City: Changing Society, Economy, and Space*, pp. 122–137. London: Routledge.

Pantusov', N. 2002. The Mausoleum of Mawlana Yusuf Sakaki. In T. Zarcone (ed.), *Saints and Heroes on the Silk Road*, pp. 173–182. Paris: Maisonneuve.

Park, C-H. 2014. *Nongjiale* Tourism and Contested Space in Rural China. *Modern China* 40 (5): 519–548.

Perz, S. G., L. Cabrera, L. A. Carvalho, J. Castilllo, and G. Barnes. 2010. Global Economic Integration and Local Community Resilience: Road Paving and Rural Demographic Change in the Southwestern Amazon. *Rural Sociology* 75 (2): 300–325.

Pickering, M., and E. Keightley. 2006. The Modalities of Nostalgia. *Current Sociology* 54 (6): 919–941.

Probst, P. 2011. *Osogbo and the Art of Heritage: Monuments, Deities and Money*. Bloomington: Indiana University Press.

Qian, M. 1988. *Zhongguo wenhua lishi daolun* (Introduction to Chinese History and Culture). Shanghai: Sanlian Press.

Qian, N. 2004. Borrowing Foreign Mirrors and Candles to Illuminate Chinese Civilisation: Xue Shaohui's Moral Vision in the Biographies of Foreign Women. In G. Fong, N. Qian, H. T. Zurndorfer (eds.), *Beyond Tradition and Modernity, Gender, Genre and Cosmopolitanism in Late Qing China*, pp. 60–101. Leiden and Boston: Brill.

Rabine, L. 1997. Dressing up in Dakar. *L'Espirt Créature* 37 (I): 84–108.

——. 2002. *The Global Circulation of African Fashion*. New York and London: Berg.

Rabinow, P. 1988. Beyond Ethnography: Anthropology as Nominalism. *Cultural Anthropology* 3 (4): 355–363.

——. 1989. *French Modern: Norms and Forms of the Social Environment*. Cambridge: MIT Press.

Reichl, A. J. 1997. Historic Preservation and Progrowth Politics in U.S. Cities. *Urban Affairs Review* 32 (4): 513 –535.

Ren, W. 1998. *La ville à l'intérieu des remparts. La protection du patrimoine et de l'amélioration de la ville historique en Chine: le cas de Xi'an*. Ph.D. dissertation, Écoles des Hautes Études en Sciences Sociales.

Ren, X. 2014. *Zhongguo Meng: Shui de Meng?* (The Chinese Dream: What does it Mean?). Xianggang: Zhonghua Shuju (Xianggang) youxiang gongsi.

Rockstrom, J. 2004. Making the Best of Climate Variability: Options for Upgrading Rain Fed Farming in Water Scarce Regions. *Water Science and Technology* 49 (7): 151–156.

Rofel, L. 1999. *Other Modernities – Gendered Yearnings in China after Socialism*. Berkeley: University of California Press.

——. 1997. Rethinking Modernity: Space and Factory Discipline in China. In A. Gupta, and J. Ferguson (eds.), *Culture, Power, Place*, pp.155–178. Durham: Duke University Press.

Ruggles, D. F., and H. Silverman (eds.). 2009. *Intangible Heritage Embodied*. New York: Springer.

Ryan, J., and S. Silvanto. 2009. The World Heritage List: The Making and Management of a Brand. *Place Branding and Public Diplomacy* 5 (4): 290–300.

Sabbon, F. 2014. The Taste of Milk in Modern China (1865–1937). In J. A. Klein, and A. Murcott (eds.), *Food Consumption in Global Perspective: Essays in the Anthropology of Food in Honour of Jack Goody*, pp. 182–208. New York: Basingstoke Palgrave Macmillan.

Salamandra, C. 2004. *A New Old Damascus: Authenticity and Distinction in Urban Syria*. Bloomington: Indiana University Press.

Salter, B., and C. Waldby. 2011. Bio-Politics in China: An Introduction. *East Asian Science, Technology and Society: An International Journal* 5 (3): 287–290.

Salvatore, A. 2009. Tradition and Modernity within Islamic Civilisation and the West. In M. K. Masud, A. Salvatore, and M. Bruinessen (eds.), *Islam and Modernity: Key Issues and Debates*, pp. 3–35. Edinburgh: Edinburgh University Press.

Sanjuan, T. 2000. *La Chine. Territores et Sociétés*. Paris: Hachette.

Schein, L. 2001. Urbanity, Cosmopolitanism, Consumption. In N. C. Chen (ed.), *China Urban: Ethnographies of Contemporary Culture*, pp. 225–240. Durham: Duke University Press.

———. 2000. *Minority Rules: The Miao and the Feminine in China's Cultural Politics*. Durham and London: Duke University Press.

Scheld, S. 2007. Youth Cosmopolitanism: Clothing, the City and Globalization in Dakar, Senegal. *City and Society* 19 (2): 232–253.

Schreiter, R. J. 2000. Is the Modernization Process Uniform in its Effect? In F. Frei (ed.), *Inkulturation zwischen Tradition und Modernität: Kontexte – Begriffe – Modelle*, pp. 297–308. Freiburg: Universitätsverlag Freiburg Schweiz.

Shaanxi Provincial Bureau of Housing and Urban-Rural Construction. 2010. *Xi'an International Metropolis Strategic Development Plan (2009–2020)*. Xi'an: Shaanxi Zhufang he Chengxiang Jianshe Ting.

Shanks, M., and C. Tilley. 1987a. *Social Theory and Archaeology*. Cambridge: Polity Press.

———. 1987b. *Reconstructing Archaeology: Theory and Practice*. Cambridge: Cambridge University Press.

Shankland, D. 2012. *Archaeology and Anthropology – Past, Present and Future*. London: Berg.

Shatzman Steinhardt, N. 1991. The Mizong Hall of Qinglong Si: Space, Ritual, and Classicism in Tang Architecture. *Archives of Asian Art* 44: 27–50.

———. 2004. The Tang Architectural Icon and the Politics of Chinese Architectural History. *The Art Bulletin* 86 (2): 228–254.

Shaughnessy, E. L. 1999. Western Zhou History. In M. Loewe, and E. L. Shaughnessy (eds.), *The Cambridge History of Ancient China*, pp. 292–351. Cambridge: Cambridge University Press.

Shen, S. 2009. *Cosmopolitan Publics: Anglophone Print Culture in Semi-Colonial Shanghai*. New Brunswick: Rutgers University Press.

Shen, Y. 2015. *Public Discourses of Contemporary China: The Narration of the Nation in Popular Literatures, Film, and Television*. New York: Palgrave Macmillan.

Shennan, S. J. 1994. *Archaeological Approaches to Cultural Identity*. London: Routledge.

Shi, L. 2009. Little Quilted Vests to Warm Parents' Hearts: Redefining the Gendered Practice of Filial Piety in Rural North-Eastern China. *The China Quarterly* 198: 348–363.

Shi, N. H. 1990. Zhongguo gudu daolun (Introduction to Ancient Capitals in China). *Shaanxi Shifan Daxue Qikang* 1.

Shirin, A. 1992. Significance of Silk Roads Today: Proposal for a Historical Atlas. In T. Umesao, and T. Sugimura (eds.), *Significance of Silk Roads in the History of Human Civilizations*, pp. 27–32. Osaka: National Museum of Ethnology.

Sifneos, E. 2005. 'Cosmopolitanism' as a Feature of the Greek Commercial Diaspora. *History and Anthropology* 16 (1): 97–111.

Silberman, N. A. 1989. *Between Past and Present: Archaeology, Ideology and Nationalism in the Modern Middle East*. New York: Henry Holt.

——. 1995. Promised Lands and Chosen People: The Politics and Poetics of Archaeological Narrative. In P. L. Kohl, and C. Fawcett (eds.), *Nationalism, Politics and the Practice of Archaeology*, pp. 249–62. Cambridge: Cambridge University Press.

Silva, K. D., and N. K. Chapagain. 2013. *Asian Heritage Management: Contexts, Concerns, and Prospects*. Abingdon and New York: Routledge.

Silverman, H. 2010. Contested Cultural Heritage: A Selected Historiography. In H. Silverman (ed.), *Contested Cultural Heritage: Religion, Nationalism, Erasure, and Exclusion in a Global World*, pp. 1–30. New York: Springer.

Sina Stock Finance. 2011. *Xi'an Qujiang Cultural Industry Investment (Group) Co., Ltd. Annual Report 2011*. Available online, http://stock.finance.sina.com.cn/bond/view/announcement_show.php?id=502325997&att==1, last accessed 1 May 2016.

Sit, V. F. S. 1996. Soviet Influence on Urban Planning in Beijing, 1949–1991. *The Town Planning Review* 67 (4): 457–484.

Siu, H. 1989. Recycling Rituals: Politics and Popular Culture in Contemporary Rural China. In P. Link, R. Madsen, and P. Pickowicz (eds.), *Unofficial China: Popular Culture and Thought in the People's Republic*, pp. 121–137. Boulder: Westview Press.

———. 1990. Recycling Tradition: Culture, History, and Political Economy in the Chrysanthemum Festivals of South China. *Comparative Studies in Society and History* 32 (4): 765–794.

Smith, G. S., P. M. Messenger, and H. A. Soderland (eds.). 2010. *Heritage Values in Contemporary Society*. Walnut Creek: Left Coast Press.

Smith, H., and W. Graves. 2005. Gentrification as Corporate Growth Strategy: The Strange Case of Charlotte, North Carolina and the Bank of America. *Journal of Urban Affairs* 27 (4): 403–418.

Smith, L. 2006. *Uses of Heritage*. New York: Routledge.

Smith, N. 1996. *The New Urban Frontier*. New York: Routledge.

Song, Q. 2012. *Local (Bendi)*. Xi'an: North-West University Press.

Song, S. Z. 1990. *Xi'an: Qin Zhong Zi Gu Di Wang Zhou* (Xi'an: Emperors from Qin and Zhou Dynasties). Taibeishi: You Shi Wenhua Shiye Gongsi.

Southall, A. 1973. *Urban Anthropology: Cross-Cultural Studies of Urbanization*. New York, London and Toronto: Oxford University Press.

Stacey, J. 1983. *Patriarchy and Socialist Revolution in China*. Berkeley, Los Angeles and London: University of California Press.

Stafford, C. 2000. *Separation and Reunion in Modern China*. Cambridge: Cambridge University Press.

Stares, S., and L. Zhi. 1996. *China's Urban Transport Development Strategy: Proceedings of a Symposium in Beijing*. Washington D.C.: The World Bank.

State Administration of Cultural Heritage. 2009. *Guojia kaogu yizhi gongyuan fa* (The National Archaeological Park Law). http://www.sach.gov.cn/sach_tabid_369/tabid/311/InfoID/22762/Default.html. Last accessed 28 March 2015.

State Administration of Cultural Heritage. 2010. *Guojia kaogu yizhi gongyuan guanli banfa* (The methods to manage National Archaeological Parks). http://www.sach.gov.cn/sach_tabid_369/tabid/311/InfoID/22762/Default.html. Last accessed 28 March 2015.

State Administration of Cultural Heritage. 2013. *Quanguo guojia kaogu yizhi gongyuan mingdan* (List of all national archaeological parks in China). http://www.sach.gov.cn/art/2013/12/18/art_59_139310.html. Last accessed 28 March 2015.

State Administration of Cultural Heritage. 2014a. *Guojia wenwu ju de zhuyao jize* (The main responsibilities of the Ministry of Cultural Heritage). http://www.sach.gov.cn/col/col1020/index.html. Last accessed 1 May 2016.

State Administration of Cultural Heritage. 2014b. *Guowuyuan guanyu di yi pi quanguo zhongdian wenwu baohu danwei mingdan de tongzhi* (The first list of national cultural heritage departments). http://www.sach.gov.cn/art/2014/5/20/art_1644_50353.html. Last accessed 1 May 2016.

State Council of the People's Republic of China. 1999. *Guowuyuan guanyu Xi'anshi zhongti guihua de pifu* (The national approval of Xi'an's overall urban plan). http://www.gov.cn/xxgk/pub/govpublic/mrlm/ 201011/t20101115_62753.html. Last accessed 1 May 2016.

State Council of the People's Republic of China. 2011. *Intangible Cultural Heritage Law of the People's Republic of China*. http://english. gov.cn/archive/laws_regulations/2014/08/23/content_281474982987 416.htm. Last accessed 1 May 2016.

Stoffle, R. W., M. N. Zedeno, and D. B. Halmo (eds.). 2001. *American Indians and the Nevada Testsites: A Model of Research and Consultation*. Washington, DC: U.S. Government Printing Office.

Strand, D. 2000. A High Place Is no Better than a Low Place: The City in the Making of Modern China. In W-H. Yeh (ed.), *Becoming Chinese: Passages to Modernity and Beyond*, pp. 98–136. Berkeley: University of California Press.

Su, X., and P. Teo. 2008. Tourism Politics in Lijiang, China: An Analysis of State and Local Interactions in Tourism Development. *Tourism Geographies* 10 (2): 150–168.

——. 2009. *The Politics of Heritage Tourism in China: A View from Lijiang*. London: Routledge.

Sugiyama, J. 1992. From Chang An to Rome: Transformation of Buddhist Culture. In T. Umesao, and T. Sugimura (eds.), *Significance of Silk Roads in the History of Human Civilizations*, pp. 55–60. Osaka: National Museum of Ethnology.

Svensson, M. 2006. In the Ancestors' Shadow: Cultural Heritage Contestations in Chinese Villages. *Working Papers in Contemporary Asian Studies* 1. Lund: Centre for East and Southeast Asian Studies, Lund University.

Swain, M. B. 2009. The Cosmopolitan Hope of Tourism. *Tourism Geographies* 11 (4): 505–525.

——. 2013. Chinese Cosmopolitanism (*Tianxia He Shijie Zhuyi*) in China's Heritage Tourism. In T. Blumenfield, and H. Silverman (eds.), *Cultural Heritage Politics in China*, pp. 33–50. New York: Springer.

Tang, Z. 2013. Does the Institution of Property Rights Matter for Heritage Preservation? Evidence from China. In T. Blumenfield, and H. Silverman (eds.), *Cultural Heritage Politics in China*, pp. 23–32. New York: Springer.

Teo, P., and B. S. A. Yeoh. 1997. Remaking Local Heritage for Tourism. *Annals of Tourism Research* 24 (1): 192–213.

Terkenli, T. S. 2002. Landscapes of Tourism: Towards a Global Cultural Economy of Space? *Tourism Geographies* 4 (3): 227–254.

Therborn, G. 2003. Entangled Modernities. *European Journal of Social Theory* 6 (3): 293–305.

Thomas, D. S. G., and C. Twyman. 2005. Equity and Justice in Climate Change Adaptation amongst Natural-Resource-Dependent societies. *Global Environmental Change* 15 (2): 115–124.

Thomassen, B. 2012. Anthropology and its Many Modernities: When Concepts Matter. *Journal of the Royal Anthropological Institute* 18 (1): 160–178.

Tobin, G. A., and L. M. Whiteford. 2002. Community Resilience and Volcano Hazard: The Eruption of Tungurahua and Evacuation of the Faldas in Ecuador. *Disasters* 26 (1): 28–48.

Tomba, L. 2014. *The Government Next Door: Neighborhood Politics in Urban China*. Ithaca and London: Cornell University Press.

Tompkins, E. L. 2005. Planning for Climate Change in Small Islands: Insights from National Hurricane Preparedness in the Cayman Islands. *Global Environmental Change* 15 (2): 139–149.

Trigger, B. 1989. *A History of Archaeological Thought*. Cambridge: Cambridge University Press.

Trigger, B. G. 1995. Romanticism, Nationalism and Archaeology. In P. L. Kohl, and C. Fawcett (eds.), *Nationalism, Politics and the Practice of Archaeology*, pp. 263–279. Cambridge: Cambridge University Press.

Tsinghua University News. 2014. *Yan Xuetong zhuoke shishi dajiangtang zonglun APEC xiangshi zhongguo guojie huanjing* (Yan Xuetong's lecture on the analysis of Asia-Pacific Economic Cooperation's influence on international relations). Available online, http://www.tsinghua.edu.cn/publish/news/4205/2014/201411211023 33682196759/20141121102333682196759.html, last accessed 1 May 2016.

Tucker, J. 2015. *The Silk Road – Central Asia: A Travel Companion.* London: I. B. Tauris & Co. Ltd.

Tyfield, D., and J. Urry. 2010. Cosmopolitan China? *Soziale Welt* 61 (3/ 4): 277–293.

Umesao, T., and T. Sugimura (eds.). 1992. *Significance of Silk Roads in the History of Human Civilizations.* Osaka: National Museum of Ethnology.

UNESCO. 1972. *Convention Concerning the Protection of the World Cultural and Natural Heritage.* Available online, http://whc. unesco.org/en/conventiontext/, last accessed 1 May 2016.

UNESCO. 1988. *The Silk Roads Project 'Integral Study of the Silk Roads: Roads of Dialogue'.* Available online, http://unesdoc.unesco.org/ images/0015/001591/159189E.pdf, last accecssed 1 May 2016.

UNESCO. 1990. *The Documentary of Desert Routes of the Silk Road from Xian to Kashgar, China.* Available online, https://en.unesco.org/ silkroad/countries-alongside-silk-road-routes/china, last accessed 1 May 2016.

UNESCO. 1997. *Information on Tentative Lists.* Available online, http://whc.unesco.org/archive/1997/whc-97-conf208-9reve.pdf, last accessed 1 May 2016.

UNESCO. 2006. *Facts about Xi'an.* Available online, https://en.unesco.org/ silkroad/content/xian, last accessed 1 May 2016.

UNESCO. 2008a. *Chinese Section of the Silk Road: Land Routes in Henan Province, Shaanxi Province, Gansu Province, Qinghai Province, Ningxia Hui Autonomous Region, and Xingjiang Uygur Autonomous Region.* Available online, http://whc.unesco.org/en/tentativelists/ 5335/, last accessed 1 May 2016.

UNESCO. 2008b. *City Walls of the Ming and Qing Dynasties Tentative List.* Available online, http://whc.unesco.org/en/tentativelists/5324/, last accessed 1 May 2016.

UNESCO. 2010. *Historic Monuments of Dengfeng in 'The Centre of Heaven and Earth'.* Available online, http://whc.unesco.org/en/list/1305, last accessed 1 May 2016.

UNESCO. 2011. *World Heritage Lists Nominations.* Available online, http://whc.unesco.org/en/nominations/, last accessed 1 May 2016.

UNESCO. 2013. *Silk Roads Cultural Route Nomination File.* Available online, http://whc.unesco.org/uploads/nominations/1442.pdf, last accessed 1 May 2016.

UNESCO. 2014a. *Evaluations of Nominations of Cultural and Mixed Properties to the World Heritage List* (ICOMOS report for the World Heritage Committee 38th Ordinary Session). Available online, http://whc.unesco.org/document/128794 on 26th May 2014, last accessed 1 May 2016.

UNESCO. 2014b. *Map of the Silk Roads.* Available online, http://whc.unesco.org/document/132728, last accessed 1 May 2016.

UNESCO. 2014c. *Silk Roads: The Routes Network of Chang'an-Tiangshan Corridor.* Available online, http://whc.unesco.org/en/list/1442, last accessed 1 May 2016.

UNESCO. 2015. Number of World Heritage Properties Inscribed by Each State Party (163). *World Heritage List Statistics.* Available online, http://whc.unesco.org/en/list/stat#s2, last acccessed 1 May 2016.

Valder, P. 2002. *Gardens in China.* Portland: The Timber Press, Inc.

Veith, I. 2002. *The Yellow Emperor's Classic of Internal Medicine.* Berkeley and Los Angeles: University of California Press.

Voss, M. 2008. The Vulnerable Can't Speak: An Integrative Vulnerability Approach to Disaster and Climate Change Research. *Behemoth* 1 (3): 39–56.

Wan, D. F., Y. G. Wang, and W. M. Zhu. 2001. A Preliminary Study on Innovation and Restructuring of Industries in Western China. *Journal of the Xi'an Jiaotong University: Social Science Series* 1 (1): 6–29.

Wang, F., and X. Zuo. 1999. History's Largest Labor Flow: Understanding China's Rural Migration inside China's Cities: Institutional Barriers and Opportunities for Urban Migrants. *AEA Papers and Proceedings* 89 (2): 276–280.

Wang, G. W. 1968. Early Ming Relations with Southeast Asia: A Background Essay. In J. K. Fairbank (ed.), *The Chinese World Order: Traditional China's Foreign Relations*, pp. 34–62. Cambridge: Harvard University Press.

Wang, H. 2006. *The Classic of Mountains and Seas.* Taibeishi: Jianduan Chuban.

Wang, J., and X-L. Liu. 2011. Tourism Resources Development Strategy of Muslim Community in Xi'an. *Xi'an Art and Science Faculty Journal* 14 (3): 49–52.

Wang, M. K. 1999. From the Qiang Barbarians to the Qiang Nationality: The Making of a New Chinese Boundary. In S-M. Huang, and C-K. Hsu (eds.), *Imagining China: Regional Division and National Unity*, pp. 43–80. Taipei: Institute of Ethnology, Academia Sinica.

Wang, T., and L. Zan. 2011. Management and Presentation of Chinese Sites for UNESCO World Heritage List. *Facilities* 29 (7/ 8): 313–325.

Wang, X., and C. Liu. 2010. The Exploration of Xi'an Beiyuan Gate Historical District Preservation Planning. *Planners* 12 (26): 50–55.

Wang, Y. P. 1992. Private-Sector Housing in Urban China since 1949: The Case of Xi'an. *Housing Studies* 7 (2): 119–137.

——. 1995. Public-Sector Housing in Urban China 1949–1988: The Case of Xi'an. *Housing Studies* 10 (1): 57–82.

——. 2000. Planning and Conservation in Historic Chinese Cities: The Case of Xi'an. *The Town Planning Review* 71 (3): 311–332.

Wang, Z. Y. 1988. *Sui Tang Wu Dai Shi* (The History of Sui and Tang Dynasty). Shanghai: Renmin Chubanse.

Watson, B. 1993. *Records of the Grand Historian of China. Qin Dynasty.* Hong Kong and New York: The Research Centre for Translation, Chinese University of Hong Kong and Columbia University Press.

White, H. 1973. *Metahistory: The Historical Imagination in Nineteenth-Century Europe.* Baltimore: Johns Hopkins University Press.

——. 1978. *Tropics of Discourse: Essays in Cultural Criticism.* Baltimore: The Johns Hopkins University Press.

——. 1992. Historical Emplotment and the Problem of Truth. In S. Friedländer (ed.), *Probing the Limits of Representation: Nazism and the 'Final Solution'*, pp. 37–53. Cambridge: Harvard University Press.

——. 2001. The Historical Text as Literary Artifact. In G. Roberts (ed.), *The History and Narrative Reader*, pp. 221–236. London and New York: Routledge.

Whyte, M. K. (ed.). 2003. *China's Revolutions and Intergenerational Relations.* Michigan: Center for Chinese Studies.

——. 2004. Filial Obligations in Chinese Families: Paradoxes of Modernisation. In C. Ikels (ed.), *Filial Piety: Practice and Discourse in Contemporary East Asia*, pp. 106–127. Stanford: Stanford University Press.

Whyte, W. 1980. *The Social Life of Small Urban Spaces.* New York: Project for Public Spaces.

Wilford, J. N. 1993. New Finds Suggest even Earlier Trade on Fabled Silk Road. *New York Times* 16 March, p. C1.

Wilkerson, J., and R. Parkin. 2013. *Modalities of Change: The Interface of Tradition and Modernity in East Asia.* New York: Berghahn Books.

Winston Yan, X. 1996. Carrying Forward Heritage: A Review of Contextualism in New Construction in Beijing. *Journal of Architectural Education* 50 (2): 115–126.

Winter, T., P. Teo, and T. C. Chang. 2009. *Asia on Tour: Exploring the Rise of Asian Tourism.* London and New York: Pergamon and Routledge.

Wittberg, P. 1992. Perspectives on Gentrification: A Comparative Review of the Literature Research. In R. Hutchison (ed.), *Research in Urban Sociology*, Volume 2, pp. 17–46. Greenwich, CT: JAI Press Inc.

Wong, D. F. K., C. Y. Li, and H. X. Song. 2007. Rural Migrant Workers in Urban China: Living a Marginalized Life. *International Journal of Social Welfare* 16 (1): 32–40.

Woo, J. K. 1964. Mandible of Sinanthropus Lantianensis. *Current Anthropology* 5 (2): 98–101.

Wriggins, S. H. 1996. *Xuanzang: A Buddhist Pilgrim on the Silk Road.* Boulder: Westview Press.

Wu, D. Y. H. 1990. Chinese Minority Policy and the Meaning of Minority Culture: The Example of Bai in Yunnan, China. *Human Organization* 49 (1): 1–13.

Wu, F. L. 2002. Real Estate Development and the Transformation of Urban Space in China's Transitional Economy, with special reference to Shanghai. In J. R. Logan (ed.), *The New Chinese City*, pp.153–166. Oxford: Blackwell.

Wu, L.Y. 1999. *Rehabilitating the Old City of Beijing: A Project in the Ju'er Hutong Neighborhood.* Vancouver: University of British Columbia Press.

Wynn, L. L. 2007. *Pyramids and Nightclubs: A Travel Ethnography of Arab and Western Imaginations of Egypt, from King Tut and a Colony of Atlantis to Rumors of Sex Orgies, Urban Legends about a Marauding Prince, and Blond Belly Dancers.* Austin: University of Texas Press.

Xi, J. 2014. *The Chinese Dream of the Great Rejuvenation of the Chinese Nation.* Compiled by the Party Literature of the Central Committee of the Communist Party of China. Beijing: Foreign Languages Press.

Xi'an City Office of Cultural Heritage. 2008. *Xi'anshi sichouzhilu shengbao shijie wenhua yichan xiangmu jianjie* (The nomination of Silk Road World Heritage sites in Xi'an). 5 June. Available online, http://www.xawwj.com/websac/cat/275/275993.html, last accessed 1 May 2016.

Xi'an City Office of Cultural Heritage. 2009. *Zhengwu gongkai* (Updates about administrative changes). http://www.xawwj.com/ptl/def/def/index_1270_2568_ci_trid_3723694.html. Last accessed 1 May 2016.

Xi'an City People's Government. 2011. *Xi'an renkou* (The population of Xi'an). Available online, http://www.xa.gov.cn/ptl/index.html, last accessed 1 May 2016.

Xi'an City Planning Bureau. 2008. *Xi'an shi guihua ju 2008 nian gongzuo zhongjie ji 2009nian gongzuo anpai* (The plan of urban planning in Xi'an city from 2008 to 2009). 2 November. Available online, http://www.xaghj.gov.cn/ptl/def/def/index_915_6236_ci_trid_43127.html, last accessed 1 May 2016.

Xi'an City Planning Bureau. 2014a. *Da Xi'an Fazhan jianluo guihua* (The development plan of Greater Xi'an). Available online, http://www.xaghj.gov.cn/ptl/def/def/index_915_6236_ci_trid_1123615.html, last accessed 1 May 2016.

Xi'an City Planning Bureau. 2014b. *Lishi jiequ* (Historical architecture). Available online, http://www.xaghj.gov.cn/ptl/def/def/index_915_6236_ci_trid_1089699.html, last accessed 1 May 2016.

Xi'an City Tourism Board. 2013a. *Xi'anshi lvyou fazhan zhongti guihua 2013–2020.* (The overall plan of Xi'an's touristic development). Available online, http://www.xatourism.gov.cn/html/xinxigongkai/detail_2013_06/27/177.shtml, last accessed 28 March 2015.

Xi'an City Tourism Board. 2013b. *Xi'an huangjin zhou youke diaochan* (Tourists' Survey of Xi'an). Available online, http://www.xian-tourism.com/article/?type=list&classid=7&page=5, last accessed 28 March 2015.

Xi'an Municipal Government. 1980. *Xi'an City Master Plan 1980–2000.* Xi'an: Xi'an City Planning Bureau.

Xi'an Municipal Government. 2005. *Xi'anshi ji wenwu mingdan* (The list of heritage sites in Xi'an city). Available online, http://www.xa.gov.cn/ptl/trs_ci_id_275986.html, last accessed 1 May 2016.

Xi'an Municipal Government. 2008. *Xi'an Municipal Government General Plan 2008–2020*. Xi'an: Xi'an City Planning Bureau.

Xi'an Municipal Government. 2014. *Xi'anshi renmin zhengfu guanyu xiugai Xi'anshi guoyou tudi fangwu zhengshou yu buchang banfa* (Announcement about the compensation of land loss from the Xi'an municipal government). Available online, http://xafz.xa.gov.cn/ptl/def/def/index_1271_2468_ci_trid_1439612.html, last accessed 1 May 2016.

Xi'an Municipal Tourism Board. 2007. *Xi'anshi lvyou fazhan jihua 2006–2020* (The Xi'an tourism development plan 2006–2020). Available online, http://www.xian-tourism.com/article/?type=detail&id=7594, last accessed 16 December 2016.

Xiang, B. 2005. *Transcending Boundaries: Zhejiangcun: The Story of a Migrant Village in Beijing*. Boston: Brill Press.

Xu, X., and Y. Chu. 2012. Attention to Culture Leading Tourism – Thoughts of Xi'an Tourism Image Positioning. *Contemporary Tourism* 2: 40–42.

Yan, Y. 1997. McDonald's in Beijing: The Localisation of Americana. In J. Watson (ed.), *Golden Arches East: McDonald's in East Asia*, pp. 39–76. Stanford: Stanford University Press.

Yang, M. 1996. Tradition, Travelling Theory, Anthropology and the Discourse of Modernity in China. In H. L. Moore (ed.), *The Future of Anthropological Knowledge*, pp. 93–114. London and New York: Routledge.

Yang, X. 1994. Urban Temporary Out-Migration under Economic Reforms: Who Moves Out for What Reasons? *Population Research and Policy Review* 13 (1): 83–100.

Yaniv, P., R. Arie, and C. Raviv. 2010. World Heritage Site – Is It an Effective Brand Name? A Case Study of a Religious Heritage Site. *Journal of Travel Research* 50 (5): 482–495.

Yao, H. Y. 2010. Xi'an fushizhang: zheli jiushi furenqu zenmele (The deputy mayor of Xi'an's plan to build a rich people's zone in the city). *Weekly Times*, 16 August. Available online, http://old.12371. gov.cn/n65551c454.aspx, last accessed 1 May 2016.

Yeh, A. G. O., and Wu, F. L. 1995. Internal Structure of Chinese Cities in the Midst of Economic Reform. *Urban Geography* 16 (1): 521–554.

Yeh, W-H. 2000. Introduction: Interpreting Chinese Modernity, 1900–1950. In W-H. Yeh (ed.), *Becoming Chinese: Passages to Modernity and Beyond*, pp. 1–30. Berkeley: University of California Press.

Yin, H., X. Shen, and Z. Zhao. 2005. Industrial Restructuring and Urban Spatial Transformation in Xi'an. In J. C. L. Ma, and F. Wu (eds.), *Restructuring the Chinese City: Changing Society, Economy, and Space*, pp. 155–174. London: Routledge.

Yin, H. T., and K. W. Liu. 2002. Thoughts on the Urban Problems of Xi'an and its Spatial Development in the 21st Century. *Human Geography* 17 (4): 85–88.

Ying, S. 2008. *Translation of 'The Song of Everlasting Regret'*. Online publication: http://www.musicated.com/syh/TangPoems/Everlasting Regret.htm. Last accessed 28 March 2015.

Yusuf, S., and T. Saich. 2008. *China Urbanizes: Consequences, Strategies, and Policies*. Washington, DC: World Bank.

Zarcone, T. 2002. *Saints and Heroes on the Silk Road*. Paris: Maisonneuve.

Zhang, H. 2007. China's New Rural Daughters Coming of Age: Downsizing the Family and Firing up Cash – Earning Power in the New Economy. *Signs* 32 (3): 671–698.

Zhang, H. N. 2001. *Shaanxi Gongye Jingru 21 Shiji* (Shaanxi's Industrial Development Entering the 21st Century). Xi'an: Shaani Remin Chubanshe.

Zhang, J. G. 2003. Beijing chengshi jingying yu chengshi guihua. (City management and city planning in Beijing). *Beijing Lianhe Daxue Qikang* 1.

Zhang, J. Y. 2014. Duan Xiannian yige beishou bobian de nengren (The ability of Duan Xiannian to change the city's destiny). *Journal of New West China*, 1 August. Available online, http://www. newwestchina.com/detailEnews.html?artId=8603, last accessed 1 May 2016.

Zhang, Li. 2001. *Strangers in the City: Reconfigurations of Space, Power, and Social Networks within China's Floating Population.* Stanford: Stanford University Press.

——. 2006. Contesting Spatial Modernity in Late-Socialist China. *Current Anthropology* 47 (3): 461–484.

——. 2012. Economic Migration and Urban Citizenship in China: The Role of Points Systems. *Population and Development Review* 28 (3): 503–533.

Zhang, Liang. 2003. *La Naissance du Concept de Patrimoine en Chine XIXe-XXe siècle.* Paris: Archiethèses Ed. Rechnerches/ IPRAUS.

Zhang, Q. F. 2004. Economic Transition and New Patterns of Parent-Adult Child Co-Residence in Urban China. *Journal of Marriage and Family* 66 (5): 1231–1245.

Zhang, W. 2012. *The China Wave: Rise of a Civilization State.* Hackensack: World Century Publishing Corp.

Zhang, X. 2000. Shanghai Nostalgia: Post-Revolutionary Allegories in Wang Anyi's Literary Production in the 1990s. *Positions* 8 (2): 349–387.

Zhang, Y. 2008. Steering towards Growth: Symbolic Urban Preservation in Beijing, 1990–2005. *The Town Planning Review* 79 (2/ 3): 187–208.

Zhang, Y. L. 2010. *Gudu Chang'an* (The Ancient Capital of Chang'An). Xi'an: Sanqin Chubanshe.

Zhang, Y. N. 2004. *Will China Become Democratic: Elite, Class and Regime Transition.* Singapore: EAI.

Zhao, F. 2011. Hexin zhichan jiazhi buming Qujiang wenlv jieke yinxiu (The uncertainties of Qujiang and its investment). *Zhongguo jingqing bao*, 11 June. Available online, http://finance.eastmoney. com/news/1354,20110611141605291.html, last accessed 1 May 2016.

Zhao, T. 2009. A Political World Philosophy in Terms of All-Under-Heaven (*Tian-xia*). *Diogenes* 56 (1): 5–18.

Zhou, Y., and L. J. C. Ma. 2003. China's Urbanization Levels: Reconstructing a Baseline from the Fifth Population Census. *The China Quarterly* 173: 176–196.

Zhu, S. G. 1996. Zhongguo qige gudu de niandai biao (The time line of the 7 ancient capitals in China). *Shaanxi Shifan Danxue Qikang* 2.

——. 2010. *Xi'an de Lishi Bianqian yu Fazhan* (The Changes and Development of the History of Xi'an). Xi'an: Xi'an Chubanshe.

Zhu, Y. 2003. Changing Urbanization Processes and in situ Rural-Urban Transformation: Reflections on China's Settlement Definitions. In A. G. Champion, and G. J. Hugo (eds.), *New Forms of Urbanization: Beyond the Urban-Rural Dichotomy*, pp. 207–228. Aldershot: Ashgate.

Zhu, Y., and N. Li. 2013. Groping for Stones to Cross the River: Governing Heritage in Emei. In T. Blumenfield, and H. Silverman (eds.), *Cultural Heritage Politics in China*, pp. 51–72. New York: Springer.

Zingel, W. P., M. Keck, B. Etzold, and H. G. Bohle. 2011. Urban Food Security and Health Status of the Poor in Dhaka, Bangladesh. In A. Krämer, M. H. Khan, and F. Kraas (eds.), *Health in Megacities and Urban Areas. Contributions to Statistics*, pp. 301–319. Heidelberg: Physica-Verlag HD.

Zufferey, N. 2008. Traces of the Silk Road in Han-Dynasty Iconography: Questions and Hypotheses. In P. Forêt (ed.), *The Journey of Maps and Images on the Silk Road*, pp.9–28. Leiden: Brill.

Zukin, S. 1987. Gentrification: Culture and Capital in the Urban Core. *Annual Review of Sociology* 13: 129–147.

Index*

archaeological ethnography 18, 72
archaeologists; amateur 53, 217
archaeology; departments of / and other institutions 14, 19-20, 40-1, 55, 58, 65, 67-8, 97, 228; disciplinary history of 17-8, 64, 66-8; in everyday life 17, 52, 54-5, 60; political uses of 46, 67, 223; versus restoration 64, *see also* social archaeology
architectural styles (dynastic); Ming 32, 171; Mingqing 95; neo-Tang 23, 82, 91-5; Qing 171; Tang 54, 94, 197, *see also* religious architecture
architectural styles (ethnic); Hui 179, *see also* religious architecture
architectural styles (regional); Chang'an 170, *see also* religious architecture
authenticity; and food 50, 173-4, 180-1, 186; and relics 49, 54, 117-8, 203; in touristic sites 48-52, 59, 103, 117, 120, 160, 162, 180, 193; of museum displays 48-51, 219

Banpo Museum 6, 28, 45n
Beijing 55, 75-6, 115, 134, 155, 162, 201, 216, 219, 221, 229-30
Bell Tower 1, 31, 37, 78, 80, 131, 192-3, 197, 203, 210-1, 216, 217
Berliner, D. xi, 226
Big Wild Goose Pagoda 6, 19, 37-8, 41n, 51, 80, 87, 110n, *112*, 113, 119-20, 125, 128, 137, 142-3, 145, 151, 158-9, 193, 199, 211
branding (city / cultural) 141, 162-3
Brumann, C. xi, 3, 12-3, 224

Buddhism 114, 119-20, 122, 126, 129, *see also* religion(s)
buffer zone 116, 143, 145, 161, 211, 224

Calligraphy Quarter 19, 24, 78, 167, 168-78, 180, 182, 183-4, 186-9, 223
Central Asia 103, 106-7, 109, 120, 125-7, 130-2, 134-5, 223
Chang'an (old); layout of 29, 59, 78, 130, 152, 200; population of 29, 31, 33, 99, 226; remains of 28-9, 53, 70, 89, 152
China Dream 231-3, 235
cities (kinds of); ancient (*gucheng*) 6, 8, 15, 19, 32, 35, 37, 54, 77, 93, 95, 130, 144, 149n, 193, 195, 203, 216-7; historic 6, 8, 41, 81, 166-7, 182, 224; international metropolis (*guoji da dushi*) 27, 33, 35, 221-3, 229-31, *see also* cosmopolitan(ism)
City Wall 6, 15, 19, 29, 31, 33n, 54, 56, 58, 75, 109, 116, 137, 144-6, 149-51, 168, 170, 177, 184, 195, 198, 201, 210, 211, 215
cityscape i, 2-3, 7, 17, 23-4, 81-2, 87, 91-6, 101, 138, 143, 192, 194, 196, 217, 222
civilization; and Chinese nationalism 23, 37, 67, 73; evidence of earliest in China 5, 27-8, 45-7, 52, 73-5, 123, 135; material (*wuzhi wenming*) and spiritual (*jingshen wenming*) 37, 46; socialist 33, 37
commercialization 25, 41-2, 48, 94, 101, 118, 137, 143, 146, 148, 154, 160, 163, 179, 180-1, 183, 186, 188, 193-4, 225
cosmopolitan(ism) i, 10, 24, 81, 96, 104, 126, 132, 198, 219-29 *passim*, 231, 233-4

Cultural Relics Protection Law 37-8, 166
Cultural Revolution 9n, 194
cultural scenic area 57, 89-91, 121, 137, 146-9, 151, 153-5, 157, 160-2, 195

Dagoba of Kumarajiva *112*, 114-5
Daming Palace 6, 19, 29, 38, 51, 53-4, 57, 68, 70-1, 87, 93, 97, 110-1, *112*, 113, 118-9, 124-8, 131, 137, 145-7, 151, 161, 199, 200, 206-8, 210, 212, 215, 237
Danfeng Gate 71, 118
Daqin Monastery Pagoda *112*, 114, 120
daughters 76, 98-9, 214, 227
demolition 15, 24, 41, 63, 93, 150, 194, 200-1, 205-6, 209-10, 213-4, 216, 224
Deng Xiaoping 9
Duan Xiannian 141, 146, 154-7, 159, 192, 210

Emperor Qin Shihuang Mausoleum 1, 51, 57, 59, 89, 228
emplotment 100-1
ethnic minorities; historical presence 114, 172, 185, 220, *see also* cosmopolitan(ism); 'foreigners'; Hui

Famen Temple *112*, 117-8, 128, 137, 145-9, 153-5, 157-8, 161, 235
Feuchtwang, S. 9-10
fieldwork i, xi, 4, 10, 19-21, 27, 41, 47-50, 56, 61, 77-8, 87, 89, 126, 140, 146, 149, 157, 159, 162-3, 169, 179-80, 184, 201, 215, 231
'foreigners' (historical) 29-31, 73, 80, 86, 125-6, 130, 221-2, 227
Forest of Steles 6, 168, 173-5, 177-8, 187, 193

Four Modernization Plan 2, 4
Four Olds 9n, 194

gender; and 'her-it-age' 98-100; education of females 97-8; female dress in the Tang 88, 97
gentrification 19, 24, 157, 193, 204-6, 208-10, 212, 214
ghost towns 24, 35, 193, 212-4
God of Fortune Temple 42, 137-8, 160
Great Mosque *112*, 120, 170-1, 179-80, 183
Green Dragon Temple 128-30

Han Chang'an city 6, 7, 19, 54-60, 89, 91, 111, 195, 199, 207
Han Chenghu 58, 89-91, 151, 195, 213
Han Dynasty 6, 29, 53-4, 57, 60, 88-90, 98, 106, 108, 111, 123-4, 151, 233, 237
Henan Province 81, 110, 113, 169, 228, 237
heritage boom 2, 10, 163, 192, 216-7
heritage preservation; (historic) stages in China 16, 33, 37, 40, 92, 194, *see also* preservation; rebuilding; reconstruction; renovation; restoration
heritage sites (classification and rankings of) 13, 22, 39, 65-6
Herzfeld, M. 165, 167
high rise zone 143, 211
Hinduism 119, *see also* religion(s)
historic conservation areas 6, 166-7, 173
historical discourse 76-7, 91
historical narration 11, 22, 91, 96, 222
history; and civilization 27, 45-7, 73, 86, 135; importance for/ relationship to Xi'an people 51-5, 77-81

Hui 4, 120, 171, 172-3, 175, 177, 179-81, 183-6, 188, 223, 228, 238

ICOMOS 43, 63, 108, 114, 118, 127, 150
intangible cultural heritage 3, 6-7, 38, 42, 48, 128
integrity 117-8, 120, 122, 220, see authenticity
Islam 4n, 119-20, 165, 170, 184, 188, see also ethnic minorities; 'foreigners'; Hui; Muslim Quarter; religion(s); religious architecture
Istanbul 3, 224-5

Japan 6, 11, 31, 80-1, 92, 118, 125-6, 129-31, 134, 228, 229n
Judaism 119, 186, see also religion(s)

Kazakhstan 104n, 107-8, 132, 135, 172, 237-8
kinship 10, 15, 98, 209, see daughters
Kleingeld, P. 233
Kunming 16, 20, 198, 217
Kyoto 6, 130, 224
Kyrgyzstan 104n, 107-8, 120, 135

Lefebvre, H. 15
Low, S. 15
Luoyang 30-1, 81, 123, 137

Manicheanism 119, see also religion(s)
Marco Polo 125
Melaka 3, 224-5
mental timeline 84-5
metro (construction of) i, 24, 198, 201-4, 216
Millward, J. A. 105-6, 126, 134
Mingde Gate 112, 115-6, 198, 211, 235

modernity; in China 11; relation to history i, 2, 8-9, 19, 186, 191, 219, 222; spatial 15-6, 18, 188; words for (modeng; xiandai) 8, 10, see also civilization
modernization; from 1990s 2-4, 7-8, 10, 32, 34, 56, 62, 91-3, 107, 138, 140, 168, 173, 178-9, 182, 184, 187, 191-2, 195, 215-6, see also Four Modernization Plan
multi-disciplinary studies 8, 17
Muslim Quarter 4n, 19, 24, 120, 165, 167-8, 170-83 passim, 185-9, 223, 228, 235

Nanjing 16, 31, 76, 138
Nara 6, 118, 130
National Archaeological Parks 57-8, 60, 68, 72-3, 89
national heritage site 38, 57, 149, 171, 228
national historic city 6, 81, 166n
national rejuvenation 231-4, see China Dream
nationalism 2-3, 11, 23, 37, 67, 73, 83, 102, 106, 163, 220-3, 228, 234
neo-Tang style 23, 82, 87, 91-2, 95, 118, 140, 145, 152, 169, 182, 217
Nestorianism 114, 119-21, see also religion(s)
nostalgia 16, 88, 193, 209, 226-8

Ong, A. 11, 139, 147
Open Door Policy 9, 32
Outstanding Universal Value 3-4, 11

patriotism 11, 39-40, 80n, 88, 234
prehistory 7, 22, 27, 45, 83
preservation (baohu); definition in Chinese 39n, 56n, 62, 150n

Qian Imperial Mausoleum 39, 52, 97, 112-3, 235
Qin Dynasty 28, 68, 70, 78-9, 84-7, 89, 101, 225-6, 237
Qingdao 16, 162
Qujiang Corporation 58, 70, 115, 117, 121-2, 138-9, 141, 143, 144, 146-51, 153-4, 156-61, 199, 204, 206, 210-1, 214, 231
Qujiang District 19, 33n, 58-60, 132, 139-45, 146n, 152, 157-60, 195, 198-9, 207, 214
Qujiang Model 23, 138-9, 141n, 142-3, 144n, 145, 147, 149, 151-61 *passim*, 223

real estate 3, 14, 23, 35, 42, 70, 115, 138, 142-3, 149, 152, 153n, 156-7, 160, 163, 183, 204, 211-2, 214, 216, 222-3, 225
rebuilding (*chongjian*); definition in Chinese 62
reconstruction (*gaijian*); definition in Chinese 62
relics; cultural (*wenwu*) 6, 10, 19, 37-8, 39n, 41, 47, 49, 54-5, 60, 61n, 166, 175, 202; national 22; protection of 37-9, 41, *see* Cultural Relics Protection Law; sacred (*śarīra*) 118, 148
religion(s) 94, 105, 119, 122, 129, 138, 147, 149, 155, 160-2, 165, 180-1, 185
religious architecture 114
renovation (*chongxiu*); definition in Chinese 62
renqi 198-200, *see* modernity, spatial
restoration (*xiufu*); definition in Chinese 62
restorers; views on archaeology and preservation 11, 19, 49, 52, 55, 60-7, 72, 203, 228
revitalization 24, 87, 90-2, 94-5, 100-1, 166, 173, 182, 184, 197, 216, 222, 231-4, *see* Calligraphy

Quarter; Muslim Quarter; Tang Imperial City Renaissance Plan; Tang Paradise; urban planning; urban renewal projects

Salamandra, C. 193-4
Shaanxi dialect 79, 187
Shaanxi History Museum 20, 41, 45n, 54-5, 66, 83-4, 91, 93, 103, 124, 126
Shaanxi Province 4, 8, 28, 31, 31n, 37-8, 40-1, 49, 57, 63, 74, 81, 86, 103-4, 110-2, 114, 119, 143-4, 147-8, 156, 159, 191, 214, 225-6
Shanghai 16, 27, 32, 75, 91, 132, 139, 216, 221, 229, 230
shop houses 3, 6, 95, 169, 171-3, 178-9, 182-3, 186-7, 223
Silk Road 18-20, 25, 70, 80, 89, 90, 103-11, 139, 152, 177-8, 181, 186, 221, 223-4, 231, 233-4, *see* Silk Roads World Heritage nomination
Silk Road Economic Belt 131-3, 135, 223
Silk Roads World Heritage nomination 6, 23-4, 38-9, 43, 104n, 104-14, 117-22, 131-2, 134-5, 147, 149-50, 171, 183
slums 24, 35, 81, 192-3, 200, 207, 209, 212, 215, 225
Small Wild Goose Pagoda 6, 19, 29, 37, 43, 87, 90, 97, 110n, *112*, 113, 119, 130
Smith, L. 12
social archaeology 18
social resilience 186-9
stock market 137-8

Tang Dynasty 6, 24, 29-31, 33, 39, 58, 70-1, 75-6, 78-80, 87, 94, 97-9, 101, 104, 111, 113, 123, 129-30, 139, 147, 170, 173-4, 198-9, 216, 223, 226n, 233, 237

Tang Females Museum 97
Tang Imperial City Renaissance Plan 82, 92, 99, 169, 182-3, 222
Tang Paradise 51, 87-8, 93-4, 97, 145, 151-2, 158-9, 196, 199
Tang Temple of Heaven 115, 235
Taoism 119, 147, 157, 162, *see also* religion(s)
Tentative List 6, 107, 108, 110-1, *112*, 113-4, 116-8, 120, 122, 128, 134
terracotta army 7, 19, 28, 47, 63, 69, 73, 75, 82, 86-8, 104, 129, 145, 165, 219; Terracotta Army Museum xi, 1, 3-4, 20, 22, 38-9, 41, 48, 51-2, 55, 57, 59-60, 64-6, 68, 71, 89, 96, 157, 220, 228
terracotta warriors 19, 48-9, 51, 61, 69-70, 86, 193, 219, 225
The Records of the Grand Historian (*Shiji*) 68, 77, 106n
tianxia 220-1, *see* cosmopolitan(ism)
tourism; and real estate development 23, 42, 138, 142-3, 149, 152, 156-7, 160, 163, 223, 225; changes in domestic 104; development in China 51; industry in Xi'an 5, 138, 223;
tradition i, 2, 4, 6, 8-9, 14, 38, 65, 67, 76, 87-8, 90, 119, 141, 173, 193-4, 204, 219, *see* Four Olds; modernity

UNESCO 2-4, 6, 12, 18, 20, 37-9, 51-2, 57, 104n, 106-9, 111, 116, 122, 135, 137, 143, 163, 171, 178, 227
urban anthropology 8, 14-5
urban planning; and nationally-led development 32; and preservation 38, 58, 61; and revitalization of Tang Chang'an 92; and tourism development 187
urban renewal projects 34, 42, 179, 181-2, 184, 188, 204, 206, 209

urban space 15, 16, 82, 100, 205, 211, 215, 223
urban transformation 20, 24, 27-8, 33, 35, 44, 138, 144, 187, 195, 201, 204, 208, 212, 221, 224

Weiyang Palace 6, 54, 91, 110n, 111, *112*, 124, 237
West Market 29, 78, 93, 98, 115, 123-4, 127-8, 133, 152, 170, 227, 231
Western Development Program 4
White, H. 100
women 56, 94, 96, 98-100, 226, *see* gender
World Heritage 1, 3-4, 6, 19-20, 23-4, 38-9, 41, 43, 47, 52, 57, 60, 86, 104-13, 116-7, 119, 121, 127, 130-2, 135-7, 147, 149-50, 154, 163, 171, 183, 219, 221, 224-5, 234, 237, *see* Silk Roads World Heritage nomination
World Heritage Convention 2, 6

Xi'an City Planning Bureau 32-3, 41-2, 82, 91-2, 99, 103, 116, 181, 183, 201-2, 214
Xi'an City Water Resources Bureau 89, 151, 213
Xingjiao Temple 6, 19, 110n, 111, *112*, 119, 121, 125, 149n, 153-5, 157, 235, 238
Xuanzang 98, 111, 121, 124-5, 153

Yellow Emperor /Emperor Huang 6, 52-3, 73, 75

Zhang, Li 217
Zhang Qian 108, 110n, 111, 123-4, 126, 130, 238
Zoroastrianism 119, *see also* religion(s)

Halle Studies in the Anthropology of Eurasia

1 Hann, Chris, and the "Property Relations" Group, 2003: *The Postsocialist Agrarian Question. Property Relations and the Rural Condition.*

2 Grandits, Hannes, and Patrick Heady (eds.), 2004: *Distinct Inheritances. Property, Family and Community in a Changing Europe.*

3 Torsello, David, 2004: *Trust, Property and Social Change in a Southern Slovakian Village.*

4 Pine, Frances, Deema Kaneff, and Haldis Haukanes (eds.), 2004: *Memory, Politics and Religion. The Past Meets the Present in Europe.*

5 Habeck, Joachim Otto, 2005: *What it Means to be a Herdsman. The Practice and Image of Reindeer Husbandry among the Komi of Northern Russia.*

6 Stammler, Florian, 2009: *Reindeer Nomads Meet the Market. Culture, Property and Globalisation at the 'End of the Land'* (2 editions).

7 Ventsel, Aimar, 2006: *Reindeer,* Rodina *and Reciprocity. Kinship and Property Relations in a Siberian Village.*

8 Hann, Chris, Mihály Sárkány, and Peter Skalník (eds.), 2005: *Studying Peoples in the People's Democracies. Socialist Era Anthropology in East-Central Europe.*

9 Leutloff-Grandits, Caroline, 2006: *Claiming Ownership in Postwar Croatia. The Dynamics of Property Relations and Ethnic Conflict in the Knin Region.*

10 Hann, Chris, 2006: *"Not the Horse We Wanted!" Postsocialism, Neoliberalism, and Eurasia.*

11 Hann, Chris, and the "Civil Religion" Group, 2006: *The Postsocialist Religious Question. Faith and Power in Central Asia and East-Central Europe.*

12 Heintz, Monica, 2006: *"Be European, Recycle Yourself!" The Changing Work Ethic in Romania.*

13 Grant, Bruce, and Lale Yalçın-Heckmann (eds.), 2007: *Caucasus Paradigms. Anthropologies, Histories and the Making of a World Area.*

14 Buzalka, Juraj, 2007: *Nation and Religion. The Politics of Commemoration in South-East Poland.*

15 Naumescu, Vlad, 2007: *Modes of Religiosity in Eastern Christianity. Religious Processes and Social Change in Ukraine.*

16 Mahieu, Stéphanie, and Vlad Naumescu (eds.), 2008: *Churches Inbetween. Greek Catholic Churches in Postsocialist Europe.*

17 Mihăilescu, Vintilă, Ilia Iliev, and Slobodan Naumović (eds.), 2008: *Studying Peoples in the People's Democracies II. Socialist Era Anthropology in South-East Europe.*

18 Kehl-Bodrogi, Krisztina, 2008: *"Religion is not so strong here". Muslim Religious Life in Khorezm after Socialism.*

19 Light, Nathan, 2008: *Intimate Heritage. Creating Uyghur Muqam Song in Xinjiang.*

20 Schröder, Ingo W., and Asta Vonderau (eds.), 2008: *Changing Economies and Changing Identities in Postsocialist Eastern Europe.*

21 Fosztó, László, 2009: *Ritual Revitalisation after Socialism. Community, Personhood, and Conversion among Roma in a Transylvanian Village.*

22 Hilgers, Irene, 2009: *Why Do Uzbeks have to be Muslims? Exploring religiosity in the Ferghana Valley.*

23 Trevisani, Tommaso, 2010: *Land and Power in Khorezm. Farmers, Communities, and the State in Uzbekistan's Decollectivisation.*

24 Yalçın-Heckmann, Lale, 2010: *The Return of Private Property. Rural Life after the Agrarian Reform in the Republic of Azerbaijan.*

25 Mühlfried, Florian, and Sergey Sokolovskiy (eds.), 2011. *Exploring the Edge of Empire. Soviet Era Anthropology in the Caucasus and Central Asia.*

HALLE STUDIES IN THE ANTHROPOLOGY OF EURASIA

26 Cash, Jennifer R., 2011: *Villages on Stage. Folklore and Nationalism in the Republic of Moldova.*

27 Köllner, Tobias, 2012: *Practising Without Belonging? Entrepreneurship, Morality, and Religion in Contemporary Russia.*

28 Bethmann, Carla, 2013: *"Clean, Friendly, Profitable?" Tourism and the Tourism Industry in Varna, Bulgaria.*

29 Bošković, Aleksandar, and Chris Hann (eds.), 2013: *The Anthropological Field on the Margins of Europe, 1945-1991.*

30 Holzlehner, Tobias, 2014: *Shadow Networks. Border Economies, Informal Markets and Organised Crime in the Russian Far East.*

31 Bellér-Hann, Ildikó, 2015: *Negotiating Identities. Work, Religion, Gender, and the Mobilisation of Tradition among the Uyghur in the 1990s.*

32 Oelschlaegel, Anett C., 2016: *Plural World Interpretations. The Case of the South-Siberian Tyvans.*

33 Obendiek, Helena, 2016: *"Changing Fate". Education, Poverty and Family Support in Contemporary Chinese Society.*

34 Sha, Heila, 2017: *Care and Ageing in North-West China.*

35 Tocheva, Detelina, 2017: *Intimate Divisions. Street-Level Orthodoxy in Post-Soviet Russia.*

36 Sárközi, Ildikó Gyöngyvér, 2018: *From the Mists of Martyrdom: Sibe Ancestors and Heroes on the Altar of Chinese Nation Building.*

38 Wang, Ruijing, 2019: *Kinship, Cosmology and Support. Toward a Holistic Approach of Childcare in the Akha Community of South-Western China.*